Minnesota
Gardener's Guide

Published by Cool Springs Press, a Division of Thomas Nelson, Inc., P. O. Box 141000, Nashville, Tennessee, 37214.

Cataloging-in-Publication information is available.
ISBN: 1591861144

First Printing 2005
Printed in the United States of America
10 9 8 7 6 5 4 3 2

Managing Editor: Ramona D. Wilkes
Editorial Assistance: Dee Maranhao
Horticulture Editor: Troy Marden
Production Artist: S.E. Anderson
Cover Designer: Sheri Ferguson Kimbrough

On the Cover: Columbine, Getty Images

Cool Springs Press books may be purchased in bulk for educational, business, fundraising, or sales promotional use. For information, please email **SpecialMarkets@ThomasNelson.com**

Visit the Thomas Nelson website at **www.ThomasNelson.com** and the Cool Springs Press website at **www.coolspringspress.net**

Minnesota
Gardener's Guide

Melinda Myers

COOL SPRINGS PRESS
A Division of Thomas Nelson Publishers
Since 1798

Dedication

This book is dedicated to my daughter Nevada who puts the smile in my life.

Acknowledgments

As I revised this book my life went through a bit of revision as well. I want to thank my wonderful friends, family, advisory board, and especially my daughter for their love and support. You held my hand through a challenging leg of my journey and helped launch me on a new path that promises to be an exciting adventure. Thanks also to Hank McBride and Ramona Wilkes of Cool Springs for their patience as I took a bit, okay more than a bit, of extra time to complete this project. And Cindy Games who listened, nudged, and helped keep me moving forward.

A SPECIAL THANKS to all the gardeners, master gardeners, horticulturists, and professionals in related fields who have so willingly shared their enthusiasm, knowledge, experience, and insight to help make this book what it is. My past twenty-five years in horticulture have been an incredible experience thanks to all of you, and I look forward to working with all of you for many years to come.

I want to thank my family and friends for their patience and support. My parents gave me the confidence to take risks and go for my dreams. Nevada, you were a gem through the task of writing yet another book. Thanks for your humor, patience, and all the help around the house. You kept me smiling all year long. I'm grateful to my friends who gave me the time to write, but didn't write me off after another year of, "Sorry, but I have to write my book." I appreciate your continued support and laughter.

Thanks to all my friends and mentors in the media and Garden Writers Association. You have helped me be a better communicator.

For the opportunity to write this and other Cool Springs Press books, I extend my thanks to Roger Waynick, Hank McBride, Cindy Games and the rest of the folks at Cool Springs Press.

Table of Contents

Featured Plants *for Minnesota*

Welcome to Gardening
in Minnesota

When I moved north over 25 years ago, I was amazed to find such a horticultural paradise in a place I had only seen as a winter wonderland on TV. I remember watching the weather reports wondering how people, let alone plants, could survive such a harsh climate. My first trip to the Twin cities, fortunately in summer, showed me a state filled with lush green trees and colorful gardens.

In the 1860's, Minnesota's new homesteaders were few in number, but blessed with many green thumbs. They brought their desire for beauty and love of plants with them as they moved west to their new homeland. Many gardeners showed off their harvest at the 1866 Minnesota State Fair and inspired the birth of the Minnesota Fruit Growers Association. Gradually the group expanded their mission and changed their name to the Minnesota State Horticultural Society. Over the years their minutes were published and soon transformed into *Northern Gardener* magazine.

At the turn of the century, focus turned from food production to ornamental plants. The increase in flower planting and use of tropical plants inside and out changed the gardening scene, with a short break to grow Victory Gardens for the WWII effort. The big explosion in landscaping came after WWII. As veterans returned home, built new houses, and started raising families. Large expanses of grass were used to create play areas for children. Shrubs ringed houses and gardens were filled with annuals and a few perennials.

In 1955, the Men's Garden Club (an affiliated club of MSHS) decided that northern gardeners needed more help and guidance for gardening in the rigors of Minnesota weather. They developed a landscape arboretum to increase research for hard ornamentals, create an interest in plants, provide a horticulture library, and promote plant testing throughout the state.

The arboretum was soon deeded to the University and has continued with the original mission. To date, hundreds of plants have been introduced, additional ornamentals have been evaluated, and thousands of Minnesota gardeners have been inspired by their plantings and educational efforts. The impact of the University of Minnesota Landscape Arboretum and The Minnesota State Horticultural Society (*Northern Gardener*) can be seen in parks, greenways, and home gardens. The expanded use of perennials and native plants has changed the suburban landscape from an expanse of lawns and sheared yews to an array of flowering trees, shrubs, ornamental grasses, and flowers.

Using This Book

Minnesota Gardener's Guide is designed to help you make the connection with nature and achieve some gardening success of your own. I wrote the book with you, the gardener, in mind. I tried to include answers to the questions gardeners are always asking me.

I selected plants that are easy to find here and are often used in gardens and yards. The information included in the pages of this volume should help you grow a healthy and attractive landscape. The *Minnesota Gardener's Guide* is divided into chapters by plant categories. These include annuals, bulbs, groundcovers, ornamental grasses, perennials, roses, shrubs, trees, turfgrass, and vines. I mixed the native plants in with plants not native to Minnesota within the appropriate category. I thought that arrangement would make the book easier to use for planning your landscape. You may be surprised to learn how many of our common garden plants are natives!

Each chapter includes an introduction with general information unique to that group of plants. Read the chapter introductions before turning to the plant entries. Every plant entry within the chapter features a plant profile for quick reference.

Getting the Most Out of Your Garden

The *Minnesota Gardener's Guide* is just a starting point. Use the basic information I have provided along with your own experience to increase your gardening success. Whether you're a beginner or a more experienced gardener, membership in the Minnesota State Horticultural Society (MSHS) is the premier source for northern gardeners like you! It is the mission of MSHS to encourage the science and practice of northern gardening through the public's enjoyment, appreciation, and understanding of plants.

Stone Border with Hostas

Thomas Jefferson, a horticulturist as well as our third president, inspired me to keep a garden journal. I read that he kept a garden journal for 50 years, entering the name, date, and source of every plant he purchased; how it grew, and when and why it was removed. I have not mastered his discipline, but as my memory fades, I am getting more motivated!

With all that said, the most important thing is to relax and have fun. If a plant dies (and it happens to all of us), look at this as an opportunity to try something new. If you put a plant in the wrong spot, move it to a new location. Gardening should be enjoyable, not a weekly chore. And when you get discouraged, think about what Thomas Jefferson said: "Though an old man, I am but a young gardener."

The Garden Environment

Weather

When I first moved North, someone told me, "If you don't like the weather, wait five minutes and it will change." They were right. Minnesota's weather is variable and often challenging for gardeners.

Garden with Urn

We base our plant selection and care on average weather conditions and expected extremes. Then weather exceptions like a drought in 1988, the floods of 1993 and 1997, severe storms and hail, and too many others to list come along.

In the twenty-five years I have lived in the North, I have yet to experience "normal" weather. There always seems to be some type of weather extreme to keep gardeners and horticulturists challenged and humble. An overview of our average weather conditions, however, may help you better plan and care for your garden.

Let's start with frost dates. On the back of every seed packet and throughout this book you will read, "Start seeds _____ number of weeks prior to the last spring frost." That date varies from May 2 to May 17 in the southern parts of Minnesota and from May 18 to June 11 in northern Minnesota. Look for the average killing frost dates on the maps provided by the Climatological Agricultural Statistics Service (see the appendix).

Now count the days between the last spring frost and the first fall frost. That will give you the number of growing days for your region. The frost-free season varies from 107 to 160 days in southern

A Perennial Garden

Minnesota and from 90 to 120 days in the northern part of the state. These are average frost dates based on one hundred years of data. Soil temperature and the frost tolerance of each plant should determine your planting date. I remember losing quite a few plants when we had a killing frost several weeks after the "normal" last-frost.

Average growing temperatures and seasonal extremes will influence plant growth and development. Some plants need warm temperatures to thrive and flower. Others become stressed or stop flowering in hot weather. Winter temperature extremes are among the major factors that influence winter survival. The U.S. Department of Agriculture hardiness zones are based on the average annual minimum temperatures. Minnesota has USDA Zones 2b through 4b. That is the rating system used by most gardeners and this book (see page 21). The Arnold Arboretum also publishes a hardiness map used by some nurseries. Check the front of plant catalogs to determine which hardiness map ratings they use.

Rainfall is also important for growing healthy plants. Most plants need an average of 1 inch of water each week. Plants need more water during the hot, dry days of summer and less during cooler periods. The type of plants grown and the care you provide influences the amount and frequency of watering. Some plants, like yucca and coneflowers, are more drought tolerant and can go longer between watering. Others, like astilbe and hostas, need moist soil and will scorch if the soil dries. Select more drought-tolerant plants if you are unable to water during dry periods. Mulching will also reduce the need to water by keeping the soil cool and moist.

Select plants that tolerate your landscape's climate to increase survival and minimize maintenance. But what about those gardeners who like to push plants to the extremes? Well, we can't change the weather, but we can modify it by creating microclimates or modifying our gardening practices.

Modifying the Climate

Microclimates are small areas that have slightly different growing conditions than the surrounding areas. Large bodies of water and nearby vegetation can alter frost dates and moderate temperatures. On the other hand, cold air sinks, creating frost pockets in valleys and other low areas. Woodlands and shelterbelts can block the northwest winter winds and reduce winter damage to sensitive plants. These areas can also shade the landscape, keeping temperatures cooler.

Use the following ideas to create microclimates. Plant windbreaks or install decorative fencing to block damaging winter winds. Grow heat-loving plants near brick buildings and walls. Even a flat warming stone in the perennial garden can add warmth for a nearby plant. Use an outdoor thermometer to track the temperatures in different parts of your garden. Record this information for future use.

Mulch can also be used effectively. Organic mulch used on the soil keeps roots cooler in the summer and warmer in the winter and minimizes soil temperature fluctuations that can stress plants. Winter mulches can be used to protect the aboveground portion of the plant. Roses, rhododendrons, and other tender plants are frequently mulched for winter protection. Apply straw, marsh hay, or evergreen branches once the ground lightly freezes. The purpose is to keep the soil temperature consistent throughout the winter. This prevents early sprouting that often occurs during our frequent, but short, midwinter thaws. Mulching also prevents drying of stems and evergreen leaves. The mulch blocks winter wind and sun to reduce moisture loss. Minnesota gardeners have access to the best winter mulch: a reliable snow cover. Even as you tire of shoveling this winter, remember that all that white stuff is protecting your plants.

Mixed Planting with Fountain Grass

A Colorful Mixture of Annuals and Perennials

Maybe it's not the cold winter that limits your gardening, but rather the short growing season. You can easily lengthen the growing season by several weeks or even a month or more. Gardeners traditionally use cold frames to get a jump on the growing season. These structures require talent to build and room to store, and they also need venting and watering. I never seem to have the time to do all that. Season-extending fabrics such as ReeMay® and other spun-bonded fabrics can make this task easier. Plant annuals or frost-sensitive perennials outside several weeks earlier than normal and loosely cover the planting bed with a season-extending fabric. The covers keep the plants warm and protect them from spring frost. Air, light, and water can all pass through the fabric, so it doesn't need to be removed for watering or ventilation. Remove the covering once the danger of frost has passed. You can also use these fabrics, bed sheets, or other material to protect plants from the first fall frost. Cover plants in the late afternoon or early evening when there is a threat of frost. Remove the frost protection in the morning. The season-extending fabric can be left in place day and night if the meteorologists predict several days of cold, frosty weather. I find the first fall frost is often followed by two weeks of sunny, warm weather. Providing frost protection will give you a few more weeks of enjoyment before our long winter arrives.

Soil

Soil is the foundation of our landscape. Not many gardeners enjoy spending the time, energy, or money it can take to build this foundation. I have to admit it's more fun to show someone a new plant than to show off my properly prepared soil. But it's a good idea to have and follow the recipe for productive soil.

The Basics

Let's start by looking at Minnesota's native soils. There are 25 major soil areas and 600 soil classifications in Minnesota. I'm going to greatly simplify this discussion with some broad generalities. I hope the soil scientists out there will forgive me!

Soil is composed of mineral material, organic matter, water, and air. The mineral matter comes from the weathering of bedrock. The bedrock in parts of Minnesota is limestone, so the soils tend to be alkaline, often called sweet, with a high pH. The other parts of the state have a granite bedrock and the soils tend to be acidic, or sour, with a low pH. The weathered bedrock combines with organic matter from dead plants, manure, and other decomposing materials. The empty spaces are filled with either water or air. It takes 100 years to make 1 inch of topsoil so handle with care.

The size, shape, and quantity of the mineral particles determine the soil texture. Clay particles are tiny and flat like plates. Water is trapped between these plate-like particles making clay soils, those with a high percent of clay particles, slow to dry. Sand particles are larger (and more angular) compared to the clay. The water runs around the particles and through the soil. This is why sandy soils, those with a high percentage of sand particles, dry out faster than clay soils. Silt particles are larger than clay and smaller than sand. They feel smooth but are not sticky. Loam soils have equal parts of sand, silt, and clay particles. These soils are better drained than clay soils and have better water-holding capacity than sandy soils.

Minnesota Soils

Soils in Minnesota range from mostly clay to sandy, to some type of loam, to the gravel and rocks dumped by the glaciers. The soils in the Red River valley are among the best agricultural soils in the United States.

That's how our state's soils began. We have greatly changed our soils since we started building homes, buildings, and parking lots. In fact, some plant and soil scientists don't call this soil, but rather "disturbed materials." When buildings are constructed, the topsoil is scraped off the lot and removed. Once the basements are dug, much of the clay, sand, or gravel subsoil is spread over the lot. Some of the building materials, many of them made from limestone, accidentally get mixed into this "soil." An inch or two of topsoil is spread, sod is laid—and is the yard is ready to be landscaped? Not at all. This conglomeration is usually poorly drained, very alkaline or acidic, and hard on most plants. Fortunately, many municipalities and customers are requiring builders to stockpile the topsoil for reapplication to the site.

Modifying the Soil

Given all this information, what do you need to do to improve your soil? Adding 2 to 4 inches of organic matter such as compost, peat moss, or aged manure will improve the drainage of heavy clay soil and increase the water-holding capacity of sandy soil. Work this material into the top 6 to 12 inches of soil. Improve the soil whenever you establish a new garden, plant your annuals and perennials, or transplant perennial flowers and groundcovers.

Do not add sand to clay soil. You need an inch of sand for every inch of soil you are trying to amend. If you add less than that, you will end up with concrete. Don't add lime to improve the drainage of alkaline soil. Lime improves drainage, but it also raises the soil pH. That increases problems with nutrient deficiencies in alkaline soil. Gypsum works only in soil high in sodium. Minnesota soils are not naturally high in sodium, so gypsum won't be effective at improving the soil drainage.

Gardeners growing plants in poorly drained, disturbed sites have a bigger challenge. These soils will take years to repair. Many gardeners give up and bring in additional topsoil. Make sure the topsoil you buy is better than that you already have. Purchase a blended or garden mix. Many garden centers and nurseries sell small quantities of topsoil. For large quantities, contact a company that specializes in topsoil. Friends, relatives, or a landscape professional may be able to recommend a reliable firm. Otherwise, check the telephone pages listings under **Soil** or **Topsoil**.

A 2-inch layer of good topsoil spread over disturbed material will not help much; water drains through the good soil and stops when it hits the bad material. A better solution is to create planting beds throughout the landscape. Large, raised planting beds and berms at least 12 inches high will give plants a good place to start growing.

Testing the Soil

Now that you have improved the soil drainage and structure, you need to develop a fertilization program. That starts with a soil test. Contact your University of Minnesota Extension Office (listed in the appendix. Extension personnel can provide you with the necessary forms and information for soil testing, or you can contact a state-certified soil testing laboratory listed in the phone book.

Take separate soil samples for each type of planting: one for the lawn, another for flowers, and a third for trees and shrubs. Remove several plugs of soil from the garden area to be tested. Take the soil from the top 4 to 6 inches, removing any surface mulch first, from different areas throughout the garden. Mix these soil plugs together and allow the mixture to dry. Send 1 cup of this soil mix to the lab for analysis. Your results will be in the mail within 2 to 3 weeks.

The soil test report tells you how much and what type of fertilizer to use for the type of plant you are growing. It also tells you the soil pH and what, if anything, should be done to adjust it.

Amending Soil pH

Soil pH affects nutrient availability. Urban soils tend to be alkaline. Iron and manganese are not readily available in these high-pH soils. The nutrients are in the soil, they are just not available to the plants. That creates problems for acid-loving plants such as rhododendrons, red maples, and white oaks. It is very difficult to lower the soil pH. Incorporating elemental sulfur and organic matter can slightly lower the pH. Using acidifying fertilizers, chelated iron and manganese, and organic mulch will help. But all of these methods can take years to lower the pH and have a minimal impact. It is much easier on you and the plant to grow species adapted to high-pH soils.

Acidic soils occur in sandy, wet organic soils in Minnesota. The phosphorus, calcium, and magnesium are tied up in these soils and are unavailable to the plants. Many gardeners add lime to raise the soil pH. Follow soil test recommendations carefully. It takes years to correct improperly limed soils. Never lime alkaline soils.

Selecting a Fertilizer

Your soil-test report will tell you what type of fertilizer to add. The main nutrients are nitrogen, phosphorus, and potassium. The percentage of each of these nutrients contained in a fertilizer are represented by the 3 numbers on the bag. For example, a 15-10-5 fertilizer has 15 percent nitrogen, 10 percent phosphorus, and 5 percent potassium.

Nitrogen stimulates leaf and stem growth. It is used in relatively large amounts by the plants. This mobile element moves through the soil quickly. You can use slow-release forms to provide plants with small amounts of nitrogen over a longer period of time. These products also reduce the risk of fertilizer burn. Excess nitrogen encourages leafy growth and discourages flowering. It also leaches through the soil, harming our lakes, streams, and groundwater.

Phosphorus is the middle number on the bag. Phosphorus stimulates root development and flowering. This nutrient is used in small amounts by the plants and moves very slowly through the soil. Excess phosphorus can interfere with the uptake of other nutrients and runoff can damage our lakes and streams. Minnesota has banned the use of lawn fertilizers containing phosphorus unless recommended by a soil test or for starting new lawns. Potassium is used in even smaller amounts by plants. It is essential in many plant processes and helps the plants prepare for winter.

Urban soils tend to be high in phosphorus and potassium. That comes from years of using complete fertilizers, like 10-10-10 and 12-12-12. Excessive amounts of one nutrient can interfere with the uptake of other nutrients. You can't remove the excess nutrients, but you can stop adding to the problem by following your soil test recommendations.

Test your soil every 3 to 5 years, or as problems arise. That will allow you to adjust your fertilizer program to your soil and the plants you are growing. This practice will save you money, improve plant growth, and help our environment.

Pest Management

Once your plants are growing, some unwelcome visitors may enter the landscape. These pests come in the form of weeds, diseases, insects, and plant-devouring wildlife. A healthy plant is your best defense against pests. Even with proper planting and care, you may need to intercede to help plants through difficult times.

Creeping Zinnia

17

Foxglove

Weed Control

You will simplify your life by eliminating existing weeds before planting. They can be removed with regular cultivation one season prior to planting. Another option is to cover the planting area with clear or black plastic for one full growing season to "solarize the weeds." A more attractive method involves wood chips and newspaper. Prepare the soil, and then spread several layers of newspaper covered with wood chips over it. You may need an extra set of hands to keep the newspapers from ending up in the neighbor's yard. The newspaper helps smother the weeds, but eventually breaks down and improves the soil. Plant through the mulch into the previously prepared soil. Or use a total vegetation killer such as Roundup® for quicker results. You can plant treated areas in 1 to 2 weeks. Remember, these products will kill any green plant they contact. Be sure to read and carefully follow label directions.

I have had good luck mulching around trees or converting lawn areas into gardens using the following technique:

Kill the grass and weeds using a total vegetation killer, leaving the dead grass in place to act as the first layer of mulch. Cover the dead grass with wood chips, twice-shredded bark, or another organic material. The dead grass eventually decomposes, adding organic matter to the soil. The organic mulch continues to control the weeds. Plant right through the mulch and dead grass.

Planting is easier the year after the dead grass layer has decomposed. You need to start with good soil for this planting method to work.Use this technique in areas with decent soil to support plant growth.

Mulch the soil after planting. This step will prevent many weed seeds from sprouting. Any that do creep through will be easy to pull. Heavily mulched soils may need some additional nitrogen fertilizer. Cultivation with a hoe or weeding tool will also work to control weeds. Be careful not to damage the roots of your garden plants.

Dealing with Diseases

Leaf spots, stem rots, mildew, and blights are just a few of the diseases found on plants. Growing the right plant in the right location will reduce the risk of infection. Proper soil preparation will help reduce rot problems. Remove infected leaves as soon as they appear. Fall cleanup will reduce disease infection the following season. Most disease problems develop in response to the weather. You will have problems some years and not others. Plants are usually more tolerant of these problems than the gardener. Contact the University of Minnesota Extension Service, the Minnesota State Horticultural Society, certified arborists, or other landscape professionals for help in identifying and controlling these problems.

Managing Insects

As you battle the insects, remember that less than 3 percent of all the insects throughout the world are classified as pests. Many more are beneficial and desirable to have in your garden. Keep in mind insecticides also kill the caterpillars that turn into beautiful butterflies and aphid-eating ladybugs. Try some environmental (and often fun) control techniques before reaching for the spray can. Always read and follow label directions carefully before using any pesticide.

Aphids are small teardrop-shaped insects that come in a variety of colors. They suck the plant juices causing the leaves to yellow, wilt, brown, curl, and become distorted. They also secrete a clear sticky substance on the leaves called honeydew. It doesn't hurt the plant but a black fungus, called sooty mold, may develop on the honeydew. You can wait and let the ladybugs move in and devour this pest or try spraying the plants with a strong blast of water. You can also use insecticidal soap, which is effective for killing softbody insects but is gentle on the plant and the environment. You may need several applications to control large populations.

Mites cause similar damage. You need a hand lens to see these pests. Like aphids, they suck plant juices and cause leaves to bronze, wilt, and brown. Don't wait to see the webs before you treat the mites. Sprays of water and insecticidal soap will help control this pest.

Slugs are slimy creatures that eat holes in the leaves of hostas and other garden plants. They feed at night, so you will notice the damage before you see the slugs. Slugs love cool, dark, damp locations and multiply quickly in wet weather. Stale beer in a shallow dish makes a great slug trap. A fellow gardener shared a good tip with me: Lay a partially filled beer bottle on its side in the garden. Tuck it out of sight under the plant leaves. The bottle keeps the beer from being diluted by rain, so it won't need frequent replacing. The slugs really do crawl in the small hole, drown in the beer, and die. Commercial slug baits are also available, but most have toxic materials and should be used with care around children, pets, and wildlife. New slug control products, such as Sluggo™, contain iron phosphate. Effective at killing slugs, but not harmful to birds and wildlife.

Animals in the Garden

Wildlife can be a nice addition to the landscape—until they start eating all the plants. Start by eliminating hiding and nesting areas, such as brush piles. Fence desirable plants. Sink fencing several inches into the ground to keep out meadow mice or voles. This rodent kills young plantings by feeding on the trunks of trees and shrubs and the crowns of some perennials. Fences must be at least 4 feet high to keep out rabbits and over 10 feet high to keep out deer. This type of deer fencing is not very practical. Many gardeners are having luck fencing small planting beds with 5-foot-tall deer fencing. You can see through to the garden while keeping out the deer, who seem to avoid small, fenced areas.

Scare tactics and repellents may provide some control, but I find urban wildlife very tolerant of the sounds and smells of humans. Vary the repellents and scare tactics for better results. And work with your neighbors—make sure one of you isn't feeding the wildlife while the other is trying to eliminate it from the neighborhood.

Next Year's Garden

If all these methods fail, there is always next year. Someone passed along to me a great definition of a green thumb gardener: The green thumb gardener is someone who grows a lot of plants, kills a few without mentioning it to others, and keeps on planting! So, take heart. If you've lost a few plants, you're probably on your way to a green thumb.

How to Use the Garden Book for Minnesota

Each entry in this guide provides you with information about a plant's particular characteristics, habits, and its basic requirements for active growth, as well as my personal experience and knowledge of the plant. I include the information you need to help you realize each plant's potential. Only when a plant performs at its best can one appreciate it fully. You will find such pertinent information as mature height and spread, bloom period and colors, sun and soil preferences, water requirements, fertilizing needs, pruning and care, and pest information.

Sun Preferences

Symbols represent the range of sunlight suitable for each plant. Full sun means eight hours or more, including midday. Part sun means six to eight hours, not midday. Part shade means four or six hours, preferably morning. Shade means less than four hours of sun. Some plants can be grown in more than one range of sun, so you will sometimes see more than one sun symbol.

Full Sun   **Part Sun**   **Part Shade**   **Shade**

Additional Benefits

Many plants offer benefits that further enhance their value. The following symbols indicate some of the more important additional benefits:

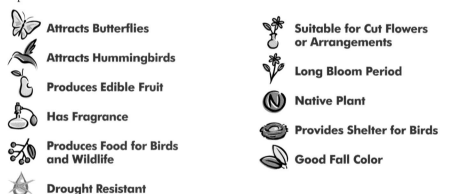

Attracts Butterflies

Attracts Hummingbirds

Produces Edible Fruit

Has Fragrance

Produces Food for Birds and Wildlife

Drought Resistant

Suitable for Cut Flowers or Arrangements

Long Bloom Period

Native Plant

Provides Shelter for Birds

Good Fall Color

Companion Planting and Design

For most of the entries, I provide landscape design ideas, as well as suggestions for companion plants to help you create pleasing and successful combinations—and inspire original compositions of your own. This is where I find much enjoyment from gardening.

My Personal Favorite

These sections describe those specific cultivars or varieties that I have found particularly noteworthy or, I recommend other good species to try. Give them a try . . . or perhaps you'll find your own personal favorite.

USDA Cold Hardiness Zone Map

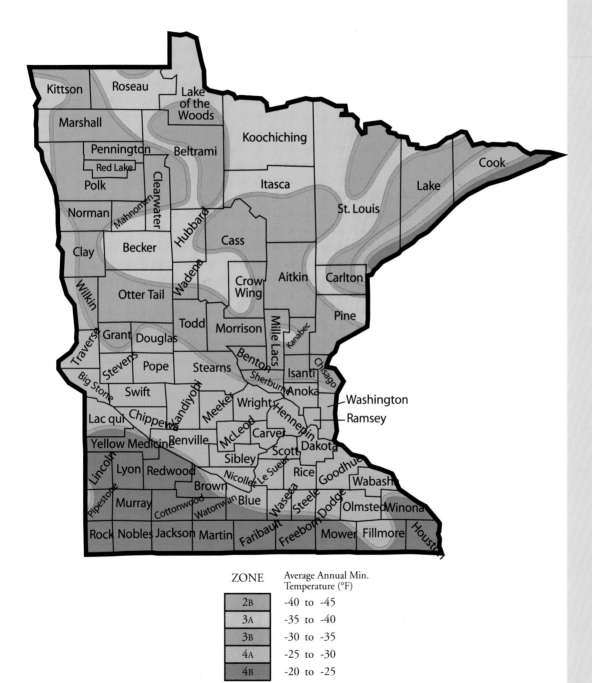

ZONE	Average Annual Min. Temperature (°F)
2B	-40 to -45
3A	-35 to -40
3B	-30 to -35
4A	-25 to -30
4B	-20 to -25

Hardiness Zones

Cold-hardiness zone designations were developed by the United States Department of Agriculture (USDA) to indicate the minimum average temperature for an area. A zone assigned to an individual plant indicates the lowest temperature at which the plant can be expected to survive over the winter.

Annuals
for Minnesota

Cosmos

The promise of spring and its colorful flowers help many a Minnesota gardener survive the snow and cold of our long, dreary winters. And that's exactly what annuals provide—beautiful hues all season long. Botanically speaking, annuals are plants that complete their life cycle (from seed to producing seeds) in a single season. Horticulturally speaking, they can be true annuals or nonhardy perennials that are replanted each year. Creating an attractive annual garden involves planning, proper planting, and a little follow-up care.

Creating a Plan

Take some time to plan before you go plant shopping. I think all gardeners are guilty of buying bargain plants or hard-to-resist selections, instead of the right plant for the intended location. I like to plan my gardens all year-round. I visit botanical gardens, attend garden tours, scour garden catalogs and magazines, and talk with other gardeners to get new ideas. I then try to apply some or parts of various ideas in my own garden designs. You may want to start a section in your garden journal listing what flower combinations work, new plants you want to try, and those to avoid. If you don't have a garden journal, now is a good time to start one.

Next, gather your family or other gardening partners together. Find out what everyone wants from the garden. You may want to include flowers for cutting, drying, or crafts. And don't forget about wildlife. Annuals are great lures for birds and butterflies, which add motion and color to your garden and may help get nongardeners interested in the landscape.

Think about creative combinations when you make your choices. I like to mix herbs like 'Purple Ruffles' basil and decorative vegetables like 'Bright Lites' Swiss chard in with my annuals. Their color and texture, not to mention their culinary value, make them great additions to the annual garden.

As you look through the catalogs and garden centers, note the All-America Selections (AAS) logo. AAS winners have performed well in test gardens across the country. The plants were selected for their superior performance by independent AAS judges. We are lucky to have five of the AAS Display gardens here in Minnesota. And check out the Proven Winners; these new introductions have been developed, selected, and tested throughout North America by a group of growers for their suitability and performance in production and the home garden. Check out their websites, www.all-americanselections.org and www.provenwinners.com for pictures and information on their winners.

Now evaluate your annual garden's location. How much sun and shade will the plants receive? What's the soil like in this particular spot? If the soil is like modeling clay or is as porous as a sandy beach, invest some time and money to improve it before you plant. A couple of inches of organic matter mixed into the top eight to twelve inches of soil makes a big difference. (For more details, see the section on improving soil in "The Garden Environment" section on pages 14 to 17.)

Think About Design

Next, select plants that serve the desired function and tolerate, or preferably thrive in, the growing conditions. Note the height and width of each plant and then make a sketch of your flower garden. Place tall plants in the center of island beds or at the back of flower borders. Shorter plants should be planted near the edge, and everything else can go toward the middle. Plant in rows for a more formal look and in masses or drifts for a more informal feel.

Don't limit your use of annuals to flower beds. Try them in containers, as a splash of color along the edge of a shrub bed, or intermingled with vegetables and perennials. Help pull your garden and landscape design together with some simple garden design strategies. Select colors that help create the feel and look you want for your landscape. Warm colors of red, orange, and yellow make large areas appear smaller, add a feeling of warmth, and attract attention. Cool colors of blue, green, and violet make small areas appear larger and give a cool peaceful feeling to the area. Use contrasting colors to create a focal point and complementary colors for continuity and blending. And remember it takes more cool-color flowers to offset a few bright orange, red, or yellow blossoms.

Repeat colors throughout the landscape through color echoing. For example, a red flower in one area can be echoed by the red foliage of a plant in another section and the red brick on the home. Color echoing increases the impact of the plants while creating a sense of unity throughout the yard.

Texture is another element that can help unify the garden or add contrast for greater impact. Fine-textured plants have dissected or grass-like foliage and airy or spike-like flowers such as baby's breath. Bold textured plants have broad leaves with round flowers like sunflowers. Repeat textures throughout the landscape to tie the garden or parts of the landscape together. Mix a few bold-textured plants in with the fine-textured plants to give the garden some punch.

"Posing" Pansies

Impatiens Border

Getting Started

Annuals can be started from seeds or purchased as transplants. Some annuals, like zinnias and marigolds, can be planted directly outside in the garden. Others, like geraniums, take a long time to mature and blossom. These should be started as seeds indoors for best results. Starting your own plants from seeds takes extra work but gives you a greater selection of new and different plant varieties. And a real sense of satisfaction.

Many gardeners prefer to buy transplants from their local garden center, greenhouse, or nursery. The extra expense provides the advantage of ready-to-plant and soon-to-bloom annuals. Select transplants with full-sized green leaves and stout stems. Avoid insect- and disease-infected plants. And this is a case where bigger isn't necessarily better. Smaller plants that aren't rootbound will suffer less transplant shock than larger-blooming, rootbound transplants.

Planting

Prepare your plants for the garden before you put them in the ground. Plants moving from the shelter of the greenhouse or your home need a little help preparing for the great outdoors. This process is called hardening off. Move the plants outdoors into partial shade. Gradually allow the soil to go drier between watering and stop fertilizing. At the same time, gradually increase the amount of light the plants receive each day. In two weeks, the plants will be ready to move to their permanent location. Many garden centers do this job for us. Ask if you're not sure.

Carefully slide the plants out of the container. Gently massage the roots before planting, to encourage them to grow out of the rootball and into the surrounding soil. Place the plant in the ground at the same level it was growing in the container.

Watering and Fertilizing

Water your new planting thoroughly, wetting the top six inches of soil. This will encourage deep, more drought-tolerant roots. Check new plantings several times per week. The small rootball growing in the soil-less mix will dry out quickly. Once established, plants need about one inch of water each week. Water thoroughly whenever the top few inches of soil are moist but crumbly. During dry periods, you will usually provide the needed water once a week to plants growing in clay soil and half the weekly rate twice a week to plants in sandy soil. You may need to water more often during hot weather and less frequently when temperatures are cool. Mulch once the soil warms to conserve moisture and decrease watering. Simply spread a thin layer of shredded leaves, evergreen needles, or other organic matter over the soil surface.

Fertilize according to soil test recommendations. If this is not available, three pounds or less per one hundred square feet of a low nitrogen fertilizer per season is sufficient for most annuals. I like to incorporate a low nitrogen slow-release fertilizer, such as Milorganite™, into the soil prior to planting. Or you can make three applications of a fast-release fertilizer once a month at a rate of one pound per one hundred square feet or according to the label directions. For more details on fertilization, see "The Garden Environment."

Overwintering

Some gardeners extend their growing season and plant life by moving a few plants indoors for winter. Simply take cuttings in late August or early September for best results, though I have been known to clip a few stems before the first killing frost. Root four-inch cuttings in moist vermiculite or perlite. Plant the rooted cuttings in any well-drained potting mix and grow as a houseplant.

You can also bring the whole plant indoors and raise it like your other houseplants. Monitor and control pests as needed. Grow the overwintering annual in a bright, sunny window or under artificial lights and keep the soil moist. Don't be alarmed if the plant drops most of its leaves. It will soon send out new leaves more suited for its indoor location.

A common, but less successful, method is dormant storage for geraniums. Most of our basements are too warm for this method to work. But that doesn't stop a determined gardener. Place plants in a cool dark location for the winter. Some gardeners knock the soil off the roots and hang the plants from the ceiling or place them in a brown paper bag. Others leave the plants in their containers. In mid-March, pot up the plants if needed and place them in a warm, sunny location. Prune back to four inches, water, and wait to fertilize until new growth appears. With some luck, you will have your favorite geranium to put out in the garden.

Stunning Coleus

Ageratum

Ageratum houstonianum

The name says it all. Ageratum is a Greek word, meaning "not old," and referring to the long-lasting blooms. Gardeners have been enjoying the longevity of this neat and tidy edging plant for many years. The compact types form tight mounds covered with flowers all season long. These are often sold as blue, white, or pink ageratums. Selecting a named cultivar will help ensure you get the size, flowering, and growth habit desired. Planted in large numbers, these annuals will provide a mass of color. The blue cultivars are often combined with red and white annuals for a patriotic display. The taller types are looser and more open. They are great for cutting and work well as fillers in perennial gardens or as part of an informal flower border. Add ageratums to the landscape to help attract butterflies to your yard.

Other Common Name
Floss Flower

Bloom Period and Seasonal Color
Spring through frost blooms in blue, lavender, white, and pink.

Mature Height × Spread
6 to 15 in. × 12 in.

When, Where, and How to Plant

Purchase ageratums as transplants or start from seeds indoors. Start seeds indoors in mid-March. Sprinkle the fine ageratum seeds on the surface of moist, sterile, seed starter mix. Gently tamp the seeds for good soil contact, but do not cover them—they need light to germinate. Keep the soil about 70 to 75 degrees Fahrenheit, and moist. Seeds will sprout in five to ten days. Transplant hardened-off seedlings outdoors after all danger of frost is past. Grow in full sun or partial shade with moist, well-drained soil. Space compact plants 6 inches apart and taller cultivars up to 9 inches apart.

Growing Tips

If placed properly, ageratums require little maintenance. Make sure the soil is slightly dry before watering. Too much water can lead to root rot. Excess fertilization can encourage leggy growth and discourage flowers.

Care

Occasional deadheading keeps the plants blooming throughout the season and improves the appearance of white cultivars as the flowers fade. Cut back leggy plants halfway to encourage more attractive growth. Powdery mildew may be a problem; avoid it by planting in a sunny area with good air circulation.

Companion Planting and Design

Ageratums make great additions to flower gardens, containers, rock gardens, or shrub borders. They combine well with dusty miller, salvia, geraniums, and marigolds. I tuck a few of the taller ones in with allium, blue oat grass, Russian sage, and other perennials.

My Personal Favorites

I prefer taller cultivars. 'Blue Horizon' grows 18 inches tall and 12 inches wide, looks good in adverse weather, and has nice long stems for cutting. 'Leilani Blue' is a newer cultivar that grows 14 to 16 inches tall and 10 to 12 inches wide. Both have big fluffy flowers that do not need deadheading. The Hawaii series is compact (6 inches) and readily available. The Artist series is a proven winner selected for its uniform growth (7 to 9 inches tall) and weather resistance. 'Blue Danube' also has uniform growth, and 'Swing Pink' is a compact (6 to 8 inches), pink-flowering cultivar.

Alyssum
Lobularia maritima

When, Where, and How to Plant

Purchase alyssum as a transplant or start from seeds indoors. Seeds should be started indoors in mid-March. Sprinkle seeds on moist, sterile seed starter mix. Gently tamp the seeds for good seed-soil contact, but do not cover them. Keep the soil at 70 degrees Fahrenheit, and moist. They will sprout in about eight days. Overwatering and deep planting can lead to damping-off of seedlings. Reduce the risk of this disease by using a sterile mix and clean containers. Seeds can be sown directly outdoors after the last hard frost. These plants will bloom much later than those started indoors. Hardened-off transplants can be planted outdoors after all danger of frost is past. Plant alyssum transplants 6 to 8 inches apart for complete and quick cover.

Growing Tips

Plants need little care when grown in moist, well-drained soil. Extreme heat may cause the plants, especially purple ones, to stop flowering. Clip back leggy plants, water as needed, but don't fertilize. Plants will begin flowering as soon as temperatures cool.

Care

Alyssum is low maintenance, free flowering, and basically pest free. Alyssum is at its peak in cool weather and will even tolerate a light frost, giving you a good fall show.

Companion Planting and Design

Try direct-seeding alyssum around spring-flowering bulbs. The alyssum will cover declining foliage and fill empty spaces. Use it as an edging plant in your annual flower beds or rose gardens. It mixes well with other container plants, spilling over the edge. Alyssum can also be used to provide some color while softening the look of steppers and planting walls.

My Personal Favorite

Plants are often sold simply as white, pink, or purple alyssum. Two commonly seen white cultivars are 'New Carpet of Snow', a 3- to 4-inch tall spreading plant, and 'Snow Crystals', a low grower with larger flowers and good heat tolerance. The 'Easter Bonnet' cultivars are compact, uniform in size, and come in pink, violet, or mixed colors.

Sweet alyssum is a longtime favorite of gardeners. The lovely fragrance makes a nice addition to any landscape. Alyssum is one of those annuals that may reseed in your garden. It's never happened to you? Maybe you cultivated it out before planting your new annuals. This is one case where procrastination is rewarded with scattered plants of alyssum. I must admit there was a period I did not plant alyssum - too common for a horticulturist's garden. But one day when helping a friend carry and plant flats of alyssum, I was reminded what I was missing. Now I include a few plants in with perennials and always have a border of parsley and alyssum at the edge of my vegetable garden. The butterflies are also glad I decided to add one of their favorites in my garden.

Other Common Name
Sweet Alyssum

Bloom Period and Seasonal Color
Spring through frost blooms in white, pink, lavender, and apricot.

Mature Height × Spread
4 to 8 in. × 10 to 15 in.

Annual Pinks

Dianthus chinensis

Garden pinks are an old-time favorite that have many relatively new, award-winning cultivars. Their informal growth habit, lightly scented flowers, and blue-green foliage make them a nice addition to the flower garden. It seems gardeners either love or hate this plant. If you have cool temperatures and well-drained soil, annual pinks will bloom all season long. Otherwise they tend to become unkempt and need a little grooming or a trip to the compost pile. Select one of the more heat tolerant cultivars for better performance during the dog days of summer. The attractive, fragrant flowers helped name this plant. The botanical name, Dianthus, comes from the Greek meaning "divine flower." The common name, pinks, doesn't refer to its flower color but rather to the frilly edges of the flowers. The flower edges appear to be cut with pinking shears.

Other Common Name
Garden Pinks

Bloom Period and Seasonal Color
Summer through fall blooms in red, pink, white, and bicolored.

Mature Height × Spread
6 to 12 in. × 12 in.

When, Where, and How to Plant

Pinks are available as seeds or transplants. Start garden pinks from seeds indoors about eight to ten weeks before the last spring frost. The seeds need moist temperatures (70 degrees Fahrenheit) to germinate within a week. Or try planting the seeds directly in the garden, after all danger of frost has passed, for a late-season flower display. Hardened-off transplants will tolerate a light frost and can be moved outdoors several weeks prior to the last spring frost. Cool summer temperatures and well-drained soil are key. Grow annual pinks in an area shaded from the hot afternoon sun. Avoid poorly drained locations. Space smaller cultivars about 6 inches apart and larger ones up to 12 inches apart.

Growing Tips

Too much moisture will kill these plants—avoid over-watering. High-nitrogen fertilizers can discourage flowering and cause tip burn on the leaves. Follow soil tests recommendations or incorporate a low nitrogen, slow-release fertilizer prior to planting.

Care

Surprisingly, our summers can actually get too hot for annual pinks. Trim back unsightly plants halfway during hot weather. Water as needed and don't fertilize. Once temperatures cool, the plants will reward you with fresh new growth and flowers. Mulch to keep roots cool. With a little protection and cooperation from nature, these plants will sometimes survive our winters.

Companion Planting and Design

Use annual pinks for early- and late-season interest. Garden pinks also provide nectar for butterflies when little else is blooming. Mix with perennials to fill in flowering voids or combine with baby's breath for an in-the-garden floral bouquet.

My Personal Favorites

There are several heat-tolerant All-America Selections-winning annual dianthus. Recent winners include 'Can Can Scarlet' with double fragrant flowers on 14 inch stems. 'Corona Magic' was selected for the cherry, lavender, and blended flowers that appear on a single plant. 'Melody Pink' is 22 inches tall and great for cutting. Older winners include the heat tolerant, compact Telstar series. The Parfait series also provides a compact growth habit with single-frilled flowers.

Begonia

Begonia semperflorens-cultorum

When, Where, and How to Plant

Place hardened-off transplants outside in late May or early June, after all danger of frost is past. Begonias can grow in a wide range of light conditions. They prefer partial shade but will tolerate full sun if the soil is kept moist. Adding organic matter to most Minnesota soils will increase the health and vigor of the plants. Wax begonia transplants can be purchased in flats or small 3- to 4-inch pots. Space small cultivars about 6 to 8 inches apart. Larger cultivars can be planted 8 to 12 inches apart. Proper spacing will help prevent disease problems.

Growing Tips

Make sure the soil is moist but not overly wet. Avoid overhead watering and remove diseased plant parts as they appear to help minimize disease problems. Avoid excess nitrogen fertilizer that can increase the risk of disease and decrease flowering.

Care

Begonia's small flowers give you a great display without regular deadheading. Wax begonias occasionally suffer from powdery mildew, botrytis blight, leaf spots, and stem rots. Good soil preparation and proper spacing of the plants can help prevent these problems. Remove diseased flowers and leaves as soon as they appear. I find deadheading during wet weather helps reduce botrytis blight and leaf spot diseases.

Companion Planting and Design

Begonias look great when used as an edging plant, en masse in a flower bed, or as an annual ground cover. Try using them in containers and hanging baskets. They perform well in many of the new planters, such as the hanging bag, pole, and vertical wall planters. Try combining with alyssum, ferns, or caladiums.

My Personal Favorites

The Cocktail series has bronze leaves, comes in a variety of colors, and tolerates full sun. The Party and Olympia series are vigorous and grow 12 to 15 inches tall. Both are available in several colors. 'Dragon Wing' is a relatively new angel wing begonia. It grows 12 to 15 inches tall and has large pendulous flowers with glossy, green, wing shaped leaves.

Begonia is a standard plant for park, municipal, business, and home landscapes. This durable choice provides attractive foliage and a season of bloom with minimal care. Most gardeners buy transplants since the tiny seeds (2 million per ounce) take more than four months to develop into flowering plants. Some gardeners extend their growing season and save a few plants for next year's garden. Simply take cuttings or move potted plants indoors for the winter (see page 25). Wax begonia leaves are glossy and come in green or bronze. The bronze-leafed cultivars tend to be more sun tolerant. Individual flowers are small and can be single or double. Though the blooms are diminutive in size, they are large in number. No matter what type you choose, wax begonias will give an impressive display.

Other Common Name
Wax Begonia

Bloom Period and Seasonal Color
Summer to frost blooms in white, red, rose, and pink.

Mature Height × Spread
6 to 12 in. × 6 to 12 in.

Cleome

Cleome hasslerana

When driving through any Minnesota city, you are bound to witness the beauty of these large, delicate flowers. Plantings of cleomes along city boulevards and in county parks are designed to catch the eyes of passersby. And that they do. The common name, spider flower, aptly describes the flower. The long stamens extend beyond the petals giving the plant a light, airy appearance. The long, thin seedpods are also attractive and add to the "spidery" look. The former botanical name, Cleome spinosa, describes the small spines on the base of the leaves. Keep these in mind when placing and weeding around the plants. One gardener told me all her guests received a prickly hug from the cleomes growing next to her front door. Cleome attracts butterflies and hummingbirds and makes a great cut flower with an interesting, often described as skunk-like, fragrance.

Other Common Name
Spider Cleome

Bloom Period and Seasonal Color
Summer through fall blooms in white, pink, rose, or purple.

Mature Height × Spread
Up to 6 ft. × 2 ft.

When, Where, and How to Plant
Start seeds indoors about six weeks before the last frost. Seeds can be purchased or collected from existing plants. Place collected seeds in the freezer for one week before planting. Provide seeds with light and warm (80 degrees Fahrenheit) temperatures for germination. Cleome transplants are usually sold in 3- or 4-inch pots. Purchased or home-grown transplants should be hardened off and then planted outdoors after all danger of frost is past. They grow in a variety of soils and full sun to part shade. Remember, these are big plants that need lots of space. Allow at least 2 feet between plants. Cleomes often reseed themselves in the garden.

Growing Tips
Although they are very tolerant of heat and drought, they will also benefit from ample moisture. Water thoroughly whenever the top few inches of soil begins to dry.

Care
Cleomes require very little maintenance. You may have to weed out a few unwanted plants the following year. These plants are self supporting (no staking required), but they do tend to slouch with age. Staking or nearby plantings can provide support if you want to contain the plants or prefer a more stiff and formal appearance.

Companion Planting and Design
This tall plant is an excellent backdrop to flower borders or a striking centerpiece in an island bed. Its large size and color can add punch to undeveloped landscapes. Use them to fill in voids left between properly spaced young shrubs or empty spaces left for future planning.

My Personal Favorites
The Sparkler series is a relatively new introductions. The smaller, 3 to 4 feet tall, plants are uniform in size, have a long bloom period, and tolerate extreme heat and sun. 'Sparkler Blush' has 4- to 6-inch flowers in pink with a flush of white, and 'Sparkler Rose' has similar rosy-red flowers. 'Helen Campbell' with white flowers and the Queen series are longtime favorites. Both grow at least 4 feet tall, and the Queen series has rose, purple, pink, white, or cherry colored flowers.

Cockscomb
Celosia argentea

When, Where, and How to Plant

Start cockscomb seeds indoors eight weeks prior to the last spring frost. The seeds need light, moisture, and 70- to 75-degree Fahrenheit temperatures to germinate. Cockscomb can be seeded directly outdoors, although plants started outdoors will bloom much later. Lightly cover the seeds and keep them moist. Move hardened-off transplants outdoors after all danger of frost is past. Wait until the soil and air are warm to avoid stunted plant growth. Cockscomb performs best in full sun and well-drained soil. Space small cultivars 6 to 8 inches apart and larger ones 12 to 15 inches apart.

Growing Tips

Once established, these are very drought tolerant plants. Water new transplants often enough to keep the soil moist. Once they are established, you will only need to water when the top few inches of soil are dry.

Care

Properly placed, celosias are low maintenance. Poorly drained soil can result in stem rot; wet weather can result in leaf spot. Mites may be a problem in hot, dry weather. A strong blast of water from the garden hose or insecticidal soap is often enough to keep mites under control. Occasionally deadhead or harvest flowers to keep the plants blooming all season long. Mist the dense blooms with water to dislodge stowaway insects before bringing indoors.

Companion Planting and Design

A mass planting of cockscomb makes a bold statement in any landscape. Try using the short, crested types as edging plants. Use the taller types of plume, crested or wheat celosia, in the middle or the back of the flower border. Celosia's drought tolerance makes it a good candidate for container gardens.

My Personal Favorite

The 2004 Gold Medal winners 'New Look Red' and 'New Look Yellow' provide a beautiful floral display all summer long with minimal care. The plume type blooms top the 12 to 18 inch tall plants. 'Prestige Scarlet's' small red-crested flowers on a medium (12 to 15 inch) plant always attract attention. *Celosia spicata* Flamingo series (tall) and 'Pink Candle' (short) plants have barley-like flower-spikes.

Bright, bold, and tough, cockscomb is a good choice for hot, dry areas. It provides a bold splash of color outdoors in the garden or indoors in a vase. The flowers can be crested like a rooster's comb (Cristata group) or plumed (Plumosa group) like a feather. Its close relative, Celosia spicata, often listed as the Spicata group, has short, narrow, barley-like flowers. The crested types remind me of brains though others say colorful coral sounds much more attractive. The cresting is the result of fasciation. This abnormal cell growth produces flatten stems and a proliferation of flower buds. All flower types come in warm colors of red, yellow, gold, orange, and pink with green, red, or bronze leaves. In fact the botanical name, Celosia, means "burned" in Greek and refers to the flower color.

Other Common Name
Celosia

Bloom Period and Seasonal Color
Summer through fall blooms in red, yellow, gold, orange, and pink.

Mature Height × Spread
6 to 30 in. × 6 to 18 in.

Coleus

Solenostemon scutellarioides

Many of you may know coleus as a houseplant first and a bedding plant second. That's the case for me. An easy-to-grow indoor plant, coleus is equally at home in the garden. The Victorians used this popular plant both ways. Coleus spent the summers outdoors with other annuals and moved indoors for winter. Pinched, groomed, and watered throughout the winter, the original plant and any offspring were moved back outdoors the following summer. This annual is grown for its colorful foliage, not its flowers. Breeding efforts have resulted in a wide variety of leaf shapes, colors, and variegated patterns. Minimal flowering and self-branching types are also available. These features result in less maintenance and a better-looking plant. The old and new sun-loving coleus cultivars show greater sun tolerance and are quite the rage.

Other Common Name
Painted Nettle

Bloom Period and Seasonal Color
Season long foliage in combinations of green, chartreuse, yellow, buff, salmon, orange, red, purple, and brown .

Mature Height × Spread
6 to 24 in. × 12 in.

When, Where, and How to Plant
Purchase coleus as transplants or start from seeds and cuttings. Start seeds indoors eight weeks before the final spring frost. Seeds need light, moisture, and 70-degree Fahrenheit temperatures to germinate. Cuttings can be taken any time indoors. Allow at least four weeks for cuttings to develop a sustainable root system before planting them outdoors. Coleus is very frost sensitive, so wait until late May or early June when all danger of frost is past before placing hardened-off transplants outdoors. Coleus prefers moist soil with lots of organic matter and performs best in partial shade. It will tolerate full shade and sun. Heavy shade causes thin and leggy plants, while full sun may cause leaves to fade and even scorch. Buy coleus as bedding plants in flats or small, 3- to 4-inch pots. Space plants 10 to 12 inches apart when planting.

Growing Tips
Water whenever the top few inches of soil are crumbly and moist. Mulching will help keep the roots cool and moist.

Care
Remove flowers as soon as they appear. This will encourage new branches to form, giving you a fuller, more compact plant. The self-branching types of coleus produce only a few flowers and require very little pruning. Slugs may be a problem on coleus grown in the shade. Coleus will die with the first fall frost. See the chapter introduction for tips on overwintering them indoors.

Companion Planting and Design
Try coleus in flower beds or containers. Planted en masse they put on quite a show. I like to back the colorful foliage with solid green plants such as hosta or single-color flowers that echo one of the colors found in the coleus leaves.

My Personal Favorites
Look for self-branching cultivars that do not require pinching. Then select a leaf shape and color combination that fits your garden design. 'India Frills' is one of my favorites. It has small, colorful, irregular leaves on a full, compact plant. 'Solar Sunrise', 'Cranberry Salad', and the Hurricane series are a few of the newer, sun-loving introductions.

Cosmos

Cosmos species

When, Where, and How to Plant

Start seeds indoors four weeks before the last spring frost. Seeds need moist, 70-degree Fahrenheit starting mix to germinate. Cosmos seeds can be planted directly outside. Plant seeds or transplants after the last spring frost. Seeds should germinate in five to ten days. Cosmos can also be purchased as bedding plants in flats. Move hardened-off transplants outdoors after all danger of frost is past. Cosmos does best in full sun and well-drained soil, although it will tolerate hot, dry conditions. Thin seedlings to and space transplants 12 inches apart.

Growing Tips

Minimal care is needed to keep the plants producing beautiful flowers. Water established plants whenever the top few inches of soil starts to dry. Avoid overfertilizing since too much nitrogen will give you tall, leafy plants that tend to fall over.

Care

Pinch back tall cultivars of Cosmos bipinnatus early in the season to promote fuller, sturdier plants. If sited correctly, these plants are fairly pest free. You may occasionally see aphids and Japanese beetles feeding on these plants. Wilt and aster yellows can be damaging. Remove infested plants as soon as they are found.

Companion Planting and Design

Add these plants to the garden, and you will be sure to attract butterflies. Dwarf cosmos plants are suitable for the flower garden and container plantings. Taller cultivars, especially those of *Cosmos bipinnatus*, can become floppy and are best used as fillers or background plants where the surrounding plants can provide support. Both species blend with a wide range of annuals and perennials.

My Personal Favorite

Cosmos bipinnatus Sonata series are dwarf plants 12 to 18 inches tall with white, pink, and red flowers. 'Sea Shells' grows 36 inches tall and has fluted flowers of white, pink, and crimson that resemble a shell. *Cosmos sulphureus* 'Cosmic Orange' is a 2000 AAS winner. The 2-inch bright orange flowers top the 12 inch tall plants. Chocolate cosmos, *Cosmos atrosanguineus*, is a perennial grown as an annual in the north and is prized for its velvety maroon-chocolate flowers and chocolate fragrance.

Neat and tidy, loose and wild, or somewhere in between: all these descriptions fit cosmos. The species and cultivar you grow will determine the look you get. Cosmos sulphureus produces single and double yellow, orange, or orange-red flowers throughout summer. A bit neater in appearance, they are suitable for formal and informal gardens. Cosmos bipinnatus is somewhat looser and informal. The finer-textured leaves and large single flowers of pink, white, red, or purple create an airy feel in the garden. The name Cosmos is from the Greek kosmos meaning "beautiful." The bipinnatus refers to the bi-pinnate, or feathery, leaves. In the other species, sulphureus refers to the sulphur-yellow flowers. Once you plant Cosmos, you will be rewarded with seedlings the following year. Keep in mind that the seedlings of hybrids will not always look like the parent plant.

Bloom Period and Seasonal Color
Summer until frost blooms in yellow, orange, red, white, pink, rose, and purple.

Mature Height × Spread
12 to 72 in. × 12 to 24 in.

Dusty Miller

Senecio cineraria

The silvery-gray foliage of dusty miller provides a nice contrast in the flower garden. The leaves can be slightly lobed or deeply divided and lacy, depending on the cultivar. It is often used as an edging plant in rose gardens. The fine-textured silvery foliage contrasts nicely with the glossy green leaves of the roses. The light-colored leaves stand out in the night landscape and make a nice foil for dark colored flowers. Include a few in the garden where they can be enjoyed even after the first fall frost. Some gardeners have managed to keep plants over winter. A little winter mulch, a protected site, and cooperation from nature results in two, three, even four seasons of enjoyment. The plants may not be pretty, but the accomplishment is great for any northern gardener.

Bloom Period and Seasonal Color
Season long foliage in silver-white.

Mature Height × Spread
6 to 15 in. × 6 to 15 in.

When, Where, and How to Plant
Seeds should be started indoors about ten weeks before the last frost. Use a well-drained, sterile seed starting mix. Spread the seeds on the surface of the mix and water. Keep the planting mix moist, not wet and at 75 degrees Fahrenheit. Use clean containers and sterile potting mix to avoid damping off disease. Place hardened-off transplants outdoors after all danger of a hard frost is past. Dusty miller prefers well-drained soil. It will tolerate light shade but NOT wet feet. Space the plants 8 to 10 inches apart.

Growing Tips
This is a low-maintenance, easy-to-grow plant when it is placed in the right spot. Avoid stem and root rot with well-drained soil and proper watering. Water the soil thoroughly and allow it to dry slightly before watering again.

Care
Trim back some of the unruly plants to keep them full and compact. Many newer cultivars have been bred to maintain a compact growth habit without shearing. Watch for small, cream or yellow, butterfly-attracting flowers that may appear late in the fall or on older plants. Clip off the flowering stems to keep the plant neat and tidy.

Companion Planting and Design
Combine dusty miller with other annuals in containers. Use the silver foliage as an eye catching contrast behind dark blue or deep purple flowers. Or use the silvery foliage to provide visual relief or continuity in a multicolored flower bed. Dusty miller is often used as an edging plant. Use it with care. I have seen its bold features create an out-of-place formal edge when it was used in an informal garden.

My Personal Favorites
Select a cultivar with your desired foliage texture, and size. 'Silver Queen', 'Silver Dust', and 'Silver Lace' are all compact, 6- to 8-inch-tall plants with lacy foliage. 'Silver Lace' has the most finely divided leaves. 'Cirrus' is slightly taller, with rounded, only slightly lobed leaves. 'Hoar Frost' has finely cut leaves on 12-inch plants. 'Snow Storm' has strap-like leaves that are more tufted in appearance.

Fan Flower

Scaevola aemula

When, Where, and How to Plant

Fan flowers are sold as seed or as bedding plants usually in 3- or 4-inch pots. Start seeds indoors six to eight weeks before the last spring frost. Grow in sterile seed starter mix that is moist and 66 to 75 degrees Fahrenheit. Or take cuttings in late spring from plants overwintered indoors. Place hardened-off transplants in the garden after the danger of frost has passed. Grow in full to part sun with moist, well-drained to dry soils. Use several plants in a container or space 20 to 24 inches apart in the garden.

Growing Tips

Fan flower is heat, drought, and salt tolerant. Water new plantings to keep the soil moist but not soggy. Allow the top few inches of soil to dry before watering established plants in the garden. Check container gardens daily and water as needed. Proper fertilization will encourage summer-long bloom (see the chapter introduction).

Care

These new comers are pest free. Avoid poorly drained soils and overwatering. Take cuttings in late summer or move healthy plants indoors for the winter.

Companion Planting and Design

This plant provides a tropical feel to containers and gardens. The green foliage is a nice backdrop for the fan-shaped flowers. I like to use it in containers or hanging baskets mixed with silver foliage trailers such as lotus vine and licorice plants. These and 'Silver Falls' *Dichondra* make nice partners when growing fan flower as an annual ground cover. I recently saw scaevola used under the large silvery leaves of cardoon. The green leaves and blue flowers peeking out from under the cardoon provided color, contrast, and eye catching appeal.

My Personal Favorites

The Proven Winner 'Blue Wonder' is probably the most readily available cultivar. It has blue flowers from planting until frost. A 2004 Proven winner, 'Whirlwind White' performs just about as well as 'Blue Wonder' but with white flowers. New cultivars of this increasingly popular annual are being developed. Check catalogs, the internet, and your favorite garden center for new introductions.

The unique flower shape and blue to violet color have helped this newcomer make a mark in northern gardens. A native of Australia, it tolerates hot dry and humid summers. The summer-long bloom is easy to maintain with minimal care. You have probably seen this low growing, spreading plant in container gardens or creeping around taller plants when used as a ground cover. I find it easy to mix this colorful yet subtle annual in just about any landscape. You may need to do a little hunting for this summer beauty, but I think you will find it well worth the effort. The name Scaevola is from the Latin word, scaevus, for "on the left side." This refers to the flowers with their petals arranged to one side much like a fan. Thus the common name fan flower.

Other Common Name
Creeping Scaevola

Bloom Period and Seasonal Color
Summer long blooms of blue, violet, white, or mauve.

Mature Height and Spread
Up to 8 in. × 36 in.

Flowering Tobacco
Nicotiana alata

Looking for a showy alternative to geraniums? This free-flowering plant will produce a floral display all season long. Flowering tobacco has star-shaped flowers with long throats. These are perfect blooms for attracting hummingbirds. Their ability to draw butterflies into the garden has given them the nickname of butterfly plant. Flowering tobacco is easy to grow. The flower clusters are held above the leaves, creating a colorful display that moves with the breeze. Many of the flowering tobacco plants are fragrant in the evening, which is another big plus. I always include a few plants near the garage or my front door for a fragrant welcome home. Don't forget to cut a few to enjoy indoors. Flowering tobacco plants will reseed themselves in your garden. Most of the seedlings tend to be taller, wider, and more fragrant than their hybrid parent.

Other Common Name
Ornamental Tobacco

Bloom Period and Seasonal Color
Summer until frost blooms in white, red, pink, lavender, green, and yellow.

Mature Height × Spread
10 in. to 5 feet × 6 to 24 in.

When, Where, and How to Plant
Start seeds indoors about eight weeks before the last spring frost. Flowering tobacco seeds need light, moisture, and 70-degree temperatures to germinate. Sprinkle the seeds on the surface of the starting mix. Lightly tamp and water the seeds. Flowering tobacco is also sold as a bedding plant in flats. Move hardened-off transplants outdoors after all danger of frost is past. They prefer moist, well-drained soil but will tolerate an occasional dry spell. Space transplants 8 to 12 inches apart depending on the cultivar. The larger cultivars need a little more space.

Growing Tips
Once it is established, it can tolerate dry periods, but even properly watered plants may appear wilted in the hot afternoon sun. So before you water, wait until the temperature cools to see if the plants recover.

Care
Though free-flowering all season long, an occasional deadheading will help keep the display fresh and full. Healthy plants will tolerate the few diseases and insects that can attack. With the increased use of flowering tobacco, we are seeing an increase in damage by Colorado potato beetles. These insects eat holes in the leaves, and large populations of Colorado potato beetles can be quite damaging. Handpicking is usually sufficient control.

Companion Planting and Design
Shorter cultivars can be planted en masse as bedding plants or used in containers. Larger cultivars serve as specimen or background plants. Even these larger cultivars can be effectively used in container plantings. Try adding a few flowering tobacco plants to the perennial garden. Their informal growth habit and smaller flowers help them fit right in.

My Personal Favorites
'Avalon Bright Pink' is a 2001 AAS winner. The bright pink flowers top the 10-inch plants. The low maintenance plants are heat and drought tolerant and provide season-long bloom. *Nicotiana sylvestris* is a big plant that produces fragrant white flowers. The plant grows 5 feet tall and does not need staking. *Nicotiana langsdorfii* 'Cream Splash' is a distinctive variety with lime green blooms.

Fuchsia
Fuchsia hybrida

When, Where, and How to Plant
Fuchsias are available as hanging baskets or in 3- to 4-inch pots. They can also be started from cuttings and seed (from specialized catalogs). Take cuttings from overwintered plants in early spring, root, pot in a well-drained planting mix, and harden off. Move hardened-off plants outdoors after all danger of frost is past. Grow fuchsias in shady locations with moist soil. Avoid hot sun and windy locations. Plant the upright types in the ground spaced 12 inches apart.

Growing Tips
Fuchsias require moist soil. Mulch will help maintain moisture. Check the soil in hanging baskets and containers once or twice a day during hot weather. Water containers thoroughly, allowing the excess to run out the drainage holes. Fertilize planters frequently throughout the summer with any flowering plant fertilizer according to the label directions (see chapter introduction regarding fertilizing). Plants in an in-ground garden should be watered whenever the top few inches of soil are moist and crumbly.

Care
Pinch back faded flowers to keep the plants blooming all summer long. Fuchsias will stop flowering during hot weather. Once the weather cools, the flowers will return. Fuchsias can be overwintered indoors like geraniums. Bring dormant, stored fuschias out of storage in late February, prune them back to old wood and grow them as houseplants. They have no serious pests, but watch for and control aphids during hot dry weather.

Companion Planting and Design
The trailing types can be planted in hanging baskets and containers. Try mixing fuchsias with other shade-tolerant plants like ferns, begonias, and sweet potato vine. Use tree-trained fuchsias as specimen or patio plants. You will need a place to winter them indoors. Upright forms can be used in containers or as bedding plants. Use the microfuchsias and minifuchsias in table top planters.

My Personal Favorites
'Thalia' and 'Gartenmeister' are the most available upright types. They have long, tubular, orange-red flowers. Check the specialized garden centers for some of the newer microfuchsias and minifuchsias.

Fuchsias are traditional favorites for shade-tolerant hanging baskets. How many of us have given or received a hanging fuchsia basket for Mother's Day? These unique flowering plants put on quite the show on a patio, porch, or shepherd's crook in that shady spot in the landscape. Consider mixing them with other shade tolerant plants for a different look. The single, semidouble and double pendulous flowers are quite ornamental, leading to the other common name—lady's eardrops (earrings). Look closely and you can see the decorative reflex sepals exposing the colorful petals and long stamens. Place one of these beauties near your hummingbird feeder to help attract these colorful flyers. I like to use the upright types in containers and in ground gardens. The tubular flowers are a bit less ornate but just as attractive to gardeners, butterflies, and hummingbirds.

Other Common Name
Lady's Eardrops

Bloom Period and Seasonal Color
Summer until frost blooms in pink, red, purple, and white.

Mature Height × Spread
8 to 36 in. × 12 to 24 in.

Geranium

Pelargonium × hortorum

The geranium is one of the most popular bedding plants. Geraniums form a mound of decorative foliage at the base. The leaves are rounded with scalloped or toothed edges and may be solid green or variegated. Either type may have a zone (a ring around the middle of the leaf) of bronze-green or red. The showy flowers are held above the leaves and can be single, semidouble, or double. There are new geranium cultivars introduced every year. The trailing geranium used in hanging baskets is the ivy geranium (Pelargonium peltatum). This plant has waxy leaves and performs best in full sun and cool conditions. Grow it in an east facing location or other area where it is sheltered from the hot afternoon sun.

Other Common Name
Zonal Geranium

Bloom Period and Seasonal Color
Summer until frost blooms in red, pink, rose, violet, salmon, and white.

Mature Height × Spread
12 to 20 in. × 12 in.

When, Where, and How to Plant
Sow seeds twelve to sixteen weeks prior to the last spring frost. Seeds need a moist, 70- to 75-degree Fahrenheit starting mix to germinate. Or start plants from cuttings taken in the spring. Geraniums are available from garden centers in 3- or 4-inch pots. Plant hardened-off transplants outdoors after all danger of frost is past. Geraniums prefer full sun with moist, well-drained soil. Space the plants 8 to 12 inches apart.

Growing Tips
Geraniums do best when kept cool and moist in well-drained soil. Mulch the soil to keep roots cool and moist and the plants at peak performance. Water established plants thoroughly whenever the top few inches of soil are crumbly and moist. Geraniums grown in containers need a little extra care. Check the soil moisture at least once a day. Fertilize planters frequently with any flowering plant fertilizer. Follow label directions.

Care
Deadhead frequently to keep the plants blooming. Though easy to grow, geraniums do have several pest problems. Check plants frequently. Bacterial leaf spot, stem rot, and botrytis blight are some of the more common diseases. Avoid these problems by purchasing disease-free plants, planting them in well-drained soil, and watering properly. Remove damaged leaves as soon as they appear. Geraniums can be wintered indoors. See the chapter introduction for details on overwintering these and other annuals.

Companion Planting and Design
Geraniums work well in containers and hanging baskets. A mass planting of geraniums will provide a season-long floral display. Try interplanting other annuals like heliotrope for a little different look.

My Personal Favorites
Choose one of the many varieties that is best suited for your garden situation. I like the Black Magic series whose flowers contrast nicely with the chocolate color leaves. The pink with dark rose centered flowers makes 'Freckles' a favorite. Consider adding scented geraniums (*Pelargonium* species) to the garden. They come in a variety of shapes, textures, and fragrances. Place these plants where you will brush against them for a fragrant surprise.

Heliotrope
Heliotropium arborescens

When, Where, and How to Plant

Heliotrope is available as seed through garden catalogs and as bedding plants in 3- or 4-inch containers. Start seeds indoors ten to twelve weeks before the last spring frost. Grow in a moist sterile potting mix kept at 61 to 68 degrees Fahrenheit. Be patient; it takes three weeks for the seeds to germinate. Plants can also be started from cuttings in early spring. Move hardened-off transplants outdoors after the danger of frost. Grow in full to part sun in moist well-drained soil. Space plants 12 inches apart in the garden.

Growing Tips

Water established plants thoroughly whenever the top few inches of soil are crumbly and moist. Check container gardens every day and water when the top few inches start to dry. Water thoroughly so the excess runs out the bottom of the pot. Incorporate a slow-release fertilizer into the container soil at the beginning of the season or use a liquid flowering plant fertilizer throughout the summer. Read and follow label directions. For in-ground plantings, follow fertilization recommendations in the chapter introduction. Mulch the soil to conserve moisture and suppress weeds.

Care

Heliotrope are fairly pest free. Purchase healthy, pest free plants to avoid problems. Monitor plants for mealybugs, spider mites, aphids, and whiteflies and control as needed. If problems arise, use insecticidal soap to keep these insect populations at a tolerable level. Many gardeners overwinter the plants.

Companion Planting and Design

I like to mix the purple heliotrope with other lesser used annuals such as Persian Shield (*Strobilanthes*) or osteospermum, or liven up traditional plantings of geranium, dusty miller, or petunias. In containers, I may add a few edibles such as 'Purple Ruffles' basil and 'Tricolor' sage.

My Personal Favorites

'Marine' is a beauty and the most readily available. It is compact, 18 inches tall, with deep violet flowers. 'Atlantis' has maintained a strong vanilla scent despite years of hybridizing. Look for the white cultivars of 'Alba' or 'White Lady'. 'Light Eyes' has lavender flowers with a lighter center.

A favorite of the Victorian era gardeners, this fragrant annual has been finding its way back into Minnesota gardens. It originally arrived here via covered wagon but now is available as seed through garden catalogs and transplants at some garden centers. The dark green leaves are slightly hairy, creating a nice backdrop for the large flower clusters. I have heard the fragrance described as somewhat like vanilla, baby powder, or licorice. I tend to smell the last. The hummingbirds and butterflies also find the flowers attractive. Some gardeners move the plants indoors for the winter. Use heliotrope in containers or combine it with common annuals for a change of pace. Used for perfumes and scenting bath water, you won't want to miss the lovely fragrance. Place it near the patio, window, or entryway where it can be enjoyed.

Other Common Name
Cherry Pie Plant

Bloom Period and Seasonal Color
Summer until frost in violet-blue, light blue, and white.

Mature Height and Spread
12 to 18 in. by 12 to 15 in.

Impatiens
Impatiens walleriana

Impatiens provide a sea of color for the shade garden. That's why it's such a popular annual. With its mound of green leaves covered with 1- to 2-inch-diameter single or double blooms, this free-flowering plant will reward you with color from summer through frost. And with minimal care. Many gardeners lacking shade envied those who were able to grow these blooming beauties. The New Guinea impatiens were introduced as sun impatiens to fill this gardening niche. I find these sun-lovers actually do best in part shade. Mulch the soil, keep the soil moist, and pinch back the plants to keep them looking good in the sun. Next time you walk through a wetland, notice our native impatiens, Jewelweed. Known botanically as Impatiens capensis *and* Impatiens pallida, *it grows to 5 feet, producing yellow and orange flowers.*

Other Common Name
Busy Lizzie

Bloom Period and Seasonal Color
Summer until frost blooms in white, red, pink, orange, and purple.

Mature Height × Spread
6 to 18 in. × 12 to 24 in.

When, Where, and How to Plant
Start impatiens from seeds twelve weeks before the last spring frost. Seeds need light, moisture, and 70-degree Fahrenheit temperatures to germinate. Be patient; it takes two to three weeks for the seeds to sprout. Impatiens is subject to damping-off disease. Use a sterile starting mix and containers and don't overwater. Impatiens is available as a bedding plant in flats or as a hanging basket. Hardened-off transplants can be moved outdoors in late May or early June after all danger of frost is past. They are very sensitive to frost. Impatiens can take some sun when they are grown in moist, organic soil. Space small cultivars 8 inches apart and larger cultivars 12 inches apart.

Growing Tips
Mulch the soil to keep the roots cool and moist. Keep the soil moist but not waterlogged. The more water and fertilizer you provide, the bigger the plants grow. Dwarf plants won't stay small if you give them extra water and nutrients.

Care
These easy-care annuals are free flowering and won't need deadheading. Leggy or tired plants can be clipped back. Leaf spot diseases and slugs can sometimes be a problem. Impatiens will die with the first fall frost. Plan to remove and replace them, or live with the void left by the frost-killed plants. You can winter your plants indoors.

Companion Planting and Design
Impatiens makes an impressive flowering ground cover under trees and shrubs. In containers and planters, it brightens up a shady spot on the deck or patio. Mixed with ferns and hosta, it adds season-long color to the perennial shade garden.

My Personal Favorites
There are many cultivars, and they increase in number yearly. Most are free-flowering, compact plants. The Fiesta and Fiesta Ole series grow 14 inches tall with double flowers that look like miniature roses. I have had good luck growing the 14-inch-tall 'Blitz' impatiens in full sun. Impatiens 'New Guinea' has attractive foliage with fewer but larger flowers. Seashell series has cupped flowers in yellow, peach, apricot, tangerine, papaya, or passion.

Licorice Vine
Helichrysum petiolare

When, Where, and How to Plant

Plants can be purchased as bedding plants in 3- or 4-inch pots. They can also be started from cuttings in early spring. Root cuttings in moist vermiculite. Move rooted cuttings to small containers filled with potting mix and grow in sunny window or under artificial lights. Seeds of certain cultivars are available and can be started indoors. Sow seeds twelve to fourteen weeks before the last spring frost. Grow in a moist sterile starting mix at 55 to 61 degrees Fahrenheit. Hardened-off transplants can be moved outdoors after the danger of frost has past. Grow licorice vine in full to part sun and well-drained soils. Place one or two plants in mixed containers and space those growing in-ground 12 inches apart.

Growing Tips

Keep the soil moist. Established plants prefer drier soil. Water thoroughly whenever the top few inches of soil begins to dry. Check container plantings daily and water thoroughly when needed. Avoid excess fertilization, which can lead to leggy growth and increase the risk of disease.

Care

Licorice plants are low maintenance and relatively pest free. An occasional caterpillar may feed on the leaves. But try to tolerate the damage—the adult butterfly is a real beauty you'll want in the garden. Leaf spot and rust can be a problem in wet soils and overfertilized gardens.

Companion Planting and Design

Licorice vine is nice as a trailer for containers and an annual ground cover in the garden. I like to combine this silver foliage plant with trailing petunias, verbena, and fan flower. These also make good annual ground-hugging plant combinations in the annual garden.

My Personal Favorites

I like them all. 'Variegatum' has gray and cream variegated leaves. 'Roundabout' is a miniature version of it. 'Limelight' has the same hairy leaves, but they are lime green. 'Icicles' is a newer cultivar with long narrow leaves and is more upright in habit. *Dichondra* 'Silver Falls' is another attractive silver foliage trailer often used in place of licorice vine in pots or as a ground cover.

This eye catching foliage plant is sure to find a place in one of your container plantings, hanging basket or as a groundcover mixed with colorful annuals. The silvery foliage is a nice foil for dark flowers and provides contract with glossy green leaves of neighboring plants. This trailing plant is native to South Africa and tolerant of heat and drought. You may find a few holes in the leaves. Don't worry about the damage. The plant produces enough leaves to share with this hungry visitor. Plus if you let them stay you will soon be rewarded with beautiful swallowtail butterflies. If you can't stand the plant damage then move the caterpillars to a nearby parsley plant. The caterpillars will get the food they need and you will still get to enjoy the butterflies.

Other Common Name
Licorice plant

Bloom Period and Seasonal Color
Colorful silver foliage all season.

Mature Height and Spread
Up to 2 feet long

Lisianthus
Eustoma grandiflorum

This is a real beauty both in the garden and as a flower arrangement lasting up to ten days in a vase. It can be a bit pricey and hard to find but is well worth the money and effort. The delicate flowers and blue green foliage resemble our native gentians. Lisianthus fits in well in both formal and informal gardens. Tuck a few in the perennial garden to fill in voids or mix with other flowers in the annual garden. The taller varieties have limited branching and look their best when staked or supported by nearby plants. Fortunately, newer dwarf and self-branching cultivars are being introduced, reducing the maintenance needs. Lisianthus flowers best and suffers fewer disease problems in warm, dry seasons.

Other Common Name
Prairie Gentian

Bloom Period and Seasonal Color
Summer until frost single, double or bicolor flowers of white, pink, red, lavender to blue, and yellow.

Mature Height and Spread
6 to 30 in. tall and 6 to 12 in.

When, Where, and How to Plant
Lisianthus is truly a biennial treated as an annual. It is slow to germinate and grow into a flowering plant. Start seeds indoors in late December or early January. Sow seeds in moist sterile starter mix at 55 to 60 degrees Fahrenheit. Grow under artificial lights and provide proper spacing to avoid disease problems. Or purchase transplants. They are sold as bedding plants in flats or in 3 or 4 inch pots. Grow in full sun to partial shade in moist, well-drained to dry soils. Space small cultivars 6 inches apart and larger cultivars 9 to 12 inches apart.

Growing Tips
Keep the soil slightly moist. Avoid overwatering, which can lead to root rot. Water plants thoroughly whenever the top few inches of soil starts to dry, but don't water leaves and flowers. This can lead to leaf spot and botrytis blight. Reduce watering once established. Follow soil test recommendation or the fertilizer recommendations at the beginning of this chapter.

Care
Taller varieties need to be staked or planted with sturdy neighbors that can provide needed support. Minimal deadheading is needed for these long-lasting flowers. Deadhead during wet weather to reduce the risk of botrytis blight. Removing diseased flowers or spotted leaves as soon as they appear, along with drier weather, will usually keep this disease under control. Avoid excess fertilizer that can increase the risk of disease and decrease flowering.

Companion Planting and Design
The airy texture of baby's breath and sweet alyssum makes for a nice container or garden combination. Tuck a few of the taller cultivars in with perennials for added color. They look nice with blue fescue, blue oat grass, and allium.

My Personal Favorites
The relatively new All America Selections winners 'Forever Blue' and its white counterpart 'Forever White' are 12 inches tall and freely branched cultivars. They showed good heat and drought tolerance and are suited to container and garden culture. The Echo series has double flowers on 18 inch plants.

Lobelia
Lobelia erinus

When, Where, and How to Plant

Lobelias are available from garden centers as bedding plants in flats. Or start your own plants from seed ten to twelve weeks prior to the last spring frost. Seeds need light, moisture, and 70-degree Fahrenheit temperatures to germinate. Plant hardened-off transplants outdoors after all danger of frost has passed. Lobelia prefers full sun, cool temperatures, and moist, well-drained soil. Mulch the soil or plant lobelia in partial shade to keep the roots cool and moist. An east location will provide sufficient light while avoiding the heat from the afternoon sun. Space plants about 6 inches apart.

Growing Tips

Keep the soil moist but not wet. Mulch the soil to keep roots cool and moist. Fertilize according to soil test results or follow general fertilization guidelines for annuals.

Care

Lobelias grow and flower best in cool weather. They often shut down and stop flowering altogether in hot weather. Lightly prune lobelias after the first flush of flowers to encourage new leaf and flower growth. Leggy plants can be pruned back halfway. Continue to water but stop fertilizing when plants heat stall.

Companion Planting and Design

Lobelias can provide splashes of color throughout the landscape. They mix well with annuals planted in the ground or in containers. Their delicate texture makes them easy to blend with perennials in the garden. Container plantings with a mixture of lobelia, geraniums, dusty miller, and spike are a traditional favorite. Lobelias are used as bedding and edging plants. They tend to go into a midsummer heat slump, so use them in areas where this will be less noticeable. Other flowers planted in the garden will draw attention away from resting lobelias.

My Personal Favorites

I find the Laguna series more heat tolerant, growing 6 to 8 inches tall. 'Crystal Palace' is a compact type with dark blue flowers and bronze foliage. 'Blue Moon' is a true blue, and 'Rosamund' has cherry-red flowers on 6-inch plants. Trailing types include the Cascade, Fountain, and Sapphire series.

Lobelia has traditionally been used in containers or as an edging plant. Cultivars can be upright types, forming 4- to 8-inch mounds. The trailing types can spread as much as 18 inches. This makes them good candidates for containers or to cascade over boulders and garden walls. The fine-textured leaves and delicate flowers add a softening touch to any garden. I like to use it as a filler plant since it often stalls out during the heat of our summers. Use it liberally in cool locations where it will flourish all summer long. Edging lobelia is a relative of our native cardinal flower, Lobelia cardinalis. This upright perennial produces spikes of red flowers. It can be found in wet areas of our southern forests and is sold for use in perennial and natural gardens.

Other Common Name
Edging Lobelia

Bloom Period and Seasonal Color
Summer to fall blooms in white, blue, rose, and purple.

Mature Height × Spread
4 to 8 in. × 6 to 18 in.

Madagascar Periwinkle
Catharanthus roseus

Though it is delicate in appearance, Madagascar periwinkle is a sturdy plant that will tolerate some of the toughest garden conditions and keep flowering. Heat, drought, and pollution won't stop the blooms, which are framed by glossy green leaves. Try using this plant when you want the look of impatiens in hot, sunny areas. They have the same neat, tidy, and mounded appearance as impatiens. They also tolerate dry shade. Whether grown in a container or mixed in with other annuals, it is sure to attract the attention of visitors and butterflies. Move a few Madagascar periwinkles indoors to extend the garden season. They often bloom when grown in a southern window or under artificial lights. Move existing plants indoors or take cuttings and start new plants for the winter. See the chapter introduction for details on how to do this successfully.

Other Common Name
Rose Periwinkle

Bloom Period and Seasonal Color
Summer to fall blooms in white, pink, rose, red, and rose-purple.

Mature Height × Spread
8 to 18 in. × 8 to 17 in.

When, Where, and How to Plant
Madagascar periwinkles are available as bedding plants in flats or in 3- to 4-inch pots. Or start seeds ten to twelve weeks prior to the last spring frost. Seeds need moist, warm conditions to germinate. Keep the starting mix at a temperature of 70 degrees Fahrenheit. It takes fifteen to twenty days for the seeds to germinate. Madagascar periwinkle can also be started from cuttings. Root cuttings in the spring. Hardened-off transplants can be placed outdoors after all danger of frost is past. Though it prefers moist, well-drained soil, established plants can tolerate heat and drought but not wet soils. Space the plants 8 to 12 inches apart.

Growing Tips
Madagascar periwinkle requires very little care. Water established plants thoroughly whenever the top few inches of soil start to dry. Plants will rot in poorly drained soils. Follow soil test recommendations, or those in the chapter introduction, for fertilizing.

Care
These plants need very little grooming to maintain their attractive appearance. Leaf spot disease and slugs may be problems during wet weather. Remove disease infested leaves and control slugs with beer traps or the less toxic iron phosphate baits.

Companion Planting and Design
Madagascar periwinkle makes a nice flowering annual ground cover or container plant. They can be planted alone or mixed with other plants for attractive in-ground or container gardens. I like to plant the bicolor Madagascar periwinkles with dusty miller or white alyssum. The dark-green glossy leaves of vinca highlight the lacy white leaves of the dusty miller.

My Personal Favorites
'Jaio Dark Red' and 'Jaio Scarlet Eye' are recent AAS winners. The first of the two has dark red flowers with a white center. It grows 15 inches tall and 20 inches wide. The latter is similar in size, but the flowers are more rosy-red with a white center. The Pretty series plants are compact, free flowering, and 12 inches tall. 'Parasol' is a 12- to 18-inch plant that produces the largest flowers that are white with a rose eye.

When, Where, and How to Plant

Start seeds indoors about four weeks before the last spring frost. Keep the starting mix moist and at a temperature of 70 degrees Fahrenheit. Seedlings will appear in about five to seven days. You can also start seeds outdoors after the last spring frost. Sow marigolds directly in a properly prepared planting bed. Lightly cover the seed with soil and keep it moist until the seeds germinate. Or purchase transplants from the garden center in flats. Plant hardened-off transplants outdoors after all danger of frost is past. Space transplants 6 to 18 inches apart in the garden. Marigolds prefer moist, well-drained soil.

Growing Tips

Marigolds are relatively low maintenance plants. Though drought tolerant, they will perform best in moist, well-drained soil. Water thoroughly whenever the top few inches of soil are crumbly but moist. Use mulch to keep the roots cool and moist. Excess fertilization can result in all leaves and few to no flowers. Follow soil test recommendation and avoid fertilizing heat stressed plants.

Care

Remove faded flowers to encourage branching and continual blooms. French marigolds will stop flowering during hot weather, but once temperatures cool, they will resume blooming. African marigolds are a little more heat tolerant, although the flowers won't look as nice in extreme heat. Rabbits and woodchucks love marigolds. Although usually problem-free, marigolds can be damaged by slugs, spider mites, aphids, and aster yellows disease.

Companion Planting and Design

Marigolds work well throughout the garden and in containers. Plant yellow marigolds with 'Victoria' blue salvia. The contrasting colors and flower forms are quite striking in the garden. I also like to use 'Purple Ruffles' basil with marigolds. Use one of the yellow or golden marigolds with maroon-tipped flowers to echo the purple in the basil leaves.

My Personal Favorites

The Signet marigold *Tagetes tenuifolia* is a compact plant with fern like leaves. It produces small single flowers all season long. 'Lemon Gem' has a lemony fragrance and small edible flowers.

Marigolds are one of the easiest annuals to grow. With very little care, you will be rewarded with season-long blooms. I think every gardener has grown at least one marigold. Perhaps you or your child started a plant in school for Mother's day. The French and African marigolds are the most popular. Both produce a colorful display. Their round flowers and warm colors command attention in any landscape. The French marigold, Tagetes patula, is a compact plant, 6 to 18 inches tall. The flowers can be single or double and up to 2 inches across. The African marigold, Tagetes erecta, is usually taller, 10 to 36 inches, with large 2- to 5-inch flowers. Triploids are a cross between the French and African marigolds. They are more heat-tolerant than the French and so keep flowering in hot weather.

Other Common Names
French Marigold, African Marigold

Bloom Period and Seasonal Color
Summer through fall blooms in yellow, orange, gold, bronze, and creamy white.

Mature Height × Spread
6 to 36 in. × 6 to 15 in.

Moss Rose
Portulaca grandiflora

Moss rose is a great choice for hot, dry locations. These plants thrive, and flower, in areas where most annuals would be lucky to survive. Their narrow, fleshy leaves give them a moss-like appearance. The flowers can be single or double. The double ones resemble a rose, thus the name, moss rose. The botanical name Portulaca comes from Latin and means "to carry milk," referring to the milky sap. And as you probably guessed, grandiflora means "large flower." Avoid planting moss roses in areas only enjoyed in the evening. Since the flowers close in low light, there won't be much of a display to see at that time. This feature also makes them an interesting addition to the garden. It might help you get some of those reluctant young gardeners interested in plants.

Other Common Name
Rose Moss

Bloom Period and Seasonal Color
Summer through fall blooms in white, yellow, orange, red, rose, and lavender.

Mature Height × Spread
4 to 8 in. × 6 in.

When, Where, and How to Plant
Start moss rose seeds indoors six weeks before the last frost. Sprinkle the seeds on the planting mix surface (don't plant deeply) and water them in. Keep the mix slightly moist and at a temperature of 70 degrees Fahrenheit. Seeds can also be planted directly outdoors after the danger of frost is past. Prepare the planting bed. Sow seeds on the surface of the soil and water them in. Or purchase moss rose bedding plants. Place hardened-off transplants outdoors after the last spring frost. Space transplants 6 to 12 inches apart. Plant moss rose in areas with full sun and well-drained soil. Once you have grown moss rose, you will be rewarded with seedlings the following season. These can be dug and moved to the preferred planting location.

Growing Tips
If placed properly, moss rose is low maintenance. Keep the roots of young transplants slightly moist. Once established, allow the top few inches of soil to dry slightly before watering. Avoid overwatering, which leads to root and stem rot problems. Minimal fertilization is needed. Follow soil test recommendations or guidelines for other annuals.

Care
Moss rose is fairly free flowering with no real pest problems. Occasional deadheading can improve the overall appearance.

Companion Planting and Design
Moss roses thrive in hot, dry conditions, making them perfect for rock gardens, hanging baskets, containers, and other hot spots in the landscape. They can be used as a ground cover or edging plant. Try direct-seeding moss rose near early-fading perennials and spring bulbs. As these perennials die back, the moss rose will fill in the void.

My Personal Favorites
Many of the new cultivars have been bred to stay open later in the day or during cloudy weather. The flowers of 'Afternoon Delight', 'Sundance Mix', and the Sundial series will stay open for most of the day. The Calypso series is probably the most readily available double-flowering moss rose. It comes in a variety of colors. 'Margarita Rosita', the 2004 AAS winner, has rose-colored semidouble flowers.

Nasturtium
Tropaeolum majus

When, Where, and How to Plant
You may be able to find transplants in flats or 3-inch pots at garden centers or farmers markets. Or plant nasturtium seeds directly outdoors in the garden after the last spring frost. Sow seeds in a prepared planting bed. Or start seeds indoors four to six weeks before the last spring frost. Plant them $1/4$ inch deep in any sterile starter mix, and keep the mix at a temperature of 65 to 70 degrees Fahrenheit. Move hardened-off transplants outdoors after the last spring frost. Grow nasturtiums in full sun in a well-drained location. Plant nasturtiums 8 to 12 inches apart.

Growing Tips
The old saying, "be nasty to your nasturtiums" is true. Excess nitrogen results in lots of large leaves and no flowers. Overwatering can lead to disease problems.

Care
Established plants need little care. In extreme heat, they may stop flowering, but once the weather cools, the blooms will resume. Aphids are the most serious pest of this plant. A strong blast of water or several weekly sprays of insecticidal soap will take care of these insects. Watch for mites, cabbage worms, and thrips. Handpick or apply Bacillus thuringiensis (*Bt*) to control cabbage worms. The aphid treatment will also keep mites and thrips under control. Leaf spot disease can be a problem. Avoid overwatering and wet foliage.

Companion Planting and Design
Nasturtium is a good choice for rock gardens, containers, and other difficult sites. The low-growing types make attractive edging plants and ground covers. Seed nasturtiums in the garden next to early-fading perennials. As the perennials die back, the nasturtiums will fill in the empty spot.

My Personal Favorites
My new favorite is the Alaska series. These nasturtiums have green leaves with creamy speckles. 'Whirleybird' is a spurless cultivar. Its single and semidouble flowers face up. They are held above the leaves and put on a good floral display. The annual canary vine *Tropaeolum peregrinum* reaches heights of 8 feet. The small yellow flowers are fringed like a bird's wing.

Nasturtium is a good plant for sunny, dry areas. Plants can be mounded, semi-vining, or climbers. The large round leaves with radiating veins are quite attractive. Unfortunately, they sometimes hide the flowers. Nasturtium leaves, flowers, and seeds are edible. They have a nice spicy flavor. In fact the common name, nasturtium, is Latin for "cress." This refers to the pungent flavor of the plant. Use the leaves and flowers in salads or as a garnish on the dinner plate. They spice up the flavor and appearance of any meal—even for a less-than-enthusiastic cook like me. Take special care when treating pests on the nasturtiums bound for the dinner table. Many insecticides are not meant for edible plants. The pest control methods mentioned here are all safe; just wash the plants before eating them.

Other Common Name
Indian Cress

Bloom Period and Seasonal Color
Summer to frost blooms in yellow, orange, red, and white.

Mature Height × Spread
12 in. × 12 to 14 in.

Pansy
Viola wittrockiana

Pansies make excellent spring and fall bedding plants whether in containers or in the garden. They are an old-time favorite experiencing a renewed interest and expanded role in the landscape. Pansies can add flowering interest to spring and fall plantings. The newer cold-hardy cultivars give us at least two seasons of interest from one planting. Plant these in fall for a colorful end to the season. When spring arrives, the pansies are already in place providing a welcome bit of color. Their flowers can be used for fragrant cuttings or pressed for crafts. They also provide needed nectar for the early- and late-season butterflies. Consider using a few of these edible flowers in your salads or as a garnish. It makes even the most inept cooks, like me, look like gourmet chefs.

Other Common Name
Viola

Bloom Period and Seasonal Color
Spring to early summer and fall blooms in white, blue, purple, yellow, dark red, rose, apricot, and brown.

Mature Height × Spread
4 to 8 in. × 9 to 12 in.

When, Where, and How to Plant
Start pansy seeds indoors in January. Place the seeds in moist media and chill in the refrigerator for one week. Seeds need moist, dark, 65-degree Fahrenheit conditions to germinate. Lower the growing temperature to 50 degrees Fahrenheit once the seeds sprout. Or plant seeds outdoors in summer for a fall display. Pansies can be purchased as bedding plants in flats, in 3- to 4-inch pots, or in planted containers. Plant hardened-off transplants outdoors in April, as soon as the soil is dry enough to work, or plant in fall. Pansies prefer full sun but perform best in cool temperatures. Grow pansies in full sun or partial shade in moist, well-drained soil. Space plants 6 inches apart in the garden, although they can be planted closer in containers.

Growing Tips
Mulch to keep the soil cool and moist. Water thoroughly and whenever the top few inches of soil are moist and crumbly. Fertilize as you do your other annual flowers.

Care
Deadhead pansies for maximum blooms. Select a heat-tolerant cultivar when using pansies for season-long interest. Even those may stop blooming during hot weather. Remove faded flowers and keep the soil moist. Unkempt plants can be pruned back. Once temperatures cool, flowering will resume. Pansies are generally pest free. Slugs and fungal leaf spots may be problems in wet weather.

Companion Planting and Design
Pansies work well in planters alone or mixed with annual or perennial plants. Use them as a ground cover around spring-flowering bulbs. This doubles your flower display and helps mask the fading bulb foliage.

My Personal Favorites
'Icicle', 'Second Season' and 'Sub Zero' pansies survive the rigors of our winters and can perform like short-lived perennials. Replace them after enjoying their fall and the following spring flower display for best results. 'Imperial', 'Maxim', 'Springtime', and 'Universal' are heat-tolerant pansy cultivars. Johnny-jump-up, *Viola tricolor*, is a close relative. It produces small flowers with 'faces' made of blue, gold, and deep violet. Once planted, it will make itself at home throughout your garden.

When, Where, and How to Plant

You may need to call around to find a garden center carrying these annuals. Believe me—it is worth the effort. Pentas are usually sold in 3- or 4-inch pots, or you can order seeds from garden catalogs and start your own plants. Sow seeds indoors about eight to ten weeks before the last spring frost. Use clean containers and a sterile starter mix. Keep it moist and 60 to 65 degrees Fahrenheit for best results. Move hardened-off transplants outdoors after the danger of frost has passed. Grow pentas in full sun with moist, well-drained soils. They will tolerate light shade but flower best in full sun. Space plants 10 to 12 inches apart.

Growing Tips

Keep the soil around new transplants slightly moist. Water established plants thoroughly whenever the top few inches of soil are moist and crumbly. Monitor soil in containers the same way but check them daily. Use mulch around plants in the garden to conserve moisture and suppress weeds. Fertilize according to soil test recommendations or follow information in the chapter introduction. Incorporate a slow-release fertilizer into the soil at time of planting. Or use a water-soluble fertilizer throughout the growing season.

Care

These annuals will flower all summer long with little or no deadheading. Though generally pest free, you may have problems with mites and aphids during hot dry seasons. A strong blast of water or several applications of insecticidal soap will reduce their populations to a tolerable level.

Companion Planting and Design

Use them alone or with other plants in containers. They are a bit pricey, so I like to scatter my investment throughout the landscape, using them much like perennials. Mix pentas with annual and perennial grasses. They also combine nicely with perennials, lisianthus, *Rudbeckia*, and salvia.

My Personal Favorites

Availability may dictate your selection. I like the dark pinks and reds in my garden. The New Look series are compact plants with red, pink, violet, or white flowers.

I always include a few of these long blooming annuals in my garden. I tuck a few in containers, add a couple to my perennial garden, and often use them next to my entranceway. I like the bold accent of the reds and the more subtle accents the pink flowers provide. You have probably seen these plants in books and magazines featuring butterflies. They are a popular plant for butterfly gardens since they are a favorite nectar source. Hummingbirds can also be seen feeding on the red and dark pink cultivars. The leaves are deeply veined and slightly hairy. They make a nice backdrop for the long-lasting and self-cleaning clusters of star-shaped flowers. Plant plenty since you will want to pick a few for garden-fresh flower arrangements.

Other Common Name
Star Cluster

Bloom Period and Seasonal Color
Summer until frost with white, pink, rose, or lilac flowers.

Mature Height and Spread
Up to 18 in. × up to 18 in.

Petunia

Petunia hybrida

I remember helping my mother deadhead the cascading petunias in our front planters. The sticky stems and my youth made this seem like torture. Fortunately, many of the new petunias have minimized the need to deadhead and have maximized the beauty. I now include petunias somewhere in my planters or garden. I enjoy their fragrance, and they help bring butterflies and hummingbirds to my garden. The grandiflora petunias are covered with larger flowers and still require some deadheading. I like the free-flowering and weather resistant blooms of the multifloras. These plants are covered with medium-sized blooms and need little deadheading. Million bells Callibrachoa looks like a small-scale petunia. This fast growing compact plant is self-cleaning and works great alone or mixed with other plants in hanging baskets and containers.

Bloom Period and Seasonal Color
Summer through frost blooms in pink, red, violet, lavender, yellow, salmon, and white.

Mature Height × Spread
6 to 18 in. × 6 to 36 in.

When, Where, and How to Plant
Start petunias from seeds indoors ten weeks prior to the last spring frost. Petunias need moisture, light, and 70 degree Fahrenheit temperatures to germinate. Or buy petunias as bedding plants in flats or hanging baskets. Place hardened-off transplants outdoors after the danger of frost is past. Grow petunias in full sun to part shade and well-drained soil. In full shade, the plants get leggy and fail to flower. In general, plant miniatures 6 inches apart, bedding types 10 to 12 inches apart, and the trailing types up to 24 inches apart when used as a ground cover.

Growing Tips
Water established petunias thoroughly whenever the top 3 to 4 inches are moist and crumbly. Use a watering wand or soaker hose to avoid wet leaves and flowers that will be more subject to disease.

Care
Remove faded flowers and clip back leggy stems to keep the plants full and flowering. The amount of grooming needed depends on the cultivar selected. The grandifloras usually need deadheading and suffer rain damage more readily than the others. Stem rot can be a problem with any petunia grown in poorly drained soil. Botrytis blight can cause flowers and leaves to brown, but regular deadheading and removal of infected plant parts is effective as a control. Flea beetles and aphids can also infest petunias, as well as tobacco mosaic virus, spread by aphids.

Companion Planting and Design
Use petunias in containers and hanging baskets or as edging and bedding plants. Trailing types work well in containers, hanging baskets, and even as ground covers weaving throughout nearby plantings.

My Personal Favorites
The 2003 AAS winner 'Merlin Blue Morn' grabbed my attention with its unique flowers that transition from a velvety blue edge to the white center. Supertunias are long blooming, compact plants. The popular Wave™ petunias are vigorous multifloras that grow and flower all season long. Stems can reach 36 inches in length, making them ideal for hanging baskets. I like 'Tidal Wave Cherry' with its outstanding red flowers and more upright undulating growth habit.

Salvia

Salvia splendens

When, Where, and How to Plant

Start salvia from seeds indoors about six to eight weeks before the last spring frost. Sow the seeds on a sterile starter medium and water in. Do not cover since these seeds need light to germinate. Avoid problems with damping off by using a sterile mix, clean containers, and not overwatering. Or buy salvias as bedding plants in flats or in 3- to 4-inch pots from the garden center. Plant hardened-off transplants outdoors after all danger of frost is past. Salvia prefers full sun with moist, well-drained soil, and cool temperatures. Space smaller cultivars 8 inches apart and larger cultivars 10 to 12 inches apart.

Growing Tips

Mulch the soil around salvias to keep the roots cool and moist. Water established plants thoroughly whenever the top few inches of soil are moist but crumbly.

Care

Deadhead to encourage branching and continual blooming. Salvias may suffer from downy and powdery mildew. Plants in full sun and properly spaced are less vulnerable. Remove infected plant parts to reduce the spread of these diseases.

Companion Planting and Design

Salvias grow well in containers or in the garden as edging, bedding, or background plants. Red salvia is an attention getter in the garden, although the intense red can be overpowering in the landscape. Temper this by planting red salvia in front of evergreens or mixed with dusty miller. Or try growing the AAS winner 'Lady in Red'. The red flowers on this compact plant are more open and less overpowering. I find it blends better with perennials and less formal landscapes.

My Personal Favorites

Carabinere, Empire, and Firecracker series are all compact plants, 10 to 12 inches tall, in a variety of flower colors. I like several of the mealycup *Salvia farinacea,* cultivars. The 18-inch 'Victoria' produces narrow violet-blue flower spikes while 'Strata' has bicolor flowers. I like *Salvia coccinea* 'Coral Nymph'. The delicate coral flowers seem to float above the foliage. Blue and Black *Salvia guaranitica* has bold foliage and blue flowers with dark blue, almost black, sepals.

Nothing grabs the garden visitor's attention like red salvia. The intense color and large flower spikes make it stand out in the landscape. Both hummingbirds and butterflies enjoy them. It is an excellent plant for making large spaces appear smaller. Use it as a focal point to accent a hard-to-find entrance, garden art, or other landscape feature. Salvia is often used to provide the red in patriotic red, white, and blue gardens. They combine well with most of the commonly grown annuals. It's a great annual for the garden or flower arrangement. I like its close relative mealycup sage, *Salvia farinacea.* Its narrower flower spike makes it easy to blend with annuals, perennials, and various gardening styles. This long bloomer needs little deadheading, and the flowers are great for fresh and dried arrangements

Other Common Names

Scarlet Sage, Firecracker Plant

Bloom Period and Seasonal Color

Summer until frost blooms in red, salmon, pink, blue, lavender, and white.

Mature Height × Spread

8 to 30 in. × 8 to 12 in.

Snapdragon
Antirrhinum majus

Snapdragons are an old-time favorite with new cultivars providing a modern update. These stately plants hold spikes of colorful flowers over whorls of narrow green leaves. The snapdragon is an impressive flower outdoors in the garden or inside in a flower vase. Harvest the flowers when the bottom third of the blossoms are open, the middle portion is just starting to show color, and the top third is in bud. This will give you the greatest vase life and encourage the plants to produce more blooms. And don't forget to put your nose in close and you may be rewarded with a light fragrance. Many newer snapdragons have open flowers for a showier flower display. Have you tried to make your snapdragons talk? Remove a single blossom from the stem. Gently squeeze the sides and watch the flower open and shut.

Other Common Name
Common Snapdragon

Bloom Period and Seasonal Color
Summer to frost blooms in white, yellow, bronze, purple, pink, and red.

Mature Height × Spread
6 to 48 in. × 6 to 24 in.

When, Where, and How to Plant
Start snapdragons from seeds indoors about ten weeks before the last spring frost. Seeds need light, moisture, and a temperature of 70 degrees Fahrenheit to germinate. Snapdragons can be direct-seeded outdoors in the spring as soon as the soil is workable. Snapdragons are available from garden centers as bedding plants in flats. Hardened-off transplants will tolerate frost but do best when planted outdoors after all danger of frost is past. Plant them in an area with moist, well-drained soil. Space small snapdragon cultivars 6 inches apart, medium cultivars 8 to 10 inches apart, and tall cultivars at least 12 inches apart.

Growing Tips
Water established plants thoroughly and often enough to keep the top few inches of moist but not wet. Mulch the soil surface to help keep the roots cool and moist. Don't fertilize the plants during hot or dry weather, when the plants stop blooming, or show signs of stress.

Care
Deadhead regularly. Remove faded flowers before too many seedpods form on the flower stem. Taller cultivars may need staking or nearby sturdy plants for support. Snapdragons may stop blooming in extremely hot weather. Prune leggy plants back and wait for an impressive fall display. A few snapdragon plants will reseed, or an occasional plant will survive a mild winter. Aphids and mites may cause leaves to curl, yellow, and eventually brown. The fungal disease rust may also cause problems.

Companion Planting and Design
Use dwarf cultivars as a ground cover, in a container, or as an edging plant. Include medium-sized cultivars in annual and perennial gardens. The tall cultivars make great background plants where it is easier to hide the stakes.

My Personal Favorites
The Floral Carpet series and the improved Floral Showers series are dwarf snapdragons, 6 to 8 inches tall. The Sonnet series is a medium (22-inch) snapdragon available in various colors. It makes a good cut flower and does not need staking. The tall Rocket series was developed for heat tolerance and makes a great cut flower.

Spike
Cordyline species

When, Where, and How to Plant
Plant spikes outdoors after all danger of frost is past. Planted containers can be moved indoors or outdoors, depending on weather. Spikes prefer full to partial sun and moist, well-drained soil. Avoid wet soil and heavy shade where the plants are more likely to develop root rot and leaf spot disease. Spikes are available from garden centers in 2- or 3-inch pots. Usually a single spike is planted in the middle of the container. Space spikes 12 to 15 inches apart when planted en masse.

Growing Tips
Spikes are very low-maintenance plants. They will thrive in properly maintained planters. Check the soil moisture in containers at least once a day. Water containers thoroughly, allowing excess water to run out the drainage holes. Fertilize planters frequently throughout the summer. Use any flowering plant fertilizer. This will keep the flowering plants, growing with the spike foliage plant, blooming. Excess nitrogen promotes lots of leaves but no flowers. This is not a problem on the spike, but it is on its planter partners. Follow label directions.

Care
Spikes are fairly pest free and tolerate temperatures in the 40s. Avoid excess moisture that can lead to root rot and leaf spot. Brown leaf tips occur in very dry soil and from the fluoride in the water. Keep soil slightly moist to correct the problem.

Companion Planting and Design
The traditional container planting includes a spike in the middle surrounded by a couple of geraniums, a few dusty millers, alyssum, and vinca vine. I have also seen spikes planted en masse in the center of an island bed for an impressive show. Other gardeners use individual spikes throughout their annual plantings, creating a scattering of vertical interest.

My Personal Favorite
Cultivars are difficult to find. Festival Grass cordyline has narrow leaves of red and purple. Consider using alternatives such as ornamental grass, bronze fennel, or vines trained on container size supports. Or try using cannas or other tropicals such as *Phormium*, dwarf papyrus, and banana for vertical accents.

Spike plants are a Minnesota favorite that have long been used as the vertical accent for container plantings. Their popularity is growing across the country. I am seeing more and more planters and gardens incorporating this plant. Many enthusiastic gardeners winter their plants indoors. One of my students shared a picture of her friend's four-year-old spike. It was 4 feet tall and lived in a half whiskey barrel planter. Strong friends help move it indoors each winter where it grows in front of a sunny window with moist soil. Each spring they move the pants outdoors to the summer garden. I take the easy way out, enjoying my spikes until the cold weather kills them or the snow flies. Then I recycle them in the compost pile and start with new plants the next spring.

Other Common Name
Dracaena

Bloom Period and Seasonal Color
Season long green foliage

Mature Height × Spread
24 in. × 15 in.

53

Sunflower

Helianthus annuus

The sunflower, native to North America, is a longtime garden favorite. The large flowers add color to the garden, and the seeds attract hungry birds, squirrels, and children. The large seeds make planting easy, and sunflower's large size gives it great kid appeal. Add to their delight by planting sunflowers in a circle to make a playhouse. Be sure to leave a little extra space between two of the plants for the door. Plant squash, beans, or morning glories between the sunflowers. These climbers will use the sunflowers as a trellis, forming walls of the playhouse. But don't relegate these flowers to the vegetable or kid's garden. Breeding programs have resulted in a variety of flower sizes, colors, and plant heights that make excellent cut flowers that readily blend into the garden.

Other Common Name
Common Sunflower

Bloom Period and Seasonal Color
Summer blooms until frost in yellow, white, and bronze, with a yellow, brown, purple, or crimson center

Mature Height × Spread
15 in. to 15 ft. × 12 to 24 in.

When, Where, and How to Plant

Start sunflowers from seeds outside after all danger of frost is past. Plant the seeds 6 inches apart and 1/2 inch deep in properly prepared soil. Thin seedlings when they are 3 inches tall, leaving 24 inches between plants. Sunflowers can also be started indoors four to six weeks before the last spring frost. Plant seeds in a starter mix keeping it moist and at 68 to 86 degree Fahrenheit temperatures. Seedlings should appear in ten to fourteen days. Transplants are sometimes in 3- or 4-inch pots. Hardened-off transplants can be planted outdoors after all danger of frost is past. Grow sunflowers in full sun with well-drained soil. Space transplants in the garden at least 24 inches apart.

Growing Tips

Water established plants thoroughly whenever the top few inches of soil are moist and crumbly. Fertilize according to soil test results or as recommended in the chapter introduction.

Care

Proper spacing will help reduce problems with leaf spot and powdery mildew—both unsightly but not life-threatening diseases. Mask the problem by growing slightly shorter plants in front of diseased leaves. Aphids may cause minor damage. Cover seedheads with cheesecloth or netting to protect the harvest from squirrels and birds. Remove the flower with 1 to 2 feet of stem attached when the back of the flower is brown. Hang it upside down until dry and brown. Harvest the seeds and store them in an airtight jar in the refrigerator.

Companion Planting and Design

The dwarf sunflowers combine nicely with amaranth, ornamental grasses, and asters. Or use them in a fall display with mums, corn stalks, and pumpkins as a fall decoration.

My Personal Favorites

'Mammoth', 'Russian', and 'Russian Giant' can reach 12 to 15 feet. The 2001 AAS winner 'Ring of Fire' produces 5-inch flowers on 4- to 5-foot plants. The chocolate-brown center is surrounded by a ring of red and then gold petals. 'Teddy Bear' is a 24-inch-tall dwarf cultivar with 5-inch-diameter double yellow flowers that remind me of dahlias.

Sweet Potato Vine
Ipomoea batatas cultivars

When, Where, and How to Plant
Sweet potato vines are available from garden centers in 3- and 4-inch pots. Some gardeners start new plants from cuttings. Move hardened-off transplants into the garden after the danger of frost has past. Grow sweet potato vines in full or part sun with moist, well-drained soil. One sweet potato vine per container is usually enough. Space plants 24 inches apart when grown in the garden as a ground cover.

Growing Tips
Water established plants thoroughly whenever the top few inches of soil are crumbly and moist. Fertilize according to soil test recommendations or as recommended in the chapter introduction. Container gardens need a bit more attention. Check planters daily and water thoroughly whenever the top few inches of soil starts to dry. Incorporate a slow-release fertilizer at the time of planting or use a water-soluble fertilizer throughout the season.

Care
Sweet potato vines are low maintenance and relatively pest free. Some gardeners overwinter the plants. Take cuttings in late summer and root in moist vermiculite or perlite. Plant the rooted cuttings in a well-drained potting mix and grow it in a sunny window, keeping the soil moist. Or, store the tuberous roots for winter. Dig them after a light frost. Clean and store them in a cool dark location. Start indoors in late winter. Take cuttings from the shoots that grow out of the tuberous roots.

Companion Planting and Design
Use the colorful foliage to complement or highlight other plants. The blue flowers of fan flower and colorful Wave™ petunias look nice against the leaves of 'Marguerite' or 'Blackie'. Persian shield, pentas, and salvia are upright annuals that combine nicely with these vines.

My Personal Favorites
'Blackie' has dark purple leaves that appear black. The lobed leaves combine well with light-colored flowers and foliage. 'Carolina Purple' has purple foliage with a more contained growth. 'Marguerite' has chartreuse, heart-shaped leaves—give it plenty of room. 'Tricolor' has smaller lobed leaves that are pink, white, and grey-green, and less vigorous.

This relative newcomer to the garden scene has some well-known relatives. The popular sweet potato vine is a cousin to the morning glory and a cultivar of the edible sweet potato. The heart-shaped or lobed foliage makes a nice trailing plant for containers and ground cover in the annual garden. First-time growers beware - one plant goes a long way. The vigorous vine will quickly fill out and engulf its neighbors. Use one sweet potato vine per pot, a less vigorous cultivar, or an equally assertive planting partner for best results. Some gardeners have overwintered the plants indoors. Some store the tuberous root for winter and start it indoors with their cannas and calla lilies. The plants survived but didn't look their best. Other gardeners had much better results using cuttings.

Bloom Period and Seasonal Color
Colorful lime green, purple, or variegated green, cream and pink foliage all season long.

Mature Height and Spread
Branches up to 3 ft. in length

55

Verbena
Verbena hybrida

With all the cultivars and related species available, there is bound to be a verbena that is right for your garden. There are upright and spreading types with various shaped leaves. The flower clusters come in a variety of colors and are quite showy. There are several related annual, biennial, and perennial verbenas. One of my favorites is the self-seeding Brazilian verbena, Verbena bonariensis. The purple bloom forms on the tip of a 4- to 6-foot stiff stem. The leaves occur on the bottom 12 to 15 inches of the stem making it a nice grow-through plant the hummingbirds love. The perennial, Verbena canadensis, is a ground hugging plant that blooms from late May till frost. Though the parent plant may die in a cold winter, they leave plenty of seeds for next year's garden.

Other Common Name
Garden Verbena

Bloom Period and Seasonal Color
Summer through frost blooms in white, lavender, purple, blue, pink, red, and apricot.

Mature Height × Spread
Up to 15 in. × up to 20 in.

When, Where, and How to Plant
Start verbena seeds indoors twelve weeks prior to the last spring frost. Chill the seeds for seven days before seeding. Plant in a well-drained sterile starter mix and maintain a temperature of 70 degrees Fahrenheit. Use sterile potting mix and clean containers and keep the starter mix slightly dry to avoid damping-off disease. Plant hardened-off transplants outdoors after the last spring frost. Grow verbena in full sun with well-drained soil. Space upright-type plants 12 inches apart and spreading types 18 inches apart.

Growing Tips
Some verbena cultivars will stop blooming during hot, dry spells. Mulch the soil to keep the roots cool and moist. Provide adequate water, and once the weather cools, the flowers will return. Avoid fertilizing during hot dry spells.

Care
Remove faded flowers to encourage branching and continual blooms. Verbenas are also subject to powdery mildew. Proper spacing and a full sun location will help reduce the risk of this disease.

Companion Planting and Design
Try a few of the spreading types in hanging baskets or used as ground covers mixed with *Helichrysum* (licorice vine), lotus vine, or *Dichondra* 'Silver Falls'. Use them in flower, rock, and butterfly gardens. I like to mix Brazilian verbena in with other plants and ornamental grasses. The flowers are a nice surprise in the garden. Mixing it into the garden also hides the foliage that can become unsightly from mildew. I let my perennial verbena crawl throughout my garden. Stray plants can be relocated to another area or to a friend's garden.

My Personal Favorite
Babylon is a proven winner selected for its compact growth that requires less deadheading. Add to this an increased tolerance to heat, drought, and powdery mildew. 'Patio' is another heat tolerant cultivar with a selection of hot colors. 'Peaches and Cream' is an All-America Selections winner with salmon and apricot flowers. The Romance series are compact plants with a dense spreading habit. 'Imagination' is one of the cutleaf spreading types and looks great in hanging baskets.

Zinnia

Zinnia elegans

When, Where, and How to Plant

Start zinnias from seeds indoors about six weeks before the last spring frost. Plant the seeds in a sterile starter mix keeping it moist at 70 degrees Fahrenheit. Direct seed zinnias in the garden after all danger of frost is past. Prepare the soil and plant seeds 3 to 6 inches apart. Thin to final spacing once the seeds are 3 inches tall. Plant hardened-off transplants outdoors at the same time. Grow them in full-sun areas with well-drained soil. Plant bedding plants at the same depth they were growing in the containers. Space small cultivars 6 to 8 inches apart and the larger cultivars at least 12 inches apart.

Growing Tips

Water thoroughly whenever the top few inches of soil are moist but crumbly. To minimum the risk of disease, avoid getting water on the leaves. Excess nitrogen fertilizer can inhibit flowering.

Care

Proper plant selection, siting, and spacing are critical to the health and appearance of zinnias. Select leaf spot and mildew resistant cultivars whenever possible. Remove faded flowers to encourage branching and continual blooms.

Companion Planting and Design

Zinnias are perfect plants for the hot, dry locations in your landscape. They work well with cockscomb, dusty miller, and annual fountain grass. Single zinnias are not as bold as the doubles and are easier to blend with other flowers. I often use them to fill in voids in perennial gardens. They also combine nicely with 'Purple Ruffles' basil and the purple alternanthera. Tall zinnias make nice background plants, and they all perform well in containers.

My Personal Favorites

The narrow-leafed zinnia, *Zinnia haageana*, also listed as *Zinnia angustifolia* and *Zinnia linearis*, is one of my favorites. This zinnia has narrow leaves with $1^1/2$-inch-wide single flowers, comes in white, yellow, and orange, and is mildew resistant. 'Profusion Cherry' and 'Profusion Orange' were selected as All-America Selections Gold-Medal winners for their low maintenance and disease resistance. Consider the 'Whirligig' or 'Zenith' if you want to include some cactus-flowered zinnias.

This eye-catching annual, in the garden or flower vase, is a longtime favorite in Minnesota gardens. Easy to start from seed indoors or right in the garden, they will quickly reach flowering size. This makes them fun for gardeners of all ages. The color and movement that hummingbirds and butterflies provide while feeding on the flowers add to their appeal. Don't let past problems with leaf spot and mildew scare you away. Many of the newer cultivars are more tolerant and even resistant to these diseases. Check out the many colors, various flower types, and plant heights available. One or more are sure to fit into your landscape. The dahlia-flowered zinnia has large double flowers with cupped petals that give it a more rounded appearance. The cactus-flowered zinnia has twisted petals and resembles the cactus-flowered dahlia.

Bloom Period and Seasonal Color

Summer to frost blooms in white, yellow, green, red, orange, apricot, rose, red, and violet.

Mature Height × Spread

6 to 36 in. × 18 to 24 in.

Bulbs *for Minnesota*

After surviving the cold and snow of a Minnesota winter, the gardening season never seems long enough. Extend your garden's bloom time by incorporating spring-flowering bulbs into your landscape. But don't stop there. Try including some of the hardy and nonhardy summer- and fall-blooming bulbs. They can add color and interest to your annual, perennial, and container gardens.

Jump start your spring garden with a few of the very early blooming minor bulbs. One year I had snowdrops (*Galanthus nivalis*) and winter aconite (*Eranthis hyemalis*) blooming in my garden on March third. Both are shade tolerant and naturalize readily. The winter aconite is first to bloom. It is three to four inches tall with yellow, cup-shaped flowers. The snowdrops appear next with their pure white flowers on six-inch plants. Glory-of-the-snow, *Chionodoxa luciliae,* will appear right before Siberian squill. The star-shaped flowers are bright blue with a white center. These early bloomers can tolerate the cold temperatures we seem to get each spring after our early spring plants start blooming. Though small in stature, these little beauties bring great hope of warmer weather to come.

For the purposes of this book, I am using the term "bulb" to include plants grown from true bulbs, rhizomes, corms, tubers, and tuberous roots. They may be hardy or nonhardy. Hardy bulbs can be left in the ground year-round. Nonhardy, sometimes called tropical bulbs, are planted outdoors each spring. You can remove them from the ground and store them indoors over the winter. The trick is finding storage areas cool enough to keep the bulbs dormant.

Selecting and Planting Hardy Bulbs

Most of us think about adding bulbs to the garden with the first big daffodil display in the spring. Unfortunately, we usually forget about planting them until the next spring when the daffodils are again in bloom. Luckily, many mail-order companies have started sending out their bulb catalogs in the spring.

Ring of Crocus

It's an easy way to order the bulbs, while you are inspired by the spring bloom, and have them delivered in the fall in time for planting. Watch for other bulb catalogs later in the season and stop by the garden centers as soon as the bulbs go on display for the greatest selection. Select firm, blemish-free bulbs. Avoid those with nicks, cuts, or soft areas. Store bulbs in a cool, dark place until it is time to plant. Bulbs should be stored in perforated plastic or mesh bags. Do not store them in closed plastic bags where they can rot.

Planting and Care

Hardy Bulbs

Most bulbs prefer moist, well-drained soil during their growing season and a bit drier soil when

Tulips Make Waves of Color

dormant in summer. Work several inches of peat moss, compost, or other organic matter into the top twelve inches of soil before planting. Organic matter helps improve the drainage in heavy clay soil and increases the water-holding capacity of sandy soil. Fertilize bulb plantings according to soil test recommendations. In general, bulbs receive enough nutrients from your regular garden fertilization program. Most garden soils do not need phosphorus, so skip the bonemeal and super phosphate. Plus bonemeal tends to attract rodents that like to feast on our bulbs. Instead, use a bulb fertilizer at the time of planting if nutrients are needed. These contain a low level of slow-release nitrogen—enough for several years.

Plant most hardy bulbs in the fall when temperatures are consistently cool, starting in early October. You can plant bulbs until the ground freezes. I think we all have planted a few in the snow and frosty soil. I don't know about you, but I have had to chip through the frozen soil to plant a few of my bulbs. One of my former students coined the manhole cover planting technique. He would outline the planting hole by picking through the frozen soil surface. He would pry the frozen soil off just like lifting a manhole cover. He would plant the bulbs in the unfrozen soil below. Water them in and then put the lid back on. He found the squirrels and chipmunks didn't bother them. I am not sure I would purposely do this—but it is a good back up plan for procrastinators like me.

In general, bulbs should be planted at a depth two or three times the vertical diameter of the bulb. Space them at least three to four times the width of the bulb apart. Water the newly planted bulbs. Avoid

Cactus-Flowered Dahlias

planting bulbs near your home's foundation, especially the south side, near a dryer vent, or close to other artificial heat sources. Bulbs planted in these spots tend to sprout early and are subject to cold damage.

Most of us have experienced the problem of a "premature spring." Every January or February, we get a week of warm weather, and bulbs start peeking through the ground just in time for the next cold wave. Prevent this by using winter mulch. Cover the ground with evergreen branches, straw, or marsh hay after the soil lightly freezes. Branches from discarded Christmas trees work great.

Remove the mulch when the air temperature hovers just above freezing or bulb growth appears. You can add, if needed, a low-nitrogen fertilizer to established bulb gardens in the early spring as the leaves appear. Don't forget to water if we have a dry spring. Remove faded flowers but leave the leaves intact so they can produce the needed energy for the plants to return and flower next year. If you need to move existing bulbs, mark their location for a fall transplant. The next best time is as the leaves start to fade, though every gardener has broken the rules and still had some success. I have moved daffodils in full bloom and had them survive and flower the next year.

Non-hardy Bulbs

Tuberous begonias, cannas, and other nonhardy bulbs require a bit different care. These "tropical" beauties can not survive our cold winters, and our growing season is often too short to get the maximum bloom time. Garden centers carry a few of these nonhardy bulbs in early spring. Check out bulb catalogs for a wider selection. Start most nonhardy bulbs indoors in mid-March for earlier bloom outdoors. Gladiolas are the exception—plant these directly outdoors. Start the others indoors in a flat filled with half peat moss mixed with half vermiculite or perlite. Keep the planting mix warm, usually around 70 degrees Fahrenheit, and moist. Move to a sunny location or under artificial lights as soon as the bulbs begin to sprout. Once they have a few leaves, move the plants to a larger container or hanging basket. Water thoroughly and often enough to keep the soil slightly moist, about the consistency of a damp sponge. Fertilize with a diluted solution of a flowering plant fertilizer.

Start hardening off transplants about two weeks before moving the plants outdoors. Stop fertilizing, allow the soil to go a bit drier, and gradually expose them to the sunlight. Move hardened-off plants to their outdoor growing location after the danger of frost has past.

Treat these plants more like annuals by keeping the soil slightly moist and fertilizing them like you do your annuals. Container plantings need to be watered daily and fertilized throughout the season. I like to incorporate a slow-release fertilizer in my containers at planting or purchase. This way every time I water I am fertilizing. No mixing or mess, and it doesn't get put off till the next time I water.

Dig the bulbs after a light frost kills the tops. Carefully lift the bulbs, remove the loose soil and allow them to dry (cure). Gently brush, don't scrub, off remaining soil, cut back foliage, and move them into storage. Pack bulbs in sand, peat moss or vermiculite in a flat, box, or other container. See specific recommendations under the individual bulbs. Be sure to label the bulb, cultivar, and its color. This will make planting much easier and less of a surprise next season.

Move bulbs to a cool dark place for the winter. Look for a corner far from the furnace, a root cellar if you are lucky, or other location where the temperatures stay close to 50 degrees Fahrenheit. Many gardeners use a spare refrigerator to store their nonhardy bulbs. Set the thermostat to the desired temperature. Check stored bulbs monthly. Remove any that are showing sign of rot. Move sprouted bulbs to a cooler location. If growth continues, pot them up, move to a sunny window or under artificial light, and grow as a houseplant until they can be moved outdoors.

Caladiums and tuberous begonias can be brought indoors and grown like houseplants. Bring them indoors before the first fall frost. Isolate them from your houseplants for several weeks. Monitor and control any insects you find before adding them to your indoor garden. Harden off in spring before moving them back outdoors.

Managing Animal Pests

Each fall it seems like the squirrels and chipmunks dig bulbs faster than you can plant. Come spring the rabbits and deer eat the flowers on whatever the other animals left behind. Sound familiar? Don't give up. The battle won't be easy, but the beauty these bulbs provide to the landscape make the battle worth the effort. Chicago Botanic Garden recommends mixing small pieces of lava rock with bulbs at planting. They find this helps discourage squirrels and other rodents. Or sprinkle naphthalene flakes or cayenne pepper on the bulbs at planting. Some gardeners swear by these repellents while others have not had success.

Another option is to cover bulb plantings with chicken wire. Dig the planting hole to the proper depth. Cover the bulbs with soil. Then lay chicken wire over the bulbs bending it down around the sides of the planting. Finish covering the bulbs. The chicken wire creates a barrier that discourages the rodents from digging. In spring, the bulbs sprout and grow through the chicken wire.

Once the bulbs sprout (come on—be positive), you can try commercial and homemade repellents, scare tactics, and barriers to protect your bulbs. I find the key to success with repellents is to apply it before the animals start feeding, reapply throughout the blooming season, and vary the products used. A variety of scare tactics such as clanging pans, motion sensitive sprinklers, and white balloons may also keep these critters under control. I live in the city and find my wildlife pests are not easily scared by human smell and sounds.

Fencing is probably the most effective but least desirable. Most of us do not want to view our garden through rabbit or deer fence. But that may be better than having no flowers to see at all. Circle the garden with a four-foot fence stretched tight to the ground to keep out rabbits. A five-foot deer fence around small gardens has been found to keep deer at bay.

If all this sounds like too much work, select bulbs that animals do not eat. Hyacinths, daffodils, allium, fritillaria, Snowflake (*Leucojum*), Camassia, and Spanish bluebells (Hyacinthoides) are larger bulbs that the animals seem to ignore. Include some animal resistant minor bulbs such as grape hyacinths, squills, winter aconite (Eranthus), snowdrop (*Galanthus),* autumn crocus (*Colchicum),* Glory-of-the-snow (*Chionodoxa*), and *Crocus tommasinianus,* which resist the deer. Not a bad list and the many newer, more unique cultivars will allow you to add plenty of variety to your garden when using these.

Forcing Bulbs

Whether planned or done out of necessity (you overbought or didn't get the bulbs planted) forcing bulbs can add beauty to both the indoor or outdoor garden. You will have best results if you purchase bulbs labeled for forcing. But don't worry—force what you have; the results will still be colorful.

Plant bulbs in a container filled with potting mix. Water and store in a cool location with temperatures between 35 and 45 degrees Fahrenheit. A

Fringed Tulip

spare refrigerator works great. No refrigerator? Then be creative with the resources you do have. One master gardener packs his potted bulbs in a Styrofoam cooler and stores them in a corner of his unheated garage. After fifteen weeks of cold, he can remove the pots as needed, place them in a cool sunny window, and get them growing indoors. Another gardener used his small water garden. Once it was drained for winter, he filled it with potted bulbs, covered the pots with straw, and placed a piece of plywood over the pond. After they were adequately chilled, he could lift the lid and take out what was needed. Or sink the pots in a vacant garden space for winter. Mulch with straw or evergreen branches after the ground lightly freezes. You can start removing the pots after fifteen weeks of cold weather. You may have to wait for a winter thaw to remove the pots from the frozen soil.

Move the chilled pots indoors to a cool location with indirect light for two weeks. Water thoroughly and often enough to keep the soil moist. Move them to a bright sunny window when the leaves are about four to six inches tall. Bright sunlight and temperatures of 68 degrees Fahrenheit will give you the best results. Most forced bulbs will start blooming three to four weeks after you remove them from storage. See www.bulb.com for specifics on individual bulbs.

Popular and Easy Irises

I like to use forced bulbs in windowboxes and containers. Our winters are too harsh to plant and grow them directly in outdoor containers. Simply force or purchase forced bulbs to place in the planters in spring. Set the potted bulbs in the windowbox or planter, cover with mulch or moss, and no one is the wiser. This is a great way to add early spring color to unplantable areas in the landscape.

Recycling Forced Bulbs

It is nearly impossible to re-force hardy bulbs since they don't replenish spent energy when grown indoors. You can recycle them in the compost pile or your outdoor garden. Planting them outdoors is a great way to expand your garden and hold onto the memory. Remove the spent flowers and continue watering forced bulbs. Fertilize with any flowering houseplant fertilizer. Keep the plants in a sunny window growing as long as possible. Reduce watering as the foliage yellows. Move the bulbs into the garden as soon as the soil is workable or store them in a cool dark place for summer. Plant the stored bulbs in fall with your other hardy bulbs. Be patient. Most forced bulbs won't bloom until their second spring in the garden.

You may want to try this with your Easter lily. Plant the bulb in a protected spot in full sun with well-drained soil. Mulch lilies, after the ground freezes, to provide extra winter insulation. With some luck you will have an Easter lily garden to enjoy in mid summer.

Allium

Allium species

Eye-catching alliums are guaranteed to get your garden a second look not only from passers-by but also from the birds, bees, and butterflies looking for a place to feed. Include an assortment of alliums in the landscape for summer-long enjoyment. Select alliums that are hardy to your area and provide the look you want in your yard. The best known is the giant onion (Allium giganteum). You have probably seen its picture in catalogues with flowers the size of the small child's head standing nearby. The 5-to-6-inch-diameter purple flower head tops a 3-to-4-foot-tall plant. These like other alliums are great in fresh or dried flower arrangements. The wonderful foliage adds texture and slight onion fragrance to the garden all season long. Mask frost-damaged foliage of the early bloomers with other plants, while highlighting allium's showy flowers.

Other Common Name
Flowering Onion

Bloom Period and Seasonal Color
Early, mid, or late summer blooms in white, purple, blue, pink, or yellow.

Mature Height × Spread
6 to 60 in. × 6 to 15 in.

When, Where, and How to Plant
Plant allium bulbs in fall. This is also a good time to dig and divide or move existing plantings. Most alliums prefer full sun to light shade and well-drained soil. Ornamental onion is often sold as a perennial plant at more specialized garden centers. Plant the bulbs at a depth of 2 to 3 times their diameter, but no deeper than 6 inches. Spacing of the bulbs varies with the species. Plant container-grown alliums at the same level they were growing in the pot.

Growing Tips
Winter mulch allium plantings with evergreen boughs, straw, or marsh hay after the soil surface freezes. Mulching will help more tender alliums make it through our difficult winters and reduce the risk of early sprouting that can result in frost-damaged foliage.

Care
Bulb rot is a common problem in cool, damp soil. You can't control the rain, but you can adjust your watering schedule. Water thoroughly and only when the top few inches begins to dry. Frost-damaged tips won't hurt the plant.

Companion Planting and Design
Smaller alliums can be used in rock gardens. Some species will reseed and naturalize. Most alliums look good mixed with perennials. The giant onion, *Allium giganteum*, is a good background plant, although I find the large flower head difficult to blend. Try surrounding this bold element with finer textured plants like threadleaf coreopsis. Or use an equally bold-textured plant like a yucca to create contrast in form.

My Personal Favorites
Ornamental onion (*Allium senescens* 'Glaucum' or *Allium montanum* 'Glaucum') is only 6 inches tall. The attractive, slightly twisted, gray-green foliage is effective all season long. The late summer flowers are 1 inch in diameter and are lilac or mauve. Turkestan onion *Allium karataviense* is a bit larger, 10 inches, with 4- to 6-inch lilac flowers gracing wide blue-green leaves that remind me of a hosta. The drumstick chives (*Allium sphaerocephalon*) is a 2-to-3-foot-tall plant with many 2-inch-diameter purple flowers. The large number of blooms makes quite a display.

Caladium

Caladium bicolor

When, Where, and How to Plant

Caladiums can be started from tubers or purchased as plants. Start tubers indoors in mid-March for an earlier display. Plant the tuber with the knobby side up in a well-drained potting mix. Keep the potting mix moist and at 70 degrees Fahrenheit. Tubers can be planted directly outdoors, no more than 2 inches deep, after all danger of frost has passed. Hardened-off transplants can be moved outdoors at this same time. Space small cultivars 12 inches apart and larger cultivars 18 to 24 inches apart. Plant a bit closer for earlier impact in the garden.

Growing Tips

Plants may suffer scorch, or leaf browning, if grown in full sun or if the soil is allowed to dry out in hot weather. Mulch to reduce this problem. Caladiums grown in planters need regular care. Check the soil moisture in planters at least once a day; twice a day during hot weather. Water containers thoroughly and fertilize regularly throughout the summer according to label directions.

Care

Caladiums are basically pest free. Dig caladiums up after the first light frost. Allow tubers to dry in a well-ventilated location. Store tubers in peat moss in a cool basement at 50 degrees Fahrenheit. Caladiums can be grown as houseplants all year long and summered outdoors in their containers or planted in the garden. Reduce maintenance by leaving the caladium in its container. Sink the pot into soil, making sure the lip of the container is even with the soil surface.

Companion Planting and Design

Caladiums make excellent bedding and container plants. Use them en masse or mixed with other shade-tolerant plants. Try combining them with shade loving annuals such as wax begonia, impatiens, and callas. They mix nicely with ferns, hosta, astilbe, ornamental sedges, and other shade loving plants.

My Personal Favorites

Select a cultivar that complements your garden's color scheme. Some cultivars, like 'White Christmas', are white with green veins. Other cultivars, like 'Pink Beauty', have red veins with speckles of bright green, pink, and white throughout the leaves.

The colorful leaves of caladium can add life to shade and indoor gardens. The arrowhead-shaped leaves are held on long stems making each leaf stand out in the garden. The leaves are a colorful mix of white, red, pink, and green. Caladiums are available as fancy- and lance-leaved types. The fancy-leaved caladiums have large leaves and are the most popular. The narrow lance-leaved types are usually dwarf and more sun tolerant. Two similar looking plants, elephant ears (Alocasia) and taro (Colocasia) are coming into popularity. Their large foliage, sometimes variegated or heavily veined provide a tropical feel to Minnesota gardens and containers. Also grown for its foliage this plant prefers shade but tolerates sun as long as they receive sufficient moisture. Taro is a food staple in Hawaii and other tropical islands. The tuberous roots are ground to make poi.

Other Common Name
Fancy-leaved Caladium

Bloom Period and Seasonal Color
Effective all season, colorful red, pink, white, and green foliage.

Mature Height × Spread
1 to 2 ft. × 12 to 24 in.

Calla Lily
Zantedeschia aethiopica

Calla lilies are a favorite cut flower and garden plant. These long-lasting blooms are commonly sold by florists and used in bridal bouquets and funeral arrangements. The showy trumpet shaped part of the flower is called a spathe. The stem-like structure in the center is a spadix. The fragrance is an added benefit. In the garden, calla flowers can brighten up a shady location. Their arrowhead-shaped leaves make a dramatic statement whether the plant is in a container, in a flower garden, or near a water garden. I was lucky enough to see them growing in their native habitat in South Africa. They flanked the banks of a stream in full bloom in early spring. Extend their colorful display by including close relatives such as Zantedeschia albo-marginata (*white flowers*) and Zantedeschia elliottiana (*yellow flowers*) that have white spots on the leaves.

Other Common Name
Arum Lily

Bloom Period and Seasonal Color
Late spring through early summer blooms in white.

Mature Height × Spread
2 to 3 ft. × 2 ft.

When, Where, and How to Plant
Plant rhizomes indoors in mid-March for an earlier outdoor flower display. Grow them in a container with well-drained potting mix. Cover the rhizomes with 3 inches of soil. Water sparingly until growth appears, then increase the watering and fertilize them. In the garden, plant rhizomes 4 inches deep and 18 inches apart. Move hardened-off transplants outdoors after the danger of frost is over. Plant calla lilies in partial to full shade. They will tolerate full sun if the soil is kept moist. Calla lilies prefer moist, organic soil. They are also available from garden centers in 3-, 4- or 6-inch pots. Plant container-grown calla lilies at the same level they were growing in the pot.

Growing Tips
Keep the top few inches of soil moist. Container plantings will need to be checked daily and watered as needed. Normal flower garden fertilization is sufficient for these plants. Add a slow-release fertilizer to the soil in container gardens for full season fertilization.

Care
Calla lilies are fairly low-maintenance plants. Remove faded flowers for a tidier appearance. Leaf spot fungal disease may be a problem in wet years. Remove infected leaves to control this problem. Dig up calla rhizomes in the fall after the first light frost. Allow the rhizomes to dry. Store them in peat moss or perlite at a temperature of 50 degrees Fahrenheit.

Companion Planting and Design
Calla lilies will grow in shallow pools or ponds, and they look nice when planted in or near water gardens. They work well in containers alone, or try using them in perennial and annual gardens. Once the calla lily has finished flowering, the leaves provide continued interest in the garden. Try mixing them with caladiums, arums, ferns, and sedges.

My Personal Favorites
'Green Goddess' has a greenish spathe with a white throat and works well in flower arrangements. 'Little Gem' is fragrant and dwarf, 12 to 18 inches tall. Calla lily 'Crowborough' produces large, 4-inch flowers and is more sun tolerant.

Canna
Canna generalis

When, Where, and How to Plant
Plant rhizomes directly outdoors in the garden after the last spring frost 3 to 4 inches deep and 1¹/₂ to 2 feet apart. Start canna rhizomes indoors in mid-March for earlier outdoor bloom. Cut rhizomes into pieces with at least 2 or 3 eyes (buds) per section. Start them in a shallow flat, or directly in a 4- or 6-inch pot filled with a well-drained potting mix. Cannas can also be purchased as transplants in 4- to 6-inch pots. Plant hardened-off transplants outdoors in well-drained soil after all danger of frost is past.

Growing Tips
Cannas do not need staking. Water thoroughly when the top few inches of soil feels moist but crumbly. Fertilize these according to soil test recommendations or as you do the other annuals in the garden.

Care
Cannas are low-maintenance plants. Remove faded flowers to maintain a neat appearance and encourage continuous blooming. Dig up rhizomes in the fall after a light frost. Cut off the stems, leaving several inches above the rhizomes. Remove any loose soil and allow them to sit for several hours. Pack the rhizomes in peat moss or sawdust and store them in a cool, 45- to 50-degree location. Divide rhizomes in the spring before planting.

Companion Planting and Design
Use smaller cultivars as bedding plants. Larger cultivars make nice background plants or vertical accents. Both work in containers. Mix with spider cleome or surround them with annual fountain grass to soften their bold texture. You can also grow cannas in containers submerged in water gardens.

My Personal Favorites
'The President' canna is consistently popular. This 3-foot-tall plant produces scarlet red flowers with glossy green leaves. The striped leaves of 'Pretoria' and 'Bengal Tiger' have gained these plants much recognition. Both are 6-foot-tall plants with orange flowers. 'Australia' with its shocking red flowers and burgundy foliage stands out in the garden, while 'Constitution' with the light pink flowers and purple-gray leaves blends easily with neighboring plants. 'Tropical Rose' is an All-America Selections Award winner.

You can't drive through parks without seeing the large, impressive cannas. These bold plants fill city boulevards and Como Park's flower beds. Their large green, bronze, or variegated leaves are covered with big, brightly colored flowers. It only takes a few plants to make a statement. This Victorian favorite is making a comeback in gardens across the country. The bold foliage and colorful flowers make a nice addition to the "tropical gardens" being created throughout the northern US. I'd like to think we are trend-setters, but perhaps we have just held onto our traditions a bit longer than the rest of the country. In any case, consider including cannas in your container or flower gardens.

Other Common Name
Canna Lily

Bloom Period and Seasonal Color
Midsummer through frost blooms in orange, yellow, white, red, and pink.

Mature Height
1 to 5 ft. × 18 to 24 in.

Crocus

Crocus vernus

Crocus is one of the first flowers to greet you in the spring. It is an easy-to-grow plant that can add weeks of enjoyment to your garden. The small plants hold their flowers above the narrow, grass-like leaves. Its early bloom period and variety of color make crocus one of the most commonly grown spring-flowering bulbs. End the season as you started it. Add autumn crocus (Colchicum) for a fall display. Plant these corms by late August. The plant produces leaves in early spring, which die back to the ground in six to eight weeks. In September, you will be pleasantly surprised when the flowers appear without leaves.

Other Common Name
Dutch Crocus

Bloom Period and Seasonal Color
Early spring blooms in white, purple, striped, and yellow.

Mature Height × Spread
4 to 6 in. × 4 to 6 in.

When, Where, and How to Plant
Plant crocus corms in the fall. They prefer well-drained soil but seem to tolerate all Minnesota soils. Place corms 3 inches deep and 4 inches apart. Plant them in groups of at least 15 to 20 for an eye catching display.

Growing Tips
Avoid overwatering that can lead to root rot. Fertilize according to soil test recommendation or as directed in the beginning of the chapter. Note the white stripe down the middle of the leaves. This identification tip will help prevent you from "weeding out" the grass-like crocus leaves.

Care
Crocuses are low-maintenance plants. Flowers will close on cloudy days or in heavy shade. Corm rot is a problem in poorly drained soil. Animals are the biggest problem the crocus faces. Squirrels and chipmunks will dig, move, and eat crocus corms. Rabbits love to nibble on the flowers and buds. Try some of the management strategies discussed in the beginning of the chapter.

Companion Planting and Design
Crocuses make an impressive spring display when planted en masse under trees, naturalized in the lawn, or throughout perennial and rock gardens. A well-manicured lawn is not the place to naturalize crocuses. You need to let the crocus foliage grow after the flowers fade. That means you must delay cutting your grass or cut it as high as possible at the start of the mowing season. Plant autumn crocus among ground covers for a fall floral surprise. They also work well in annual, perennial, and rock gardens.

My Personal Favorites
Showy crocus, *Crocus speciosum*, a fall-flowering crocus, is easy to grow and hardy statewide. It flowers in fall before the leaves are fully developed. Golden crocus, *Crocus chrysanthus*, flowers earlier than the Dutch crocus, helping to extend the flowering season. Try *Crocus tommasinianus* if you are plagued with squirrels. And for the cooks in the group, note that *Crocus sativus* is the source of saffron. It takes 7000 flowers to make 3 ounces—no wonder it is so expensive!

Crown Imperial
Fritillaria imperialis

When, Where, and How to Plant
Plant this scaly bulb in fall after the temperatures are consistently cool and before the ground freezes. Moist well-drained soil is a must for winter survival. Add organic matter to the top 12 inches of soil to ensure good drainage in heavy soils and to increase water holding capacity in sandy soils. Many gardeners plant the bulbs on their sides to avoid water collecting in the center that can cause bulb rot. Plant the bulbs 6 inches deep and 8 to 12 inches apart. Fritillarias are said to prefer shade, but I find they grow just fine in full sun in our northern climate.

Growing Tips
Supplement rainfall in dry springs. Water thoroughly whenever the top few inches of soil begin to dry. Allow the soil to stay drier in summer. Incorporate a bulb fertilizer at the time of planting if supplemental nutrients are needed.

Care
Winter survival is the biggest challenge. Cover plantings with a layer of straw, marsh hay, or evergreen boughs after the soil surface freezes. Avoid bulb rot with soil preparation and by planting the bulb on its side. Leaf spot and rust are occasional problems in wet springs.

Companion Planting and Design
Crown imperial's shade tolerance makes it a good addition to the shade garden. Mix it with hosta and other shade lovers that will cover the fading foliage in late spring. This tall plant makes a nice vertical accent in larger bulb plantings. I have seen wonderful plantings in the Netherlands where they had fritillaria surrounded by a mix of hyacinths and daffodils that were skirted with lower growing daffodils and grape hyacinths. Or tuck a few in with shrubs or as part of the perennial border.

My Personal Favorite
For those farther north or looking for the more unusual, try checkered lily *Fritillaria meleagris*. This close relative of crown imperial is hardy to Zone 3, grows 9 to 15 inches tall, and has mottled flowers that look checked. Grow it in moist soils with full sun to light shade.

The name suggests royalty, but some gardeners see a bit of Dr. Seuss in the flower. The tall plants are crowned with downward facing, bell-shaped flowers. The tuft of short grass-like leaves that top the flowers remind some of a Dr. Seuss character. Whatever you see, you will enjoy their stately appearance in the mid-spring garden. The lily-like plant fits both formal and informal garden styles. The light musky (skunky), smell won't bother you in the garden but is probably why animals leave this bulb alone. Once I made the mistake of leaving a box of these bulbs in my kitchen waiting for planting. A search of the kitchen revealed that the unidentifiable smell was coming from the bulbs, not something that died in my pantry. Increase the longevity and your enjoyment by planting these in well-drained soil.

Other Common Name
Fritillaria

Bloom Period and Seasonal Color
Mid-spring with orange or yellow flowers.

Mature Height × Spread
3 to 4 ft. × 1 ft.

Zones
Hardy to Zone 4

Daffodil

Narcissus species and hybrids

Daffodils are guaranteed to brighten up any spring landscape. They are one of the easiest bulbs to grow. Select several different cultivars for variety and extended bloom. The daffodil's distinctive flowers stand out from their strap-like leaves. So is it a daffodil, jonquil, or narcissus? Narcissus is the scientific name that is often used as its common name. Daffodil is a common name introduced and spread by English-speaking people. Jonquil is actually a species of this plant, Narcissus jonquilla. Whatever you call it, consider forcing it for your indoor enjoyment. And plant plenty of daffodils so you have extra to use as cut flowers indoors. Keep daffodils separate from other cut flowers. The plant sap that leaks from the daffodils' cut stems will plug the cut ends of other flowers. This blocks their intake of water and shortens their vase life.

Other Common Names
Narcissus, Jonquil

Bloom Period and Seasonal Color
Early to mid-spring blooms in yellow, white, orange, pink, and green.

Mature Height × Spread
6 to 24 in. × 6 to 12 in.

When, Where, and How to Plant
Plant daffodil bulbs in the fall. They tolerate clay soil but perform best in areas with well-drained soil. Plant the bulbs 5 to 6 inches deep and 6 to 12 inches apart. In areas with sandy soil, you can plant daffodils up to 8 inches deep. Use closer spacing for smaller cultivars and quicker display. The wider spacing works for larger cultivars and naturalizing. The greater the spacing, the longer you have before the bulbs become overcrowded.

Growing Tips
Daffodils prefer moist soils in spring but drier soils during their dormant period in summer. Add organic matter to improve drainage. Excess nitrogen can result in lots of leaves and no flowers.

Care
Animals leave this poisonous bulb alone. Remove faded flowers for a tidier look and leave the foliage on the plant until it yellows but at least six weeks after flowering. Bulb rot can be a problem in poorly drained soil. Poor flowering can be caused by excess shade, overcrowding, overfertilizing, and cold-temperatures injury to the buds. Move the daffodils, divide them, and avoid high-nitrogen fertilizers to fix the first three problems. Winter-mulch the plants that are prone to early sprouting or move them away from the house and other artificial heat sources. A hot spell at the time of flowering can prevent flower buds from opening or shorten the floral display.

Companion Planting and Design
Daffodils can be planted in perennial gardens, around trees and shrubs, or naturalized in woodland landscapes. Use smaller species in rock gardens. Mix daffodils with daylilies or hosta to mask the daffodil leaves during summer. I also like to mix daffodils with Virginia bluebells.

My Personal Favorite
There are more daffodils than you can imagine, and many of them don't even look like a typical daffodil. Some have very short or double trumpets. Daffodil flowers may be all one color or a combination. Some daffodils are better for naturalizing, others are more fragrant, and still others may be better for forcing. Pick the one that fits your taste and design.

Dahlia

Dahlia hybrids

When, Where, and How to Plant

Plant dahlia tuberous roots indoors in mid-March for early bloom outdoors. Each section must have at least one eye, the point of new growth. Or plant tuberous roots directly in the garden after the last spring frost. Prepare the top 12 inches of the soil before planting. Plant the tuberous roots 4 inches deep. Lay the root on its side with the eye pointing up. Stake tall cultivars at planting time to avoid injuring the tuberous root. Cover the root with soil. Dahlia plants are available in 4- to 6-inch pots from garden centers. Place the plants several inches deeper in the ground than the dahlias were growing in the container. Grow dahlias in a location with full sun to light shade in moist, well-drained soil.

Growing Tips

Mulch dahlias to keep the soil cool and moist. Make sure the plants receive adequate moisture and nutrients throughout the growing season. Move dahlias into storage after the first light frost. Pack the roots in sand and store in a cool (35 to 40 degrees Fahrenheit) dry place for winter.

Care

Pinch out the growing tips and deadhead for shorter, bushier plants. To get larger blooms, train the plants to one major stem, removing side shoots as they develop. Next, remove all the flower buds that develop along the stem. Leave one bud on the end of each stem. Insects such as mites, aphids, leafhoppers, and thrips can cause damage. Insecticidal soap will usually control these pests.

Companion Planting and Design

Tall dahlias make excellent background plants. Plant medium and short dahlias in small groupings throughout annual and perennial gardens. I like to use these with ornamental grasses, threadleaf coreopsis, or other fine textured plants.

My Personal Favorites

Flower types vary from the single, daisy-like flowers to the double-flowering, decorative types. The cacti flowers have twisted petals; the ball dahlias look like pom-poms, and the water lily dahlias resemble water lily flowers. Annual or bedding dahlias are smaller, less expensive, and flower from seed in the first year.

Ever been to a dahlia show? I am always amazed at the wide range of flower sizes, types, and colors available. But don't let the high-quality exhibition flowers scare you away. With proper planting and routine maintenance, you can put on your own dahlia show right in the garden. In fact, the latest trend is to use dahlias, like mums, for your fall floral display. Forget the hassle of starting them indoors – rather, plant the tuberous roots directly in the garden each spring. The later bloom is a nice way to end the garden season. No matter when they bloom, dahlias will bring added value to your garden. They are a good nectar source for hummingbirds and butterflies, which add motion and color to the landscape. And the beautiful flowers look good on the plant or in a vase indoors.

Other Common Name
Garden Dahlia

Bloom Period and Seasonal Color
Midsummer to frost blooms in white, pink, red, orange, and yellow.

Mature Height × Spread
1 to 5 ft. × 12 to 24 in.

Gladiolus
Gladiolus hortulanus

Popular as a cut flower, the gladiolus is often relegated to the back row or cutting garden. Consider incorporating this plant into your landscape. Its attractive flowers can create a colorful vertical accent in the flower garden. And plant plenty so you can bring some indoors to enjoy. Extend their vase life by cutting the flowers in early morning or evening. Cut them when the bottom third of the flowers have just opened, the middle third just starting to open and the top third still in bud. Leave at least a third of the leaves on the stem to restore energy to the corm for next season's bloom. Leave some flowers in the garden to help bring hummingbirds and butterflies to the landscape. So try planting gladiolus where the flowers, hummingbirds, and butterflies can be seen and enjoyed.

Other Common Name
Gladiola

Bloom Period and Seasonal Color
Summer blooms in white, yellow, pink, red, orange, purple, blue, and green.

Mature Height × Spread
1 to 5 ft. × 6 to 8 in.

When, Where, and How to Plant
Plant gladiola corms outdoors in the spring as soon as the soil is workable. Gladiola will bloom in 60 to 120 days, depending on the cultivar. Stagger planting every two weeks through the end of June to extend your bloom and cutting time throughout the season. Use the earlier-blooming cultivars for your late-June plantings. Plant gladiola in full sun and well-drained soil. Plant corms 3 to 6 inches deep and 3 to 6 inches apart. The larger the corms, the deeper and farther apart they should be planted.

Growing Tips
Gladiola need about 1 inch of water per week during the growing season. You may need to supplement rainfall during dry spells. Fertilize according to soil test or as you do your annual plants.

Care
Purchase and store only pest-free corms. Some gardeners treat corms with insecticides and fungicides prior to storage. Read and follow all label directions; label the stored corms as pesticide treated to remind you to wear gloves when handling them. Dig up the corms in the fall after the leaves have turned brown. Dry corms, then cure in a location at 80 degrees Fahrenheit for up to four weeks. Sort and discard old or shriveled corms and store the remaining ones uncovered in a cool well-ventilated location at 40 degrees Fahrenheit.

Companion Planting and Design
Their strong vertical forms can be difficult to blend in the garden, but I know one gardener who planted a group of gladiola in her garden and used a piece of white lattice (parallel to the ground) as a grow-through stake. The strong features of the lattice structure balanced the sturdy vertical features of the gladiola. Try softening the gladiola with fine-textured plants such as baby's breath, threadleaf coreopsis, and cosmos.

My Personal Favorite
The large-flowered hybrids grow 2 to $4^1/_2$ feet tall. They produce long flower spikes with large flowers and come in a variety of colors. The miniature and butterfly hybrids are $1^1/_2$ to 4 feet tall. Each corm produces several slender flower spikes filled with small flowers.

Grape Hyacinth
Muscari botryoides

When, Where, and How to Plant

Plant grape hyacinth bulbs in the fall. They are flexible but prefer full sun to partial shade and cool, moist, well-drained soil. Plant the bulbs 3 inches deep and 4 inches apart. Plant them in groups of at least 15 to 20 for good impact. Several hundred will really grab your attention.

Growing Tips

Make sure new plantings are well-watered before the ground freezes. Supplemental watering may be needed during dry springs. Water thoroughly when the top few inches of soil are crumbly and moist. Allow the soil to go drier when the bulbs are dormant in summer.

Care

Grape hyacinths are low-maintenance plants. The leaves will persist and continue to grow most of the season. They usually die back in late summer and reappear in fall, making some gardener's nervous. That's not a problem; you just need to plan for it. Grape hyacinths multiply quickly. They will need dividing every four or five years in the late summer or fall.

Companion Planting and Design

Plant in large masses for an impressive spring display. Mix with other, taller bulbs such as daffodils and tulips that bloom at the same time to double the blooming impact, or plant cultivars that bloom later to extend bloom time. Plant them under trees and shrubs or let them naturalize in wooded landscapes or grassy areas. Use small cultivars in the rock garden. An idea for yard art: Kuegenhoff Gardens in the Netherlands uses grape hyacinths in winding patterns, like a river, throughout their plantings.

My Personal Favorites

The Armenian grape hyacinth, *Muscari armeniacum*, is a larger and more vigorous plant than the common grape hyacinth. It is often sold as grape hyacinth in some catalogues and garden centers. It is only hardy to Zone 4. Plant *Muscari botryoides album* for a white-flowering grape hyacinth. The plumed grape hyacinth, *Muscari comosum* 'Plumosum', has a really different look. The flowers on this grape hyacinth are shredded and look like plumes or tassels.

Though small in size, the grape hyacinth can create great interest in the landscape. This easy-to-grow bulb is resistant to animals and multiplies quickly. I once sent my parents a bag of bulbs. Three years later my dad gave me back three bags of grape hyacinth bulbs and a request not to return the favor. The name Muscari is derived from the Turkish name for this plant. Botryoides means like a bunch of grapes, which certainly describes the flowers. The flowers are nice additions to forced bulb containers and miniature cut-flower arrangements. I let the seed pods develop on my grape hyacinths. I think the translucent pods add interest to the garden and to dried flower arrangements. The vigorous grape hyacinth won't be weakened, but you will have even more plants as they reseed.

Other Common Name
Common Grape Hyacinth

Bloom Period and Seasonal Color
Early to mid-spring blooms in blue and white.

Mature Height × Spread
6 to 9 in. × 4 to 6 in.

Hyacinth
Hyacinthus orientalis

Hyacinths are sure to brighten up a landscape or room with their large flowers and sweet fragrance. Use this plant outdoors in the garden or force it indoors. Either way, it will make a colorful addition to your spring bulb display. Just be careful when using them indoors. Their fragrance can be overpowering. One semester I transported my pot of hyacinths from campus to campus for demonstration. Despite the cold weather I drove with my windows down due to the overwhelming fragrance. Purchase pre-cooled bulbs or force your own by giving them twelve to fifteen weeks of cool (35 to 45 degrees Fahrenheit) temperatures to initiate flowering. Sales of hyacinths are on the rise. Many gardeners and landscapers are using these animal resistant bulbs in place of tulips and other deer and rabbit favorites.

Other Common Name
Dutch Hyacinth

Bloom Period and Seasonal Color
Early to mid-spring blooms in blue, violet, white, rose, pink, yellow, salmon, and apricot.

Mature Height
6 to 10 in. × 6 in.

When, Where, and How to Plant
Plant hyacinth bulbs in the fall. Grow them in areas with full sun and moist, well-drained soil. Add organic matter to improve the drainage of clay soil and increase the water-holding capacity of sandy soil. Purchase medium-sized bulbs, which will produce nice-sized flowers that are less likely to flop and require staking. Keep the bulbs in a cool, dark place until you are ready to plant. Plant the bulbs 6 inches deep and 6 to 9 inches apart. Even a small grouping of 6 or 9 bulbs can put on a good show.

Growing Tips
Mulch the soil to keep the bulbs cool and moist spring through fall. Water thoroughly whenever the top few inches of soil starts to dry. Fertilize according to soil test results or as recommended for other hardy bulbs.

Care
Hyacinths are basically pest free but generally short lived in our area. They need cool summers and moist, well-drained soil to flourish and multiply. Remove faded flowers to allow all the energy to go into the bulb instead of into seed formation. Flowers will tend to get smaller each year. Replace hyacinths every 3 or 4 years for the best flowering display. Hyacinths are subject to bulb rot. Plant them in well-drained locations and add organic matter to heavy clay soil to avoid this problem.

Companion Planting and Design
The stiff habit and large flowers give the hyacinth a formal look. Use mass plantings for an impressive spring display. I use small groupings of hyacinths scattered throughout my perennial gardens to maintain my informal design. Consider mixing hyacinths with daffodils, tulips, or winter hardy pansies.

My Personal Favorites
'Gipsy Queen' has a nice coral-colored flower that combines well with 'Pink Charm' daffodil. The flower spike covered with double raspberry-red florets of 'Hollyhock' inspired the name. A close relative, *Hyacinthoides hispanica* known as Spanish Bluebells, Spanish squills, or wood hyacinth have a more open spike of blue, bell-shaped flowers. This is a good addition to the shade garden.

When, Where, and How to Plant

Plant iris rhizomes in midsummer through early fall, preferably by September 1st so the plants can develop roots before winter. Mulch late plantings after the ground lightly freezes. Plant iris in full sun and well-drained soil, just below the soil surface with the leaf fan facing outward. Each rhizome should contain at least 1 fan of leaves. Plant iris singly or in groupings of three. In groupings, set the rhizomes next to each other (fan facing out), and the groupings at least 24 inches apart. Smaller cultivars can be spaced closer.

Growing Tips

Water thoroughly whenever the top few inches of soil are crumbly and moist. Avoid high-nitrogen fertilizers that promote leaf growth and discourage flowering.

Care

Taller cultivars will need staking. Poor flowering can result from excess fertilizer, low light, overcrowding, and recent transplanting. Remove spent flowers. Divide overcrowded iris in midsummer. Dig rhizomes and cut them into smaller pieces containing at least 1 set of leaves and several large roots. Cut the leaves back to 6 inches. Discard any damaged or insect-infested rhizomes. Iris borer is the biggest problem for bearded iris. Remove any borers found during summer transplanting. Removing old foliage in the fall eliminates the egg-laying site of the adult moth. Remove leaf spot-infested leaves when found.

Companion Planting and Design

Mix iris with perennials for late spring and early summer interest. Healthy, sword-shaped leaves can provide a vertical accent in the summer garden. Iris combine nicely with fine textured plants such as ornamental grasses, threadleaf coreopsis, and baby's breath,

My Personal Favorites

The Siberian iris, *Iris sibirica*, tolerates moist soil, partial shade, and is less susceptible to iris borer. It grows 2 to 4 feet tall with long, grass-like leaves, which look good all summer. The crested iris *Iris cristata* is an early bloomer that also tolerates moist soil and shade. The short foliage persists all season, creating a nice ground cover. The reblooming (remontant) iris such as 'Immortality' will often produce a second set of flowers in the fall.

The stately beauty of the iris can fill in the blooming void between spring-flowering bulbs and early summer perennials. Its wide range of heights and colors makes this versatile plant work in any garden. The flowers consist of 3 inner segments or standards, which are usually upright. The 3 outer drooping segments are called falls. The miniature dwarf bearded iris is the first to bloom. It is 4 to 10 inches tall, which makes it a good choice for the rock garden. The standard dwarf bearded iris blooms about seven to ten days later. It is 10 to 15 inches tall. The intermediate iris is the next to bloom and grows to 15 to 28 inches tall. The tall bearded iris is over 28 inches tall and the last to bloom. Include a variety of bearded iris to extend the flowering period.

Other Common Name
Bearded Iris

Bloom Period and Seasonal Color
Late spring to early summer blooms in wide range of colors.

Mature Height × Spread
4 to 48 in. × 6 to 12 in.

Lily
Lilium species

The classic lily is as at home in the informal garden as it is in a more formal setting. Lilies are a little more challenging than daffodils and crocuses, but the flowers will convince you they are worth the effort. Be sure to include enough plants for cutting. The beautiful, fragrant flowers are a great addition to any arrangement. The Asiatic and oriental hybrids are the most readily available. The Asiatic cultivars tend to be hardier than the oriental types. Their flowers are usually unscented and may face up, out, or down. The oriental hybrids usually produce lots of showy fragrant flowers that can be trumpet-shaped, bowl-shaped, flat faced, or with recurved petals. Many florists are forcing the Asiatic and oriental hybrids into bloom for Easter. This Easter lily alternative can then be added to the perennial garden.

Other Common Name
Hardy Lily

Bloom Period and Seasonal Color
Early to midsummer blooms in white, yellow, orange, red, and pink.

Mature Height × Spread
2 to 6 ft. × 8 to 12 in.

When, Where, and How to Plant
Plant lily bulbs in the fall. Purchase and plant pre-cooled lily bulbs in the spring outdoors as soon as the soil is workable. Lilies are also sold as plants during the growing season. Plant whenever they are available. Grow lilies in full sun and moist, well-drained soil. Add organic matter to heavy clay soil to improve drainage. Plant lily bulbs at a depth 2 to 3 times their height. Use the minimum planting depth for lilies growing in clay soil. The deeper the bulb is planted, the greater the risk of bulb rot. Plant lilies at least 3 times their width apart.

Growing Tips
Mulch the soil to keep lily roots cool and moist. Avoid overwatering, especially in clay soil, since that can lead to root rot.

Care
Lilies are subject to bulb rot. Proper soil preparation and watering will help prevent this problem. Deer, rabbits, and groundhogs will eat the plants down to ground level. Repellents and scare tactics may help keep these pests at bay. Apply a winter mulch after the ground freezes for added insulation and for help in getting the plants through our challenging winters.

Companion Planting and Design
Use lilies in large masses, small groupings, or as individual plants scattered throughout the garden. Tall lilies make excellent background or specimen plants. Mix any of the lilies with ornamental grasses, Russian sage, and other perennials. They are quite attractive growing up through or behind shorter plants.

My Personal Favorites
'Star Gazer' is a popular oriental lily suitable in the ground and in container gardens. The red, star-shaped flowers have recurved tips and are marked with darker spots. I also like the Turk's cap lily, *Lilium martagon*. Hardy to Zone 3 and more shade tolerant, this is an excellent choice for northern gardeners. The tiger lily, *Lilium lancifolium* (formerly *Lilium tigrinum*), is a long-time favorite. The tiger lily produces lots of orange-red flowers with spotted recurved petals. It also tolerates some shade and moist soils. It propagates readily from offsets (bulblets) and bulbils produced on the stems.

When, Where, and How to Plant

Plant bulbs in the fall. They prefer well-drained soil but seem to tolerate less than ideal conditions. Plant the bulbs 3 inches deep and 4 to 6 inches apart. Plant them in groups of at least 15 to 20 for good impact.

Growing Tips

Squills tolerate most soils and our climate well. Like other bulbs, they prefer moist soils when growing and a bit drier in the summer. They typically receive enough nutrients when you fertilize the lawn or garden they are growing in.

Care

If properly placed, squills are low-maintenance and basically pest-free plants. Crown rot can cause plants to wilt, yellow, and die. Improve soil drainage prior to planting to avoid this problem. Most gardeners have too much success—complaining that their squills have taken over the garden and moved into the lawn. I think the lawn may be a better place for this plant. Squills brighten up the spring lawn without damaging the grass. Unlike most bulbs, squills tolerate mowing once the flowers have faded. But be aware that once you have them in the lawn they are difficult to remove. Broadleaf weedkillers won't work on these plants. Overcrowded bulbs can be lifted and divided every four to five years.

Companion Planting and Design

Naturalize squills in lawn areas and wooded landscapes, include them in rock gardens, or plant large drifts around trees and shrubs. Mix with ground covers to add a boost of color before the ground covers get growing. Plant them in areas where they have room to grow. Squills multiply quickly and can take over the spring garden. I like to mix them with daffodils, tulips, or hyacinths to double my bloom appeal.

My Personal Favorites

Scilla siberica 'Alba' is a white-flowering Siberian squill. 'Spring Beauty' has large, blue flowers. They are held above the leaves on taller spikes than the straight species. Two-leaved squill, *Scilla bifolia*, is another true blue flowering squill. It grows 3 to 6 inches tall and naturalizes well in sun or partial shade.

Picture a sea of true blue flowers in the midst of the bluegrass in your front lawn. This is just one of the many uses of the Siberian squill. Its true blue color is hard to beat in the early spring garden. These early-blooming bulbs are easy to grow and hardy throughout Minnesota. They are prolific, so give them lots of room or plan on digging and sharing them with friends and family. A few or a mass of these plants are pretty to look at and safe to touch, but do not eat them. All parts of the squill contain digitalis-like substances that are toxic if eaten. The animals seem to know—they leave these bulbs alone. A true blue flower that the animals don't eat I think I can put up with a little thinning as needed.

Other Common Name
Siberian Squill

Bloom Period and Seasonal Color
Early spring blooms in blue and white.

Mature Height × Spread
6 in. × 4 to 6 in.

Tuberous Begonia

Begonia tuberhybrida

Bold, beautiful, and made for the shade, tuberous begonias can add a lot of color and texture to container and shade gardens. These plants can be upright or pendulous in habit. The large green leaves provide an attractive backdrop for the flowers, which are usually double and can be up to 6 inches in diameter. I do not recommend planting tubers directly outside in the garden. If they are planted outside too early, the tubers will rot. If they are planted after all danger of frost is past, you miss the majority of the flowering season. Extend the season by moving these begonias indoors before the first fall frost and growing them as houseplants for the winter. Grow them in moist soil, in a sunny window. I've met gardeners who have kept the same plant going for over five years.

Other Common Name
Tuberous Rooted Begonia

Bloom Period and Seasonal Color
Summer until light frost blooms in orange, red, yellow, and pink.

Mature Height × Spread
10 to 24 in. × 24 in. × 8 to 12 in.

When, Where, and How to Plant
Plant tubers indoors in mid-March. Place tubers rounded-side down (indented side up) in a shallow flat or container filled with a soilless mix. Keep the mix warm and moist. Or purchase plants from the garden center in hanging baskets or 3- to 4-inch pots. Plant hardened-off transplants outdoors after all danger of frost is past. Careful: Tuberous begonias are very frost sensitive. Grow them in moist, well-drained soil in full to part shade 6 inches apart. Three plants are usually enough for a full flowering hanging basket. Avoid windy locations where the stems may break.

Growing Tips
Mulch to keep soil cool and moist. Check the soil moisture in hanging baskets and containers at least once a day. Check pots twice a day during hot weather. Water containers thoroughly, allowing excess water to run out the drainage holes. Fertilize planters frequently throughout the summer.

Care
Powdery mildew, botrytis blight, and downy mildew can be problems. Proper spacing will increase air circulation and reduce disease. If problems continue, plant in a little more light. Botrytis blight and downy mildew are common problems in wet seasons. Plants will scorch (brown leaf margins) when grown in full sun. Remove faded or infected flowers and leaves as soon as they appear. Tuberous begonias will not survive outdoors in Minnesota. After the first light frost, dig, dry, and store in peat moss at 45 to 50 degrees Fahrenheit.

Companion Planting and Design
Plant them en masse for a colorful display in the shade garden. Try adding sweet alyssum or impatiens to a container. This makes for an appealing new look.

My Personal Favorites
The Non Stop series is a seeded type that has received a great deal of attention. It is a compact plant that grows 12 inches tall and wide. It produces 3-inch-wide double flowers of red, pink, apricot, orange, white, or yellow. I like the unique flowers of 'Pin-Up'. This Flueroselect winner has 4-petaled white flowers with a dark pink edge on a compact 10 inch plant.

Tulip
Tulipa species and hybrids

When, Where, and How to Plant

Plant tulip bulbs in the fall. Plant tulips as late as possible to avoid fall sprouting. Grow tulips in full sun and well-drained soil. Plant bulbs 5 to 6 inches deep and 6 to 9 inches apart. Those with sandy or well-drained soils can plant tulips 8 inches deep.

Growing Tips

Water tulips thoroughly whenever the top few inches of soil are crumbly and moist. This will ensure an attractive floral display during dry springs. Mulch the soil to keep bulbs cool in the summer. Excessive heat can result in poor flowering the following spring. Standard bulb fertilization is sufficient.

Care

Leave the foliage in place for at least six to eight weeks after the tulips bloom. Tulips are subject to several rot diseases. Add organic matter to poorly drained soils prior to planting to reduce the risk of rot disease. Deer and rabbits are major pests of this plant. They will eat the flowers and trample the plants. Squirrels, mice, and chipmunks will dig, move, and eat tulip bulbs. See the chapter introduction for tips to keep them away. Tulip hybrids tend to be short lived. Include some of the longer-lived species tulips or plan on replacing the short-lived hybrids every few years.

Companion Planting and Design

Tulips can be planted en masse or scattered throughout the perennial garden in small groupings. Include small species and cultivars in rock gardens. Don't forget to plant extra tulips for cutting. I have several interplanted with perennials. I like to see my tulips popping out of *Brunnera* or *Lamium*. Mix them with pansies or smaller bulbs for a double layer of flowers.

My Personal Favorites

It's hard to pick a favorite. Here are just a few I like. The mid-spring bloomer 'New Design' has variegated foliage and soft pink blossoms. 'Candy Club', another mid-spring tulip, has 4 or 5 white with violet blush flowers on each stem. *Tulipa tarda* is a small, early blooming species tulip that has attractive seedpods for extended appeal.

Tulips are a sure sign of spring for most gardeners. Whether forced in a pot or grown in the garden, tulips can provide color and interest throughout the season. Select early-, mid-, and late-spring blooming tulips for a continuous display and choose the sizes, bloom types, and colors that best fit your landscape design. The early tulips tend to be shorter, while the late spring tulips are taller, reaching heights of 36 inches. Tulips come in single and double flowers. You may have heard about "tulipomania." In the early 1600s, the Dutch became obsessed with the tulip. It was seen as a status symbol, and people started trading money, possessions, and even family businesses for these bulbs. A virus caused a streak in the flower color, which increased the excitement over and value of the tulip.

Bloom Period and Seasonal Color

Early through late spring blooms in all colors.

Mature Height × Spread

4 to 36 in. × 6 to 8 in.

Ground Covers *for Minnesota*

Ground covers are a great alternative to grass for shady locations or hot, dry areas, and they also create a better environment for our trees and shrubs. They are less competitive than grass with the trees and shrubs for water and nutrients, and ground covers help keep the tree roots cool and moist.

All of the advantages of ground covers make them a very appealing choice for home owners. But before you tear out your lawn, let's talk about some important things to consider for ground cover care.

Installation and Maintenance

Many established ground covers are relatively low maintenance, but remember that no plant is maintenance free. As much as I prefer ground cover to grass, you can mow down or spray weeds in the lawn. You have to pull the weeds that invade your ground covers.

Periwinkle

Increase your success and decrease maintenance by investing time and effort during planting and establishment of ground covers. First, eliminate the existing grass and weeds. You can remove weeds with or without the help of chemicals. Cut an edge around the area to be planted in ground cover. Use a sod cutter to remove the grass and weeds or treat the area with a total vegetation killer. Remember, these products kill anything green that they touch. Read label directions before treating the area. Follow label directions and wait the recommended time, anywhere from four to fourteen days, before tilling the treated area.

I have another suggestion for patient gardeners who prefer a non-chemical approach. Edge the bed and cut the existing grass short. Cover with several layers of newspaper and then woodchip mulch. The covered grass will die, and the newspapers will decompose over the following few months. Brush aside the mulch to plant individual ground cover plants.

Take a soil test. It will tell you how much and what type of fertilizer to add. Work the recommended fertilizer and 2 to 4 inches of organic matter such as compost, aged manure, or peat moss into the top 6 to 12 inches of the soil. This will improve drainage in heavy clay soil and increase the water-holding capacity in sandy soil.

Planting

Many ground covers are planted under trees and shrubs. Planting in these areas requires extra care. Do not add soil on top of the roots or deeply till the soil surrounding established trees and shrubs. That can injure or kill the trees and shrubs. Start by killing or removing the grass around established plantings.

Dig a hole larger than the ground cover's rootball and plant it in the existing soil. Broadcast the recommended fertilizer over the soil surface and water in. Next, mulch with an organic material such as shredded leaves, twice-shredded bark, pine needles, or cocoa bean shells. As the mulch breaks down, it will improve the soil below. Be patient; it takes plants longer to fill in this type of planting.

Ground covers growing under trees and shrubs may need a little extra fertilizer and water to help them compete with tree roots. But don't overdo it. Too much water and fertilizer is also bad for your plants. Your soil test will tell you what type of fertilizing you should do once the plants are established. In general, ground covers need 1 pound of actual nitrogen per 1000 square feet. This is equal to 4 pounds of ammonium sulfate (21-0-0), 10 pounds of a 10 percent nitrogen fertilizer and 16 pounds of Milorganite (6-2-0). I like to use a slow-release low nitrogen fertilizer in spring to avoid injury and provide season long results.

Water new plantings thoroughly and often enough to keep the soil moist. Many established ground covers can survive on natural rainfall. You may need to lend a hand during drought. For best results, water established plants thoroughly but only when the top 4 to 6 inches starts to dry.

Weeds are the biggest problem these plants face. Mulch ground cover plantings to reduce weed infestation, or plant the ground covers a little closer so they will fill in quickly to crowd out the weeds. Planting closer means more plants and more money, and the ground covers may need dividing sooner. Remove weeds as soon as they appear, especially when the ground covers are getting established. Once the ground cover fills in, there will be fewer weeds.

Does all this sound like too much work? Just picture this: a carpet of green or variegated leaves covered with fragrant and colorful flowers. Bluegrass can't do that. So invest some time and hard work now for years of beauty.

Pachysandra Along a Walkway

Barren Strawberry

Waldsteinia ternata

Barren strawberry is a tough, low-growing ground cover. Its evergreen leaves provide year-round interest. In the spring, the plants are covered with bright yellow flowers that turn into small, dry, brown fruits. These don't look like strawberries and are not edible. Waldsteinia fragaroides is a closely related species that is also sold as barren strawberry. It is a larger plant with dull green leaves and a looser, more informal look. This barren strawberry is native to Minnesota. It would be a good choice for gardeners interested in using native plants. False or mock strawberry, Duchesnea indica, is often confused with barren strawberry. This plant does produce red strawberry-like fruit, which is tasteless but ornamental. This aggressive grower can overtake the landscape. So check the label and scientific name before you purchase a barren strawberry. You don't need to make more work for yourself.

Other Common Name
Yellow Strawberry

Bloom Period and Seasonal Color
May through June blooms in yellow.

Mature Height × Spread
4 to 6 in. × 18 in.

Zones
Hardy to Zone 4

When, Where, and How to Plant
Plant barren strawberries in the spring for best results. Winter-mulch late plantings after the ground freezes to help this ground cover through the first tough winter. They prefer moist, well drained soil but will tolerate a wide range of conditions. Dig a hole larger than the rootball and plant barren strawberry at the same level it was growing in the container. Water thoroughly to remove air pockets and settle the soil. Mulch with woodchips, shredded leaves, or other organic matter. Barren strawberry plants are available in flats and containers. Plant them at the same level they were growing in the pots. Space plants 1 foot apart. Divide and plant divisions in the spring once the plant has finished blooming.

Growing Tips
Established plants growing in partial shade are drought tolerant, while those growing in full sun should be watered during extended dry spells. Mulch new plantings to conserve moisture and reduce weeds. Minimal fertilization is needed. Try using a slow-release low nitrogen fertilizer to avoid poor flowering and overly aggressive growth.

Care
Once established, barren strawberries are low-maintenance plants. The only serious pests are weeds. Remove weeds as they appear. Once the strawberries fill in, they will crowd out the weeds and cut down on the time spent weeding. Lift and divide overgrown plants, which often have dead centers or fail to bloom. Use a shovel or garden fork to dig out the plants. Cut the clump into several sections and replant the divisions at 12-inch intervals in a prepared spot.

Companion Planting and Design
Barren strawberries make good ground covers in tough locations and under trees and shrubs. Add some spring flowering bulbs for an extra splash of color.

Personal Favorite
Fragaria 'Pink Panda' is one of the ornamental strawberries. It has one-inch bright pink flowers in spring, occasionally followed by edible red fruit. Although it's rated hardy to Zone 5, I do know some Zone 4 gardeners who have small plantings. Good drainage is critical for winter survival in any northern garden.

Barrenwort

Epimedium rubrum

When, Where, and How to Plant

Plant barrenwort in the spring for best results. This gives it plenty of time to get established before winter. Mulch late plantings for winter after the ground lightly freezes. Divide plants in the spring or early summer after the new leaves reach full size. These plants will tolerate full sun as long as the soil is kept moist. Barrenwort needs moist, well drained soil. Barrenwort plants are available from garden centers and perennial nurseries in flats and containers. Prepare the site prior to planting. Plant barrenworts at the same level they were growing in the pots. Space plants 9 to 12 inches apart. Division is needed only if you want to start new plants for other areas. Dig, divide, and replant in the spring or early summer after the new leaves are full size.

Growing Tips

Water the plants during dry periods. Mulching will help conserve moisture and lengthen the time between waterings. Give these slow growers, and those competing with tree roots, a boost of fertilizer. Use a low-nitrogen fertilizer in the spring. Follow soil test recommendations or directions in the chapter introduction.

Care

Barrenworts are slow growers, which gives fast-growing weeds an opportunity to move into the planting. Pull weeds as they appear. Avoid cultivating near the plants, which could damage the barrenwort's shallow roots. Once the barrenworts fill in, they will crowd out the weeds and reduce the time you spend on this task. Cut back old foliage in late winter or early spring before new growth begins. This will make the flowers more visible.

Companion Planting and Design

Use Barrenwort in small groupings, mixed with other shade lovers, in rock gardens, or under trees where grass won't grow. Sedges, hostas, and ferns make a nice backdrop for the delicate heart-shaped leaves.

My Personal Favorites

Yellow barrenwort, *Epimedium* × *versicolor* 'Sulphureum', grows 10 to 12 inches tall and has yellow instead of red flowers. This cultivar is more tolerant of dry, shady sites than the other barrenworts. Try cultivars of Young's barrenwort, *Epimedium* × *youngianum* for smaller gardens.

Barrenwort's changing character can provide year-round interest in your landscape. The new growth emerges green with a touch of red. The heart-shaped leaves are held on wiry stems, giving them a delicate, airy appearance. The red flowers emerge in May or June as the new leaves develop. In the fall, the leaves will turn reddish bronze. Old leaves persist through the winter, adding interest to the winter perennial garden. Add to your enjoyment by using them as cut flowers. Use them in small containers alone or as a filler with other flowers. Pick partially opened flowers in the morning or evening for best results. You will be pleasantly surprised by their vase life. Barrenwort is a long-lived plant. It can remain in the same location for many years.

Other Common Name
Bishop's Hat

Bloom Period and Seasonal Color
May blooms in red.

Mature Height × Spread
8 to 12 in. × 8 to 12 in.

Zones
Hardy to Zone 4

Bishop's Weed

Aegopodium podograria 'Variegatum'

Bishop's weed is lovely to look at, but make sure you really want it before you put the first plant in the ground. The common name gives us some insight into this plant. People believed that bishop's weed was so persistent that it would make a bishop swear. Anyone trying to eliminate the plant would agree. Its tough nature helped it gain its way into the landscape. The variegated leaves help brighten heavily shaded areas in the landscape. The flowers rise above the leaves and remind me of the flower of Queen Anne's lace. Bishop's weed plants are long lived with little care. The species Aegopodium podograria is solid green and even more aggressive than the variegated cultivar. I would avoid using this plant in the landscape. This is a tough plant that should be reserved for the most difficult situations.

Other Common Name
Silveredge Goutweed

Bloom Period and Seasonal Color
June blooms in white.

Mature Height × Spread
1 ft. × spreading

When, Where, and How to Plant

Plant container-grown goutweed any time during the growing season. It can be divided, and the divisions can be planted in early spring or early fall. Bishop's weed can tolerate a wide range of conditions. Its leaves will tend to scorch or brown when it is grown in full sun. Bishop's weed grows in all types of soil, including wet and dry. It grows well in deep shade and is able to compete with the trees for water and nutrients. Plants are commonly available in flats and containers. Plant them at the same level they were growing in the pot. Space plants at least 1 foot apart. They will fill in the area within two years.

Growing Tips

Mulch the soil and water during drought to minimize scorch. Avoid excess fertilization, which will only encourage this plant.

Care

Bishop's weed tends to look unkempt and develops brown leaves in August. Prevent this problem by mowing the plant back to 6 inches two or three times during the summer. That will eliminate the flowers while keeping the plants compact and tidy. This fast-growing ground cover can easily outgrow the weeds. Remove any weeds that do manage to get through. Prune out any green shoots as soon as they appear. Your biggest task is controlling this plant. Remove stray plants as soon as they leave their planting beds. Stray plants can be dug up or spot treated with a total vegetation killer. Edge planting beds prior to chemical treatment. That will prevent the chemicals from damaging the plants you want to keep.

Companion Planting and Design

Bishop's weed is a substitute for the grass that won't grow under Norway maples. I prefer to limit its use to contained areas, such as planting beds between the house and sidewalk. Surrounding it with concrete is the best way to keep it under control.

My Personal Favorites

Consider using a less aggressive ground cover such as variegated pachysandra, vinca, or deadnettle for shady areas. Use sedums in hot dry areas for attractive flowers and foliage.

Bugleweed

Ajuga reptans

When, Where, and How to Plant

Plant container-grown bugleweed in the spring or early summer to allow the plants to become established before our tough winters. Bugleweed can be grown in sun or shade but flowers best in full sun with moist, well drained soil. Avoid open or exposed areas where this plant may suffer winter kill. Bugleweed plants are available from garden centers and perennial nurseries in flats and containers. Space plants 12 inches apart. Divisions can be made any time, but you will get the best results if plants are divided in spring or early summer.

Growing Tips

Mulch new plantings to conserve moisture and reduce weeds. Water established plants during drought. Minimal fertilization is needed to keep these plants healthy. Broadleaf weed killers applied to the lawn will help control stray bugleweed.

Care

Bugleweed is a quick-growing plant that will eventually crowd out the weeds. Remove weeds as they appear. Cut off or mow faded flowers to prevent reseeding and to keep the plants looking good. Lift and divide crowded plants. These fast growers may need to be divided as often as every two to three years to avoid overcrowding and reduce the risk of crown rot. Overgrown plants often have dead centers or fail to bloom. Use a shovel or garden fork to dig out the plants. Cut the clump into several sections. Replant the divisions at 12-inch intervals in a prepared site. Bugleweed is susceptible to crown rot. Avoid this disease by growing plants in well-drained soil.

Companion Planting and Design

Bugleweed is a quick, mat-forming plant that works well under trees, in rock gardens, or as a ground cover in large beds. Avoid growing it next to lawn areas where its aggressive nature can be a problem. Interplant with hostas. The bugleweeds help keep down the weeds until the hostas fill in.

My Personal Favorites

Ajuga reptans 'Catlin's Giant' is one of the largest bugleweed cultivars. It has 8-inch bronze leaves and blue flowers. 'Bronze Beauty' has green-bronze foliage that turns glossy deep purple in fall and winter. The leaves of 'Burgundy Glow' are green, white, and dark pink.

Bugleweed is a beautiful evergreen ground cover. The strap-like leaves create a thick mat of green, bronze, or variegated foliage. New and interesting cultivars are continually appearing in garden centers. These come in a variety of leaf and flower colors. Select a cultivar that is hardy to your location and complements the landscape design. The foliage creates a nice backdrop to the spikes of purple-blue flowers that appear in May. This member of the mint family spreads in all directions by stolons. These horizontal stems lie on the soil surface, producing new plants along the way. One healthy plant can fill a 3-square-foot area in season. You'll need to regularly edge the planting beds to slow the spreading bugleweed.

Other Common Name
Ajuga

Bloom Period and Seasonal Color
May through June blooms in violet and blue-purple.

Mature Height × Spread
6 to 9 in. × 24 to 36 in.

Deadnettle

Lamium maculatum

Deadnettle is such an ugly name for such a pretty plant! The green and white foliage brightens up shady locations all season long. The delicate rose-purple flowers rise above the leaves for added beauty in May and June. Deadnettle works equally well in large or small ground cover plantings. Once established, it will grow well in the dry shade found under Norway maples and other dense shade trees. Minnesota gardeners lost a few deadnettle, along with other plants, in the winter of 2002-2003. I found that most gardeners looked at it as nature helping to thin the planting. My lamium quickly filled in by the end of the following summer. Deadnettle is similar to variegated yellow archangel. Both plants have similar growing requirements and uses. Deadnettle tends to grow in a clump form, while variegated yellow archangel is more spreading.

Other Common Name
Lamium

Bloom Period and Seasonal Color
May through midsummer blooms in rose-purple.

Mature Height × Spread
8 to 12 in. × 3 ft.

Zones
Hardy to Zone 4

When, Where, and How to Plant
Plant container-grown deadnettle plants any time throughout the growing season. Divide plants in early spring for best results. The leaves may scorch or brown if grown in full sun. It prefers moist, well drained soil and will become open and a bit leggy in dry conditions. Prepare the soil prior to planting as described in the chapter introduction. Dig a hole larger than the rootball and plant deadnettle in the existing soil. Mulch the soil with organic matter. Deadnettle plants are available from garden centers and perennial nurseries in flats and containers. Plant them at the same level they were growing in the pot. Space these plants 12 to 18 inches apart.

Growing Tips
Mulch new plantings to conserve moisture and reduce weeds. Water new plantings during dry periods. Check established plants during drought periods. Water thoroughly whenever the top few inches dry.

Care
Spotted deadnettle is basically pest free. Weed control is critical in the first year, so remove weeds as they appear. Once established, deadnettle will quickly fill in, keeping weed growth to a minimum. Prune plants growing in dry shade to encourage fuller, more compact growth. Lift and divide overgrown plants, which often have dead centers or fail to bloom. Use a shovel or garden fork to dig out plants. Cut the clump into several sections. Replant divisions at 12-inch intervals in a prepared site.

Companion Planting and Design
Deadnettle makes an excellent ground cover for shaded areas. Use it under trees where grass won't grow. I also like to use it as an edging plant or in rock gardens. It can be a little aggressive for some garden settings, so pick its neighbors carefully. The attractive foliage of deadnettle has made it a popular addition to hanging baskets and containers.

My Personal Favorite
'Beacon Silver' and 'White Nancy' are probably the two most popular deadnettle cultivars. 'Beacon Silver', also sold under its German name 'Silbergroschen', has pink flowers. Its silver leaves with narrow green borders really stand out in the shade. 'White Nancy' looks like 'Beacon Silver' but has white flowers.

English Ivy
Hedera helix

When, Where, and How to Plant
Plant container-grown English ivy in the spring for best results. Dig and replant rooted stems early in the season. Grow English ivy in a protected site away from the drying winter wind and sun. Good spots include the east side of a house or wall, or any other location that blocks cold winter winds and shades the plant from the winter sun. English ivy also needs moist, well drained soil. Established plantings will tolerate dry conditions. Space plants 12 inches apart. Cut back transplants to 6 inches tall. Use rooted cuttings and divisions to fill in bare areas. Root cuttings in July through September. These should also be spaced at 12-inch intervals.

Growing Tips
Mulch new plantings to conserve moisture and reduce weeds. Make sure new plantings receive adequate water. Once established, English ivy can tolerate dry conditions.

Care
This plant can be a fast grower in the right location. Remove weeds as they appear. Established plantings require little weeding. Prune established plants in early spring. Tip pruning will remove winter damage and keep plants in bounds. Use a rotary mower on its highest setting or shears for heavy rejuvenation pruning. Leaf spot and powdery mildew, as well as mites and aphids, can cause problems on these plants. Plant ivy in areas with good air circulation to minimize disease problems. Sanitation, and raking and removal of diseased leaves, will help reduce these problems. Insecticidal soap will help with insect control, although several applications may be needed. Winter mulch ruins the evergreen appeal but can aid in winter survival. Cover plants with straw or evergreen boughs after the ground freezes. This is especially helpful for new plantings, late plantings, and those in less protected sites.

Companion Planting and Design
Use English ivy as a ground cover under trees and shrubs. It can also look attractive growing over boulders and other structures.

My Personal Favorites
Look for hardy cultivars. 'Bulgaria' is one of the hardiest cultivars based on testing done in Minnesota. 'Thorndale' has larger leaves and is also hardy to Zone 4.

Planting beds and structures covered with English ivy create a warm, cozy look in any landscape—if the ivy is green, healthy, and growing. English ivy is at its northern limits here, but hardy cultivars planted in the right location can add charm to southern Minnesota gardens. Boston ivy (see Vines) is the plant that covers homes and outbuildings throughout Minnesota. Take a closer look at both and you will see the difference. Boston ivy has more of a grape-leaf shape while English ivy is finer in texture. In fact, you may recognize it as the ivy many of us have grown as a houseplant. It is amazing that some of its cultivars are hardy outdoors in Minnesota. It is listed as an invasive plant in other states but is not a problem here in the cold north.

Other Common Name
Ivy

Bloom Period and Seasonal Color
Year round foliage in green.

Mature Height × Spread
6 to 8 in. × spreading

Zones
Hardy in Zone 4

Ginger
Asarum species

Can't grow anything under that spruce tree? Try wild ginger. Both European and wild ginger can take heavy shade and moist conditions that most plants won't tolerate. The ginger flower often goes unnoticed. It is a greenish-purple or brown, bell-shaped flower. The large leaves mask the flowers lying on the soil surface. Wild ginger Asarum canadense *is native to Minnesota, hardy throughout the state and tolerant of the rigors of northern gardens. European ginger,* Asarum europaeum, *is an evergreen and is only hardy in Zones 4 and 5. The spicy fragrance given off by their cut leaves, flowers, and rhizomes gave these plants their common name. Though not related to the cooking ginger,* Zingiber officinale, *European settlers candied or dried the roots of wild ginger to use in cooking.*

Other Common Names
Wild and European Ginger

Bloom Period and Seasonal Color
Early May blooms in greenish-purple or brown.

Mature Height × Spread
6 to 12 in. × 12 in.

Zones
Vary by species

When, Where, and How to Plant
Plant container-grown ginger in early spring. Divisions can be made and planted before growth. Both European and wild ginger prefer full to dense shade but will tolerate partial shade. Plant them in moist soil with lots of organic matter. They prefer an acid soil, but I have had luck growing them in the high pH soil of southern Minnesota. Grow the European ginger in a protected location for best results. Ginger plants are available in containers. Plant them at the same level they were growing in the pot. Space plants 8 to 12 inches apart. Divisions can be made in early spring before new growth.

Growing Tips
Mulch new plantings with shredded leaves, twice-shredded bark, pine needles, or another organic matter. The mulching will help conserve moisture, reduce weeds, and add organic matter to the soil as it breaks down. Water ginger during dry periods. Water thoroughly, wetting the top 6 inches of the soil. Water again when the soil just starts to dry.

Care
These are low maintenance, pest-free plants. I find European ginger a bit more challenging. It is more particular about the growing conditions, often struggles through the winter, and is slow to establish. Canadian ginger will tolerate the rigors of northern gardens. Remove weeds as they appear.

Companion Planting and Design
Use them as ground covers under trees and shrubs. The glossy green leaves of European ginger reflect the light and help brighten shady locations. Wild ginger is hardier and is a good choice for native woodland gardens. Both European ginger and wild ginger combine well with ferns, hostas, astilbe, and other shade-tolerant plants. The native wild ginger, *Asarum canadense* (shown) has large, deeply veined, kidney-shaped leaves.

My Personal Favorite
I prefer the easy-to-grow native wild ginger, *Asarum canadense.* It has large, deeply veined, kidney-shaped leaves that provide textural interest in the garden. Wild ginger dies back for the winter but is hardy throughout the state. Siberian bugloss, *Brunnera macrophylla*, provides a similar texture as wild ginger. This 15- to 18- inch-tall plant has blue forget-me-not-like flowers in spring.

Lily-of-the-Valley
Convallaria majalis

When, Where, and How to Plant
Plant lily-of-the-valley pips (shoots that appear on the rhizome) in the spring. Plant container-grown plants any time during the growing season. They prefer moist, well drained soil, although they will tolerate most soil conditions. Keep in mind that any plant this tough is usually a weed problem in good garden settings. Do not grow this plant along with less assertive plants. Though a tough plant, lily-of-the-valley benefits from proper soil preparation. Space container-grown plants or divisions with several pips 6 to 8 inches apart. Space single pips 3 to 4 inches apart. With proper care, the planting area will be filled in by the end of the second season.

Growing Tips
Mulch and water the plants during dry periods. Give plants growing under trees a yearly application of fertilizer in early spring to help them compete with tree and shrub roots.

Care
Remove old foliage in the spring before new growth begins. Plants grown in dry, sunny locations tend to brown out in midsummer, but the plants will survive. Leaf spot and stem rot can be problems during wet seasons. These diseases cause brown spots to develop on the leaves and stems. Severe infestations can cause the plants to die back to ground level. Remove and destroy infected foliage. Remove all leaves in the fall to reduce the source of disease for next season. Divide the plants in the spring every four or five years to maintain a good flower display.

Companion Planting and Design
Lily-of-the-valley is an effective ground cover in shady areas where nothing else will grow. Use lily-of-the-valley on a shady slope to cover the soil and reduce erosion.

My Personal Favorites
There are quite a few cultivars available. The hybrids are often less aggressive than the species. Try 'Flore Pleno' if you want double white flowers. For a bigger plant, try 'Fortin's Giant'. It has longer leaves and bigger flowers. The variety *rosea* has pink flowers. For interesting foliage, try 'Albostriata', 'Aureovariegata', or 'Variegata'. They all have some type of yellow, cream, or white variegation on their leaves.

Lily-of-the-valley is an old-time favorite. Its fragrant, white, bell-shaped flowers and adaptability have helped this beauty remain part of modern landscapes. The flowers brighten the shade gardens and flower arrangements. Though delicate in appearance, these are one of the few plants that will grow in the small, shaded areas between homes in the older sections of urban areas. It also tolerates the heavy shade and often dry conditions found under trees and shrubs. But any plant that can survive these difficult areas usually needs to be contained. Limit use of this assertive plant to areas surrounded by concrete, edging, or other physical barriers. Its aggressive nature has helped lily-of-the-valley become an invasive plant in Minnesota forests. Avoid using this plant in landscapes near native woodland areas.

Bloom Period and Seasonal Color
May to mid-June blooms in white.

Mature Height × Spread
8 in. × spreading

Moneywort

Lysimachia nummularia

The adaptability and fine texture of moneywort make this a useful ground cover. The bright, ground hugging, green leaves are round like coins. In June, the planting will be covered with yellow buttercup-like flowers. The green leaves persist late into the fall. This attractive ground cover tolerates light foot traffic and a variety of growing conditions. I had moneywort plant itself in my yard. I left a flat of divisions sitting in the backyard waiting to be planted. The stems grew over the flat and into the surrounding soil. I now have a backyard filled with this ground cover. Though it tends to wander through the garden, I find that the other plants are able to compete. A fast grower, moneywort is an invasive plant that has naturalized in the eastern United States. Avoid using this plant in landscapes near natural wetlands and springs.

Other Common Name
Creeping Jenny

Bloom Period and Seasonal Color
June blooms in yellow.

Mature Height × Spread
2 to 4 in. × spreading

When, Where, and How to Plant

Plant seeds in early spring. Dig and divide plants in early spring or late summer. Plant container-grown plants any time during the growing season. Moneywort will tolerate a wide range of conditions. It prefers shade with moist to wet organic soil. Plants grown in full sun need to be kept moist. Space plants 15 to 18 inches apart.

Growing Tips

Water moneywort during dry spells. Mulch plantings to conserve moisture and reduce weeds. Minimal fertilization is needed.

Care

Moneywort can take over in the right growing conditions. Monitor the planting, pruning back and pulling plants that have overstepped their bounds. Hand pulling or broadleaf weed killers will control plants that creep into the lawn. Remove weeds as they appear. Moneywort will quickly fill in the area and eliminate this maintenance task. Lift and divide overgrown plants in early spring or late summer. Use a shovel or garden fork to dig them out. Cut the clump into several sections. Replant the divisions at 12-inch intervals in a prepared site. Moneywort sawfly can devour lots of the leaves in early summer. Handpick when these worm-like insects are found. Fortunately, healthy plants will tolerate their feeding. Insecticides can be used for major infestations.

Companion Planting and Design

Use moneywort under trees and shrubs. I have it creeping through my perennial gardens. Other larger, more robust plants can hold their own with this ground cover. A friend used the golden moneywort as a ground cover in her shade garden. The chartreuse leaves made the hostas and other shade plants stand out. Use it to soften structures in the landscape. Let it cascade over a wall, crawl between steppers, or climb in a rock garden.

My Personal Favorite

I like the yellow-leafed form, *Lysimachia nummularia* 'Aurea' (shown). Get the best foliage color by growing it in full sun or light shade. The leaves tend to be more chartreuse in shade. Since it is less vigorous than the straight species, you should remove any of the more aggressive green sprouts that appear.

Mother of Thyme
Thymus serpyllum

When, Where, and How to Plant
Start seeds of thyme indoors in early spring. Germination requires light and 55- to 60-degree temperatures to germinate. Lift and divide established plants in the spring. Plant container-grown thyme throughout the growing season. I like to get it in the ground early so it has time to get established before winter. You can also take cuttings of new growth to root and plant later in the summer. Grow thyme in full sun and well-drained soil. Add 2 to 4 inches of organic matter to heavy clay soils to improve drainage. It will tolerate light shade but does best in full sun and poor, dry soil. Space plants 6 to 18 inches apart.

Growing Tips
Only fertilize if your plants show signs of nutrient deficiencies. Excess fertilizer results in tall, weak, and unattractive growth. Avoid over-watering. Wet soil will lead to root rot and winter dieback.

Care
Winter dieback can be a problem in extremely cold winters or poorly drained locations. Fortunately, stems will often root and survive even when the parent plant dies. Prune back plants in the spring after leaves begin to sprout but before flowering begins. Don't disturb the rooted stems you want to keep. Spring pruning will remove winter damage and give the plants a neat appearance. Root rot can be a problem when thyme is over-watered or grown in poorly drained soils. Lift and divide overgrown plants. Use a shovel or garden fork to dig out plants in spring or early summer.

Companion Planting and Design
Use thyme as a ground cover on slopes, in rock gardens, near walkways, and between steppers where it can be seen. The lovely fragrance and attractive flowers add to its landscape value. Thyme will tolerate light traffic, which will release its fragrance. People have used thyme with stone walkways in place of the traditional bluegrass lawn.

My Personal Favorites
For color try 'Albus' with white flowers, 'Coccinea' with red flowers, or 'Pink Chintz' with pink flowers. 'Elfin', as its name implies, is small, 2 by 5 inches, and slow growing.

Thyme has long been used for its fragrance and flavor. History is full of examples of how Roman soldiers, European royalty, and common folks used this fragrant herb in cooking and as a deodorant. In the garden, women's long skirts would brush over the thyme ground cover releasing its fragrance and masking less desirable odors. Mother of thyme is a close relative of the thyme most used for cooking. Its creeping growth habit makes it a good ground cover for sunny, dry locations. Add attractive leaves and a summer-long bloom, and you have a ground cover fit for most landscapes. Established thyme needs very little care. I like the aroma-therapy the plant provides. There is great confusion over this plant. It is listed under several different botanical names. That may be why there is some variability in the plants sold as creeping thyme or mother-of-thyme.

Other Common Name
Creeping Thyme

Bloom Period and Seasonal Color
Summer blooms in purple.

Mature Height × Spread
3 to 6 in. × 18 in.

Pachysandra
Pachysandra terminalis

Pachysandra is probably one of the most commonly used ground covers. Its glossy green leaves provide year-round interest. In the spring, the leaves are topped with fragrant white flowers. It is often used in mass plantings under trees and shrubs in both formal and informal gardens. Pachysandra is a good ground cover for shady areas with appropriate soil conditions. Keep this evergreen plant looking good all winter by growing it in areas that remain shaded year-round. Over the winter, the leaves can become tattered or totally drop from this plant. It is taller and less vigorous than the Japanese pachysandra and works best in small areas.

Other Common Name
Japanese Spurge

Bloom Period and Seasonal Color
April to May blooms in white.

Mature Height × Spread
6 to 8 in. × spreading

Zones
Hardy to Zone 4.

When, Where, and How to Plant
Plant divisions and rooted cuttings of pachysandra in the spring or early summer. Plant container-grown plants any time during the growing season. Earlier plantings allow transplants to get established before winter. Plants will yellow when grown in full sun. Winter wind and sun can also cause yellowing. Avoid winter damage by planting this evergreen ground cover in a protected location or winter-mulch plantings in exposed sites. Pachysandra needs moist, well-drained soil to thrive. Prepare the soil prior to planting. Dig a hole larger than the rootball and plant pachysandra in the existing soil. Mulch the soil with organic matter. Plant container plants at the same level they were growing in the pot. Space plants 12 inches apart.

Growing Tips
Mulch new plantings to conserve moisture and reduce weeds. Water plants thoroughly when the top few inches are moist and crumbly. Fertilize plants in the spring according to soil test results.

Care
Remove weeds as they appear. Mulching will help reduce weeds and improve the soil. Leaf blight, root rot, and euonymus scale can be devastating problems. Proper soil preparation, placement, and care will help prevent these problems. Remove blight-infected leaves as soon as they appear. Water in the morning or late afternoon to avoid wet leaves at night. Treat euonymus scale when the young shell-less scales are active. This coincides with the beginning of Japanese tree lilac and catalpa bloom. Use insecticidal soap at that time and then twice more at ten- to twelve-day intervals. Soil-applied systemic insecticides labeled for this pest can be applied in the fall.

Companion Planting and Design
Grow this ground cover under trees and shrubs. It can be used in small or large ground cover beds on flat or sloped surfaces.

My Personal Favorites
The 'Green Carpet' cultivar of Japanese pachysandra is a low-growing plant. The compact growth and deep green leaves make this the preferred choice for many landscapers. The less vigorous 'Variegata' has mottled white foliage. Use this choice for small locations or to create contrast in shade gardens.

When, Where, and How to Plant

Plant container-grown potentillas throughout the summer. Dig and divide overgrown plantings in the spring. Grow potentillas in full-sun or partially shaded locations. They need good drainage and tolerate infertile soils. Proper soil preparation is critical when planting potentilla in clay soil. Work at least 2 inches of organic matter into the top 6 to 12 inches of soil. Space plants 6 to 12 inches apart, depending on the species. Space divisions 6 to 12 inches apart.

Growing Tips

Water new plantings as needed until they are established. Most species are drought tolerant once established. All benefit from supplemental watering during extended dry periods. Mulch new plantings to conserve moisture and reduce weeds. Avoid excess fertilizer than can lead to poor growth and reduced flowering

Care

Remove weeds as they appear. Some species benefit from pruning whenever the plants appear unkempt. With a shovel or garden fork, lift and divide overgrown plants. These often have dead centers or fail to bloom. Cut the clump into several sections and replant the divisions at 12-inch intervals in a prepared site. Root rot and winter dieback is common in heavy and poorly drained soils. Improve drainage or use a more suitable ground cover in these areas.

Companion Planting and Design

Use potentilla for rock gardens, on dry slopes, or as a ground cover in open, rocky areas. I saw a wonderful combination of blue fescue and potentilla. The potentilla covered the ground beneath the grass. The yellow potentilla flowers peeked through the blue leaves of the fescue. It was a nice texture and color combination—good for full sun and dry locations.

My Personal Favorites

Spring cinquefoil, *Potentilla verna,* is deciduous, grows 2 to 3 inches tall, and has yellow flowers in late spring. Use it in dry wall plantings or as a low-growing ground cover. It is hardy to Zone 4. Use Wineleaf cinquefoil, *Potentilla tridentata,* as a ground cover in rock gardens and on dry slopes. This hardy evergreen spreader is 2 to 6 inches tall with white flowers. Hardy to Zone 3.

Potentilla is a good ground cover for sandy and rocky soils. The growth habit and dissected foliage is similar to barren strawberry. Select a species best suited for your growing conditions and your landscape design. Some cinquefoils lose most or all of their leaves for the winter, while others are evergreen. Flowers are typically yellow or white, although there are some newer red-flowering cultivars. These plants are related to the popular summer-blooming shrubs used in many Minnesota landscapes. A close look at the flowers will help you see the family connection. The name Potentilla comes from the Latin word potens *meaning powerful. The word refers to the medicinal properties this group of plants is suppose to have.*

Other Common Name
Cinquefoil

Bloom Period and Seasonal Color
May to June blooms in white or bright yellow.

Mature Height × Spread
3 to 10 in. × 12 to 24 in.

Sweet Woodruff
Galium odoratum

Don't let the delicate appearance of sweet woodruff fool you. Its bright green, fragrant leaves will cover the ground from early spring through late fall. The white flowers cover the plant for several weeks. Consider adding a little patch to your garden or put a large planting under some trees and shrubs. Place it somewhere you can enjoy the fragrance and blooms. Try adding a planting near the patio or deck or garden bench. I have mine under a serviceberry tree near my front door. The fragrance greets me on warm summer evenings. It's a little landscape aromatherapy to end my work day. Extend its fragrant impact by adding dried leaves to potpourris and sachets. The fresh leaves and flowers have long been used to flavor May wine and other spring drinks.

Other Common Name
Woodruff

Bloom Period and Seasonal Color
May and June blooms in white.

Mature Height × Spread
6 to 8 in. × spreading

Zones
Hardy to Zone 4

When, Where, and How to Plant
Plant container-grown sweet woodruff throughout the season. Dig, divide, and plant divisions from established plantings in early spring for best results. Woodruff prefers shade and moist, well-drained soil but tolerates a wide range of conditions. It tends to burn out in full sun and dry locations. Reduce maintenance and improve the plants appearance by growing it in full to part shade with moist soils. Space plants 12 inches apart.

Growing Tips
Keep the soil near new plantings moist, but not wet. Water established plants thoroughly and only when the top few inches of soil feel crumbly and moist. Mulch new plantings with shredded leaves or other organic matter to conserve moisture and reduce weeds. Apply a low-nitrogen fertilizer in the spring to improve flowering.

Care
Woodruff will quickly cover an area; just remove weeds as they appear. Woodruff maintains an even and attractive growth habit throughout the summer. You can clip it back several times during the summer to create a more formal appearance. Poor flowering and a fungal leaf spot may be a problem on rare occasions. Remove disease-infected leaves. In severe cases, you will need to remove infected plants, amend the soil with organic matter, and wait for the surrounding plants to fill in the bare spots. Lift and divide overgrown plants. Cut the clump into several sections and replant the divisions at 12-inch intervals in a prepared site.

Companion Planting and Design
In shady spots, it makes a nice edging or rock garden plant. Try using it under crabapples for double blooming pleasure. Or mix it with hostas as a spring-flowering backdrop.

My Personal Favorites
Sweet woodruff was formerly listed as *Asperula odorata*. Both groups of plants are called woodruff or bedstraw. *Galium odorata* is the best choice for use as a ground cover. *Galium triflorum* is native to moist forests. It has a taller, looser habit but has the same nice fragrance. The dried vanilla scented leaves were often used to stuff mattresses, thus the common name bedstraw.

Variegated Yellow Archangel

Lamium galeobdolon 'Variegatum'

When, Where, and How to Plant

Plant container-grown variegated yellow archangel any time during the growing season. Dig and divide established plantings in early spring. This ground cover prefers moist, well-drained soil while adjusting to its new location. Established plants are tolerant of well-drained to dry soil. Variegated yellow archangel will grow just about anywhere it is planted. Space the fast-growing plants 2 to 3 feet apart.

Growing Tips

Mulch new plantings to conserve moisture and reduce weeds. Established plants only need supplemental water during extended dry periods. Water thoroughly and only when the top few inches of soil starts to dry. Minimal fertilization is needed for this assertive plant.

Care

Yellow archangel is basically pest free. Remove weeds as they appear, but in a short time, the yellow archangel will be able to crowd them out. Shear plants back to 6 inches in midsummer to promote compact growth. Containing this plant will be your biggest maintenance task, although proper siting will help reduce this problem. Contain the plants by pruning back any stems that grow out of the planting bed. Plants that creep into the lawn can be dug up or controlled with broadleaf lawn weed killers. Lift and divide overgrown plants in early spring. Use a shovel or garden fork to dig out plants. Cut the clump into several sections and replant the divisions 2 to 3 feet apart.

Companion Planting and Design

Use this aggressive grower in difficult areas. The poor conditions will help to contain its rampant growth. Or plant variegated archangel in contained areas, such as planting beds between the house and sidewalk. The variegated leaves help brighten up shady locations and contrast nicely against the dark green leaves of other plants. It can also be used in planters, hanging baskets, or as a houseplant.

My Personal Favorite

Lamium galeobdolon 'Herman's Pride', is a popular cultivar. It has narrower green leaves with regular silver variegation. This cultivar has more of a clump form and upright habit and is less aggressive than 'Variegatum'.

Need a plant for dry shade? Variegated yellow archangel could be the plant you are looking for. It will quickly fill in those difficult shaded locations. This plant may be the solution to growing plants under Norway maples and evergreens. Its variegated leaves will help brighten the deep shade, and the bright yellow flowers will liven up the landscape in late May through June. Just plant it where you can keep an eye on it—variegated archangel tends to move around the landscape without waiting for your permission. The variegated yellow archangel can be found listed under several botanical names including Galeobdolon luteum and Lamiastrum galeobdolon. The former name Lamiastrum means "somewhat resembling lamium." I guess the botanist took a closer look and decided it looked enough like a lamium to change the name again.

Other Common Name
Yellow Archangel

Bloom Period and Seasonal Color
Late May to June blooms in yellow.

Mature Height × Spread
12 to 18 in. × spreading

Zones
Hardy to Zone 4

Vinca

Vinca minor

Gardeners seem to be on a never-ending search for blue flowers. Periwinkle, as the name implies, can be added to this list. Vinca's periwinkle blue flowers can brighten the often dreary days of May. Its glossy evergreen foliage provides year-round interest in Minnesota landscapes. Use it to cover a small piece of ground or as a ground cover under trees and shrubs. This shade-tolerant plant hugs the ground as it vines through the garden. I grow several different varieties of vinca in my garden. I allow them to intermingle and creep beneath my other plants, around boulders, and fill in areas that need livening up. An assertive plant in the garden, it is starting to spread into forests throughout our state. Watch for and remove stray plants. Those living and gardening near natural areas should avoid this plant.

Other Common Name
Periwinkle

Bloom Period and Seasonal Color
May blooms in blue.

Mature Height × Spread
6 in. × spreading

Zones
Hardy to Zone 4

When, Where, and How to Plant
Plant container-grown plants any time during the growing season. Dig and divide established plantings in the spring for best results. Vinca will tolerate full sun, but the leaves will be dull and pale green. Grow plants in an area protected from winter wind and sun to avoid winter burn. Vinca grows best in moist, well-drained soil. Good drainage (and so proper soil preparation) is critical for growing success since the plants will not tolerate soggy conditions. Plant vinca and mulch the soil with organic matter. Space plants 6 to 14 inches apart. It will take two years for the plants placed at 12-inch intervals to fill in a bed. Pinch back vincas at planting time. This promotes branching and a denser cover.

Growing Tips
Mulch new plantings to conserve moisture and reduce weeds. Water plants during dry periods. Fertilize as needed in the spring.

Care
Remove weeds as they appear. Once the vinca fills in, it will crowd out the weeds. Keep the plants looking thick and vigorous by shearing them in the spring. Lift and divide overgrown plants. Replant the divisions 6 to 14 inches apart in a prepared site. Vinca is susceptible to canker, leaf spot, and root rot. Avoid these problems by growing vinca in areas with good air circulation and good drainage. Remove any infected leaves as soon as they appear.

Companion Planting and Design
Use vinca as a ground cover under trees and shrubs. It also works well in rock gardens and sloped areas. I like to mix spring- and fall-blooming bulbs in with this ground cover. It gives you added bloom and makes for a nice surprise in the landscape.

My Personal Favorites
There are several white-flowering forms including 'Alba' and 'Bowles White'. 'Alba Variegata' has white flowers with green- and yellow-variegated leaves. 'Argenteovariegata' has light violet-blue flowers with white and green leaves. Try 'Atropurpurea' if you want dark purple flowers. 'Illumination' is a recent introduction with bright golden foliage edged in green.

Wintercreeper
Euonymus fortunei

When, Where, and How to Plant

Plant container-grown plants any time during the growing season. Grow wintercreeper in areas with full or partial shade and moist, well-drained soil. They will tolerate full sun in the summer, but evergreen types can be damaged by winter sun and wind. Space plants 12 to 24 inches apart.

Growing Tips

Water established plants thoroughly and whenever the top few inches are crumbly and moist. Apply fertilizer in spring, if needed, according to soil test recommendations.

Care

Proper cultivar selection and plant placement are the best ways to reduce maintenance and keep this plant healthy. Select cultivars and varieties that are hardy for your location. Prevent winter injury by growing this plant in a protected site or east exposure, safe from winter wind and sun. Cover exposed and tender plants with evergreen boughs or straw for winter. Prune trailing forms of wintercreeper in the spring. Use your lawn mower on the highest setting for quick results. Scale insects and crown galls are the worst pest problems. Treat the shell-less immature scale with an insecticide when the Japanese tree lilacs are just starting to bloom. Repeat the application twice at ten- to twelve-day intervals. Or use a soil-applied systemic insecticide in fall. Read and follow label directions. Crown gall is caused by bacteria that causes golf ball-like nodules on the roots and stems. Prune out stems beneath the gall and disinfect tools with denatured alcohol between cuts. Remove and destroy badly infected plants.

Companion Planting and Design

Use euonymus as ground cover under trees and shrubs or in large planting beds. The small-leafed varieties look nice in rock gardens, while the variegated types make nice specimen plantings.

My Personal Favorite

Purpleleaf wintercreeper, *Euonymus fortunei* var. *coloratus*, is the most popular and readily available trailing euonymus. It is hardy in Zone 4b. The evergreen leaves turn purple in winter. It grows 6 to 18 inches tall and benefits from winter protection. Most of the small leafed variegated cultivars are not reliable in Zone 4 unless they have constant snow cover.

Trailing types of wintercreeper can be grown as ground covers under trees and shrubs. The small leaves and trailing growth habit can soften walls, raised beds, and other structures in the landscape. Wintercreeper will root wherever its stems touch the ground. This makes it easy to propagate new plants. Wintercreepers are semi- or fully evergreen. The trailing types tend to produce few, if any, flowers or fruits. This urban tolerant plant can be seen growing in challenging locations in both business and home landscapes. Its tough nature has allowed wintercreeper to escape cultivation and spread into wild areas around the state. Select sterile types that pose less of a threat to our native areas. Watch for and remove stray plants. Those of you living near natural spaces should avoid growing this plant.

Other Common Name
Wintercreeper Euonymus

Bloom Period and Seasonal Color
Seasonal or year-round foliage in green or variegated.

Mature Height × Spread
2 to 18 in. × spreading

Zones
Hardy to Zone 4

Ornamental Grasses *for Minnesota*

In the last twenty years, ornamental grasses have become an important part of the American gardening scene. With their long, narrow leaves, these distinctive plants provide motion and sound in a landscape. A gentle breeze makes the tall moor grass flowers dance and the switch grass rustle.

Most ornamental grasses bloom at some point during the growing season. The flowers on some, such as blue fescue, are secondary to the foliage, while those of others, such as silver grass, steal the show from the greenery. The seedheads also add winter color to an otherwise barren garden since the dried leaves and flowers often remain intact on the plant. They also can be enjoyed in a vase indoors.

One of the biggest and most desired ornamental grasses is pampas grass. If you have traveled to California, the southeastern United States, or the arid dome in Milwaukee, Wisconsin's Mitchell Park Conservatory (the Domes), you have seen this plant. It grows up to ten feet tall, producing large white, silver, or pink flowers. Many plants go by the name pampas grass, but the variety I just described is *Cortaderia selloana* and is not hardy in Minnesota.

Selecting Ornamental Grasses

It is important to select ornamental grasses that are best suited to the growing conditions in your area. Most grasses prefer full sun and well-drained soil. A few, like *Hakonechloa*, will tolerate shade and moist soils. Some of these grasses are relatively new to the upper Midwest. Many Minnesota gardeners, gardening professionals, and researchers have been evaluating ornamental grasses and their cultivars for winter hardiness. Those gardening in Zone 3 or trying to push plant hardiness can do a bit of their own research. Try a few of the hardiest grasses in protected sites in your landscape. Remember cold temperatures, snow cover, and soil drainage all influence the ornamental grasses' ability to survive our harsh winters. You may have better or worse results in the microclimates of your own garden.

Prairie Dropseed

Many of the ornamental grasses are substantial plants, so it's important to allow sufficient space for them to grow and bloom. I have quite a few grasses in my small city lot, but I use single specimens of various species and varieties to add interest, texture, and sound. In larger settings, ornamental grasses make great screens, as well as background or hillside plantings. However, remember your screen will be missing from the late winter, when you trim back the plants, through early summer, when they again reach full size.

Consider light in placing grasses. Not just for growth but also beauty. Sunlight glistening through fluffy or icy seedheads can provide added beauty. Combine ornamental grasses with trees, shrubs, and other perennials that provide winter interest. This will give you a nice garden rather than a lone plant to view in winter.

Planting Basics

Many ornamental grasses come in containers that are one gallon or larger. That means you will need a shovel, not a trowel for planting. Dig the planting hole the same depth and two to three times wider than the rootball. Plant the grass at the same level it was growing in the container. Gently loosen potbound and girdling roots before filling the hole with soil. Established grasses rarely need watering or fertilizing except in extreme droughts or where the soil is sandy. Follow soil test recommendations when fertilizing

Japanese Blood Grass and Miscanthus in Autumn

ornamental grasses. If these aren't available, err on the side of moderation. Most grasses need little to no fertilizer when grown in well-prepared soil that is top-dressed every other year with compost.

Cut back ornamental grasses in late winter before growth begins. I use hand pruners for my small plantings. A weed whip or electric hedge trimmer will make larger jobs go much faster. Compost the debris. Spring is a good time to dig, divide, and transplant ornamental grasses that are overgrown, dead in the center, or performing poorly.

Ornamental grasses can make a big impact in the home landscape. With proper selection, you can use ornamental grasses to add low-maintenance, year-round interest to your landscape.

Blue Fescue

Festuca cinerea

Blue fescue has long been used in Minnesota perennial gardens and landscapes. This small grass is a good fit in large and even small city lots. Blue fescue forms a tuft of narrow, blue-green leaves that contrast nicely with bold textured perennials and shrubs. Its colorful, fine texture blends well in rock and perennial gardens. Or try using it en masse as a ground cover. This salt-tolerant plant is a good solution for garden areas subjected to winter de-icing salts. I have seen it growing successfully in boulevard plantings, parking lot islands, and ground cover beds next to salted sidewalks. Use it in areas where its evergreen foliage can be enjoyed throughout the winter—when it's not buried under a blanket of snow!

Other Common Name
Gray Fescue

Bloom Period and Seasonal Color
Midsummer blooms in blue-green followed by beige seedheads.

Mature Height × **Spread**
6 to 10 in. × 10 in.

Zones
Hardy to Zone 4

When, Where, and How to Plant

Plant container-grown blue fescue during the growing season. I prefer spring and early summer. That allows the grass time to become established before our harsh winter. Divide and transplant blue fescue in the spring. Plant blue fescue in well-drained soil. Add organic matter to soil with a heavy clay content to improve drainage. Blue fescue is available in pots from perennial nurseries, garden centers, and catalogues. Space the plants 1 foot apart or a bit closer together for a denser, ground cover effect.

Growing Tips

Blue fescue is a relatively low-maintenance plant. Avoid over-wateringing and over-fertilizing, which can lead to poor growth, root rot, and dead plants.

Care

Blue fescue can be short-lived in Minnesota. Try dividing these plants every three or four years to increase vigor. Or replace them with new plants as needed. Although blue fescue is an evergreen, parts of the plant turn brown during the winter. You can trim back the older leaves in late winter before growth begins, or just let the new growth mask the old leaves as they fade away. I have done both, and my plants looked fine and remained healthy either way.

Companion Planting and Design

This small grass makes a good edging plant, ground cover, or addition to the rock garden. The fine texture creates a nice contrast to bolder, coarser-textured plants. The blue-green foliage makes blue fescue a nice addition to any garden. Try combining this plant with one of the purple-leaved coral bells or hardy geraniums. Blue fescue also works well in rock gardens. I have allowed my moneywort ground cover to creep through the blue fescue. The contrasting green leaves and yellow flowers make an attractive display. Or substitute a yellow-flowered creeping potentilla for the moneywort.

My Personal Favorites

'Elijah Blue' is an excellent cultivar that grows 8 inches tall and has powdery blue foliage. 'Sea Urchin' ('Seeigel') is 6 inches tall with sea green foliage. *Festuca amethystina* is slightly bigger and more tolerant of clay soils.

Blue Oat Grass
Helictotrichon sempervirens

When, Where, and How to Plant

Plant container-grown blue oat grass during the growing season. I prefer planting in spring and early summer, which gives the grass time to get established before our harsh winter. Divide and transplant blue oat grass in the spring. Plant blue oat grass in areas with full sun and well-drained soil. It is more tolerant of clay soil than blue fescue, but I still add organic matter to soil with a high clay content. Plant container-grown blue oat grass at the same level it was growing in the pot. Gently loosen potbound and girdling roots before planting. Space the plants 24 to 30 inches apart.

Growing Tips

Blue oat grass is a low-maintenance plant. Avoid over-wateringing and over-fertilizing. Too much water and nitrogen can lead to root rot and plant decline.

Care

Rust, a fungal disease, can occasionally be a problem during wet, humid weather. Adjust watering if necessary and remove infected leaves as soon as they appear. The disease usually clears up in drier weather. Blue oat grass is evergreen, although the leaves may turn brown during a particularly harsh winter. I find it holds its color better than blue fescue. You can trim back the older leaves in late winter before new growth begins, or just let the new growth mask the old.

Companion Planting and Design

Blue oat grass is larger and slightly coarser than blue fescue. Use it as a specimen plant in flower beds. It combines well with bolder, coarse-textured perennials. One of my favorite, though quite accidental, combinations is 'Husker Red' penstemon planted behind blue oat grass. The bronze foliage, white flowers, and red seedpods of the penstemon create a nice contrast with the blue oats.

My Personal Favorite

Check perennial nurseries, garden centers, and catalogues for available cultivars. 'Sapphire Fountain' ('Saphirsprudel') was introduced from Germany in 1982. It tolerates windy sites and is more resistant to rust.

Blue oat grass is an excellent and dependable grass for Minnesota gardens. The botanical name gives some clues to its identity. Helictotrichon is from helix *which means "spiral" and* trichos *meaning "hair." Sempervirens means "evergreen." This aptly describes the tufts of thin, slightly twisted leaf blades of evergreen blue oat grass. Try including this large tuft of blue grass in your perennial garden. Blue oat grass is a more reliable plant than blue fescue and performs better in the heavy clay soil of southern Minnesota. It also has better winter interest. Its larger size makes it easier to see through the snow, and the leaves tend to hold their blue color better than blue fescue.*

Other Common Name
Ornamental Oats

Bloom Period and Seasonal Color
Early summer blooms in pale blue followed by beige seedheads.

Mature Height × Spread
2 to 3 ft. × 2 to 3 ft.

Zones
Hardy to Zone 4

Bluestem

Schizachyrium scoparium

Little bluestem, also sold as Andropogon scoparius, *was a major element in Minnesota's native prairie landscape, and its beauty and year-round interest have helped this native grass find its way into the home landscape. The fine-textured green to blue-green foliage fits well in naturalized or perennial gardens. The late-summer flowers quickly give way to showy silvery-white seedheads and striking orange-red fall color. This short grass forms loose, upright clumps. Its compact size makes it a practical choice for even the smallest city lot, like mine. If you like natives but don't have room for a prairie, try incorporating this and other natives into your perennial gardens. This creates a less abrupt transition from formal to naturalized, readily blends with surrounding yards, and is easier to manage on a smaller plots.*

Other Common Name
Little Bluestem

Bloom Period and Seasonal Color
Fall blooms in pinkish-white.

Mature Height × Spread
1 1/2 to 3 ft. × 2 ft.

When, Where, and How to Plant
Plant container-grown little bluestem during the growing season. I prefer spring and early summer, which gives the grass time to become established before our harsh winter. Divide and transplant little bluestem in the spring. Seed large plantings of little bluestem in the spring or fall. The seed must be stratified (cold treated) to germinate. Little bluestem and short prairie seed mixes are available from several quality prairie seed companies in Minnesota. Purchase clean seed that is free of stems, fluff, bracts, and leaves. Although clean seed costs more, you get more seed and less debris for the money. Quality companies will provide soil preparation and planting guidelines. Plant little bluestem in areas with well-drained soil. Add organic matter to heavy soils to improve drainage. Space plants at least 2 feet apart.

Growing Tips
When placed in an appropriate spot, little bluestem requires very little maintenance. Avoid over-fertilizing. Plants tend to flop over when they receive excessive nitrogen or are grown in nutrient-rich soils.

Care
Cut down old stems in the late winter before growth begins. Poor growth will occur in wet, poorly drained soils. Dig up struggling plants in the early spring and move them to a location with better drainage, or add organic matter to the soil to improve drainage before replanting.

Companion Planting and Design
Little bluestem can add year-round interest to the garden. The fine-textured green to blue-green foliage fits well in naturalized or perennial gardens. Combine them with asters, coneflowers, and other natives. A mass planting of little bluestem can be quite impressive in a large landscape.

My Personal Favorites
Look for local strains of little bluestem for seeding and natural plantings. 'Blaze' has a russet-red fall color. Big bluestem, *Andropogon gerardi*, is a much larger (4 to 7 feet or taller) cousin to little bluestem. It is the primary grass of the tall grass prairies. Its heat- and salt-tolerance as well as attractive seedheads and red-purple fall color make it a good choice for large landscapes.

Feather Reed Grass
Calamagrostis acutiflora 'Stricta'

When, Where, and How to Plant

Plant container-grown feather reed grass during the growing season. I prefer to plant in the spring and early summer, which gives the grass time to get established before our harsh winter. Divide and transplant feather reed grass in the spring. It prefers moist, well-drained soil but will tolerate clay and wet soil with good drainage. Plant at the same level it was growing in the pot. Gently loosen potbound and girdling roots before planting. Space plants at least 2 feet apart.

Growing Tips

Feather reed grass is a low-maintenance plant. It is one of the tougher, more reliably hardy ornamental grasses. Water established plants only during extended droughts. Water thoroughly, moistening the top 6 inches of soil. Wait until the top 4 inches of soil is cool and crumbly before watering again.

Care

It has no serious insect or disease problems. Cut it back to just above ground level in late winter before growth begins. Divide plants as they outgrow their location or when divisions are needed for other garden areas.

Companion Planting and Design

Feather reed is stiffly upright. This makes it a good choice for a background plant or as a vertical accent in the landscape. Use it as a low screen to block the view of a compost pile, neighbor's doghouse, or storage area. Its moisture tolerance makes it suitable for placement alongside a pool or pond. Feather reed grass is also salt tolerant. Mix feather reed grass with other perennials and shrubs to expand your landscape's seasonal interest. One of my favorite sites includes feather reed grass, Siberian iris, black-eyed Susans, 'May Night' salvia, daylilies, and sedum 'Autumn Joy'.

My Personal Favorites

Overdam feather reed grass, *Calamagrostis acutiflora* 'Overdam' ('Oredam'), is also stiffly upright, a bit shorter (24 to 30 inches), and has variegated leaves. Korean feather reed grass, *Calamagrostis arundinacea brachytricha*, has the same growth habit but tends to be a little shorter and flowers later in the summer. It combines nicely with purple coneflower.

Feather reed grass has demonstrated its hardiness, durability, and beauty for many years in Minnesota landscapes. The wheat-like seedheads and stiff, upright leaves provide year-round interest. Feather reed grass is tall enough to demand attention in a large yard yet small enough to fit into more limited spaces. This tough plant tolerates a wider range of growing conditions than most grasses. I have observed it growing and thriving in difficult sites subject to stressful winters, droughty summers, de-icing salt, clay soil, and reflected heat. A custard stand I visit uses feather reed grass in a narrow planting bed between a wall and the parking lot, and it always looks good, especially while you're checking out the flavor of the day.

Other Common Name
Reed Grass

Bloom Period and Seasonal Color
July blooms in pink.

Mature Height × Spread
4 to 5 ft. × 2 ft.

Zones
Hardy to Zone 4

Fountain Grass

Pennisetum setaceum

Fountain grass is an annual that is bound to brighten up both flower beds and container gardens. Look for these lovely plants when traveling down boulevards or through Minnesota parks. This traditional favorite always generates attention from locals and visitors alike. It forms an upright clump up to 3 feet tall, but in container gardens, the limited root area keeps plants shorter. Its light airy texture makes it a perfect filler in annual, perennial, and container gardens. Try it in place of spike plant for a vertical accent in your planters. Fountain grass has feathery foxtail flowers that extend beyond the leaves. In late fall, the seedheads will shatter and the leaves will brown, but the plant form will remain intact and provide winter interest.

Other Common Name
Annual Fountain Grass

Bloom Period and Seasonal Color
Midsummer through fall blooms in pink to purplish-pink.

Mature Height × Spread
3 ft. × 18 to 24 in.

When, Where, and How to Plant

Sow seeds indoors in late winter. Keep the starting mix moist and at a temperature of 70 to 80 degrees. The seeds will germinate in three to four weeks. Plant hardened-off transplants in the spring after all danger of frost is past. Space plants 1 or 2 feet apart. Excessive shade can result in poor flowering and floppy plants. Fountain grass prefers moist, well-drained soil but will tolerate a wide range of conditions including clay soil. Fountain grass is difficult to find. Check with the more specialized garden centers in your area.

Growing Tips

Fountain grass is a low-maintenance garden plant, but specimens grown in containers need extra attention. Check the soil moisture in container gardens at least once a day. Water the containers thoroughly, allowing excess water to run out the drainage holes. Fertilize planters frequently throughout the summer. In the garden, water thoroughly whenever the top 4 inches of soil feels cool but crumbly.

Care

Fountain grass is relatively pest free. No deadheading is needed to keep this plant covered with flowers throughout the growing season.

Companion Planting and Design

Include fountain grass in containers. It provides vertical interest and is a good substitute for the traditionally used spike plant. Use fountain grass en masse or mixed with annuals and perennials. Its fine texture softens the bold texture of plants such as cannas and spider cleome. The feathery flowers and fine leaves create an attractive contrast to the bold texture of sedum 'Autumn Joy.' The colorful purple leaves and flowers of red fountain grass complement the bronze centers of the yellow-flowered 'Becky Mix' black-eyed Susans.

My Personal Favorites

I like the red-leafed varieties that are often listed as *Pennisetum setaceum* 'Rubrum', 'Cupreum', or 'Purpureum'. I have had mixed results with the hardy fountain grasses. Perennial fountain grass (*Pennisetum alopecuroides*) is marginally hardy in Zone 4a. Oriental fountain grass (*Pennisetum orientale*) is slightly less hardy. Both look similar to the annual form. The oriental fountain grass has blue-green leaves and pink flowers.

When, Where, and How to Plant

Plant container-grown hakonechloa during the growing season. Divide and transplant hakonechloa in the spring. This is one of the few ornamental grasses that will tolerate shade and moist soil. Add organic matter to heavy clay soil to improve drainage and to sandy soil to increase its capacity to hold water. Plant hakonechloa early in the season and in a protected location to increase its chances of winter survival. Space plants 18 to 24 inches apart.

Growing Tips

Keep the soil moist throughout the season. Mulching will help conserve water and minimize weeds. Water thoroughly whenever the top few inches of soil start to dry. Hakanochloa can also be used in container plantings. Check the soil moisture in container gardens at least once a day. Fertilize planters frequently throughout the summer using any flowering plant fertilizer.

Care

Hakonechloa is a low-maintenance plant. It is slow to get established, so be patient! Leaf scorch or brown-leaf edges can occur on plants grown in full sun or in dry soil. Loss of variegation is common in heavily shaded areas. Extremely cold and fluctuating winter temperatures as well as poor drainage can kill this plant. Use a winter mulch to help it survive the cold. Cover the plants with evergreen boughs, straw, or marsh hay after the ground freezes. Remove the mulch in the spring. Hakonechloa will not survive the winter in a container garden. Sink the pot into the soil for the winter.

Companion Planting and Design

Use it as a specimen plant near the front of a border. The variegated leaves brighten up shady areas in the landscape. I like to mix the colorful narrow foliage with the bold leaves of hosta. Hakonechloa also combines well with ferns and astilbe.

My Personal Favorite

I prefer the variegated cultivar, but those in cold regions may want to start with Hakone grass, *Hakonechloa macra*. It has bright green foliage and tends to be more vigorous and hardier than the variegated hakonechloa. It has a similar growth habit and pink fall color.

Very few grasses tolerate moist shady conditions, but this one does. Its variegated foliage forms attractive mounds in the flower garden. The bamboo-like foliage also makes this grass suitable for Japanese gardens. Pink flowers appear in late summer. Though it's not very showy, I find the light, airy flowers a nice addition to the overall appearance. The flower display is followed by a pink tinge of fall color. Buy an extra plant or two for your container gardens. You will need a bit of extra care to overwinter these plants, but the extra effort will be worth it when you hear the oohs and ahhs from your friends. Consider this plant if you're looking for something different for your shade or container garden.

Other Common Name
Golden Variegated Hakonecholoa

Bloom Period and Seasonal Color
Late summer blooms tinged with pink.

Mature Height × Spread
20 to 24 in. × 20 to 24 in.

Zones
Hardy to Zone 4b

Miscanthus
Miscanthus sinensis species

This is one of the most dramatic ornamental grasses for the landscape. A tall plant with fluffy white seedheads provides fall and winter interest. Some gardeners call this hardy pampas grass, a common name shared by several grasses. Those with small yards can include a few specimen plantings, and those with large landscapes may want to use this plant en masse. I find this plant a valuable asset in my yard. It provides the height of a shrub without the width, making it great for narrow screens and vertical accents. Cultivars vary in height, bloom time, hardiness, and foliage effect. Do NOT plant Chinese silver banner grass (Miscanthus sacchariflorus). Though tolerant of wet areas, this unmannered grass will take over your landscape and nearby natural areas as it has throughout the Midwest.

Other Common Names
Silver Grass, Eulalia

Bloom Period and Seasonal Color
Fall blooms in pale pink to red.

Mature Height × Spread
3 to 7 ft. × 4 ft

When, Where, and How to Plant
Plant container-grown miscanthus during the growing season, preferably in spring and early summer so the grass has time to become established before winter. Space plants at least 3 feet apart. Divide and transplant miscanthus in the spring. Miscanthus prefers moist, well-drained soil. It will tolerate clay soil, although I prefer to add organic matter to the soil prior to planting. In shady areas, it tends to flop over and flower poorly.

Growing Tips
Plant miscanthus in a protected location to increase winter hardiness. Plants are slow to emerge in spring, so be patient. Root prune to invigorate sparsely leaved miscanthus plants struggling after a hard winter. Take a sharp spade and cut through the crown and roots in two directions. The plant will fill in by the following season.

Care
Miscanthus is a low-maintenance plant. Lift and divide every four or five years when the center of the plant dies out or becomes floppy. Rust, a fungal disease, can occasionally be a problem during wet, humid weather. Adjust watering if necessary and remove infected leaves as soon as they appear. Cut the plants back in late winter before new growth begins.

Companion Planting and Design
Use these large grasses as screens, hedges, or background plants. Individual plants make good specimens in the landscape, in a flower garden, or near water. One of my favorite combinations includes tamarisk, *Hydrangea paniculata* 'Tardiva', boltonia, and silver feather miscanthus. You can't go wrong with this grass among most perennials, shrub roses, and flowering shrubs.

My Personal Favorites
Red flame miscanthus, *Miscanthus sinensis* var. *purpurascens*, is one of the hardiest (Zone 4), grows 4 to 5 feet tall, flowers in August, and turns orange-red in the fall. Maiden grass, *Miscanthus sinensis* 'Gracillimus', grows 5 to 6 feet tall and is grown for its fine foliage. The cold weather often arrives before its late season blooms. Variegated miscanthus, *Miscanthus sinensis* 'Variegatus', is somewhat shade tolerant, grows 5 to 6 feet tall, and is hardy to Zone 4a.

Moor Grass
Molinia caerulea

When, Where, and How to Plant
Plant container-grown moor grass during the growing season. I prefer spring and early summer so the grass has time to get established before our harsh winter. Divide and transplant moor grass in the spring. It prefers moist, well-drained soil. Moor grass is available in pots from perennial nurseries, garden centers, and catalogs. It is slow to get established, so purchase larger plants for quicker results. Plant container-grown moor grass at the same level it was growing in the pot. Gently loosen potbound and girdling roots before planting. Space plants 18 to 24 inches apart.

Growing Tips
Native to the wet lowlands of Eurasia, this grass prefers moist soil. Mulch the soil surrounding the grass to help keep roots moist. Water as needed during dry spells.

Care
Moor grass is a low-maintenance plant. It is slow to get established. Use larger plants and divisions to get flowers in the first or second year. Moor grass is self cleaning. The leaves and flower stems drop from the plants in the winter. A little spring cleanup may be all that is needed.

Companion Planting and Design
Moor grass forms dramatic tufts of foliage 1 to 2 feet tall and wide. The flowers shoot several feet above the plant. The fine, airy blooms allow you to see through to the rest of the garden. That feature makes moor grass a good choice as a specimen plant or in a small grouping in the perennial garden. Try planting moor grass in front of a dark background, like evergreens, to highlight its flower display.

My Personal Favorites
Variegated purple moor grass, *Molinia caerulea* 'Variegata' (shown), is 18 to 24 inches tall. The flowers rise 6 to 12 inches above the white-striped foliage. This shorter plant makes a nice edging, ground cover, or rock garden plant. Tall moor grass, *Molinia caerulea* subsp. *arundinaceae*, foliage grows 2 to 3 feet tall. The cultivars 'Skyracer' reaches 7 to 8 feet in bloom while 'Transparent' is shorter, 5 to 6 feet in bloom, with seemingly transparent flower stems.

Use moor grass to add motion and color to your perennial garden. Native to the wet moorlands of Eurasia, it is more tolerant of wet soils than most grasses. Moor grass forms a tuft of green leaves that easily blends with other plants. The real surprise comes in midsummer when the flowers shoot several feet above the foliage. The purple flowers are open, airy, and blend well with the background. This, along with the shorter foliage, makes it easy to use throughout the flower garden and landscape. In the fall, the leaves and flowers turn yellow, creating a colorful display. This grass does not have outstanding winter interest, but its other assets more than compensate for that. It was named for Chilean botanist Juan Ignacio Molina.

Other Common Name
Purple Moor Grass

Bloom Period and Seasonal Color
Midsummer blooms in purple.

Mature Height × Spread
1 to 2 ft. × 1 to 2 ft.

Zones
Hardy in Zones 4 and 5

Prairie Dropseed
Sporobolus heterolepis

This beautiful native grass is suited to any landscape. Its smaller size fits into any size landscape while providing year-round beauty. In late summer, the grassy leaves are topped with fragrant delicate flowers. The seedheads persist through winter, capturing dew and ice crystals to add a little sheen to the garden. This is what sold me on the plant. The leaves turn a yellow-orange in fall and eventually fade to beige; they provide motion, sound, and beauty in the winter landscape. This grass is equally at home in a perennial, rock, or naturalized garden. I like to tuck a couple of these in amongst my perennials. Or consider adding several to create an impressive winter display. Look for a sunny spot with well-drained soils for this beauty.

Other Common Name
Dropseed

Bloom Period and Seasonal Color
Summer pale-pink blooms.

Mature Height × **Spread**
3 to 3¹/₂ ft. × 24 in.

When, Where and How to Plant
Grow prairie dropseed in full sun and well-drained soils. Plants can be started from seeds in spring or fall. Select quality seed free from debris. Though it costs more, you are paying for seed not the debris you don't need. Purchase seed from a quality source that provides detailed information on soil preparation and planting rates. Plants are also available from some garden centers and catalogs. Plant bare-root plants as soon as they arrive and container plants throughout the season. Dig a hole 2 to 3 times wider than the root ball. Plant prairie dropseed at the same depth it was growing in the nursery. Loosen any tangled roots and girdled roots before planting. Backfill with existing soil, gently tamp, and water in well.

Growing Tips
This native takes several years to dig its roots in and start blooming. So be patient. Water recent transplants often enough to keep soil slightly moist. Once established, these plants are fairly drought tolerant and only need occasional watering during drought.

Care
This native grass is low maintenance and basically pest free. Allow the plants to stand for winter interest. Cut them back in late winter and compost the leaf debris.

Companion Planting and Design
Use as a specimen or plant en masse. The airy foliage looks great with ornamental shrubs and dwarf conifers. Or add prairie dropseed to your perennial garden. It looks good with airy perennials such as coreopsis and boltonia as well as the bolder plants of heliopssis and sedum. And don't forget to look to nature for some ideas. Try combining it with its native companions such as aster, coneflowers, and rudbeckia. Or try a mass planting. A hillside covered with prairie dropseed is a site and fragrance to behold. Or line a walkway or flank an entrance where visitors will delight in the beautiful texture and late summer fragrance of this grass.

My Personal Favorite
There has been no improvement on nature. Try this beautiful native in your landscape.

When, Where, and How to Plant

Plant bare-root sedges as soon as they arrive. Container-grown sedges can be planted throughout the season. I prefer spring or early summer so they can get established before the summer heat and winter cold. Most sedges prefer full to part shade and moist to wet soils. Hardiness has been a concern with many of the ornamental types. Look for hardier introductions and try planting just one or two before investing in large numbers. It may take you several tries to find the best location.

Growing Tips

Check soil moisture throughout the season. Most sedges prefer moist soils and may need supplemental watering. Hardiness can be a bigger problem in clay soils that stay excessively wet in winter. Add organic matter to clay soils to improve drainage while maintaining moisture.

Care

Native sedges are low maintenance if planted in the proper environment. The ornamental sedges are a bit more difficult to grow successfully in our climate. Place these in microclimates that have the right soil, moisture, and shelter in the winter. Let plants stand for winter. They provide interest and increases hardiness. Cut back the dead foliage in spring or allow the new leaves to grow through the old.

Companion Planting and Design

Sedges are good alternatives for grass in moist shady areas. Use it as a ground cover under shade tolerant viburnums and dogwoods. Or mix in a few spring wildflowers. And don't forget to add a few sedges to the shade or hosta garden. The fine-texture leaves provide a colorful contrast to the bold leaves of hosta.

My Personal Favorites

Carex morrowii 'Bowles Golden' was the standard ornamental sedge for northern gardens. The chartreuse foliage brightens the shade and looks great against the large blue-green leaves of hosta. My new favorite is *Carex morrowii* 'Ice Dance'. The wider leaves with white variegation add color and interest to the garden. I have been watching this one grow and survive in our climate for the last few years.

You may have heard the old saying "sedges have edges." Their triangular stem gives their identity away. Though not a true grass this, look-alike tolerates moist shade that most grasses detest. These clump growing plants with long narrow leaves make nice fillers, ground covers, and specimen plantings. Their fine texture creates a welcome contrast to the bold textures of hosta, ginger, and ligularia often found in shade gardens. Consider replacing sparse lawns and bare spots in wet shaded parts of the landscape with sedges. Use Carex pennsylvanica or other native sedges to create a no mow grass-like look for these challenging areas. Check garden centers and catalogs where you will find many of the native sedges moving into the garden and new cultivars being introduced. Hardiness varies with species.

Other Common Names

Ornamental Sedges.

Bloom Period and Seasonal Color

Late spring or early summer, green turning brown.

Mature Height × Spread

6 to 24 in. × 6 to 24 in.

Spike Grass

Spodiopogon sibiricus

Spike grass adds form and color to the landscape. Back this plant with a fence, an evergreen, or another plant that will highlight its bamboo-like appearance. Use this medium-sized grass as a specimen, a small summer screen, or as a background plant. Its flowers appear in summer, starting out purple and then turning fuzzy and brown. They are held high over the foliage, giving it a light airy appearance. Spike grass flowers look good in the garden or cut and added to fresh arrangements. The leaves turn purplish brown in fall. Winter impact of spike grass is limited since the flower heads shatter and the plants eventually collapse during cold weather, but the outstanding show this hardy plant provides makes it worthy of space in any garden.

Other Common Names
Silver Spike Grass, Frost Grass

Bloom Period and Seasonal Color
Summer blooms in purple turning brown.

Mature Height × **Spread**
4 to 5 ft. × 2 ft.

Zones
Hardy to Zones 4

When, Where, and How to Plant
Plant container-grown spike grass during the growing season. I prefer spring and early summer to give the grass time to become established before our harsh winter. Divide and transplant spike grass in the spring. Spike grass will tolerate some light shade, but the plants will flop over when they are grown in excess shade. Grow this grass in moist, well-drained soil. Once established, it is somewhat drought tolerant. Plant container-grown spike grass at the same level it was growing in the pot. Gently loosen potbound and girdling roots before planting. Space plants at least 2 feet apart.

Growing Tips
Spike grass is a low-maintenance plant. Provide moisture during extended drought periods. Avoid excess fertilization that can make this and most ornamental grasses floppy. Follow soil test results or, better yeat, just top-dress the soil with several inches of compost every other year.

Care
The plants tend to collapse over the winter. A little spring cleanup is usually all that is needed. Dig and divide when the grass outgrows its location or when you want more plants for other garden areas.

Companion Planting and Design
Back this plant with a fence, an evergreen, or another plant that will highlight its bamboo-like appearance. The leaves on this upright grass are held perpendicular to the stems. This gives it the look and feel of a tropical plant, such as bamboo, and makes spike grass a perfect choice for Japanese gardens. Try using it as a specimen plant or in groups in the landscape or in a perennial garden. One of my favorite plantings at Boerner Botanical Gardens included spike grass. They backed this plant with tamarisk and tardiva hydrangea. The bed included variegated miscanthus, sedum 'Autumn Joy', and Japanese blood grass. The red and pink hues helped tie together this diverse group of plants. It was a magnificent fall display.

My Personal Favorite
I am not aware of any cultivars but find the straight species worthy of a spot in my small landscape.

Switchgrass

Panicum virgatum

When, Where, and How to Plant

Plant container-grown switchgrass during the growing season. I prefer spring and early summer, which gives the grass time to become established before winter. Divide and transplant switchgrass in spring. Space plants 30 to 36 inches apart. Seed large areas of switchgrass in the spring or fall. Switchgrass and prairie seed mixes are available from several quality prairie seed companies in Minnesota. Purchase clean seed that is free of stems, fluff, bracts, and leaves and is from a local source. The quality companies will provide soil preparation and planting guidelines.

Growing Tips

Shade-grown plants tend to be more open and fall over. Move them to a sunnier location. Switchgrass prefers moist soil but will tolerate wet to dry soil and exposure to de-icing salt.

Care

Switchgrass is a low-maintenance plant. The biggest problem is keeping plantings under control. Plants spread by seeds and rhizomes. Weed out strays and dig and divide sprawling clumps to keep them under control. Cultivated varieties are much less aggressive. Rust and fungal leaf spot may occasionally occur. Adjust watering if necessary and remove infected leaves as soon as they appear.

Companion Planting and Design

Use it near roadsides, paved areas, and walkways that are salted in winter. Switchgrass also works well as a specimen plant, background plant, or as a mass planting. Try combining switchgrass with plants you would see it with in nature. The bold textures of coneflowers, black-eyed Susans, sunflowers, and goldenrods contrast nicely with the light, airy appearance of switchgrass.

My Personal Favorites

Heavy metal switchgrass, *Panicum virgatum* 'Heavy Metal', is a narrow, upright plant that grows 3 to 5 feet tall. It has metallic-blue leaves that turn bright yellow in the fall. 'Northwind' is stiffly upright with blue foliage and reaches heights of 6 feet. 'Shenandoah' is 36 inches tall with bright red foliage that appears in June, followed by red flowers later in summer. 'Strictum' is 5 feet tall and narrowly upright with green foliage.

Bring a little of Minnesota's native prairie into your backyard. Plant some switchgrass as a backdrop for a flower garden, as a screen, en masse, on a hillside, or as part of a native garden. The straight species will spread by underground rhizome and seed, so give it plenty of room to grow. Use some of the cultivated varieties in your perennial gardens. Switchgrass grows in tall, upright clumps. The colorful flowers look like fireworks exploding 1 to 2 feet above the leaves. This "flowerworks" display is complemented by the beautiful golden-yellow fall color. And watch for the wildlife that enjoys this plant. Finches feed on the seeds, and the larvae of Leonard's skipper (Heperia leonardus) *and tawny edge skipper* Polites themistochies *feed on the leaves.*

Other Common Name
Panicum

Bloom Period and Seasonal Color
Midsummer to late summer blooms in pink to red to silver.

Mature Height × Spread
3 to 8 ft. × 3 ft.

Perennials *for Minnesota*

Perennials have become an important part of Minnesota landscapes. No longer relegated to a single garden in the back, they are now being used throughout the yard. Many people have eliminated their lawns and replaced them with perennial plantings. Others have ripped out the yews and junipers around the foundation and replaced them with perennials and other ornamental shrubs. Some gardeners have added just a few plants as ground covers or specimens in their existing landscape. Whether you are adding a few or a few hundred perennials, proper selection, planting, and care are essential to gardening success.

Soil Preparation

Start by evaluating the planting location. Take a soil test to find out how much and what type of fertilizer you need to apply. Your local University of Minnesota Extension Service can provide soil test information. Recent research has shown that perennials growing in a well prepared garden need little if any additional fertilizer. You can incorporate a low-nitrogen, slow-release fertilizer in the soil just prior to planting. Use no more than one pound of a ten percent and two pounds of a five percent nitrogen fertilizer per one hundred square feet.

Check the soil drainage. Dig a hole twelve inches deep and fill it with water. Allow the water to drain and fill the hole again. If it takes more than one hour to drain the second time, you need to amend the soil. Soils that drain too quickly, sandy and rocky types, need amending to increase the soil's ability to hold water. Add two to four inches of organic matter to the top six to twelve inches of garden soil to improve drainage and increase water holding capacity. Till the compost, peat moss, aged manure, or other organic matter and fertilizer into the soil prior to planting. Create a raised bed or relocate the garden if the site is subject to standing water or extremely poor drainage. All the time and energy spent in preparation will pay off in healthy plants, less maintenance, and years of enjoyment.

Aster

Designing the Garden

Most gardeners are looking for perennials that can be planted once, will bloom all season, and require no maintenance. They don't exist. But selecting the right plant for the existing growing conditions will give you a good looking garden with the least amount of work.

Once you have a list of potential plants for the garden, check out their bloom period. You can design your landscape so something is always blooming in every part of the yard. Or you may prefer peak areas of interest that change throughout the season. You may have one garden or a section of a garden that looks great for a short period of time. As it fades, another area comes into full bloom and becomes the new focal point. Place the gardens in areas where you will get the most enjoyment when they are at their peak. Design your plantings to fit your lifestyle and needs.

Now look at your design realistically. Most people take on more than they can maintain. I always have bigger plans and more plants than I have time available. Beginning gardeners or those with limited time should start small. Design beds with easy access for planting and maintaining. Try using fewer types but more of each type of perennial in your garden. That design strategy will result in an easier to maintain garden that will provide a bigger overall effect. Don't forget to plan for some winter interest. Seedpods and evergreen leaves can add impact and attract birds during our longest season—winter.

Mix of Coneflowers and Daylilies

Plant Choices

Perennials are sold bare root, container grown, and field potted. Bare-root perennials are plants sold without any growing media on the roots. Store them in a cool, but not freezing, location until you are ready to plant. Keep the roots moist and packed in peat moss, sawdust, or another similar material. Move dormant bare-root plants into the garden as soon as the soil is workable and ready for planting. Pot up bare-root plants that begin to grow in transport or storage. Grow in a sunny window indoors or outdoors in the protection of a coldframe. Move these plants into the garden after hardening off, and the danger of severe weather has passed.

Container-grown plants are grown and sold in pots. Some are grown outdoors and can be planted as soon as they are purchased. Others are grown in greenhouses and need to be hardened off, toughened to outdoor conditions, before planting. Store potted perennials in a shaded location until they can be planted in the garden. These small pots need to be watered daily. Water and allow the potted plants to drain prior to planting. Remove container-grown plants from the pot. Loosen potbound roots to encourage root development into the surrounding soil. Plant these at the same level they were growing in the container.

Sedum 'Autumn Joy' with Petunias

Field-potted plants are grown in the field and potted for delivery as they are dug. The freshly potted plants often lack a cohesive rootball. Minimize problems by digging the hole first. Cut off the bottom of the pot and set it into the planting hole. Adjust planting depth so the crown, the point where the stem joins the roots, is even with the soil surface. Slice down the side and peel away the pot. Backfill, gently tamp, and water to eliminate air pockets.

Check all new plantings for soil settling. Perennials often die when the soil settles and their roots are exposed. Fill in low spots and cover exposed roots as needed.

Care

Proper soil preparation, plant selection, and planting will help reduce maintenance requirements. Perennials need about an inch of water per week. Once established, many perennials will only need supplemental watering during extended dry periods. Water whenever the top four inches of soil are crumbly and slightly moist. This is usually about once a week in clay soils and twice a week in sandy soil when the weather is dry. Moisten the top six inches to encourage deep drought-resistant roots. Mulch perennials with a one- to two-inch layer of organic material such as cocoa bean shells, twice-shredded bark, shredded leaves, or pine needles. It conserves moisture and reduces weed problems.

Weeds are a major pest. They compete with perennials for water and nutrients and often harbor insect and diseases. Pull these invaders as soon as they appear. The perennials will be able to crowd out most weeds by the second or third summer. You may need to enlist help controlling quackgrass, bindweed, and other hard-to-control perennial weeds. Spot treat with a total vegetation killer such as Roundup® or Finale®. These materials are absorbed by the leaves and move through the plant killing the roots and all. Protect nearby plants that can also be killed by these herbicides. Once the chemical touches the soil, it won't harm the plants.

Deadheading and pruning can help control growth, increase flowering, and reduce pest problems. Some plants require a lot of work, and others perform fine on their own. Some cultivars require less maintenance and have fewer problems than the species. Select the perennial and its cultivars that best fit your growing conditions and maintenance schedule.

Remove all disease- and insect-infested plant debris in the fall to reduce the source of infection for next year. Leave the seedheads and healthy foliage for winter interest, to attract birds and increase hardiness. My major cleanup comes in the spring before new growth begins. I look forward to getting into the garden in late March after a long winter and before the busy garden season gets underway.

Perennials can be divided to improve their health and appearance or to start new plants. Divide perennials that are too big for the location, flower poorly, flop over, or open in the center. In general, lift and divide spring-flowering plants in late summer and fall-flowering plants in the spring. Summer bloomers can be divided in spring or late summer.

Winter-mulch new plantings and tender perennials. Cover the plants with evergreen branches, straw, or marsh hay after the ground lightly freezes. Remove the mulch in the spring as new growth begins. Winter-mulching keeps the soil temperature consistently cold. That eliminates frost heaving caused by the freezing and thawing of soil throughout the winter. Frost heaving damages plant roots and can even push perennials right out of the soil.

Despite the long list of chores, perennial gardening can be relatively low maintenance and worth the effort. The best part, I think, is the seasonal change. It is so exciting to watch the first plants peek through the cold soil in the spring. The garden continues to grow and change through summer and fall. And in winter, the snow-covered seedheads, rustling foliage, and visiting birds will add a new dimension to the season.

Phlox

115

Artemisia

Artemisia species

The fragrant, silver leaves of artemisia can brighten any garden all season long. White sage, Artemisia ludoviciana, and silvermound, Artemisia schmidtiana 'Nana', are two of the more popular artemisias. White sage is native to Minnesota and hardy to Zone 4. Like all artemisias, it needs full sun and well-drained soil. It is 2 to 3 feet tall and can be floppy in moist, fertile soil. You will see this used in wreaths and dried arrangements. Silvermound, Artemisia schmidtiana 'Nana', is a shorter member of this group. It forms a neat, tidy mound 12 to 18 inches tall. Use this as an edging or rock garden plant. Silvermound is rated hardy throughout Minnesota. This group of plants is commonly called wormwood for their past use as an ant- (in cupboards) and moth- (in clothing) repellent.

Other Common Name
Wormwood

Bloom Period and Seasonal Color
Season-long silver foliage.

Mature Height × Spread
1 to 3 ft. × 1 to 3 ft.

When, Where, and How to Plant

Plant bare-root perennials in the spring after the danger of severe weather has passed. Plant hardened-off, container-grown, and field-potted perennials any time during the growing season. Artemisia must be grown in well-drained soil. Avoid fertile soils where plants tend to become floppy. Add organic matter to clay soil to improve drainage. These plants will rot in poorly drained soil during wet seasons. I visited a trial of these plants at the Chicago Botanic Garden at the end of a very wet growing season. The field was a mass of brown leaves, not a pretty sight. On the other hand, I saw a beautiful planting of white sage at a botanical garden in Denver. The plants were full, upright, and healthy in this sunny, dry location. Space plants 15 to 24 inches apart.

Growing Tips

Avoid excess fertilization. Too much nitrogen makes these plants open up in the center and flop over.

Care

Pull weeds as soon as they appear. Established artemisia will be able to crowd out most weeds by the second or third summer. Divide fast-growing artemisias every few years to control the spread and keep the plants healthy. Artemisias tend to open up in the center and flop over. Prune plantings once or twice a season before flowering to encourage shorter, stiffer growth and to prevent open centers on the low growing, mounded types.

Companion Planting and Design

Use artemisias next to dark flowers or plants with glossy green leaves. The contrast makes both plants stand out. Shorter species make nice edging and rock garden plants. The taller ones make a nice backdrop for many other perennials. Combine artemisia with blue- and pink-flowering perennials and roses for rich, attractive mixtures.

My Personal Favorite

'Oriental Limelight' is a relatively new introduction. It has attractive green with yellow variegated leaves and grows to 36 inches tall. Rated hardy to Zone 3 this plant can get a bit aggressive in the garden, so monitor with shovel and shears in hand. Plant 'Oriental Limelight' near yellow flowers to highlight its attractive foliage or next to a blue spruce for a rich color and texture combination.

When, Where, and How to Plant

Plant bare-root perennials in the spring after the danger of severe weather has passed. Plant hardened-off, container-grown, and field-potted perennials any time during the growing season. Plant less hardy species and cultivars early in the season to give them time to get established before winter. Grow asters in well-drained soil. Prepare the soil before planting. Plant asters at least 2 feet apart with the crown even with the soil surface.

Growing Tips

Water new plantings thoroughly whenever the top 4 inches are crumbly and moist. Mulch asters to conserve moisture and reduce weed problems. Avoid excess fertilization that can reduce flowering and increase floppy growth.

Care

Pinch back tall asters to 6 inches throughout June. Cut the stems above a set of leaves to reduce toppling and encourage full, compact growth with lots of flowers. Taller species may still need staking. Or use grow-through stakes or sturdy neighboring plants for added support. Divide asters every three years to control the growth of taller plants and increase the vigor of less hardy species. Let the plants stand for winter to increase hardiness and add a little winter interest. Cover the base of less hardy asters with evergreen branches, straw, or marsh hay after the ground freezes. Asters are susceptible to wilt and powdery mildew. Remove wilt-infested plants. Proper spacing and placement will minimize problems with powdery mildew, which won't kill the plant but just looks bad.

Companion Planting and Design

Asters make great additions to perennial and cut-flower gardens. Use them with ornamental grasses and goldenrod for a dramatic fall display.

My Personal Favorites

'Purple Dome' is a compact cultivar of New England Aster, *Aster novae-angliae*, that grows 18 inches tall and can spread to 36 inches wide. It remains a nice mound all season with no pinching required. 'Alma Potschke' is another New England aster guaranteed to grab your attention. Its bright pink flowers seem to leap out of the garden. It grows 3 to 4 feet tall and usually needs staking.

Asters can add a last flash of color to the landscape before the snow falls. They are equally at home in formal and naturalized gardens. Include asters in your garden design to help attract butterflies, for use as cut flowers, and for a little winter interest. A little early season care or garden design can keep these stately beauties upright and attractive. Select the color and size that best fits your landscape design and is hardy in your area. The New England Aster, Aster novae-angliae, is among the most well-known asters. It is native and grows 4 to 6 feet tall. The New York aster, Aster novi-belgii, grows 3 to 5 feet tall. Asters are more than a pretty plant. They were used to dye wool a greenish gold color and are the flower for the month of September.

Other Common Name

New England Aster

Bloom Period and Seasonal Color

Late summer through fall blooms in purple, white, and pink.

Mature Height × Spread

2 to 5 ft. × 1 to 3 ft.

Astilbe
Astilbe species

Looking for a shade garden alternative to hosta and impatiens? Astilbes can add color, attractive foliage, and texture to the shadier side of your landscape. Select a variety of astilbes with different bloom times to provide summer-long color. Leave seedheads of late bloomers intact. They will persist over winter adding additional texture and interest. Astilbes make great cut flowers and are even grown as flowering potted plants in some areas. Cut astilbe when the flowers are halfway open for the maximum vase life. The light feathery flowers and fern like foliage make this a great filler plant in the vase or shade garden. Select an area with moist soil and partial shade for the best looking plants with minimal care. Or use the more drought tolerant dwarf Chinese astilbe for late summer bloom.

Other Common Name
False Spirea

Bloom Period and Seasonal Color
Summer blooms in white, pink, red, salmon, and lavender.

Mature Height × Spread
1 to 4 ft. × 2 to 3 ft.

When, Where, and How to Plant
Plant bare-root astilbe in the spring after the danger of severe weather has passed. Plant hardened-off potted perennials any time during the growing season. Plant them early in the season, prior to September 1st, to give them time to get established before winter. Grow astilbe in moist, well-drained soil. No matter where it is planted, astilbe needs moist, not wet, soil for best results. Prepare the soil prior to planting. Add several inches of organic matter to help improve both drainage and the water-holding capacity of the soil. Plant small cultivars 12 to 15 inches apart and larger cultivars at least 24 inches apart.

Growing Tips
Moisture and fertilization are the keys to growing healthy astilbes. Water thoroughly whenever the top 3 to 4 inches of soil are crumbly and moist. Mulch the soil surface with a 1- or 2-inch layer of organic material to keep the roots cool and moist and to suppress weeds. Fertilize astilbe in the spring before growth begins or in the fall as plants are going dormant. Use a low-nitrogen, slow-release fertilizer to help get them growing.

Care
Deadheading will not encourage reblooming but tidies up the summer garden. Seedheads add a bit of winter interest. Let healthy foliage stand for the winter. This helps increase hardiness, and the stems catch the snow for added insulation. Regular dividing every three years seems to help revitalize astilbe.

Companion Planting and Design
Use astilbe for its foliage and flower effect in shade gardens. Shorter cultivars work well in shady rock gardens with moist soil. Try using astilbes with ferns and hosta. The combination of foliage shape, texture, and color make for an attractive display.

My Personal Favorites
Flamingo astilbe, Astilbe × arendsii 'Flamingo' has full, pink flowers atop glossy green leaves. The slightly fragrant flowers appear in June through July. The drought tolerant dwarf Chinese astilbe, a small, 12- to 15-inch-tall plant, makes a great ground cover or edge for the perennial garden. It has a rosy-lavender flower in mid- to late summer.

Beebalm
Monarda didyma

When, Where, and How to Plant

Plant dormant bare-root plants as soon as the soil is workable. Plant hardened-off transplants throughout the season. Place in an area with moist soils and full sun for healthy and attractive plants. Those grown in shade are more susceptible to powdery mildew and tend to spread faster. Add organic matter to the soil to improve drainage in clay soils and water holding ability in sandy soils. Space plants at least 2 feet apart.

Growing Tips

Drought-stressed plants are less attractive and more susceptible to powdery mildew. Water plants thoroughly whenever the top 3 to 4 inches of soil are moist and crumbly. Mulch the soil with shredded leaves, evergreen needles, or other organic matter to conserve moisture and reduce weeds. Avoid high nitrogen and excess fertilization that can increase disease, reduce flowering, and promote faster growth on this naturally assertive plant.

Care

Remove $^1/_4$ of the plant stems in early spring to increase light penetration and air circulation through the plant. This reduces problems with powdery mildew and encourages stiffer stems. Deadhead for added bloom and to limit unwanted seedlings. Allow a few late blooms to go to seed for winter interest. Remove unwanted seedlings in early spring to keep plantings contained. The young leaves are easy to identify by their citrus-mint fragrance. Divide plants every three years or as needed to control its spread.

Companion Planting and Design

The bold red flowers stand out nicely against an evergreen background. Mix with swamp sunflower, coreopsis, or other yellow flowers to create a bold focal point. Use a tall ornamental grass or deciduous plant behind beebalm to create a nice combination for year-round interest.

My Personal Favorites

To reduce your frustration, try one of these cultivars with good mildew resistance. The hybrid 'Raspberry Wine' has rich raspberry color. 'Cambridge Scarlet' has bright scarlet flowers. 'Marshall's Delight' has a long bloom period and rosy-pink flowers. 'Blue Stockings' (not a true blue) has violet-blue flowers.

This lovely flower fits in formal, informal, or naturalized settings. The unique, almost Dr. Seuss-like in character, flowers sit atop fragrant foliage. The tubular flowers attract hummingbirds, butterflies, and, as the common name suggests, bees. Cut a few flowers to enjoy in a vase indoors. Allow seedheads to develop later in the season. They add texture and interest to the winter garden. The fragrant foliage adds a little aroma therapy as you thin and weed your way around the plant. This species is native to the Eastern United States. Our native wild bergamont, Monarda fistulosa, has lilac-purple to pale pink flowers and is hardy to Zone 3. Beebalm leaves have long been steeped to make tea. In fact, it is still used in Earl Grey tea.

Other Common Name
Monarda

Bloom Period and Seasonal Color
Summer blooms in red or violet.

Mature Height and Spread
Up to 4 ft. × 3 ft.

Zones
Hardy to Zone 4

Bellflower
Campanula species

Bellflowers have long been used in perennial gardens. Their beautiful, blue-and-white, bell-shaped flowers are unmistakable. The commonly grown bellflowers are native to Europe and Asia. There are several bellflowers native to Minnesota. The tall bellflower Campanula americana is native to moist, shady locations. The same goes for Marsh bellflower, Campanula aparinoides, which can be found in swamps and grassy swales throughout the eastern United States. You may find the common harebell Campanula rotundifolia in cedar glades. The European or creeping bellflower, Campanula rapunculoides, has long spikes of blue bell-shaped flowers and has widely naturalized in Minnesota. This tall garden plant spreads by rhizomes and seeds, quickly engulfing a perennial garden and escaping into nearby natural areas. Be persistent, it takes several years to get this plant out of the garden. Avoid problems by not planting it in the garden.

Other Common Name
Harebells

Bloom Period and Seasonal Color
Late spring to summer blooms in blue, white, and purple.

Mature Height × Spread
6 to 36 in. × 6 to 36 in.

When, Where, and How to Plant
Plant bare-root bellflowers in the spring after the danger of severe weather has passed. Plant hardened-off, container-grown, and field-potted perennials any time during the growing season. I prefer spring and early summer planting to give the bellflowers time to get established before winter. They need moist soil with good drainage. Bellflowers have a difficult time surviving the winter with wet feet. Add several inches of organic matter to the top 12 inches of soil prior to planting. Space them 12 to 24 inches apart.

Growing Tips
Healthy bellflowers require minimal care. Water thoroughly whenever the top 3 to 4 inches of soil are moist and crumbly. Mulch the soil to keep the roots cool and moist and to help reduce weed problems. Avoid excess nitrogen fertilizer.

Care
Some species, like the clustered bellflower, may need to be staked even when properly fed. Cut back floppy plants after blooming to encourage fresh compact growth. Removing faded flowers will encourage repeat blooming and reduce problems with reseeding. Be careful not to remove the developing buds. Divide overgrown and poorly flowering bellflowers in early spring for best results.

Companion Planting and Design
Use campanulas in formal or more naturalized settings. The stately spikes of flowers on upright forms create a vertical accent or serve as background plants in the landscape. The mounded type of bellflowers easily blend with other flowers, and they work well in rock gardens or as edging.

My Personal Favorites
There are perennial and biennial forms of bellflowers. Some like Canterbury bell, *Campanula medium*, are biennials that reseed and appear to be perennial. The Clips series of Carpathian bellflower, *Campanula carpatica*, 6- to 12-inch plants, are covered with white, blue, or dark-blue flowers throughout the summer. I have seen these thrive in a sunny rock garden and mixed with ground covers in partial shade. Serbian Bellflower, *Campanula poscharskyana*, forms a 12-inch mound, covered with pale blue flowers in late spring and early summer. It often continues throughout the summer.

Black-eyed Susan
Rudbeckia species

When, Where, and How to Plant
Sow seeds in early spring or fall. Sprinkle seeds on prepared soil, lightly rake, tamp, and water to ensure good seed-soil contact. Plant bare-root black-eyed Susan plants in the spring as soon as the soil is workable. Plant hardened-off transplants any time during the growing season. They tolerate a wide range of soils but prefer full moist, well-drained soil and full sun. Space plants at least 2 to 3 feet apart.

Growing Tips
Water new plantings thoroughly whenever the top few inches of soil are moist and crumbly. Once established, these plants can tolerate dry periods. Mulch them with 1 to 2 inches of organic material to conserve moisture and reduce weed problems. These perennials need minimal fertilization. Proper soil preparation and spreading of 1 to 2 inches of compost over the soil surface every other year provides all the nutrients this plant needs.

Care
Black-eyed Susans are low-maintenance plants. They will quickly grow and crowd out weeds. Rudbeckias will bloom continuously summer through fall without deadheading. As the flowers fade, the attractive seedheads provide fall and winter interest. Powdery mildew can be a cosmetic problem on some species. Select mildew-resistant plants and grow them in areas with full sun and good air circulation. Several fungal and a bacterial leaf spot diseases have recently attacked rudbeckias. Remove infested leaves and do a thorough fall cleanup. If the problem continues, treat plants as they emerge in spring with a copper containing fungicide. Follow label directions.

Companion Planting and Design
Combine with other native plants and grasses for a naturalized or meadow effect. Combine with tall red angelica or Porcupine grass (*Miscanthus sinensis* 'Strictus') for a bit of color echoing in the garden.

My Personal Favorites
The great coneflower, *Rudbeckia maxima*, has large bluish-green leaves and reaches heights of 5 to 6 feet when in bloom. *Rudbeckia nitida* 'Herbstonne' has large yellow flowers on 7-foot-tall plants. The native three-lobed coneflower (*Rudbeckia triloba*) blooms longer than 'Goldsturm' and grows 2 to 3 feet tall.

Black-eyed Susans are sure to attract the attention of your neighbors as well as passing butterflies and birds. Their dramatic yellow flowers brighten formal, informal, and naturalized plantings. These plants will bloom continuously throughout summer and fall without deadheading. As the flowers fade, the attractive seedheads form. Leave these intact for winter interest. You and the finches will enjoy them all winter long. The common black-eyed Susan, Rudbeckia hirta, *is susceptible to powdery mildew and tends to be a short-lived perennial. It easily reseeds, so its presence will be long-lived in the garden. Many of the new introductions like* 'Prairie Sun', 'Becky Mix', *and* 'Goldilocks' *are being sold and used as annuals.* Goldsturm Rudbeckia (Rudbeckia fulgida var. sullivantii 'Goldsturm') *has become one of the workhorses of the perennial garden. It is compact, 24 inches tall, and mildew resistant.*

Other Common Names
Gloriosa Daisy, Rudbeckia

Bloom Period and Seasonal Color
Summer and fall blooms in yellow with black centers.

Mature Height × Spread
24 to 36 in. × 18 to 48 in.

Bleeding Heart

Dicentra spectabilis

Bleeding heart is an old-fashioned favorite among gardeners. Many of us include this plant more for sentimental than ornamental reasons. Perhaps your grandmother or a favorite neighbor grew bleeding hearts when you were a child. In any case, the beautiful, heart-shaped flowers add interest and color to shade gardens. Use the flowers for cutting or check with your florist who may sell them as potted blooming plants. Bleeding heart is a fun plant for kids. Pull a flower apart to reveal a dancing lady, slippers, bathtub, sword, and other items that combine to make great stories. Check children's gardening books for the many stories associated with this plant. Or better yet, make up a few of your own. Check out the flowers on its cousin, our native Dutchman's breeches (Dicentra cucullaria), to see where this spring bloomer gets its name.

Other Common Name
Japanese Bleeding Heart

Bloom Period and Seasonal Color
Spring to early summer blooms in rose-red and white.

Mature Height × Spread
2 to 3 ft. × 3 ft.

When, Where, and How to Plant
Plant bare-root bleeding hearts in the spring after the danger of severe weather has passed. Plant hardened-off, container-grown, and field-potted perennials whenever plants are available. Grow bleeding hearts in partial to full shade with moist soil. The plants will turn yellow and go dormant earlier when they are grown in full sun and dry soils. Space plants 24 to 30 inches apart.

Growing Tips
Bleeding hearts are relatively low-maintenance plants. Water plants thoroughly whenever the top few inches of soil are crumbly and moist. Mulch the soil with a 1- to 2-inch layer of organic material. This helps conserve moisture and reduce weed problems.

Care
Remove faded flowers to encourage a longer bloom period and discourage reseeding. Young seedlings can be moved in early spring to a desired location, or share them with your perennial gardening friends. The leaves will yellow and brown and the plants go dormant in July. Prune bleeding heart plants back halfway after flowering to avoid the summer dormancy. The pruned plants send up new foliage that stays green throughout the season. Plants can stay in the same location for many years. Divide plants in early spring to start new plants or to reduce the size of those that have outgrown their location.

Companion Planting and Design
These large plants need lots of room. Make plans to cover the bare spot left when these plants die out in midsummer. I like to keep them towards the back of my garden, making their midsummer departure less noticeable. Combine them with hosta, ferns, and other shade tolerant perennials.

My Personal Favorites
Fringed bleeding heart, *Dicentra eximia*, is a good plant for the garden and landscape. It grows 12 to 18 inches tall and wide. Its lacy foliage stays green all summer long. These plants are covered with flowers in early summer but continue producing blooms all season long. It makes a nice edging or ground cover plant. 'King of Hearts' has blue-green foliage and rosy-pink flowers throughout the summer.

Butterfly Weed
Asclepias tuberosa

When, Where, and How to Plant

Sow purchased seeds in early spring. Sprinkle seeds on prepared soil and lightly rake to cover the seeds. Tamp and water to ensure good seed-soil contact. Thin seedlings as needed. Butterfly weed is difficult to transplant, so plant seeds in their permanent location. Plant hardened-off, container-grown, and field-potted perennials anytime during the growing season. Grow butterfly weed in well-drained soil. Established plants tolerate drought and perform well in poor soil. Space plants 12 inches apart.

Growing Tips

Water new plantings thoroughly whenever the top few inches of soil are crumbly and moist. Mulch the soil to conserve moisture and reduce weed problems. Established plants are drought tolerant. This native plant needs little fertilizer.

Care

Butterfly weed is slow to establish. The seedlings that plant themselves often do the best. They seem to find the perfect spot and thrive. Move, propagate, transplant, and divide butterfly weed in early spring. Dig deep to avoid damaging the taproot. Butterfly weeds are late to emerge in the spring. Mark their location by leaving last year's stems stand or with plant labels or spring-flowering bulbs. Remove the first set of flowers as they fade to encourage a second flush of blooms. Allow the second flush of flowers to set seed for added interest and additional plants. Aphids are a problem. Many of the insecticides that kill these will harm visiting butterflies. Let the ladybugs take care of the aphids. If that doesn't work, spot-spray the aphids with insecticidal soap, but don't spray caterpillars.

Companion Planting and Design

Use in perennial gardens or naturalized areas. Butterfly weed competes with grass, making it a good addition to meadow and prairie plantings. The orange flowers combine nicely with blue-flowered plants such as the wild petunia (*Ruellia*).

My Personal Favorites

Most plants have orange flowers, but there are some available with red or yellow blooms. The cultivar 'Gay Butterflies' has all 3 flower colors. Swamp milkweed *Asclepias incarnata* is native, hardy to Zone 3, and tolerates moist soils.

This is no "weed" that needs to be removed from the garden. It is a beautiful plant that deserves a home in most landscapes. The deep orange flowers and the monarchs they attract brighten the landscape from midsummer into fall. Watch for the black-green-and-yellow-striped "Packer" caterpillars (as my daughter used to call them). They feed on the leaves, form cocoons, and soon turn into beautiful adult butterflies that nectar on the flowers. Kids and adults love to watch this amazing process. A side benefit for the butterfly is that the toxins in the plant make the butterfly distasteful to their predators. Don't use insecticides on this plant if you want to enjoy the monarch butterflies. Butterfly weed is native to Minnesota and is now available as plants and seeds from garden centers, perennial nurseries, and catalogs. It is hardy to Zone 4.

Other Common Name
Milkweed

Bloom Period and Seasonal Color
Summer into fall blooms in orange, red, and yellow.

Mature Height × Spread
18 to 30 in. × 12 in.

Catmint

Nepeta × faassenii

No, I haven't gone crazy. The right cultivar of catmint can provide long lasting bloom without taking over the garden. Catmint's fragrant gray-green foliage is covered with lavender to blue flowers from June through August. Use this plant as a substitute for lavender. Its hardy Zone 3 nature makes it much easier to grow in Minnesota. I have heard mixed reports on how attractive this plant is to cats. One gardener told me she found her cat rolling in this plant every morning. She was so frustrated she placed thorny rose prunings in the middle of the plant. The next morning the stems were removed and the cat was contentedly lying in the catmint. I have had no problems with my plant and the many stray cats that seem to love to visit my landscape.

Other Common Name
Nepeta

Bloom Period and Seasonal Color
Late spring through fall in lavender-blue.

Mature Height and Spread
18 to 30 inches tall × 10 to 30 inches

When, Where, and How to Plant
Plant dormant bare-root plants as soon as the soil is workable. Hardened-off transplants can be planted anytime throughout the growing season. Grow catmint in full sun with well-drained soils. Add several inches of organic matter to heavy soils to improve drainage. Plant catmint at the same depth it was growing in the nursery. Water for soil settling, and cover exposed roots as needed. Space plants 18 to 24 inches apart.

Growing Tips
Water new plantings thoroughly whenever the top 3 to 4 inches of soil are moist and crumbly. Mulch the soil to conserve moisture and suppress weeds. Established plants are drought tolerant. Overwatering and rainy seasons can lead to yellow foliage and floppy growth. Proper soil preparation and top-dressing with compost every other year usually provide sufficient nutrients for these perennials. Avoid high nitrogen fertilizers that can lead to floppy growth.

Care
Select sterile and less aggressive cultivars. They offer all the beauty without fighting to keep the plant inbounds. Deadheading is not needed for repeat bloom. Remove spent flowers for a tidier appearance or to prevent reseeding. Cutback floppy plants by two thirds after the first flush of blooms. This encourages more compact growth and prevents open centers.

Companion Planting and Design
Use catmint as a ground cover or edging plant with roses. Sedums and yellow daylilies also make good planting partners. The light airy foliage and flowers are easy to blend and make catmint a great filler in full-sun perennials gardens.

My Personal Favorites
'Six Hills Giant' is a large, up to 30 inches tall and wide, clump forming catmint with sterile seeds. Use it as an edge or specimen plant in the landscape. I have seen it flanking the ends of a garden bench, effectively anchoring the bench into the garden. 'Walker's Low' is a mounding spreader that does not seem to grow out of control. Not real low, it grows 24 by 24 inches and looks great as an edge for the rose garden.

Columbine
Aquilegia hybrids

When, Where, and How to Plant
Plant bare-root perennials in the spring as soon as the soil is workable. Plant hardened-off transplants any time during the growing season. Grow columbine in full to part sun with moist soil. Plants will deteriorate in dry soil and rot in overly wet conditions. Space plants 12 inches apart.

Growing Tips
Columbines are fairly low-maintenance plants. Water thoroughly whenever the top few inches of soil are moist and crumbly. Mulch the soil to help conserve moisture and reduce weed problems. Proper soil preparation and top-dressing with compost every other year usually provide adequate nutrients.

Care
Remove faded flowers to encourage rebloom. Deadheading also prevents reseeding of hybrids whose unpredictable offspring can overrun the garden. A few seedheads left on the plants add winter interest. Columbine seldom needs dividing. You can divide plants in late summer and preferably by September 1 to become re-established by winter. Leafminers are the biggest pest. These insects feed between the upper and lower leaf surfaces leaving a white, snake-like pattern in the leaves. It doesn't hurt the plant; it just looks bad. Cut severely damaged plants back to ground level after flowering to encourage fresh new foliage. Columbine sawfly is a more recent pest problem. It eats the leaves causing the gardeners, not the plants, great stress. Remove and destroy the problem insects by hand. If you must use an insecticide, follow all label directions.

Combination Planting and Design
Combine with ferns, hosta, and other shade-loving plants. Mix them with these and other perennials to mask the foliage that tends to deteriorate over the summer.

My Personal Favorites
The new hybrids tend to be short lived. Think of it as a way to try many new plants in limited space. The 'Biedermeier Strain' grows 12 inches tall with short, spurred, white, pink, or purple flowers. The popular 'McKana Hybrids' grow 30 inches tall and come in a variety of colors. 'Song Bird' cultivars are 24 to 30 inches tall with vibrant flowers that brighten up the garden.

This delicate beauty holds its own in any garden. The blue-green leaves make a nice base for the long, flowering stems. The flowers can be single or bicolored with long or short spurs. You, the hummingbirds, and butterflies will enjoy the flowers from late spring through early, even mid-, summer. Be sure to include them in the garden where you can sit and watch the hummingbirds feed. Plant extras so you can pick a few to enjoy indoors as well. The native columbine, Aquilegia canadensis, *has red and yellow nodding flowers. It is easy to grow, self-seeds, and will quickly fill in shady areas. Columbine is the symbol for folly. If you look closely at the flower you may see a jester's cap. Or perhaps you see an eagle's claw, as the botanical name* Aquilegia *means eagle.*

Other Common Name
Aquilegia

Bloom Period and Seasonal Color
Late spring to early summer blooms in yellow, red, pink, blue, purple, and white.

Mature Height × Spread
1 to 3 ft. × 1 to 2 ft.

Coralbells

Heuchera sanguinea

Coralbells are rugged plants that provide year-round interest in the landscape. Use them as ground covers, edging plants, or specimens in sun or shade locations. The foliage looks good throughout the growing season and in mild winters. The small bell-shaped flowers are held high above the leaves. These light, airy blooms allow you to see through to the back of the border. And don't forget to bring a few of the flowers indoors to enjoy in floral arrangements. Most gardeners select hybrids and cultivars with attractive foliage and flowers. Cultivars are available with white, red, and pink flowers. They may have green-to-purple, plain, or variegated foliage in a wide range of shapes. There are over 50 species of coralbells native to North America. Our native Alum root, Heuchera richardsonii, has green flowers and coarse textured leaves.

Other Common Name
Alum Root

Bloom Period and Seasonal Color
Late spring to early summer blooms in red, pink, and white.

Mature Height × Spread
12 to 20 in. × 12 to 20 in.

When, Where, and How to Plant
Plant bare-root perennials in the spring after the danger of severe weather has passed. Plant hardened-off perennials in the spring and early summer to allow the plants to get established and reduce the risk of frost heaving. Coralbells perform best in partial shade with moist, well-drained soil. They will tolerate dry shade. Heavy shade allows nice foliage but fewer flowers. The purple-leafed cultivars tend to scorch in the hot afternoon sun. Space plants 12 inches apart.

Growing Tips
Water thoroughly whenever the top 3 to 4 inches of soil is moist and crumbly. Mulch them with a 1- to 2-inch layer of organic material to conserve moisture and reduce weeds. Proper soil preparation and top-dressing with compost every other year usually provide sufficient nutrients.

Care
Shallow-rooted coralbells are subject to frost heaving. Plants are pushed out of soil as the ground freezes and thaws over the winter. To prevent this, mulch the plants in early winter after the ground freezes. Check coralbells in the spring and replant frost-heaved plants so the crown is just below the soil surface. Coralbells need dividing about every three years to prevent woody stems or when they outgrow their location. Divide in spring to allow plants time to reestablish before winter. Remove browned leaves in the spring before new growth begins. The green ones can be left in place. Deadhead coralbells to encourage season-long bloom.

Companion Planting and Design
Use them as ground covers, edging plants, or rock garden plants in sun and shade locations. The purple-leafed forms look nice with blue oat and fountain grasses. Mix coralbells with ferns, salvias or veronicas, and threadleaf coreopsis.

My Personal Favorites
Heuchera × 'Plum Pudding' has both attractive foliage and flowers. The silvery marked, plum-colored leaves provide the base for the pink, bell-shaped flowers that appear in June. 'Palace Purple' forms a mound of red-purple foliage and was named the 1991 Perennial Plant of the Year. Heucherella is a cross between Heuchera and foamflower (*Tiarella*).

Coreopsis
Coreopsis species

When, Where, and How to Plant

Plant bare-root coreopsis in the spring after the danger of severe weather has passed. Plant hardened-off, container-grown, and field-potted perennials any time during the growing season. Grow coreopsis in moist, well-drained soil. Established plants of most species will tolerate dry conditions. Space plants 12 inches apart.

Growing Tips

Proper soil preparation, plant selection, and planting will help reduce future maintenance. Keep the soil around new plantings moist, but not wet. Water thoroughly whenever the top 3 to 4 inches begin to dry. Mulch to conserve moisture and reduce weeds. Avoid high nitrogen fertilizer and excess fertilization that can decrease flowering and increase floppiness.

Care

Many of the coreopsis species need deadheading. This encourages a second flush of flowers and reduces problems with self-seeding. One plant of mouse ear coreopsis has turned into many plants scattered throughout one of my perennial gardens. A little spring weeding and deadheading will keep this plant in check. Divide overgrown and floppy plants in the spring. The threadleaf coreopsis is not as aggressive as others and seldom needs deadheading. Dig and divide threadleaf coreopsis (*Coreopsis verticillata*), about every four years to increase vigor and eliminate deadheading.

Companion Planting and Design

Use coreopsis in the perennial, wildflower, or naturalized garden. They look nice when grown with salvias, ornamental grasses, and sedums.

My Personal Favorites

Threadleaf coreopsis is my first choice. This attractive plant tolerates drought and needs no staking. Dig and divide the plant every few years to eliminate the need for deadheading. The cultivar 'Zagreb' is 12 to 18 inches tall with clear yellow flowers. 'Moonbeam' is slightly larger and less hardy in heavy soils. *Coreopsis rosea* has fine foliage and pink flowers. It tends to take over in dry soils and die in poorly drained soils. Give 'Limerock Ruby' a try. The season-long, dark red flowers make it worth the risk of just one season of beauty.

Coreopsis is a good choice for sunny, dry gardens. The small daisy-like flowers are great for cutting and for attracting butterflies. Use them in formal and informal perennial gardens or in wildflower and naturalized plantings. Beginning gardeners and those who want low-maintenance gardens will like threadleaf coreopsis. Its fine-textured foliage is covered most of the season with small, yellow flowers. And—the best part—it requires no deadheading for season-long bloom. The name coreopsis comes from the Greek words koris *meaning a bug and* opsis *meaning resemblance. The seeds are thought to look like ticks. Thus the common name, tickseed. There are over 100 species of tickseed that are native to the United States (including the Hawaiian Islands) and tropical Africa. Coreopsis tripteris and C. palmata can be found in our dry prairies.*

Other Common Name
Tickseed

Bloom Period and Seasonal Color
Late spring to late summer blooms in yellow.

Mature Height × Spread
18 to 36 in. × 18 to 36 in.

Cranesbill Geranium

Geranium sanguineum

Use this long-blooming plant to provide several seasons of interest in your landscape. The fragrant, lobed leaves form an attractive mound. The white, pink, or lavender blooms appear in late spring through early summer. Sporadic flowers follow throughout the remainder of the season. Watch for hummingbirds and butterflies looking for a meal from this garden beauty. Take a close look at the seedheads to reveal the source of this plant's common name. They resemble a crane's bill. In the fall, the leaves turn red and will often persist through a mild winter. Try the cultivar 'Max Frei' for a longer season of bloom on a smaller, 8-inch plant. Geranium × 'Rozanne' has larger, cup-shaped, deep blue flowers that tolerate the heat and brighten the garden all summer long. Use Geranium × cantabrigiense 'Biokovo' for dry shade.

Other Common Name
Perennial Geranium

Bloom Period and Seasonal Color
Late spring through summer blooms in pink, lavender, and white.

Mature Height and Spread
8 to 15 in. × 24 in.

When, Where, and How to Plant
Plant dormant bare-root geraniums in early spring as soon as the ground is workable. Plant hardened-off transplants anytime during the growing season. Grow perennial geraniums in full sun or partial shade locations with moist well-drained soils. Established plants will tolerate drought. Amend the soil prior to planting. Space plants 18 to 24 inches apart.

Growing Tips
Water the soil thoroughly whenever the top 3 to 4 inches are crumbly and moist. Mulch the soil with 1 to 2 inches of an organic material to conserve moisture and suppress weeds. Minimal fertilization is needed when the soil is properly prepared and top-dressed with compost every other year.

Care
Deadheading will not increase the sporadic bloom. Trim plants back after the main flower display or when the leaves are spotted, discolored, or unkempt. Use a hedge clipper to prune plants back to about 4 inches, exposing the basal growth (young leaves near soil surface). These new leaves will grow quickly, giving the plant a fresh new look for the remainder of the season and throughout the winter. Geraniums occasionally suffer from leaf spot and rust. As a control, clip back the plants and perform a good fall cleanup. Dig and divide geraniums when they outgrow their location. Or use a sharp spade and just remove a portion of the outside edge of the plant.

Companion Planting and Design
Geraniums make nice ground covers, edging plants, and additions to the rock garden. Mix them with dwarf conifers or use them to hide the ugly ankles of small deciduous shrubs. Plant them with bearded iris, ornamental grasses, and other perennials.

My Personal Favorites
Bigroot geranium (*Geranium macrorrhizum*) produces pink and white flowers from May through June and sporadically the rest of season. The plant has lobed leaves and forms a mat; it grows 12 to 18 inches high and 18 inches wide. The fragrant foliage looks good all season, turning red in fall. This species is more heat and drought tolerant than the crane's bill geranium. 'Variegatum' has magenta pink flowers and creamy variegated leaves.

When, Where, and How to Plant

Plant dormant bare-root daylilies in spring as soon as the soil is workable. Plant hardened-off transplants any time during the growing season. Grow in full sun to partial shade. Pastel-colored daylilies tend to fade in full sun, and poor flowering and floppy growth may occur in heavy shade. Daylilies prefer moist, well-drained soil, but will tolerate a wide range of conditions including heavy clay. Space plants $1^1/_2$ to 3 feet apart.

Growing Tips

Water thoroughly whenever the top 3 to 4 inches of soil are moist and crumbly. Mulch the soil to conserve moisture and suppress weeds. Established plants are fairly drought tolerant. Most daylily cultivars grow fast and need minimal fertilization. Excess nitrogen can cause unattractive growth and poor flowering. Repeat bloomers benefit from regular division and light fertilization in spring.

Care

Daylilies are tough plants that are often sold as low maintenance selections. This is misleading for gardeners who like things neat and tidy. Each daylily flower lasts one day, fades, and then hangs on the stem. Daily deadheading is needed for meticulous gardeners. Once all flowers have bloomed, remove the flower stem back to the leaves. Animals also love the blossoms. Scare tactics and repellents can be used to discourage these pests. Use a repellent labeled for food crops if you plan on eating the blossoms. Pull out or clip back discolored foliage in mid- to late summer. Established daylilies form a tangle of thick fleshy roots that make digging and dividing difficult for the gardener. Divide plants every three years to make this job easier.

Companion Planting and Design

Use daylilies as ground covers, cut flowers, edibles, or in the perennial border. They combine nicely with Russian sage, ornamental grasses, and sedum.

My Personal Favorites

Select a variety of daylilies including early, mid-, and later summer bloomers to have daylily flowers all season long. Plant 'Stella d'Oro', 'Happy Returns', or another repeat bloomer for several bursts of flowers in one season. 'Strawberry Candy' is a repeat bloomer with coral-pink flowers and a strawberry-red eye. Hardy throughout the state.

Daylilies are versatile plants that can fit in any garden. The long, grass-like leaves are effective all season. The individual flowers last a day, but the flower display can last up to one month on an individual plant. The newer, repeat-blooming hybrids provide a summer-long floral display. Enjoy them indoors as cut flowers. Select stems with tight buds for a longer flower display or remove fresh blossoms and place them on tables around the house for an evening of enjoyment. Some daylily flowers are fragrant, and they all are edible. Use them fresh, in salads, stuffed and cooked, or in soups. The orange daylily (Hemerocallis fulva), often called ditch lily, is seen growing wild in drainage ditches and other areas in Minnesota. Deadhead or remove seedpods from garden daylilies to keep these plants from invading our native grasslands.

Other Common Name
Hemerocallis

Bloom Period and Seasonal Color
Summer through fall blooms in most colors.

Mature Height × Spread
1 to 4 ft. × 2 to 3 ft.

Delphinium

Delphinium elatum

Stately spikes of blue-and-white delphinium flowers stir up visions of an English cottage garden. These visions may have enticed you, like many gardeners, to add these high-maintenance plants to your garden. Every time you see a beautiful flowering plant or a bouquet of blossoms, you are ready to try again. Join the club. Some gardeners buy flowering plants and treat them like annuals. If they return, they consider it a bonus. I have also met gardeners who have no problem growing these sometimes picky plants. One gardener asked me for advice—her delphiniums were only 8 feet instead of their normal 12-foot height! Handle these plants with care. The seeds and young plants are poisonous if eaten. The leaves may irritate gardeners with sensitive skin, so wear gloves when working with delphiniums.

Other Common Name
Larkspur

Bloom Period and Seasonal Color
Early to midsummer blooms in blue, purple, white, red, pink, and yellow.

Mature Height × Spread
4 to 6 ft. × 2 ft.

When, Where, and How to Plant
Plant hardened-off perennials in the spring and early summer so the delphiniums have time to get established before winter. Grow delphiniums in full sun in moist, well-drained soil. Good drainage is essential for winter survival. Place the plants in a protected site with good air circulation. This environment will increase winter survival and reduce wind damage and pest problems. Space plants 24 inches apart.

Growing Tips
Delphiniums are difficult plants to grow. Proper soil preparation and watering are critical to establish and grow healthy delphiniums. Water thoroughly whenever the top few inches of soil are moist and crumbly. Mulch plants with a 1- to 2-inch layer of organic material to conserve moisture, keep roots cool, and reduce weed problems. Fertilize delphiniums lightly in the spring as growth begins and again in the summer, after you clip back the faded foliage.

Care
Deadhead flowers to encourage a second flush of blossoms. Prune back plants once all the flowers have faded to encourage new growth and blossoms. Consider skipping the fall bloom the first year to increase the chance of winter survival. Stake tall cultivars to prevent flopping and wind damage. Regular division improves plant vigor and hardiness. Divide in early spring as growth begins. Check plants frequently for insects and disease problems. They are susceptible to powdery mildew, blight, leaf spot, crown rot, canker, aphids, mites, borers, and leafminers. Buy healthy transplants and grow them in the right conditions to minimize pest problems.

Companion Planting and Design
These plants make a great backdrop for other perennials, or as a vertical accent or specimen plant. Mix them with threadleaf coreopsis, beebalm, and most other perennials.

My Personal Favorite
The New Millenium hybrids are bred for strong stems and greater survival in our tough growing conditions. They grow 4 to 6 feet tall and come in a variety of colors. Or try the shorter Belladonna delphinium, *Delphinium × belladonna.*

When, Where, and How to Plant

Plant bare-root ferns in the spring after the danger of severe weather has passed. Hardened-off, container-grown, and field potted plants can be planted anytime during the season. Plant tender ferns early in the season to give them time to get established before winter. Most ferns prefer shady locations with moist soil. Prepare the soil prior to planting. Add several inches of organic matter into the top 8 to 12 inches of soil. Spacing depends on the species grown and varies from 12 to 36 inches.

Growing Tips

Water ferns thoroughly whenever the top few inches of soil are crumbly and moist. Mulch ferns with an organic material to conserve moisture, improve the soil, and reduce weed problems. Proper soil preparation and top-dressing with compost every other year are usually all you need to keep ferns healthy and attractive.

Care

Fast growing ferns benefit from division while slow growing ones seldom need attention. Divide overgrown ferns in the spring as growth begins. Let fronds stand for winter. This adds beauty to the winter garden and increases winter hardiness. You can prune out old fronds in late winter or allow the new growth to mask the old leaves.

Companion Planting and Design

Use taller ferns as background plants in the shade garden. Lower-growing ferns can be used as ground covers and edging plants. Ferns combine well with hosta, astilbe, ginger, daylilies, and other shade lovers.

My Personal Favorites

Japanese painted fern, *Athyrium niponicum* 'Pictum', is a good fern for beginning and perennial gardeners. This clump-forming fern works well as a ground cover or edging plant for shady areas. The fronds are gray-green with a maroon stalk and a silver flush to the leaves. This low-maintenance fern was selected as the 2004 Perennial Plant of the Year and is hardy to Zone 4. The hayscented fern *Dennstaedtia punctilobula*, interrupted fern *Osmunda claytoniana*, and lady fern *Athyrium filix-femina* all tolerate the sun, but provide shade from afternoon sun and keep soil moist for best results.

Ferns have always been an integral part of the natural landscape. Their wonderful texture, shades of green, and interesting form can add interest to shady gardens. You may know the ostrich fern, Matteuccia struthiopteris, that can be found growing along the foundations of many Minnesota homes. Its long lacy upright fronds reach heights of 5 feet. These fast growers quickly fill the space provided. You may also know that ostrich ferns will brown out in the heat and drought of midsummer. Minimize scorch by planting them in a north or east location, mulching, and keeping the soil moist. This native fern is hardy throughout Minnesota. But this is not the only choice. Ferns come in a variety of sizes, leaf shapes, and textures. Some are even suited for the sun, making them a plant for any garden.

Other Common Names
Japanese Painted Fern, Ostrich Fern, Cinnamon Fern

Bloom Period and Seasonal Color
Season long foliage in shades of green.

Mature Height × Spread
1 to 5 ft. × 1 to 3 ft.

Foxglove
Digitalis purpurea

As promised, I have included foxglove and hollyhocks in this edition, for those who asked. Foxglove is truly a biennial, but it reseeds readily and stays in the garden for years. The drooping tubular flowers appear on one side of the stem at the top of this large stately plant. You may recognize the botanical name Digitalis *from the heart medicine. Though used as medicine, all parts of the plant are toxic and should not be eaten. This part of the botanical name comes from Latin and means "finger of the glove." Maybe you can see the reference as you look at the flowers. The common name has its basis in English superstitions. A northern legend says that bad fairies gave the blossoms to the fox to cover his toes and muffle his steps while hunting.*

Other Common Name
Fairy Glove

Bloom Period and Seasonal Color
Late spring to early summer with white, pink, mauve, rust, and yellow.

Mature height and Spread
2 to 5 ft. × 1 to 2 ft.

When, Where, and How to Plant
Plant hardened-off transplants early in the season. Sow seeds directly in the garden in late spring or early summer up to two months prior to the first fall frost. These plants will bloom the following year. Or start seeds indoors in spring. Sow seeds in warm (70 degrees Fahrenheit) moist sterile starter mix. It takes fifteen to twenty days for germination. Most foxglove will self-seed in the garden. Grow foxglove in partial shade with moist, well-drained soil. Though it will grow in a wide range of soils, it does not tolerate wet or dry conditions. Space plants 15 to 18 inches apart.

Growing Tips
Water established plants whenever the top few inches of soil are crumbly and moist. Do not over mulch or treat with a pre-emergent weedkiller. This can prevent self-seeding and eventually eliminate foxglove from the garden. Proper soil preparation and care as outlined in the chapter introduction are sufficient for keeping these plants healthy and attractive.

Care
Poorly drained soils and overzealous weeders are the biggest threat to these plants. Proper soil preparation, plant placement, removal of infected plant parts, and proper spacing are the best way to prevent disease problems. Powdery mildew, leaf spot, and stem rot can be an occasional problem. Japanese beetles and aphids may also cause damage. Control as needed. Learn to identify the small seedling stage of this plant. If mistaken for a weed and removed—you will have no plants next season.

Companion Planting and Design
Foxglove is a great backdrop for the shade garden. It works well in a cottage-style or woodland garden. Mix it with ferns, hosta, astilbe, ginger, and other shade loving plants.

My Personal Favorites
I always look for the hardiest as well as the beauty in the group. Strawberry foxglove, Digitalis × mertonensis is just that. The plant is hardy to Zone 3 and is topped with a spire of rose colored flowers. Divide this plant after flowering every two years for longevity.

Gayfeather

Liatris spicata

When, Where, and How to Plant

Plant gayfeather rhizomes in the spring or fall. Place the woody corm or rhizome 1 to 2 inches below the soil surface. Plant hardened-off, container-grown, and field-potted perennials any time during the growing season. Grow gayfeather in full sun and well-drained soil. These plants will tolerate some light shade, but not wet feet. Space plants 15 to 20 inches apart.

Growing Tips

Gayfeathers are low maintenance plants. Water thoroughly whenever the top few inches of soil start to dry. Once established, these plants are very drought tolerant. Mulch new plantings to conserve moisture and reduce weed problems. Avoid excess nitrogen, which can lead to floppy growth and poor flowering.

Care

Deadhead plants when most of the flower spike has bloomed. Cut the flower stem back to the first whorl of leaves; this will encourage a second flush of flowers. Let flowers dry and form their fluffy seedheads. The plants will self-seed if the seedheads are left alone. I have supplied gayfeathers to several friends, a park, and all my gardens from one plant. Gayfeather plants seldom need staking. Those grown in rich, moist soil or shade are more likely to topple. Use commercially available grow-through stakes or surrounding plants to provide support. Divide (and give away) overgrown gayfeathers in the spring as growth begins.

Companion Planting and Design

Mix gayfeather with other sun-loving perennials. Its upright growth habit makes it a good vertical accent and background plant for the perennial garden. Or combine it with grasses and other native plants to create a naturalized garden.

My Personal Favorites

The cultivar 'Alba' produces white flowers, and 'Kobold' is a compact cultivar. Its smaller size, 18 to 30 inches tall, makes 'Kobold' easier to blend into most home gardens. The profusion of dark purple flowers will provide enjoyment in the garden and flower vase. Several species are native to Minnesota prairies. The most common include the tall blazing star, *Liatris pycnostachya,* and rough blazing star, *Liatris aspera.*

Though native to the prairies, this plant is equally at home in the perennial garden. Gayfeather's whorls of dark green leaves are topped with spikes of purple, rose, or white flowers. These are more than just pretty plants. They attract wildlife to the garden and make long-lasting cut flowers. In winter, birds will stop by to feed on the seeds hidden in the fluffy seedheads. This native has also been an important crop in the floral industry. It is grown around the world for use as a cut flower. Some are produced right here in Minnesota. Don't confuse this with the invasive loosestrife. A closer look will help you tell the two apart. Gayfeather flowers open from the top down. Purple loosestrife with its shorter and broader leaves have purple flowers that open from the bottom up.

Other Common Name

Blazing Star

Bloom Period and Seasonal Color

Midsummer to fall blooms in lavender, rose, and white.

Mature Height × Spread

12 to 36 in. × 18 in.

Hollyhocks
Alcea rosea

As promised, here is the second of the pair of plants, hollyhocks and foxglove, which gardeners asked me to include in this edition. Hollyhock is classified as a biennial or short-lived perennial. Don't worry about them disappearing. They reseed readily, and you will have plenty for your landscape and 20 of your closest friends. These tall plants have large leaves at the base and are topped with hibiscus-like flowers. Many gardeners like this old fashioned favorite as much for the childhood memories as for its beauty. I remember making hollyhock dolls with my grandmother. The open flower was the skirt, an unopened bud the head and a pair of rolled leaves made green sleeve covered arms. The hollyhocks in my yard were a gift from a friend—another memory growing in my backyard.

Other Common Name
Althea

Bloom Period and Seasonal Color
Midsummer to early fall in white, yellow, pink, red, lavender, and nearly black.

Mature Height and Spread
Up to 8 ft. × 2 ft.

When, Where, and How to Plant
Start hollyhock seeds indoors in late February or March if you want flowers the first summer. Keep the sterile starter mix moist and 60 to 70 degrees Fahrenheit. Or start them outdoors in spring or early summer at least two months prior to the first fall frost. These plants will bloom the following summer. Plant hardened-off transplants outdoors when the danger of frost has passed. Container-grown plants are also available. Grow hollyhocks in full sun and well-drained soils. Space plants 18 to 36 inches apart.

Growing Tips
Water plants thoroughly whenever the top few inches of soil are crumbly and moist. Keep foliage dry to minimize disease problems. Apply water directly to soil with a watering wand or drip irrigation. Or water early in the day if overhead watering is the only option. Avoid excess nitrogen fertilization that can increase risk of disease.

Care
Lacy leaves are a common sight. These are not a prized cultivar but rather the feeding damage of a caterpillar, sawfly, or Japanese beetle. Remove insects as they are discovered or just tolerate them. Orange and brown spots on the leaves are also commonly found. Rust disease, not life threatening, is the culprit, and fall clean up and a bit drier weather will help reduce the symptoms.

Companion Planting and Design
Use these stately beauties against a wall or fence. Add a bird bath for some extra charm. Try mixing in some ornamental grasses, tall daylilies, and Russian sage. I use medium-sized plants in front of the hollyhocks to mask the insect- and disease-riddled foliage.

My Personal Favorites
I like the romantic color of 'Peaches and Dreams'. It grows 5 to 6 feet tall and displays peach-yellow flowers throughout July and August. The deep purple, almost black flowers of 'Nigra' are quite unique. One of the 2004 AAS winners is 'Queeny Purple' hollyhocks. It blooms the first season from seeds started in February or March. The double purple flowers are on short, 20 to 30 inch plants. The smaller size is easier to blend in most gardens.

When, Where, and How to Plant

Plant bare-root perennials in the spring after the danger of severe weather has passed. Plant hardened-off, container-grown, and field-potted perennials any time during the growing season. Grow hosta in shady locations with moist, organic soil. Your plants will have the best leaf color in partial shade. Avoid afternoon sun that can cause leaf edges to brown or scorch. Hosta prefer rich organic soil. Spacing depends on size of the variety grown.

Growing Tips

Hosta are low-maintenance plants. Water established plants thoroughly whenever the top few inches of soil are crumbly and moist. Hosta will scorch in dry soil. Mulch them with a 1- to 2-inch layer of organic material to conserve moisture and reduce weed problems.

Care

Early-sprouting hosta may suffer frost damage. New growth will help mask some of the browned leaves. Many gardeners remove the flowers as they sprout or as the flowers fade to improve their appearance. I like to leave the seedheads for winter interest and to attract birds. You can divide hostas almost anytime during the growing season. Mulch fall-divided plants for added winter protection. Slugs and earwigs are the major pests. Beer-baited traps tucked under the hosta leaves will help capture the slugs. The newer iron phosphate based baits seem to provide good slug control. Hosta with thicker and heavier leaves such as 'Inniswood' tend to resist slug damage. Crumpled paper or tubes can be used to trap earwigs. Deer and rabbits love hosta. Repellents, scare tactics, and fences around small perennial plantings may help, or you can replace hosta with lungwort *Pulmonaria*. It looks similar to hosta and tolerates shade.

Companion Planting and Design

Use hosta alone or in groupings in shade gardens. Combine hosta with ferns and astilbes for an interesting shade garden. Or use them en masse as a ground cover or edging plant.

My Personal Favorites

There are too many hosta for me to narrow down all of my favorites. A few include 'Guacamole', 'Great Expectations', 'Thunderbolt', 'Drinking Gourd', and 'Inniswood'.

Hosta are low-maintenance, quick-growing, shade-tolerant perennials. These features have helped make hosta one of the most popular perennials in the landscape. The variety of leaf sizes, shapes, colors, and textures adds to its landscape value. Plant hosta where you can enjoy hummingbirds nectaring on the flowers in summer, juncos feeding on the seeds in winter or the sometimes fragrant flowers. Gather design ideas with a visit to the University of Minnesota Landscape Arboretum. Their hosta glade beneath the sugar maples provides a beautiful respite on a hot summer day. The arboretum is also the home of the International Hosta Registry, where new cultivars are enrolled, and the national display gardens of the American Hosta Society. Hosta enthusiasts may want to join the American Hosta Society, 338 E. Forestwood Street, Morton, IL 61550.

Other Common Name
Funkia

Bloom Period and Seasonal Color
Summer and fall blooms in white and lavender.

Mature Height × Spread
2 to 36 in. × 36 in.

Joe Pye Weed

Eupatorium fistulosum

Bold and beautiful has been a trend for the past decade or two. Joe Pye Weed provides just that in the garden. The large plants provide fresh color to the late summer and fall landscape. Their towering size and dramatic flower heads provide an architectural accent in the perennial garden, shrub bed, or mixed border. Add to that a long bloom period, low maintenance, and butterfly appeal and you have a valuable plant for most landscapes. It loves moisture and makes an attractive addition to the rain garden. Several species of Eupatorium go by the common name of Joe Pye Weed. They are all similar in appearance, and some taxonomists group them together while others prefer to keep their identities separate. They're native throughout the U.S., so you can find these plants growing in moist pasturelands, woodland edges, and along streams.

Other Common Name
Queen of the Meadow

Bloom Period and Seasonal Color
Mid to late summer through fall, purple flowers.

Mature Height and Spread
Up to 8 ft. × 3 ft.

When, Where, and How to Plant

Plant bare-root perennials in spring as soon as severe weather has passed. Container-grown plants can be added to the garden anytime during the growing season. Plants can be grown from seed. Start seeds indoors in a moist starter mix at 55 to 60 degrees Fahrenheit. Hardened-off transplants can be moved outdoors after the danger of frost. Grow Joe Pye Weed in full sun with moist soil. Plants growing in shade tend to grow tall and leggy, and those growing in droughty soils are not as robust and attractive. Space plants 3 feet apart.

Growing Tips

Keep soil moist for best results. Water thoroughly whenever the top few inches are moist and crumbly. Mulch to conserve moisture and suppress weeds. Minimal fertilizer is needed for this robust plant.

Care

Cut plants back to 6 inches in early June to reduce the height by several feet. The cultivar 'Gateway' is free flowering and requires little or no deadheading. Dig and divide overgrown plants in early spring. Regular division keeps the plants vigorous and more free-flowering (less deadheading needed). Leave the seedheads and plants for winter interest. You may occasionally see leaf spot disease or powdery mildew. Good cleanup and better weather are usually sufficient to control these diseases.

Companion Planting and Design

This is a beautiful background plant or focal point of the garden. It is equally at home in the formal garden or the rain garden. Try growing it near a water feature. It loves the moist soil, and the strong architectural features provide a nice accent to the water garden. Joe Pye Weed combines nicely with other large flowers such as heliopsis, Russian sage, *Rudbeckia nitida*, and miscanthus grass. Or anchor it to the garden with smaller ornamental grasses and daylilies.

My Personal Favorites

'Gateway' is a relatively smaller, 5 to 6 feet tall, cultivar that provides a long period of bloom with no deadheading needed. The smaller scale and low maintenance make it a great landscape plant. Pinch these plants back in early June for fuller growth.

Mum

Chrysanthemum × morifolium

When, Where, and How to Plant

Plant bare-root perennials in the spring after the danger of severe weather has passed. Plant hardened-off, container-grown, and field-potted perennials in the spring or late summer. Spring planting increases plant hardiness and overwintering success. Grow mums in full sun with moist, well-drained soil. Increase winter hardiness by growing them in protected sites with good drainage. Space plants 2 to 3 feet apart.

Growing Tips

Most mums are not reliably hardy in Minnesota. Select hardy cultivars mentioned below. Plant mums in properly prepared soil in spring or early summer for healthy plants that are more likely to survive the winter. Water established plants thoroughly whenever the top few inches of soil start to dry. Fertilize mums early in the growing season according to soil test recommendations.

Care

Pinch back taller cultivars for compact growth and increased flower production. Start pinching mums in late May or early June. Cut plants back just above a set of leaves to a height of 6 inches. Stop pinching by late June so blooming will occur prior to snowfall. Leave the plants intact for the winter for increased hardiness. The stems help capture snow and insulate the plants. For added protection, cover plants with a few evergreen branches after the ground freezes.

Companion Planting and Design

Many botanical gardens, estates, and home gardeners treat mums as annuals. Use them alone for a splash of fall color or en masse for a more formal, breathtaking display. I like to use mums in containers. A few plants go a long way in brightening up the landscape.

My Personal Favorites

'My Favorite Mum'™ is really my favorite mum. Bred at the University of Minnesota, this plant is hardy to Zone 3. I have seen it successfully grown in Minnesota and Green Bay Botanical gardens. Several colors are available, and the plants are becoming easier to find. A garden mum relative *Chrysanthemum × rubellum* is hardier. 'Clara Curtis' has rosy-pink flowers and grows 2 to 3 feet tall. 'Duchess of Edinburgh' has dull-red flowers.

Mums are often called "the last smile of the departing year." It's a good description of their frost-tolerant fall flower display. One plant can provide over a hundred blossoms for cutting and garden use. Consider adding a few mums to your perennial gardens or annual flower display. A single fall flower show will convince you they are well worth the price. They can be single or semi-double like the daisy, anemone, brush, or spoon types. The double-flowering pompons, quill, spider, or buttons tend to be more rounded with many more petals. Many gardeners have given up growing mums as perennials. They simply buy new plants each fall for a late season floral display. Plant mums with bulbs to add two seasons of bloom with one planting. Or you can plant mums in spring or grow hardier cultivars to increase your success.

Other Common Names
Hardy Mum, Garden Mum

Bloom Period and Seasonal Color
Late summer through frost blooms in yellow, orange, rust, red, bronze, white, and lavender.

Mature Height × Spread
1 to 2 ft. × 1 to 2 ft.

Oriental Poppy
Papaver orientale

I think I fell in love with poppies when I saw Georgia O'Keefe's picture of the red and orange flowers. The flowers are just as beautiful in the garden as they are in her picture. They are a little difficult to get started, but your efforts will be rewarded with years of enjoyment. Poppies make great cut flowers. Cut the flowers when the bud is in an upright position. Some floral designers singe the end of the stem, while others feel it is unnecessary and possibly detrimental. See what works best for you. Don't forget to pick the dried seedpods to use in wreaths and dried arrangements. Select cultivars propagated from root cuttings to maintain the true characteristics of the plant. Many places start their plants from seed and can't guarantee the quality and growth characteristics of each plant.

Other Common Name
Poppy

Bloom Period and Seasonal Color
Late spring to early summer blooms in orange-red, red, pink, and white.

Mature Height × Spread
1 to 4 ft. × 2 ft.

When, Where, and How to Plant
Plant hardened-off, container-grown, and field-potted poppies any time during the growing season. Plant and divide poppies in August and September when the plants are somewhat dormant. Grow poppies in a sunny location with good drainage. Poppies do not respond well to transplanting, making them difficult to establish. However, once established, they are very long lived. Good soil drainage is critical for growing success. Minimize transplanting stress by carefully handling the plants. Plant poppies at the same depth they were growing in the containers and 2 feet apart.

Growing Tips
Established poppies are low-maintenance plants. Winter-mulch new plantings with evergreen branches after the ground lightly freezes. This will help them through their first winter and increase establishment success. Many gardeners, including me, are not successful on their first attempt at planting poppies. It has taken me several tries to find the best spot to successfully grow poppies.

Care
Deadheading is not necessary and will not encourage a second flush of flowers. You can leave the large, attractive seedheads for added interest. Remove the faded leaves in midsummer. A small rosette of leaves may develop in the fall. Leave these in place over the winter. New growth in the spring will cover any of the leaves damaged during cold weather. Pull, don't dig, weeds as soon as they appear. Cultivation can damage the poppy's roots.

Companion Planting and Design
Used en masse, these large flowered plants will steal the show. I have seen them used effectively in naturalized settings and formal gardens. Plan for the void left by these earlier bloomers. By midsummer, the plants dry up and die back to ground level. Plant late-blooming perennials, such as baby's breath, nearby to fill the void left by the poppy.

My Personal Favorite
Get out the catalog and start your wish list. I like the watermelon pink flowers of 'Watermelon'. Try 'Allegro' with its bold orange-red flowers and dark markings at the base of the flowers. 'Prince of Orange' has more orange than red flowers.

Peony
Paeonia hybrids

When, Where, and How to Plant
Plant rhizomes in the fall before the ground freezes or in the spring after the danger of severe weather has passed. Plant hardened-off, container-grown, and field-potted perennials any time during the growing season. They will tolerate light shade but will fail to bloom in excess shade. Peonies will survive in heavy clay soil but need good drainage. Plant the rhizomes with the buds (eyes) 2 inches below the soil surface. Space peonies at least 3 feet apart.

Growing Tips
Water established peonies whenever the top few inches of soil are crumbly and moist. Mulching not only helps conserve moisture and reduce weeds, it can also help reduce some soil-borne diseases. Properly prepare the soil, add mulch, and top-dress with compost every other year for healthy and attractive plants.

Care
Once established, peonies can remain in place for many years. Removing the large terminal bud results in many smaller flowers on each stem. These are less subject to flopping. Removing the side buds and leaving just the terminal results in fewer, but larger, blossoms. Using a peony cage, provide support to peonies in full bloom. Plants can fail to bloom the spring after transplanting and when grown in too much shade, planted too deep, or over fertilized. Peonies are subject to several fungal diseases. Remove faded flowers and infected parts as soon as they appear. This, combined with fall cleanup, will usually control disease problems.

Companion Planting and Design
Use them as specimen plants, mixed with shrubs in foundation plantings, or as a background plant for other flowers. Mix with dwarf conifers, low growing ornamental grasses, and other perennials.

My Personal Favorites
There are lots of beautiful cultivars available. I like the single flowering 'Seas Shell Pink'. The fragrant flowers are held on sturdy stems that don't need staking. This new release won the American Peony Society's gold medal. Fern leaf peony *Paeonia tenuifolia* has cutleaf foliage and impressive red flowers. 'Bartzella' is the result of a cross between the tree and herbaceous peony. The large yellow flowers are incredible.

Peonies provide a long season of interest in the landscape. The new growth comes up red and soon turns green as the leaves enlarge. The large flowers can be single, semi-double, or double. Many are fragrant, and all of them work well as cut flowers. Once the flowers fade, the leaves remain green and attractive throughout the season. In the fall, the leaves turn a nice purple before dying back to the ground. Select the peony cultivar with the color and flower type that is best suited to your landscape. Choose a cultivar with fragrance if this is a desired feature. Some retailers sell unnamed peonies. This can result in a plant that is not suited to your likes and the landscape design. Check with quality garden centers, perennial nurseries, and catalogs for named cultivars.

Other Common Name
Chinese Peony

Bloom Period and Seasonal Color
Late spring to early summer blooms in white, pink, red, and salmon.

Mature Height × Spread
3 ft. × 3 ft.

Phlox
Phlox species

Use a few creeping phlox plants to give your spring landscape a little pizzazz. The bright flower display often leads gardeners to convert their front gardens to this plant. But remember, it will just be green the remainder of the season. Creeping or moss phlox, Phlox subulata, grows 3 to 6 inches tall and creeps along the ground. One plant can quickly cover a 2-foot-square area. Its evergreen foliage and early spring bloom make it a popular perennial. Garden phlox, Phlox paniculata, is another popular phlox. This perennial grows 3 to 4 feet tall. It makes a nice background, cut flower, or specimen plant in the perennial border. Try substituting the more mildew-resistant wild sweet William (Phlox maculata) for garden phlox. They look very similar, but wild sweet William is resistant to powdery mildew.

Other Common Name
Creeping or Garden Phlox

Bloom Period and Seasonal Color
Spring or summer to fall blooms in blue, purple, pink, rose, red, and white.

Mature Height × Spread
3 to 48 in. × 24 in.

When, Where, and How to Plant
Plant bare-root perennials in the spring after the danger of severe weather has passed. Plant hardened-off, container-grown, and field-potted perennials anytime during the growing season. Creeping phlox is often sold as half flats rooted in sand. These can be planted as is or divided into smaller sections. Grow phlox in full sun with moist, well-drained soil. Creeping phlox prefer well-drained soils and are drought tolerant. Space creeping phlox 12 inches apart and garden phlox 18 to 24 inches apart.

Growing Tips
Water new plants often enough to keep the roots moist but not wet. Established plants will need less frequent watering. Water them thoroughly whenever the top few inches of soil are moist and crumbly. Mulch the soil to conserve moisture and to suppress weeds. Established creeping phlox can tolerate drier soils. Minimal fertilization is needed.

Care
Cut back creeping phlox halfway after flowering. This keeps the plants full and attractive and often encourages additional flowers later in the season. Deadhead garden phlox to extend the bloom time. Powdery mildew is the biggest problem of garden phlox. Select mildew-resistant cultivars such as 'David' whenever possible. Remove 1/3 of the stems in the spring to improve air circulation and reduce mildew problems. Remove and discard all infected leaves throughout the season. Fall cleanup will also help reduce mildew problems. Deer love phlox. Repellents, netting, and fencing can help reduce the damage. Vary controls and be persistent.

Companion Planting and Design
Use tall garden phlox for added color in the back of the perennial garden. Use creeping phlox as an edging plant, in rock gardens, or trailing over a wall. Both combine nicely with other perennials such as coreopsis, salvia, Russian sage, and ornamental grasses.

My Personal Favorites
The Flame series of phlox provides all the beauty of garden phlox on a smaller disease resistant plant. Several species are native to Minnesota. Wild blue phlox, *Phlox divaricata*, creeps on the ground. It is 8 to 10 inches tall with blue flowers in spring.

Purple Coneflower
Echinacea purpurea

When, Where, and How to Plant

Sow seeds outdoors in the fall or early spring. Spread seeds on prepared soils, rake to cover seeds, gently tamp, and water. These plants will bloom in several years. Plant bare-root perennials in the spring after the danger of severe weather has passed. Plant hardened-off, container-grown, and field-potted perennials any time during the growing season. Grow purple coneflowers in full sun with well-drained soil. They will tolerate light shade, but excess shade will cause poor growth and flowering. Avoid rich soil and excess fertilizer that can cause the plants to topple and flower poorly. Space plants 24 inches apart.

Growing Tips

Established coneflowers are heat and drought tolerant. Water new plantings often enough to keep the soil slightly moist. Water established plants thoroughly during extended dry periods.

Care

Purple coneflowers will grow and prosper with very little care. Cut the plants back halfway in mid-June. Pruning will reduce the plant size and delay flowering. Try pruning just half of your plants to extend the bloom time with pruned and unpruned plants. Deadheading is not necessary but will give the plants and garden a neater appearance. Stop deadheading by early September to allow seedheads to form. Coneflowers suffer from some leaf spot diseases. Remove the yellow and wilted stem or the whole plant when these symptoms appear. Surrounding plants will quickly fill in the vacant area. I find a thorough cleanup is sufficient to control this problem.

Companion Planting and Design

Combine coneflower with Russian sage and ornamental or native grasses. The finer textured plants help the coneflowers blend into the perennial or naturalized garden.

My Personal Favorites

The clear pink flowers and shorter plant makes 'Kim's Knee High' a favorite in my garden. The orange coneflower 'Meadowbrite' is a recent introduction. The orange flowers and light fragrance have created much interest. The 1998 perennial plant of the year, 'Magnus', has large flowers with flat, dark purple petals.

Purple coneflower is as at home in its native environment as it is in the home landscape. A few coneflowers can create a mass of color in the fall garden or cutflower arrangements. Their large, daisy-like flowers will help attract butterflies, and the seedheads will attract birds to the landscape. Start small since one plant goes a long way. I learned this the hard way when my small city lot was soon overrun with the offspring of one purple coneflower. I still have purple coneflower in my yard—I just share or compost extra plants to maintain planting space for other perennials. You may recognize the name from the drugstore shelves. This plant has long been used to cure colds, scurvy, and snake bites. It is still used today to treat colds.

Other Common Name
Hedge Coneflower

Bloom Period and Seasonal Color
Summer through fall blooms in purple and white.

Mature Height × Spread
2 to 4 ft. × 2 ft.

Russian Sage

Perovskia atriplicifolia

Russian sage was the 1995 Perennial Plant of the Year. Its silvery stems and foliage make a nice backdrop or filler in the perennial garden. Russian sage is a good plant for beginning gardeners and those who want low-maintenance plants. The foliage has a nice sage-like fragrance when crushed. The airy blue flowers appear in midsummer and last all season long with no deadheading needed. This drought tolerant plant tolerates alkaline soil and so far appears to be deer resistant. Try using young plants and small cultivars as a vertical accent in container plantings. Bury the container or move it into an unheated garage for winter. I like to transplant mine into the garden. I get to enjoy the plant in my garden and then have a good excuse to go plant shopping for its replacement the following spring.

Other Common Name
Azure Sage

Bloom Period and Seasonal Color
Midsummer through fall blooms in blue.

Mature Height × Spread
3 to 5 ft. × 3 to 4 ft.

Zones
Hardy to Zone 4

When, Where, and How to Plant
Plant bare-root Russian sage in the spring after the danger of severe weather has passed. Plant hardened-off, container-grown, and field-potted perennials any time during the growing season. Grow Russian sage in full sun and well-drained soil. Good drainage is essential for vigorous growth and winter survival. Plants will flop in wet soil and shade. Space plants 30 to 36 inches apart.

Growing Tips
Russian sage is a low-maintenance plant. Once established, it is very drought tolerant. Water established plants thoroughly during extended droughts. Avoid excess fertilizer that can lead to floppy growth and poor flowering.

Care
Russian sage tends to topple as it reaches full size. Surround it with other plants to provide some needed support. Pruning the plants early in the season will encourage more compact growth. Cut the plants back halfway when they are 12 inches tall. Or try one of the more compact cultivars that are less likely to flop. Leave the Russian sage plants standing for winter interest. The silvery stems and some of the foliage will last throughout the winter. Spring pruning is needed to remove the dead stems and encourage sturdy new growth. It will still be fragrant when you prune it in spring. Cut the stems back to just above a healthy bud 4 to 6 inches above ground level.

Companion Planting and Design
Russian sage provides year-round interest in the landscape. Its fine leaves and flowers give it an airy texture, making it a good filler plant. Mix Russian sage with coarser-textured plants, such as purple coneflower and black-eyed Susan.

My Personal Favorites
'Little Spire' has all the beauty of Russian Sage in a smaller package. It grows 30 inches tall with the same attractive leaves and flowers of the full-size plant. 'Longin' is narrower and more upright than the species. The leaves are silver, but not as finely divided. Try growing 'Filigran' for a more compact, 30-inch-tall, and finer-textured plant. 'Blue Spire' Russian sage produces a profusion of violet-blue flowers on 4 foot plants.

Salvia
Salvia species

When, Where, and How to Plant
Plant bare-root salvias in the spring after the danger of severe weather has passed. Plant hardened-off, container-grown, and field-potted perennials any time during the growing season. Grow salvia in moist soil with good drainage. Plants tend to flop in excess shade and rich soils. Space plants 18 inches apart.

Growing Tips
Perennial salvia performs best in moist, well-drained soil. Once established, the plants will tolerate dry conditions. They grow better and flower longer in cool temperatures and moist soil. Mulch the soil with a 1- to 2-inch layer of organic material such as cocoa bean shells, twice shredded bark, shredded leaves, or pine needles. Mulch helps to conserve moisture, keep soil cool, and reduce weed problems. Avoid excess fertilizer than can lead to floppy growth and poor flowering.

Care
Deadhead salvia to extend the bloom time. Remove the faded flower stems back to the side buds and stems. Prune salvia back halfway after flowering. Some salvia become floppy and open in the center during flowering. In that case, skip the deadheading and prune plants back after the first flush of flowers. Keep the soil moist after pruning. Leave plants standing for winter to increase hardiness. The overwintering stems capture snow for mulch and are less likely than cut stems to collect water and freeze. Divide overgrown salvia in spring.

Companion Planting and Design
Use the taller species as background plants. Salvias are nice, long-blooming plants for the perennial garden. Combine them with threadleaf coreopsis, Rudbeckia, daylilies, and lamb's ears.

My Personal Favorites
There are several species and hybrids called perennial sage. Select a cultivar that holds it shape and is best suited for your landscape. The sky blue flowers and reblooming nature of the 18-inch-tall Salvia × superba 'Blue Hill' makes this a must have perennial. 'May Night' ('Mainacht') is a long bloomer that stays nice and compact. It produces indigo-blue flowers on 18-inch-tall plants. 'East Friesland' is another compact form and grows 18 inches tall with dark violet flowers.

Salvia has been a standard plant in perennial gardens for years. The spikes of blue and pink flowers add charm to the garden and color to flower arrangements. Plant a few of these long blooming perennials near the window or patio so you can enjoy the butterflies and hummingbirds that come to visit. This plant also has an interesting history outside the garden. People have used this for healing problems with the liver, stomach, and heart as well as controlling fever and plague. You are more likely to use its perennial cousin Salvia officinalis outside the garden This is the sage usually grown in the herb garden and used for cooking. I often use it in perennial gardens. The colorful leaves and interesting texture make it a nice edging or specimen plant.

Other Common Names
Perennial Salvia, Perennial Sage

Bloom Period and Seasonal Color
Summer blooms in blue, violet, and rose-pink.

Mature Height × Spread
2 to 3 ft. × 3 to 4 ft.

Sedum
Sedum species

Sedums have long been known and used for their ability to grow in difficult locations. Many of the newer sedums are being grown for their impressive flowers and colorful foliage. Sedum × 'Autumn Joy' is probably the most popular sedum on the market, though 'Purple Emperor' (see My Personal Favorites) is on its heels. The thick, fleshy leaves of 'Autumn Joy' are topped with large, flat-flower clusters in late summer. They start out pale pink, deepen to a rosy red, and then turn a rust color after the first frost. The dried seedheads persist, adding interest to the winter landscape. Two-row stonecrop, Sedum spurium, and orange stonecrop, Sedum kamtschaticum, are low growing and have long been used in rock gardens and as ground covers.

Other Common Name
Stonecrop

Bloom Period and Seasonal Color
Summer and fall blooms in yellow, pink, red, and white.

Mature Height × Spread
2 to 24 in. × 2 to 24 in.

When, Where, and How to Plant
Plant bare-root sedums in the spring after the danger of severe weather has passed. Plant hardened-off, container-grown, and field-potted perennials any time during the growing season. Sedums are tough plants that tolerate a wide range of conditions. They grow best in well-drained soil. Some sedums can tolerate light shade, but they will become open and leggy in heavy shade. Sedums will tolerate heavy clay soil as long as they are not kept excessively wet.

Growing Tips
Sedums are low-maintenance plants. Water new plants often enough to keep the soil moist but not wet. Established plants are very drought tolerant. Water these thoroughly during extended periods of drought. Avoid overwatering and overfertilizing, which can lead to floppy growth and root rot.

Care
Divide overgrown sedums any time during the season. Spring division will allow plants to get established before summer and fall bloom. Dig, divide, and replant by September to help them get established before winter. Some of the large sedums like 'Autumn Joy' can become floppy. Grow in full sun with well-drained soil to avoid this problem. Control floppiness on problem plants with proper pruning. Pinch back 8 inch tall stems to 4 inches in June. Let the plants stand for winter interest. Railroad enthusiasts harvest dried flowers to use as small scale trees in their railway landscape.

Companion Planting and Design
Sedum × 'Autumn Joy' and 'Purple Emperor' can be used as an edging plant in rose and perennial gardens. Used as a specimen or en masse, it gives an impressive fall flower display. Use the low-growing sedums in rock gardens or as ground covers. Combine sedums with roses, low-growing grasses, daylilies, and yucca.

My Personal Favorite
'Purple Emperor' sedum provides contrast and season-long interest. The combination of smoky purple-red foliage and dusty-red flowers on a 15-inch plant has captured the eye of many gardeners. 'Vera Jameson' is another purple-leafed plant. The round leaves and pink star shaped flowers form a colorful mound in the perennial garden.

Shasta Daisy

Chrysanthemum × superbum

When, Where, and How to Plant

Plant bare-root shasta daisies in the spring after the danger of severe weather has passed. Plant hardened-off, container-grown, and field-potted perennials in the spring or early summer. Grow shasta daisies in full-sun, moist, well-drained soils. Good drainage is important for winter survival. Space plants 18 to 24 inches apart.

Growing Tips

Keep the soil moist, but not wet, throughout the growing season. Water established plants thoroughly whenever the top few inches of soil are crumbly and moist. Mulch the soil to conserve water, keep the roots cool, and suppress weeds. Keep shasta daisies healthy with a light fertilization in the spring.

Care

Shasta daisies tend to be short lived. They do great for several years, and then one spring they don't come back. Regular dividing seems to keep the plants vigorous and prolongs their life. Divide shasta daisies in early spring every two to three years. Staking is often needed for the species and taller cultivars. Spring pruning will help encourage more compact growth. Pinch back tall cultivars to 6 inches in late May or early June. This will delay flowering by one to two weeks but eliminates the need for staking. Deadheading will prolong blooms. Cut faded flowers back to side buds. Prune back plants to the new growth once flowering has finished. This will encourage more leaf growth with some sporadic blooms throughout the remainder of the season.

Companion Planting and Design

Shasta daisies provide a long season of bloom. Use them in cottage, perennial, and cutting gardens. They combine well with perennial salvia, veronicas, yarrow, coreopsis, beebalm, and ornamental grasses.

My Personal Favorites

Northern gardeners should consider 'Alaska' shasta daisy. It tends to be longer lived, benefits from staking or pruning, and is hardy to Zone 4. 'Becky' and 'Switzerland' are tall cultivars that do not need staking. 'Snow Lady' is an AAS winner that grows 10 to 18 inches tall with single flowers. 'Silver Princess' is another compact plant. It grows 12 inches tall and produces lots of flowers.

Shasta daisies provide a profusion of white flowers from summer until frost. The large daisy-like flowers are good for cutting, attracting butterflies, or providing a long season of bloom in the garden. The plant produces plenty of flowers to enjoy indoors and out. Originally named Chrysanthemum × superbum, *it was one of the many members of the* Chrysanthemum *group to be renamed. Shasta daisy became* Leucanthemum × superba; *however, the name change was appealed and the plant is once again* Chrysanthemum × superbum. *You may see it listed both ways. The common name Shasta Daisy goes back to its place of origin. Luther Burbank, credited for its introduction, did much of his breeding and research in California near the white peaks of Mount Shasta. The white flowers of the daisy were reminiscent of the snow covered mountain peak.*

Other Common Name

Daisy

Bloom Period and Seasonal Color

Summer until frost blooms in white with yellow center.

Mature Height × Spread

1 to 3 ft. × 1 ft.

Zones

Hardy to Zone 4

Veronica
Veronica species

Veronicas are versatile plants that fit into many garden situations. Veronica is native to Europe and Russia. Spike speedwell, Veronica spicata, grows 10 to 36 inches tall and has spikes of white, blue, or red flowers. The 'Red Fox' cultivar flowers for five to six weeks. It grows 15 inches tall and does not need staking. I can't say the same for 'Blue Fox'. The cultivar 'Icicle' produces white flowers most of the summer and is 18 to 24 inches tall. Woolly speedwell, Veronica spicata subsp. incana, has blue flowers and gray leaves. Harebell or prostrate speedwell, Veronica prostata, is a creeping form. It forms a mat 6 inches high and 16 inches wide. Veronica austriaca subsp. teucrium 'Crater Lake Blue' forms a mat 12 to 15 inches tall and wide with beautiful blue flowers in early summer.

Other Common Name
Speedwell

Bloom Period and Seasonal Color
Late spring to summer blooms in blue, red, and white.

Mature Height × Spread
4 to 36 in. × 6 to 24 in.

When, Where, and How to Plant
Plant bare-root veronicas in the spring after the danger of severe weather has passed. Plant hardened-off, container-grown, and field-potted perennials any time during the growing season. Plants tend to flop open in the center when grown in heavy shade. Most veronicas prefer full to part sun but will tolerate partial shade. They all need well-drained soils, especially for winter. Space plants 18 to 24 inches apart.

Growing Tips
Water established plants thoroughly whenever the top few inches of soil are crumbly. Mulch to keep the well-drained soil moist and weed-free. Use organic materials such as cocoa bean shells, twice-shredded bark, shredded leaves, or pine needles. Proper soil preparation and top-dressing with compost is usually enough to keep the plants healthy and attractive. Avoid excess nitrogen, which can increase floppy growth and decrease bloom.

Care
The upright types of veronica tend to open in the center and flop. Select cultivars with sturdier stems that resist flopping. Staking will help keep taller cultivars upright and attractive during blooming. Or cut them back by half after flowering. The new growth forms a compact and attractive mound. Deadhead to extend the flower display. Clip off faded flowers back to side buds or leaves. Pruning should be done after this second flush of flowers. Divide floppy and overgrown veronicas in the spring. Most cultivars benefit from being divided every two or three years.

Companion Planting and Design
The lower growing types are good edging plants and ground covers. Use the mat type between steppers for added interest. The upright types add color to the cutting, butterfly, and perennial garden. Combine with threadleaf coreopsis, Rudbeckias, and ornamental grasses.

My Personal Favorites
Veronica × 'Royal Candles' has rich violet-blue flowers that look like candles. It blooms May through June and is hardy to Zone 4. Deadhead for repeat bloom. The Perennial Plant of the Year for 1993 was Veronica 'Sunny Border Blue'. It produces light blue, spike-like flowers.

Virginia Bluebell
Mertensia pulmonarioides

When, Where, and How to Plant

Virginia bluebells are available as plants or tuberous roots. I find most gardeners get their bluebells from friends and family who are thinning out these plants. Plant tuberous roots in spring or fall with the growing point 1 to 2 inches below the soil surface. Plant hardened-off, container-grown, and field-potted perennials any time during the growing season. The leaves die back in late spring, so summer and fall planting is a matter of trust. Virginia bluebells prefer shady locations with moist, organic soil. Space plants 12 inches apart.

Growing Tips

Virginia bluebells are low-maintenance plants. They either grow and take over the area or never quite get established. Proper soil preparation and post-transplant care will aid in establishment. Make sure new plantings receive enough water to keep the soil moist but not wet. Water established plants thoroughly whenever the top few inches of soil are crumbly and moist. Mulch with shredded leaves or other organic matter to improve the soil and keep it moist.

Care

Pull weeds as soon as they appear. Divide bluebells in early spring as new growth emerges. Regular dividing will prevent the bluebells from taking over the garden. Leaf spot is an occasional problem in extremely wet seasons. Clean up and a bit drier weather will usually control this seldom seen problem.

Companion Planting and Design

Plant them at the edge of a wooded area or naturalized shrub planting. Yellow daffodils and bluebells make a nice color combination. The large leaves of Virginia bluebells die back soon after flowering and leave empty space in the garden. Mix Virginia bluebells with later emerging perennials like hosta and ferns to fill in these voids.

My Personal Favorites

Add a few white-flowering 'Alba' for a change of pace. They look nice mixed with the blue flowered bluebells or combined with other spring-blooming bulbs. Oyster plant, *Mertensia maritima*, is low growing, 4 inches tall, and hardy throughout the state. It has blue-green leaves and bright blue flowers in early summer.

The leaves of Virginia bluebells, also listed as Mertensia virginica, *peek through the cold soil in early spring. The heart-shaped leaves quickly expand as the plant reaches a height of 12 to 24 inches. The pink flower buds open into blue bell-shaped flowers. Virginia bluebell is one of the early spring bloomers that let us know winter is on its way out. Gardeners either love or hate Virginia bluebells that often do a little too well in the garden. Some gardeners don't like the way the plant creeps into areas it was not invited. I find a little digging and dividing keep it in check.* Mertensia paniculata *is native to the forests of Minnesota. This relative of Virgina bluebells can grow up to 3 feet tall. The bell-shaped flowers start out white or pink and turn blue.*

Other Common Name
Bluebell

Bloom Period and Seasonal Color
Early spring blooms in blue.

Mature Height × Spread
12 to 24 in. × 18 in.

Yarrow

Achillea filipendulina

The golden flowers of fernleaf yarrow can be enjoyed in the garden or indoors in fresh and dried flower arrangements. The fern-like foliage has a spicy odor and adds interest to the perennial garden from spring through early winter. Fernleaf yarrow, Achillea filipendulina, *grows 3 to 4 feet tall and seldom needs staking. Common yarrow,* Achillea millefolium, *is a plant you will see listed in weed books, wildflower books, and garden catalogues. It is native to some of Minnesota's prairies but can become a weed in the landscape. Gardeners like the red, yellow, white, and orange flowers. Select a non-invasive cultivar to minimize your workload. Use* Achillea millefolium *with caution. It took me twelve years to weed out seedlings of 'Summer Pastels'.* Achillea *was named for Achilles, the hero of Homer's Illiad. Supposedly he fed yarrow to his soldiers to help clot the blood from their wounds. Researchers have found blood clotting chemicals in the plant.*

Other Common Name
Fernleaf Yarrow

Bloom Period and Seasonal Color
Summer blooms in yellow, white, cream, pink, red, orange, and salmon.

Mature Height × Spread
1 to 4 ft. × 3 ft. and spreading

When, Where, and How to Plant
Plant bare-root yarrow in the spring after the danger of severe weather has passed. Plant hardened-off, container-grown, and field-potted perennials any time during the growing season. Grow yarrow in full sun with well-drained soil. Yarrow is able to thrive in hot, dry locations where other plants are lucky to survive. Plant yarrow at the same level it was growing in the nursery or container. Space plants 2 to 3 feet apart.

Growing Tips
These plants tend to flop when grown in shade or overfertilized gardens. Water new plantings often enough to keep the soil moist but not wet. Established plants are drought tolerant. Water during extended drought when the top few inches of soil are dry. Mulching helps conserve moisture and suppress weeds. Avoid excess fertilization, which leads to floppy growth.

Care
Deadhead yarrow to remove unattractive seedheads and to encourage longer blooming. This also reduces reseeding of the more invasive yarrow species. Prune plants back to fresh new growth after the final bloom. The foliage will continue to look attractive into the winter. Fernleaf yarrow grown in the proper conditions does not need staking. Common yarrow will become leggy and topple over without pruning. Prune plants back halfway in early June and after the first and second flush of flowers. This will also prevent seeding. Divide overgrown, leggy, or poorly flowering plants in the spring. Common yarrow benefits from division every two to three years.

Companion Planting and Design
Combine fernleaf yarrow with Shasta daisies, garden phlox, salvia, veronicas, and ornamental grasses. Use them in the perennial garden, naturalized gardens, or areas where nothing else will grow.

My Personal Favorites
Fernleaf yarrow, 'Coronation Gold' is a shorter cultivar that is very heat tolerant. It makes an excellent dried flower. The hybrid *Achillea* 'Moonshine' has bright yellow flowers and silvery gray feather-like foliage. This compact plant grows 24 inches tall and works well in perennial gardens.

When, Where, and How to Plant

Plant bare-root yucca in the spring after the danger of severe weather has passed. Plant hardened-off, container-grown, and field-potted perennials any time during the growing season. I prefer spring or early summer to give the plants time to get established before winter. Grow yucca in well-drained soil. Space plants 24 inches apart.

Growing Tips

New plantings benefit from regular watering until the root system becomes established. Once established, plants are very heat and drought tolerant. Water established plants during extended droughts whenever the top few inches of soil is dry. Proper soil preparation and top-dressing with compost every other year will keep the plants healthy. Avoid excess nitrogen which can prevent flowering.

Care

Yuccas thrive and put on the best flower display during hot, dry summers. Clip off faded flowers for a neater appearance. Leave the evergreen leaves and seedheads in place for winter interest. The new growth in the spring will mask the fading leaves. Or for a tidier look, remove older leaves as new leaves appear. Yucca will occasionally suffer from leaf spot diseases, mostly in cool wet seasons. Remove infected leaves to reduce the spread. Cleanup is usually an adequate control. Deer like to eat this plant. Protect the plants if deer are a problem in your landscape.

Companion Planting and Design

I find yucca challenging to blend into the landscape. Try using it as a vertical accent in the garden or shrub bed. The tall flower stalk is quite impressive and will temporarily steal attention from the rest of the landscape. Use the yellow-variegated variety with black-eyed Susans or threadleaf coreopsis for a bit of color echoing. Use any of the yuccas in the corner of the garden or with a boulder to create a focal point.

My Personal Favorites

'Golden Sword' has a yellow stripe down the middle of the green leaves. 'Bright edge' is just the opposite: the yellow is along the edge of the green leaves. 'Variegata' has blue-green leaves with white margins. These become pink-tinged in the winter.

Yucca may bring visions of the desert, and those are the conditions it prefers: hot, dry areas where other plants fail to thrive. In fact, a walk by the yucca planting at the Minnesota Landscape Arboretum makes you feel like you were transported to the southwest. They combined yucca with prickly pear cactus and threw in a few boulders as accents. Proper planning is important when introducing this strong architectural feature into the garden. The sword-shaped leaves, vertical growth habit, and the large cluster of bell-shaped flowers held on long stems 5 to 8 feet above the ground can be challenging to blend into a Minnesota garden. Soften the strong features with airy plants like threadleaf coreopsis or complement them with other bold plants like allium.

Other Common Name
Adam's needle

Bloom Period and Seasonal Color
July blooms in white; evergreen foliage.

Mature Height × Spread
2 to 3 ft. in foliage × 3 ft. wide up to 12 ft. tall in bloom

Roses *for Minnesota*

For years, roses have been providing fragrance and beauty to Minnesota landscapes. There are hundreds of varieties to choose from in just about every size and color. No wonder it was selected as our national floral emblem in 1987.

The beauty, fragrance, and sentimental appeal of roses make them a favorite among gardeners. The pest problems and lack of hardiness of some of the most beautiful roses make them a great source of frustration as well. As a plant doctor, I have the opportunity to advise many gardeners about what is eating, discoloring, or killing their roses. In addition, many of the popular hybrid tea roses require more care than most gardeners are willing to give.

So why include roses? They provide a long season of bloom in the landscape and colorful bouquets indoors. With proper siting and care, you can keep pest problems to a minimum and increase winter survival. Many gardeners are willing to put forth a little extra effort to grow spectacular hybrid teas. Some rose growers forego the pampering and treat the less hardy roses as annuals. They plant, tend, and enjoy the colorful display throughout the season. If the plants survive the winter, it is an added benefit. If not, it is a chance to try some new cultivars. Others, like me, focus on the hardier, more pest resistant roses. Keep checking catalogs and garden centers for showier, hardier, and more pest-resistant plants. More varieties are being introduced every year.

For best results, roses should be grown in moist, well-drained soil where they receive good air circulation and at least six hours of sun per day. Select a site with morning sun, such as an east-facing location, that will dry morning dew off the leaves, thus helping reduce disease problems. Look for a protected spot to help them survive cold Minnesota winters.

Buying Roses

Roses are available from catalogues, garden centers, and nurseries. The best selection is found in garden catalogues that specialize in roses. Roses are available bare root and in containers. Bare-root roses are often sold according to grades 1, 1^1/$_2$, and 2. Grade 1 plants are the most expensive with 3 or 4 heavy canes that are about 18 inches long. Grade 1^1/$_2$ and 2 plants have a smaller root system and fewer canes that are shorter and thinner. Store bare-root plants in a cool, shaded, frost-free location until they can be planted outdoors. Heel them in, outdoors in a protected location, or pack the roots in peat moss or sawdust to keep them from drying out.

Early-sprouting plants require special

Hybrid Tea Rose
'Double Delight'

handling. Pot up bare-root plants that have begun to grow in storage. Move these and any greenhouse-grown or early-sprouting container plants to a sunny location free from frost. Provide water as needed. Gradually introduce the plants (harden off) to the outdoor conditions. Plant outdoors once danger of frost has passed.

Planting Roses

Soil preparation is critical to successful rose growing. Spread 2 to 4 inches of organic matter over the soil surface and work it into the top 6 to 12 inches of soil. Plant bare-root roses in the spring while they are still dormant. Soak the roots for twenty-four hours before planting. Container plants can be planted any time the ground is not frozen. Plant early in the season to allow container-grown plants to get well established before winter.

Many roses are grafted. A bud from the desired plant is attached to a hardy root system. The bud graft is the swollen knob where all the branches are formed. This portion of the plant is very susceptible to winter damage. Plant the graft 2 inches below the soil surface for added winter protection. Roses grown on their own roots can be planted at the same level they were growing in the container. Dig the planting hole at least 2 times wider than the root system. For bare-root roses, create a cone of soil in the middle of the planting hole. Set the roots on top of the cone so the graft is 2 inches below the surface and the roots are positioned over the cone and throughout the hole. Container roses should also be handled with care since they may have been recently potted and lack a cohesive rootball. Minimize root disturbance by cutting away the pot. First, cut off the bottom of the container. Set the plant (pot and all) in the planting hole, making sure the graft will be 2 inches below the soil surface. Now slice the side of the pot and peel it away, leaving the rootball intact. Fill the hole with soil and water. Mulch and keep the soil moist, but not wet, throughout the growing season.

Maintenance

Roses do best when they receive 1 inch of water per week from rainfall or irrigation. Mulch roses with an organic material to conserve moisture, reduce weed problems, and improve the soil.

Test the soil to determine its nutrient content and then fertilize roses according to the test recommendations. In lieu of a test, apply a low-nitrogen fertilizer in spring once new growth is well established, and again four to six weeks later. Complete fertilizers such as 10-10-10 and 12-12-12 can be used in soils deficient in phosphorus and potassium. Additional fertilizing can be done as needed, but do not fertilize after August 1 since late-season fertilization can contribute to winter damage.

Pruning requirements vary for each type of rose. (Refer to individual entries for details.) For all roses, remove the suckers that form from the rootstock of grafted roses. Cut suckers below the soil to discourage resprouting.

Cutting roses for arrangements and deadheading faded flowers is another form of pruning. When properly done, pruning will encourage strong, new growth and repeat blooms. Prune flowering stems back to the first 5-leaflet leaf. You can prune back farther on established plants, but be sure to always leave at least two 5-leaflet leaves behind.

Pests

Roses are subject to many insect and disease problems. Select the most pest-resistant cultivars available. Black spot, powdery mildew, and rust are the most common disease problems. Remove infected leaves as soon as they appear. Fall cleanup will also help reduce the source of disease for the next growing season. Many gardeners spray disease-susceptible plants with a fungicide on a regular basis. New plant-derived, more environmentally friendly products are being introduced on the market. Check with your local garden center for availability in your area. Insect pests including aphids, mites, leafhoppers, beetles, sawflies, and caterpillars feed on the leaves of rose bushes. Aphids, mites, and leafhoppers suck plant juices, causing leaf discoloration and curling. Several applications of insecticidal soap will control these pests. Handpicking or applying insecticides appropriate for roses will take care of the others that chew holes in leaves or flowers. Deer and rabbits are also fond of roses. Using scare tactics, repellents, and fencing may provide relief from these bigger pests. Whenever using pesticides, select a product specifically for use on roses. And always read and follow label directions carefully.

Winter Protection

There are as many ways to protect roses from winter weather as there are rose gardeners, but proper timing is the key to the success of each method. We often protect the roses when WE get cold NOT when the roses need it. Wait to cover rose bushes after we have had a week of consistently freezing temperatures. Start removing winter protection in the spring when the mercury again starts hovering near freezing. Limit fall pruning. Remove only just what is needed to apply winter protection. Save extensive pruning until spring.

Hybrid tea roses need extra care to survive Minnesota winters. There are several methods for protecting roses. You can do nothing and hope for the best. Some winters this actually works. I find the soil mound method works well. Wait until that week of cold to start mulching plants. Loosely tie the soil mound method works well. Wait until that week of cold to start mulching plants. Loosely tie the canes. Many gardeners surround the plants with chicken wire sunk into the ground (prior to the ground freezing) to hold the soil and mulch in place and keep rodents out. Cover the bottom 8 to 10 inches of the rose plant with soil. (You may need to raid the compost pile, bring in soil, or dig it from an unfrozen bare spot in your landscape.) Let the soil mound freeze and then mulch with evergreen branches, marsh hay, or straw.

For rose beds, I prefer the leaf method. Before the ground freezes, surround planting beds with 4-foot-high fence of hardware cloth. Sink the fencing several inches into the soil to keep out the rodents. Prune roses back to 18 inches once the ground freezes, then fill the rose bed with 3 feet of tightly packed dry leaves. Remove the leaves in spring and recycle them in your compost pile or use as mulch in the garden.

Rose cones are a favorite but often misused technique. The same timing applies to this method. Prune back roses to fit under the cone. Mulch roses and cover with cone. Anchor to hold the cone in place. Be sure to ventilate cones on sunny winter days.

The Minnesota Tip method is much more labor intensive but has the greatest survival rate. In fall use a spade to cut through the roots, about a foot from the stems, on one side of the plant. Tip the plant over so it is laying flat on the ground. Cover with soil. Once the soil covering freezes, mulch with straw or evergreen boughs for added insulation. This method works well for climbers and tree roses.

Roses growing in pots need even more care. In fall, sink the pot in a vacant part of the garden. Once cold weather arrives use one of the above winter protection methods. Or move the rose, pot and all, into an unheated garage. Pack insulating materials around the pot for added insulation. Water the soil anytime the soil is thawed and dry. Or move the plant indoors into a cool sunny location and grow it like a houseplant for the winter.

Tree roses are grafted in two places and need special winter care. Grow them in a pot and winter as above or follow the recommendations for winter care of climbing roses. A little extra work but worth it if you want your tree rose to survive the winter.

Winter damaged roses may die back to ground level. Those growing on their own roots will recover and eventually regain the mature size. Grafted roses suffer a different fate. If the graft union survives the plant will send out new growth with the desirable flowers. If the tender bud graft dies and the roots survives you end up with thick, thorny stems and no or red flowers. You can either enjoy the surprise or replace it with the desired rose.

There are many wonderful roses, too many to mention here. Look for hardy, pest resistant introductions that fit your landscape and garden design. Contact your nearby Botanical Garden for their list of favorite roses, check out the All-American Rose Selections (http//www.rose.org/) and American Rose Society (http://www.ars.org/) websites and then start creating your own list of favorites.

Climbing Rose

Rosa × hybrida

The climbing rose is a jack-of-all-trades in Mother Nature's garden. An arbor covered with a colorful and fragrant climbing rose can provide a warm welcome to your guests. Another climbing rose can provide a discreet and attractive disguise for an unattractive, old chain link fence. The possibilities are endless. Use climbers as vertical accents, flowering specimens, or screens. Climbing roses are grouped into two major categories. The ramblers are big, fast-growing, hardy roses. Rambling roses are an old variety, a kind everyone's grandmother seemed to grow. They bloom profusely early in the season and require very little care and no winter protection. Rambling rose flowers are small and grow in clusters. New disease-resistant and repeat-blooming hybrids are being introduced. The large-flowered climbing roses grow slower. Climbers come from a variety of sources including mutations of hybrid tea, grandiflora, and multiflora roses.

Other Common Names
Ramblers and Pillars

Bloom Period and Seasonal Color
Once or repeat blooming in summer; various flower colors including red, pink, salmon, yellow, and white.

Mature Height and Spread
6 to 20 ft. × 3 to 6 ft.

When, Where, and How to Plant

Plant bare-root and container-grown climbing roses early in the season. Climbers, like all roses, grow best in full sun and moist, well-drained soil. Plant climbers near a fence, trellis, or arbor that is large and sturdy enough to handle the size and weight of the mature plant. Grafted climbers should be planted with the graft union 2 inches below the soil surface. Non-grafted climbers can be planted at the same level as they were grown in the nursery. See the chapter introduction for more on planting. Plant climbers 4 to 10 feet apart.

Growing Tips

Train and attach climbers to their support. Loosely tie the stems to the support with twine. Keep the training simple, since many climbers must be removed and protected from our harsh winter conditions.

Care

Only prune dead and damaged wood during the first few years. All climbers should be pruned after flowering, and plants should not be cut back for winter protection. Each spring, cut only the dead stems back to ground level. After blooming you can remove 1/3 of the older canes. Single bloomers can be pruned back by 2/3 of their size. Trim side branches by 2/3 also. Prune after flowering throughout the season. This improves air circulation and reduces problems with powdery mildew. After temperatures hover near the freezing mark for about a week, remove non-hardy climbers from their support. Tie canes together to make the job more manageable. Bend or tip the roses over and lay them on the ground. Cover the entire plant with soil. Once the soil covering freezes, mulch with straw, marsh hay, or evergreen branches.

Companion Planting and Design

Use roses as a backdrop for perennial gardens, as a fragrant screen for a patio or deck, or to cover an arbor. Train them along a fence or other structure.

My Personal Favorites

'William Baffin', a large shrub rose that can be trained as a climber, is a low-maintenance repeat bloomer with deep pink flowers and good pest resistance that needs no winter protection. 'New Dawn' is hardy, disease-resistant, and has survived unprotected in Zone 4.

Floribunda

Rosa × hybrida

When, Where, and How to Plant

Plant your floribundas early in the season in a sunny, well-drained location. Use floribunda roses in mass plantings, hedges, or borders. Or add them to your perennial gardens, shrub beds, or other rose plantings. If your floribunda is grafted, plant it with the graft union 2 inches below the soil surface. Non-grafted floribundas can be planted at the same level as they were grown in the nursery. Follow planting guidelines in the introductions to roses.

Growing Tips

Many of these, like hybrid teas, are subject to insect and disease problems. Monitor plants throughout the season. Remove any insects or diseased leaves as soon as they are found. A thorough clean-up in fall will also reduce future pest problems. Any pesticides you use should be specific to roses.

Care

Provide adequate water and fertilization. Prune floribunda roses in the spring as buds swell but before growth begins—about the same time the forsythia bloom. Prune plants back to 10 inches if any above-ground growth survived. Make pruning cuts 1/4 inch above an outward-facing bud. Otherwise, prune plants to ground level. You can seal pruning cuts to keep out cane borers. Deadhead roses throughout the season to encourage new blooms and thick sturdy growth. Stop deadheading toward the end of the season to slow down new growth and help with winter hardiness. Though hardier than hybrid teas, many floribundas benefit from winter protection. (See the chapter introduction.) Some gardeners choose to do nothing.

Planting Combinations and Design

Mix floribunda roses with your perennials or shrubs for a little extra summer color. A few floribundas can liven up any foundation planting.

My Personal Favorite

'Nearly Wild' (often listed as a shrub rose) has been a popular choice in recent years. This 2- to 3-foot shrub is covered with medium pink flowers in late spring or early summer and again later in the season. Its small size, light fragrance, and Zone 4 hardiness make it a good addition to most Minnesota landscapes.

Floribundas produce long-blooming clusters of flowers on stems suitable for cutting. These hybrids resulted from crossing polyantha and hybrid tea roses. The polyanthas gave these plants increased hardiness, while the hybrid teas gave them larger attractive flowers. Both varieties contributed to the floribundas long blooming season. This group of roses requires much the same care as hybrid teas. Both suffer from a wide range of pest problems and most floribundas, like hybrid teas, are grafted and require winter protection. But don't let this scare you away. This small shrub packs a lot of punch throughout the season. Select one of the hardier, more pest-resistant cultivars available in a variety of colors. And don't forget to stop and smell the roses – many of the floribundas are fragrant.

Bloom Period and Season Color
Summer with a variety of flower colors available.

Mature Height and Spread
3 ft. × 3 ft.

Grandiflora
Rosa × hybrida

Grandifloras are a relatively recent introduction to the rose family. These, along with the hybrid teas, polyanthas, and floribundas, make up the modern roses. Their name gives you a clue to their best attribute, big (grand) flowers (flora). These hybrids were developed by crossing hybrid teas and floribunda roses. The flowers are similar in shape to the hybrid tea and grow on long stems making them good for cutting. The long lasting flowers, extended bloom time, and increased hardiness are compliments of the floribunda parent. Individual flowers are smaller than the hybrid teas yet larger than the floribundas. They are usually double and grow in small clusters. Most lack fragrance, but a variety of colors is available. Watch for the best flower display later in the season.

Bloom Period and Season Color
Summer blooms with a variety of solids, blends, and bicolor flowers.

Mature Height and Spread
4 to 5 ft. × 3 to 4 ft.

When, Where, and How to Plant
Plant grandifloras early in the season, which gives the rose time to get established before winter. Like all roses they prefer full sun and moist, well-drained soil. Good air circulation will help reduce disease problems. These large plants can be used as background plants in a flower garden or mixed with other roses and shrubs. Prepare the soil prior to planting. Grandifloras are usually grafted and should be planted with the graft union 2 inches below the soil surface.

Growing Tips
Deadhead roses throughout the season to encourage new blooms and thick, sturdy growth. Stop deadheading toward the end of the season to slow down new growth and help with winter hardiness.

Care
Water and fertilize as recommended. Do not fertilize after August 1. Mulch the soil to conserve moisture and control weeds. Prune roses in the spring as buds swell, before growth begins. Start by removing dead and diseased wood. Prune back to healthy live portions of the canes where the center of the stem is white. This may be to ground level some years. If needed, prune the roses back to the desired height. Next, thin out the center of the plant. Remove old and crossed canes first. Cut back stems 1/4 inch above an outward-facing bud. You may want to seal pruning cuts to keep borers out. Winter protection is needed statewide. (See chapter introduction for details). Grandifloras, like many other roses, are subject to insect and disease problems. The susceptibility varies by cultivar. Watch plants for signs of insects and disease and control as needed.

Companion planting and Design
Grandiflora roses are great combined with a white picket or ornamental iron fence, and their structure make a welcoming entrance, a colorful backdrop, or a focal point in the landscape.

My Personal Favorites
Like many people, I vote for 'Queen Elizabeth'. This grandiflora was the second most popular rose (after the hybrid tea 'Peace') of the twentieth century. Nearly thornless, it produces pink flowers through most of the growing season.

Hybrid Tea

Rosa × hybrida

When, Where, and How to Plant

Like all roses, hybrid teas benefit from early season planting in sunny, well-drained locations. Grow hybrid teas in rose gardens, in containers, as specimen plants, or incorporate them into planting beds. Prepare the soil prior to planting. Hybrid teas are usually grafted onto a hardy rootstock and should be planted with the graft union 2 inches below the soil surface. New own-root (non-grafted) hybrids are just entering the market. See the chapter introductions for general rose planting guidelines.

Growing Tips

Deadhead roses throughout the season to encourage new blooms and thick, sturdy growth. Stop deadheading toward the end of the season to slow down new growth and improve winter hardiness.

Care

Water and fertilize as needed. Prune hybrid tea roses in the spring as buds swell but before growth begins. Rose growth begins about the same time the forsythia bloom. Start by removing dead and diseased wood. Prune back to healthy, live portions of the canes where the center of the stem is white. Some years, the pruning may go to ground level. Prune the roses to the desired height then thin out the center of the plant. Remove old and crossed canes first. Cut stems back 1/4 inch above an outward-facing bud. You can seal pruning cuts to keep out borers. Hybrid teas need winter protection throughout Minnesota, though some gardeners choose to do nothing.

Companion Planting and Design

Take your cue from the florist and mix baby's breath with your hybrid teas. You have a ready made bouquet right in the garden. Or edge the rose bed with one of the tame catmints such as 'Walker's Low' and 'Six Hills Giant' or annual sweet alyssum.

My Personal Favorites

With hundreds of hybrid teas on the market and more being added each year, it is impossible to pick just one. The wonderful fragrance of the dark red 'Mister Lincoln', 'Double Delight', and 'Veterans Honor', and the wonderful blended colors of 'Tropicana', 'Peace', and 'Tropical Sunset' place these on my list of favorites.

When you say roses, hybrid teas are the plants most people picture. Their beautiful, large flowers put on quite a show in the garden or in a vase. But there is a price for their beauty. Hybrid tea roses require some time and effort on your part. If you are willing to do the work, you will be rewarded with flowers throughout the summer. Proper selection, planting, placement, and care will help increase hardiness and decrease pest problems. Consider incorporating one or more of the All America Rose Selections (AARS) winners in your landscape. These award-winning roses were tested at more than 25 sites throughout the country. Test and display gardens and their locations are available at the AARS website: www.rose.org. Winners were selected as the best roses based upon flower form, pest resistance, fragrance, growth habit, and other features.

Other Name

Rose bush

Bloom Period and Seasonal Color

Summer in a wide range of colors, blends, and bicolors.

Mature Height and Spread

4 to 5 ft. tall × 3ft. wide

Miniature Rose
Rosa × hybrida

Miniatures are just that: miniature versions of hybrid teas or floribunda roses. Miniatures are usually sold as container plants. They are valued for their hardiness, free-flowering nature, and versatility. These small roses will fit in any landscape. Look for the American Rose Society Award of Excellence next time you shop for miniature roses. Contestants are grown and evaluated over a two year period at designated gardens throughout the United States. Winners are selected for their outstanding performance in such areas as novelty, bud and flower form, plant habit, quantity of blooms, vigor, foliage, and disease/insect resistance. One of these may be just the winner you are looking for.

Bloom Period and Seasonal Color
Summer in a variety of colors.

Mature Height and Spread
6 to 24 in. × 8 to 24 in.

When, Where, and How to Plant
Plant them in spring and early summer to give them time to get established before winter. Plant in full sun and moist, well-drained soil. Try using these small roses as an edging plant in the garden or as a specimen in a rock garden. Their small size makes them perfect for windowboxes or containers. Move container plantings indoors or to a protected location for the winter. Or you may want to try growing miniatures as a flowering houseplant in a south window or under artificial lights. Miniatures are grown on their own roots, so plant them at the same level they were grown in the nursery.

Growing Tips
Even though miniatures are hardier than the hybrid teas, many benefit from some winter protection. This is especially true in northern Minnesota. (See chapter introduction for details.)

Care
Just like all roses, miniatures benefit from adequate water and fertilization. Do not fertilize after August 1. Start pruning miniature roses after winter protection is removed and the buds swell but before growth begins. Prune to open the center by removing twiggy growth. Cut the plants back to the desired height. Make cuts 1/4 inch above an outward-facing bud. You can seal pruning cuts to keep borers out. Deadhead roses throughout the season to encourage new blooms and thick sturdy growth. Stop deadheading toward the end of the season to slow down new growth and help with winter hardiness. Miniatures are subject to insect and disease problems. Susceptibility varies with the cultivar, so reduce problems by selecting the most pest-resistant cultivars available.

Companion Planting and Design
I have combined miniature roses with sweet alyssum, lobelia, and other annuals for an interesting container combination. Or plant them in their own container as an accent on a patio or deck.

My Personal Favorites
The Sunblaze series of miniature roses includes golden yellow, lavender, hot pink, raspberry, and salmon flowering varieties. Most are fragrant and grow to about 2 feet tall. The eye-catching orange scarlet flower of 'Gizmo' and white 'Gourmet Popcorn' blooms are worth considering.

Shrub Rose
Rosa species and hybrids

When, Where, and How to Plant

Shrub roses are usually sold as container plants; however, small plants may be available bare root. Plant bare-root roses in the spring while they are still dormant. Container plants can be planted any time the ground is not frozen. I prefer to plant in the spring and early summer, giving the rose time to get established before winter. These hardier roses are much more tolerant of late-season planting than other roses. Grow shrub roses in full sun and moist, well-drained soil. Their size and growth habit will help determine their suitability for use as climbers, hedges, specimens, borders, and for winter interest. Plant shrub roses at the level they were grown in the nursery.

Growing Tips

Don't deadhead single blooming shrub roses. Allow the fruit (rose hips) to develop and provide interest from summer through fall and winter. Stop deadheading repeat bloomers in the late summer to allow their colorful fruit and hips to develop.

Care

Shrub roses require much less care and less pruning. Fertilize as needed in the spring after new growth has developed. Mulch to conserve moisture and reduce weed problems. Remove dead and crowded stems in the spring before growth begins and cut back older stems to keep growth in bounds. Shrub roses are generally resistant to insects and disease and do not need winter protection. Select one hardy for your part of Minnesota.

Planting Companions and Design

One of my favorite low-maintenance combos was at the Chicago Botanical Gardens. They used Russian sage (*Perovskia atriplicifolia*) in the center of the bed surrounded with a lower growing, repeat blooming rose such as 'Carefree Delight'.

My Personal Favorites

'Knock Out' and 'The Fairy' have to be my two favorite shrub roses. My third, 'William Baffin', is listed under climbing roses. 'Knock Out' has raspberry to cherry-red flowers that bloom all season. No winter protection is needed in southern Minnesota, though some winter dieback has been experienced in northern regions. 'Starry Nights' brightens up the landscape with its white flowers.

Most Minnesota gardeners think of shrub roses as hardy, pest-resistant roses with limited landscape appeal. You may be surprised to find that many shrub roses, especially some of the new introductions, also have showy flowers, longer and repeat bloom, attractive fruit, and good fall color. In general, shrub roses have smaller flowers with fewer petals than the hybrid teas. But their vigor, hardiness, and low maintenance make them a good choice for many gardeners. Some shrub roses bloom only once, while others repeat one or more times throughout the summer. Shrub roses also provide winter interest with their attractive fruit. All roses produce hips (small crabapple-like fruit), but the shrub roses are most prolific, and the hips are on display all winter long. High in vitamin C, the fruits have long been used for jam, jelly, and tea.

Other Common Names
Hardy Rose

Bloom Period and Seasonal Color
Early summer blooms (some repeating throughout) in variety of colors.

Mature Height × Spread
2 to 8 ft. tall and wide

159

Shrubs *for Minnesota*

Picture your landscape filled in with shrubs that provide
structure and year-round interest. Develop a plan
for planting and maintaining the shrubs you
are about to invest your time and money in.
Select the right plant for the location to
minimize maintenance and increase beauty. Make sure the
shrubs you choose will fit the space and tolerate the growing
conditions in your area.

What to Do First

Once you have determined what plants you want and where they will be
placed, do a little preventative maintenance. Call Gopher State One Call at
1-800-252-1166 throughout Minnesota. Gopher State is a free utility-locating service. They will mark
the location of any underground utilities in the planting area. Give them three working days to complete
the task. This is an important step for your safety and pocketbook. Digging into a utility line can be
expensive and even deadly.

Buying and Planting

While waiting for Gopher State One Call, visit a nursery or garden center to select your plants. Store
your plants in a cool, shady location until they can be planted. Mulch the roots of bare-root plants and
the rootballs of balled-and-burlapped plants to keep the roots moist. Water these mulched roots and
container plants daily.

Plant bare-root shrubs as soon as possible after purchase. Dig a shallow hole wide enough to
accommodate the roots. The planting hole should be just deep enough to let you plant the shrub at the
same level it was grown in the nursery. Fill the hole with existing soil and water.

Balled-and-burlapped plants should also be planted as soon as possible after purchase. Dig the
planting hole the same depth as the rootball, but several feet wider. Set the shrub in the hole, remove the
twine, and cut away the burlap. Fill the hole with existing soil and water.

Containerized plants may have been grown in the pot or dug out of the nursery and then potted.
Dig a planting hole the same depth and two to three times wider than the rootball. Container-grown
shrubs should be removed from their pot. Roll the pot on its side or squeeze the container to make it
easier to slide the plant out. Loosen or slice through circling roots. Place the shrub in the hole at the same
depth it was grown in the nursery. Fill the hole with existing soil and water.

Potted plants usually lack a cohesive rootball. Minimize root damage by cutting the bottom off the
pot. Place the shrub, pot and all, in the hole at the same depth it was growing in the nursery. Now cut
away the remainder of the container. Fill the hole with soil and water.

Care

New plantings need help to become established. Be sure they receive about an inch of water each week.
You may have to water if nature doesn't take care of the job. Established shrubs will need to be watered
during drought conditions. Thoroughly water the soil when the top few inches begin to dry. This is

about once a week in clay soils and twice a week in sandy soil. Some container-grown shrubs are planted in soilless mixes. The rootball of these shrubs will dry out faster than the surrounding soil. You will need to water the root system more frequently than the surrounding soil to keep both moist, but not wet.

Mulch the soil to conserve moisture and reduce weed problems. Use a two- to three-inch layer of wood chips, shredded bark, or other organic materials. These help improve the soil as they decompose. Don't bury the base of the shrub and do not use weed barrier fabrics under these organic mulches. Weeds end up growing into the fabric, creating a real mess in several years.

Water and Fertilizing

Wait a year to fertilize new shrub plantings. Follow your soil test recommendations for the type and amount of fertilizer to use. If this information is not available, you can use a nitrogen fertilizer such as 16-8-8 or 21-0-0 at a rate of two pounds per one hundred square feet of shrub beds. I prefer a low nitrogen, slow-release fertilizer like Milorganite. It releases small amounts of fertilizer to the plants throughout the growing season. The formulation is also goof proof, eliminating damage caused by overfertilization. Young shrubs can be fertilized in late fall after the plants are dormant or in early spring before growth begins. Fertilizing every few years encourages rapid growth on young shrubs. Established shrubs need little if any fertilizer.

Pruning

Pruning is a regular part of maintenance. Just be sure you have a plan before taking the pruning saw to your plants. Prune shrubs to remove diseased and damaged branches, encourage flowering, improve bark color, control size, and shape the plants. Spring-flowering plants like lilacs and forsythia should be pruned right after flowering. Others can be pruned any time during the dormant season. I prefer late winter or early spring. That timetable gives you the opportunity to enjoy the plant's winter interest and to repair winter damage at the same time you do routine pruning; it is also better for the plant.

The place you make the cut is also important to the health of the plant. Prune above outward-facing buds, where branches join other branches, or to ground level. These cuts will close more quickly to keep out pests.

Pruning can help correct unattractive growth. You may have seen shrubs with all the leaves at the top and bare stems at the bottom. Use renewal pruning to avoid this problem. Remove about one-third of the older, thicker canes to ground level each year for several years. You can also reduce the height of the remaining stems by one-third. Renovate overgrown shrubs by cutting all the stems back to several inches above the ground. There are some species, however, that will not tolerate this drastic pruning.

Shrubs are often sheared, a process that is easy on the gardener but hard on the plant. Shearing leaves stubs that make perfect entryways for disease and insects. It's better for the plant if you use a hand pruner and selectively remove out-of-bound branches. Hedge plants should be pruned so the top is several inches narrower than the bottom. This allows light to reach all parts of the plants and helps keep leaves on the bottom of the shrub.

With proper selection and care, your shrubs will give you years of enjoyment.

Alpine Currant
Ribes alpinum

Alpine currant hedges are found in both old and new landscapes. Their small leaves, dense growth habit, and tolerance for shearing make them popular. Alpine currants are usually sold as container-grown plants. The flowers are green and go unnoticed. Nurseries typically sell male plants, which are more disease resistant and do not form fruit. I have occasionally seen inedible, red fruit on female alpine currant plants (the female in this photo is blessed with more fruit than average). The fall color is usually a poor yellow. The straw colored twigs and bright white buds add a bit of interest to the winter landscape. Alpine currants can be grown unsheared. You may not recognize this plant when grown in its natural round and spreading shape. Use unsheared plants in mass, mixed with other shrubs, or to provide some year-round structure in the perennial garden. This natural look blends easily with other shrubs, foundation plantings, and perennials.

Other Common Name
Currant

Bloom Period and Seasonal Color
Insignificant blooms; deciduous.

Mature Height × Spread
3 to 5 ft. × 3 to 5 ft.

When, Where, and How to Plant
Plant alpine currants throughout the season. Grow in full sun or shade in any good soil. They are very tolerant of the alkaline soils of southern Minnesota. Dig a hole the same depth as, but wider than, the rootball. Loosen any circling roots, backfill with the existing soil, and water the plants. Plant alpine currants 3 feet apart.

Growing Tips
Water new plantings thoroughly whenever the top 4 to 6 inches of soil is moist but crumbly. Wait a year to fertilize new plantings according to soil test recommendations. Fertilize young alpine currants every two or three years to encourage rapid growth. Established shrubs need very little, if any, fertilizer.

Care
Prune alpine currants in the spring before growth begins. Remove the older canes to ground level to encourage new growth at the base of the plants. You can also prune back the remaining overgrown stems by one-third. Alpine currants will tolerate shearing. Shear them so the top of the hedge is narrower than the bottom, which allows light to reach all parts of the hedge. Cut back overgrown plants to several inches above ground level. Alpine currants are susceptible to anthracnose. This is a common problem in cool, wet weather. Rake and destroy infected leaves as they fall. Cleanup and drier weather will help control this disease.

Companion Planting and Design
Alpine currants are usually used as sheared hedges. Sheared plants are also used around flowerbeds and herb gardens to create a formal landscape. Add a few unsheared plants to your shrub or mixed border.

My Personal Favorites
Clove currant, *Ribes odoratum*, is native to Minnesota and hardy in Zone 4. It produces showy fragrant, yellow flowers on a 6- to 8-foot-tall shrub. It is an alternate host for white pine blister rust. Don't grow it near white pine trees. 'Green Mound' is a dwarf cultivar of alpine currant. It grows 2 to 3 feet tall and wide, with good leaf spot resistance. You may find it listed as 'Nana', 'Pumila', or 'Compacta'.

Arborvitae
Thuja occidentalis

When, Where, and How to Plant
Plant balled-and-burlapped arborvitae as soon as possible after they are purchased. Plant container-grown plants by October 1. Plants grown in heavy shade tend to become loose and open. Avoid open areas and those exposed to drying northwest winter winds. Arborvitaes prefer moist, well-drained soil. Native arborvitae will grow in both wet and dry soil, but the cultivated plants are not as tolerant of these extremes. Plant shrubs the same depth they were growing in the nursery or container. Fill the hole with existing soil and water.

Growing Tips
Water plants thoroughly whenever the top 4 to 6 inches of soil are crumbly and moist. Mulch the soil to help conserve moisture and reduce weed problems. Wait at least one year to fertilize new plantings according to soil test recommendations. Once established, arborvitaes need little, if any, fertilizer.

Care
Prune in the spring before growth begins, or in midsummer during their semi-dormant period. You can shear the sides and top of the plants to control their size. Overgrown specimens can be topped but will be more subject to damage from heavy snow loads. Reshape the topped shrub as new growth fills in. Multistemmed arborvitae tend to split apart under the weight of heavy snow. Prevent the problem by loosely tying the upright stems together in the fall. Arborvitae foliage often browns during the winter. Reduce the damage by keeping plants properly watered and growing in protected areas. You can repel deer with repellents, scare tactics, and fencing.

Companion Planting and Design
This plant is commonly used in long rows as a hedge or screen. Use small clusters of arborvitae to block views and provide shelter. Mix them with deciduous shrubs for added interest.

My Personal Favorite
'Technito' is a new introduction from Johnson's and Bailey's nurseries. This smaller form of 'Techny' grows to 4 feet in ten years. It has dense, dark growth that resists winter burn and does not need shearing. Variegated varieties also exist. Pick a cultivar suited to your landscape and climate.

Arborvitaes are popular evergreen shrubs. They are a favorite of deer and gardeners alike. This Minnesota native can be found growing in our northern forests. Though not a true cedar, Cedrus, it is often called white cedar by northern gardeners. The scaly foliage is soft, flattened, and reminds me of fans. You will find it used as a screen, foundation plant, or tall evergreen hedge. Be aware that the American arborvitae is a tall plant reaching a height of 40 feet or more. Many homeowners found this out the hard way as the arborvitae quickly outgrew its spot in the landscape. American arborvitae also tends to turn a bit yellow-brown in the winter. Arborvitaes need minimal pruning if the right size cultivar is selected. Select one that is right for your landscape and holds its green color throughout the year.

Other Common Name
White Cedar

Bloom Period and Seasonal Color
Evergreen foliage.

Mature Height × Spread
3 to 40 ft. × 4 to 15 ft.

Barberry

Berberis thunbergii

If you have ever walked into a barberry plant, you understand why they make effective barriers. The fine thorns are guaranteed to keep people out or make the trespassers pay. This dense, rounded shrub is covered with bright green leaves that turn a brilliant orange to red in the fall. The yellow flowers aren't showy, but the small, red fruit will add color to the winter landscape. Choose from a variety of cultivars in different sizes and foliage colors. Consider the Korean barberry, Berberis koreana, if you want a larger shrub, 4 to 6 or more feet tall. It creates a colorful barrier with an abundance of flowers and fruit and a colorful fall display. Seedlings of Japanese barberry have been found in our native forests. Avoid planting these if you live near native woodland areas.

Other Common Name
Japanese Barberry

Bloom Period and Seasonal Color
Fall foliage in orange to red.

Mature Height × **Spread**
3 to 6 ft. × 3 to 6 ft.

When, Where, and How to Plant
Container-grown plants transplant easily throughout the season. Plant balled-and-burlapped plants as soon as possible after they are purchased. The red- and yellow-leafed forms are not as colorful in the shade. Barberries need well-drained soil. They can tolerate dry soil and urban conditions. Space plants 2$^{1}/_{2}$ to 3 feet apart. Backfill with existing soil and water the plants.

Growing Tips
Water thoroughly whenever the top 4 to 6 inches of soil begins to dry. Established plants are drought tolerant. Wait a year to fertilize new plantings according to soil test recommendations. Once established, barberries need little, if any, fertilizer.

Care
Prune barberries in late winter or early spring before growth begins. Come prepared with thorn-proof gloves and clothing. Many gardeners shear barberries to spare themselves the pain. Results are better if barberries are hand pruned to their natural shape. Remove $^{1}/_{5}$ of the older stems each year. Prune them back to ground level or to a strong, low shoot. Remove dead wood. The older growth produces the best fall color, so the less pruning the better the color will be. Barberries are fairly pest free when grown in full sun and well-drained soils. Wilt and canker problems are often found on barberries growing in poorly drained soil. Prune out the diseased and dead branches as soon as they appear. Disinfect your tools between cuts.

Companion Planting and Design
Use as hedges, in groupings, or as a colorful accent. I have seen 'Crimson Pygmy' sheared into a small hedge around a formal annual garden. Use them in the mixed border to provide structure and seasonal interest.

My Personal Favorites
Select a barberry that fits the size and style of your landscape design. 'Royal Burgundy' has rich maroon foliage that doesn't burn in summer. The leaves of 'Sunsation' start out green and turn yellow as they mature. 'Rose Glow' has rose-pink foliage mottled with reddish-purple splotches that matures to a deep reddish purple.

Blue Spirea
Caryopteris × clandonensis

When, Where and How to Plant

Plant container-grown plants in spring through early summer to get them established before our harsh winter. These tend to be short-lived plants in the north, so use them in an area with easy access - just in case. Grow in full sun to partial shade in moist, well-drained soils. They tolerate most soils, but good drainage, especially in winter, will increase survival. Carefully slide the plant out of the pot. Set it in a hole the same depth as but wider than the rootball. Loosen circling roots, backfill with existing soil, and water. Keep soil around new plantings moist but not wet. Space 2¹/₂ to 3 feet apart.

Growing Tips

Water established plants whenever the top 4 to 6 inches is moist but crumbly. Apply an organic mulch to help conserve moisture and reduce weed problems. Wait a year to fertilize new plantings. Avoid excess fertilization that stimulates growth more likely to be winter killed. Consider using a slow-release, low nitrogen fertilizers.

Care

Winter kill is the only real problem. Proper siting and care along with cooperation from nature will help with this plant's longevity. Let the plants stand for winter. This will add winter beauty to the landscape and increase winter survival. Cut blue spirea down to 4 to 6 inches in late winter or early spring. The plant will quickly reach its full size and begin flowering in late summer.

Companion Planting and Design

The gray foliage combines nicely with a wide range of shrubs and flowers. Plant near 'Tardiva' hydrangea for a nice white and blue flower combination. Or skirt it with white alyssum or Corydalis lutea for season-long interest.

My Personal Favorites

I have 'Blue Mist' *Caryopteris* growing in my yard. I like the powder blue flowers. I cut the plant back in late winter, and it usually grows to 2¹/₂ to 3 feet tall and wide each summer. 'Dark Knight' is pretty readily available. It is similar in size with deep purple flowers.

This lovely shrub is heading north to add some late season color to our landscapes. I have seen it listed as hardy in Zone 6 and sometimes in Zone 5. Being a typical northern gardener with "Zone envy" I had to give it a try. That was over ten years ago. My plant has not only survived a difficult planting location, it also rewarded me with offspring to enhance my landscape and share with other gardeners. I have seen this plant growing in Zone 4 gardens. The top usually dies back, so treat it like butterfly bush and Russian sage. The blue-gray foliage is a nice addition to the perennial border. The true blue flowers can't be beat for a late summer through fall display. Bees love this plant. I have my blue spirea by the front entrance, and no one has been bothered.

Other Common Name
Caryopteris

Bloom Period and Seasonal Color
Late summer through frost with blue flowers.

Mature Height × Spread
3 ft. × 3 ft.

Boxwood

Buxus microphylla var. *koreana* × *Buxus sempervirens* cvs.

Boxwood hedges evoke thoughts of English gardens. These broadleaf evergreens have long been used as sheared hedges in the formal landscapes of Europe and the southern United States. You may know that large-leafed boxwood Buxus sempervirens are not hardy in Minnesota. Winter damage is the biggest concern with boxwood. Northern gardeners need to select a hardier, small-leafed boxwood, such as Buxus microphylla var koreana. This is the hardiest boxwood, and its hybrids (Buxus microphylla koreana × Buxus sempervirens) and cultivars were bred to be more tolerant of Minnesota winters. Consider adding a few boxwoods to your shade garden or shrub bed. Left to grow naturally, they blend well with a variety of perennials and shrubs in more informal garden designs. Take a close look at boxwoods in the spring. They produce small, white flowers that are hard to see. Their lovely fragrance, however, makes a second look, or should I say sniff, worthwhile.

Other Common Name
Korean Boxwood

Bloom Period and Seasonal Color
Spring blooms in white; evergreen foliage.

Mature Height × Spread
3 ft. × 3 ft.

Zones
Hardy in Zone 4

When, Where, and How to Plant
Plant balled-and-burlapped plants soon after they are purchased. Plant container-grown boxwood in the spring and early summer. Grow boxwood in protected locations for best results. Dig a hole the same depth as, but wider than, the rootball. Plant the shrub at the same depth it was growing in the nursery. Space plants 2$\frac{1}{2}$ to 3 feet apart. Remove any twine and cut away burlap on balled-and-burlapped plants. Backfill with existing soil and water the plants.

Growing Tips
Water thoroughly whenever the top 4-6 inches of soil is moist and crumbly. Mulch with wood chips, shredded bark, or another organic material to keep the roots cool and moist, reduce weed problems, and improve the soil. Keep cultivators and tillers away from boxwoods and their roots. Water new and established plants thoroughly in the fall before the ground freezes. Wait a year to fertilize new plantings, following soil test recommendations for the type and amount of fertilizer to use.

Care
Unsheared boxwoods require very little pruning. Cut long branches back to a side branch in mid-summer. Remove winter damage and do more severe pruning or shearing in early spring before new growth appears. A burlap wrap, decorative wind break, or cylinder of hardware cloth filled with evergreen boughs or straw can reduce winter damage on more tender cultivars or plants exposed to winter wind and sun.

Companion Planting and Design
Use them as a hedge, edging plant, or as part of a formal garden. They are naturally compact, dense growers with a round growth habit. Too often they are sheared beyond recognition. Use them as the framework of your mixed border or evergreen foil in a shady rock garden.

My Personal Favorites
'Wintergreen' is probably the hardiest. This compact grower maintains its evergreen color. 'Green Velvet' has small, dark green leaves and grows 3 feet tall and wide. 'Green Gem' is a slow growing, dense boxwood that stays about 2 feet tall and wide. 'Chicagoland Green' (Buxus × 'Glencoe') is a sister to 'Green Velvet' but is faster growing.

Burning Bush

Euonymus alatus

When, Where, and How to Plant

Plant balled-and-burlapped burning bushes as soon as possible after purchasing. Plant container-grown plants throughout the season. Grow plants in full sun or part sun for the best fall color. They will tolerate shade, but the fall display may be less than spectacular. Euonymus tolerate a wide range of soil conditions but need good drainage to perform well. Plant the shrub at the same depth it was growing in the nursery. Loosen circling roots, backfill and water. Space plants 4 to 6 feet apart.

Growing Tips

Water thoroughly whenever the top 4 to 6 inches of soil begins to feel crumbly and moist. Mulch to conserve water and reduce weeds. Wait a year before fertilizing new plantings and follow soil test recommendations. Once established, these plants need little, if any, fertilizer. Overfertilization can inhibit fall color.

Care

Burning bush needs very little pruning. Prune established plants in the spring before growth begins. Do not prune back to ground level. Euonymus caterpillar build webby nests in the shrubs that they feed upon. Physically remove the webs and insects, or spray the plant with *Bacillus thuringiensis* (Bt), an environmentally friendly insecticide. Yellow leaves and branch dieback occur on plants grown in poorly drained soil. Rabbits love euonymus. Fencing is the most effective way to prevent damage.

Companion Planting and Design

Euonymus is used in a variety of ways. It makes an excellent hedge, screen, specimen plant, and foundation planting. Add it to the mixed border for good fall color and winter texture.

My Personal Favorites

'Chicago Fire' is hardy to Zone 3, has decorative orange fruit, colors up early in fall, and grows 8 to 10 feet tall. The 'Nordine Strain', often sold as 'Koreana', is much hardier than 'Compactus' and grows only 5 to 8 feet tall. 'Rudy Haag' is a true dwarf selection (4 to 5 feet) that is basically seedless and has consistent fall color. Burning bush seedlings have been found in our native forests. Avoid growing this nonnative euonymus near our natural areas.

Burning bush is best known for its brilliant fall color. Its bright red leaves are among the first to appear in the autumn landscape. I will never forget a boat ride around Lake Geneva. The hillside was a blaze with burning bush. I think everyone on board went home and bought a plant or two. But the show doesn't end there. Once the leaves drop, the corky, winged stems are apparent and become even more attractive when they are covered with snow. Compact euonymus, Euonymus alatus *'Compactus', is the most frequently used cultivar. The name is a bit misleading as it grows 10 feet tall. Too many gardeners have removed this compact plant once it overgrew their bay window. It often suffers winter injury. Select one of the hardier compact cultivars for Minnesota landscapes.*

Other Common Name
Winged Euonymus

Bloom Period and Seasonal Color
Early fall foliage in red.

Mature Height × Spread
15 ft. × 15 ft.

Butterfly Bush
Buddleja davidii

Picture an arching shrub covered with flowers from July through frost. Now add some flashes of additional color provided by butterflies and hummingbirds. Does this garden dream sound too good to be true? It's not. The butterfly bush can give you all this interest and more all year long. A quick pruning job in late winter is all the maintenance needed. In early spring, the new growth bursts from the ground and quickly grows to its mature size. By July, the flowers appear and continue through frost. The flowers are 6 to 12 inches long and resemble lilac flowers. They have a light, fruity fragrance. There is one little drawback—winter kill. But the year-round enjoyment these sometimes short-lived plants provide is well worth the investment.

Other Common Name
Summer Lilac

Bloom Period and Seasonal Color
July through frost blooms in purple, white, pink, and yellow.

Mature Height × Spread
5 to 8 ft. tall and wide

Zones
Hardy to Zone 4

When, Where, and How to Plant
Plant bare-root shrubs in the spring before growth begins. Plant container-grown plants in the spring and early summer. Grow butterfly bush in full sun or light shade with moist, well-drained soil. Remove container-grown plants from the pot and loosen potbound roots. Plant the shrub at the same depth it was growing in the nursery, backfill and water. Space plants 4 to 5 feet apart.

Growing Tips
Water thoroughly whenever the top 4 to 6 inches are crumbly and moist. Mulch the soil to help conserve water and reduce weed problems. Wait a year to fertilize newly planted butterfly bushes. Follow soil test recommendations for the amount and type of fertilizer to use. Butterfly bush benefits from regular fertilizing.

Care
Leave the plants stand for winter. The seedheads and plant form add to your landscape's winter interest and increase hardiness. Some gardeners add a layer of woodchips or other winter mulch for added insulation. Prune the plants back to 4 to 6 inches above ground level in late winter or early spring. Make your cuts at a slight angle above a bud. These plants are not long lived in the landscape. They will die out after an extremely harsh winter. My first planting lasted five years, and my second one is on its seventh season. Don't give up on your plants too soon. They often emerge late so wait until the soil warms before replacing them.

Companion Planting and Design
This large shrub can be used alone or grouped in shrub beds and perennial gardens. Plant it where you can sit and watch the butterflies and hummingbirds that visit.

My Personal Favorites
The Petite series grow 3 to 4 feet tall and come in a variety of colors. It's the perfect size for small yards and perennial borders. Nanho series grows 4 to 5 feet tall and wide. It comes in purple, white, and blue. 'Pink Delight' grows 5 to 8 feet tall and has large, deep pink flowers. 'Black Knight' has very dark purple flowers and may be hardier than the others.

Chokeberry
Aronia melanocarpa

When, Where and How to Plant

Plant container-grown plants anytime during the growing season. Grow chokeberry in full sun to partially shaded locations. They tolerate a wide range of soil, including wet and dry, but prefer moist, well-drained soils. Carefully slide the plant out of the pot. Set it in a hole the same depth as, but wider than, the rootball. Loosen circling roots, backfill with existing soil, and water. Keep soil around new plantings moist but not wet. Space 2¹/₂ to 3 feet apart.

Growing Tips

Water established plants thoroughly whenever the top 4 to 6 inches of soil are moist and crumbly. Wait a year to fertilize new plantings. Avoid excess nitrogen, which can limit flowering and fall color.

Care

The chokeberries tend to sucker and form a colony. Give them plenty of space to take advantage of this growth habit. Remove older canes to ground level in late winter. This encourages new growth at the base. Regular renewal pruning controls the overall size. This is a fairly pest-free plant that tolerates a wide range of growing conditions. You may see problems with leaf spot or powdery mildew in wet seasons when diseases are prevalent. Rake and destroy infested leaves as they drop.

Companion Planting and Design

Use this as an accent plant with evergreens. The flowers, fruit, and fall color add life to evergreen screens and hedges. Add a few to the mixed border as part of the framework and for seasonal interest.

My Personal Favorites

Several dwarf cultivars are available. 'Autumn Magic', 'Morton', and 'Viking' are about ¹/₂ to ²/₃ the size of the straight species. All have good fall color. Viking blooms a bit earlier and produces larger fruit that is great for attracting wildlife. The red chokeberry, *Aronia arbutifolia*, is a bit larger than the black fruited, glossy chokeberry. It has the same seasonal appeal, just on a larger plant that reaches 6 to 10 feet tall and 3 to 5 feet wide. Its cultivar 'Brilliantissima' (shown) produces an abundance of fruit, exceptional scarlet fall color, and almost waxy leaves.

As northern gardeners, we need to make the most of all four seasons. Certain plants help us get through our long winters once the growing season has passed. Chokeberries do just that. Their white spring flowers greet the new season. The glossy green foliage is a nice addition to shrub beds, foundation plantings, and mixed borders. The black fruit persists through much of the winter, adding beauty to the landscape and food for the birds. The fall color is a beautiful wine to red. This beautiful shrub is also tough. It can tolerate wet and dry soils and full sun to partial shade. You will get the best fall color and flowering in full sun, though I have seen them perform pretty well in partial shade. And it is hardy to Zone 3. You can't beat that.

Other Common Name
Glossy Chokeberry

Bloom Period and Seasonal Color
White flowers in spring.

Mature Height × Spread
3 to 5 ft. × 5 ft. or more

Cotoneaster

Cotoneaster species

Low growing, spreading, weeping, or tall and upright: *these terms all describe the popular plant cotoneaster. With the many sizes and forms available, it can be used in a variety of ways throughout the landscape. Many gardeners pronounce its name cotton easter, but is really pronounced ko (long o) to(long o) ne (long e) as'ter (like the flower). Most of the varieties provide year-round interest. Spring flowers, glossy summer foliage, good fall color, and winter fruit give you plenty of show from one plant. You have probably seen the popular cranberry cotoneaster Cotoneaster apiculatus used as a ground cover, cascading over a wall, or trailing down an embankment. It is hardy in Zone 4. The hardy and urban-tolerant hedge cotoneaster stands upright to form a hedge in your yard or colorful planting along the freeway.*

Bloom Period and Seasonal Color
Spring to summer blooms in white and pink.

Mature Height × Spread
1¹/₂ to 25 ft. × 6 to 15 ft.

When, Where, and How to Plant

Cotoneaster tends to be shallow rooted and does best when it is grown in containers or balled and burlapped. Plant balled-and-burlapped plants after they are purchased. Plant container-grown plants throughout the season. They tolerate a wide range of soil conditions, as long as the soil is well drained. Cotoneasters are tough plants that tolerate dry soil and roadside salt. Plant cotoneaster at the same depth it was growing in the nursery, loosen circling roots, backfill with soil, and water. Spacing varies with each variety.

Growing Tips

Water thoroughly whenever the top 4 to 6 inches of soil starts to dry. Wait a year to fertilize new plantings according to soil test recommendations. Established cotoneasters need little, if any, fertilizer.

Care

Established shrubs can be pruned in late winter or early spring before growth begins. Remove old, diseased, and damaged stems at ground level. You can prune back overgrown shrubs by one-third. Rabbits live under and will feed on cotoneaster. Fencing is the best control option but is often not practical. A variety of repellents and scare tactics may discourage the rabbits.

Companion Planting and Design

Use low-growers as a ground cover, bank cover, trailer over a wall, or as edging plant for a shrub bed. Allow low-growers to weave in and out of creeping ground covers. Upright forms can be used as background plants and screening.

My Personal Favorite

Cranberry cotoneaster forms 3-foot-high by 3- to 6-foot-wide mounds of dark green leaves that turn a bronzy-red or purplish color in the fall and persist into November. The pinkish-white flowers appear in late May and early June. Red cranberry-like fruit develops in the fall. Hedge cotoneaster, *Cotoneaster lucidus*, is upright from 6 to 10 feet and is hardy throughout Minnesota. The leaves turn yellow, orange, and red in the fall. The flowers are pinkish white, and the fruit is black. *Cotoneaster divaricatus* and rock cotoneaster, *Cotoneaster horizontalis*, are medium-sized plants with a spreading growth habit. Many-flowered cotoneaster, *Cotoneaster multiflorus*, is covered with showy white flowers in May.

When, Where, and How to Plant

Plant bare-root dogwoods in the spring before growth begins, balled-and-burlapped plants as soon as possible after they are purchased, and container-grown plants throughout the season. Most prefer moist soil, and many tolerate wet sites. See planting directions in the chapter introducton. Spacing varies with variety.

Growing Tips

Water thoroughly whenever the top 4 to 6 inches of soil feels crumbly and moist. Mulch to help conserve water and reduce weed problems. Wait a year to fertilize new plantings. Regular fertilization will encourage rapid growth on young shrubs. Once established, little fertilizer is needed.

Care

Prune established shrubs in late winter or early spring. Remove old, diseased, or damaged canes on redtwig, gray, and variegated dogwoods at ground level. Color coded for pruning, the older stems of redosier turn brown. Renewal pruning helps stimulate new brightly colored stems. You can prune back overgrown shrubs by one-third. Stressed plants can suffer from scale insects and drought-induced cankers. Proper watering and regular pruning of the discolored, cankered stems will reduce these problems. Disinfect tools between cuts of diseased plants.

Companion Planting and Design

Use redtwig dogwood for bank stabilization, along streams and in natural settings. Gray dogwood makes a great hedge and screen. Give it plenty of room to grow. Pagoda dogwoods make a nice accent on the shady corner of a house. They complement formal and Japanese garden styles as well as an informal mixed border.

My Personal Favorites

I miss the flowering dogwoods, *Cornus florida*, of southern Ohio. A few northern gardeners try to grow these Zone 5 beauties. Even if the tree survives, the plant seldom flowers. Kousa dogwood, *Cornus kousa*, performs better. Rated hardy for Zone 5, a few gardeners grow it successfully in Zone 4 with flowers and fruit. Gray dogwood, *Cornus racemosa*, is another native. This rapid spreading plant tolerates dry or wet soil and sun or shade.

Our Minnesota native dogwoods have become prominent plants in our landscapes. They can be used in natural settings or formal gardens. The flower show may not compare with the flowering dogwood of the south, but the Minnesota dogwoods make up for it by providing food and shelter for the birds and year-round interest in the landscape. Redtwig or Redosier dogwood, Cornus sericea, is probably the best known. This native has bright red stems and can be found in natural areas and landscapes. Redosier dogwoods are spreading shrubs that tolerate moist to wet sites. Pagoda dogwood, Cornus alternifolia, is a larger native dogwood with a spreading growth habit. It prefers shade and moist soil. This dogwood provides year-round interest with its attractive growth habit, cream-colored flowers, blue fruit with persistent red stems, and maroon fall color.

Bloom Period and Seasonal Color
Spring to summer blooms in white, yellow, and pink; fall foliage in red, orange, and yellow.

Mature Height × Spread
5 to 15 ft. × 5 to 15 ft.

Forsythia
Forsythia hybrids

The bright yellow flowers of forsythia signal the start of spring. Most forsythias are hardy through Zone 4, but the flower buds are frequently killed in Minnesota winters. You usually have great flowering after a mild winter or from the snow line down. Snow-covered flower buds are protected from the cold winter temperatures. Fortunately, there are newer varieties with hardy flower buds that will flower in spring despite our cold winter temperatures. Select hardy types bred for reliable flowering. Meadowlark forsythia, Forsythia × 'Meadowlark', grows up to 9 feet tall and is hardy in Zones 3b through 5. It has bright yellow flowers and an added benefit of purplish fall color. 'Northern Sun' is another large forsythia reaching heights of 8 to 10 feet.

Bloom Period and Seasonal Color
Early spring blooms in yellow.

Mature Height × Spread
1 to 10 ft. × 4 to 10 ft.

When, Where, and How to Plant
Plant bare-root forsythia in the spring before growth begins, balled-and-burlapped plants as soon as possible after they are purchased, and container-grown plants throughout the season. Forsythia prefer full sun and well-drained soil. They will tolerate any pH, as well as urban conditions. Follow planting directions in the chapter introduction. Space depends on the size and spread of the cultivar grown.

Growing Tips
Water thoroughly whenever the top 4 to 6 inches is moist and crumbly. Mulch the soil to help conserve moisture and reduce weed problems. Wait a year to fertilize young plants according to soil test recommendations. Once established, shrubs need little, if any, fertilizer.

Care
Prune established shrubs in the spring after flowering. Remove $1/3$ of the older stems at ground level. You can cut back overgrown stems by $1/3$, or cut all the stems back to several inches above ground level. Lack of flowers is the major problem on forsythia; this is caused by cold temperatures, poorly timed pruning, excess nitrogen, and too much shade. Select a hardy type for reliable bloom. Prune right after flowering, or you'll be removing the flower buds and eliminating spring bloom. Avoid excess fertilization and grow in full sun for best results. Bring a bit of spring indoors by forcing a few forsythia branches. Select stems with lots of plump flower buds. Pound the cut ends and submerge the stems in water overnight. The next morning place the stems in fresh water and store at 60 to 70 degrees Fahrenheit until blooming starts in about two weeks.

Companion Planting and Design
Plant in shrub beds, add a few to the mixed border, or use as a bank cover in areas where the spring floral display can be enjoyed. It's a nice backdrop for early blooming tulip or daffodil varieties that complement yellow forsythia blooms.

My Personal Favorite
'Sunrise' is a variety with hardy flower buds. This dense plant grows 5 feet tall and wide, tolerates urban conditions, and is hardy in Zone 4b.

Fragrant Sumac
Rhus aromatica

When, Where, and How to Plant
Fragrant sumacs are usually sold as container plants. Plant throughout the growing season. They tolerate a wide range of soil conditions but prefer well-drained to dry soil. Follow planting directions provided in the chapter introduction. Loosen any circling roots, backfill the hole with existing soil, and water the shrub. Space plants 3 feet apart.

Growing Tips
Once established, these plants are drought tolerant and can survive with normal rainfall. Water thoroughly during extended dry spells whenever the top 4 to 6 inches of soil starts to dry. Mulch the soil to help conserve moisture and reduce weed problems. Wait a year to fertilize new plantings. Once established, fragrant sumac needs little, if any, fertilizer.

Care
Established shrubs can be pruned in early spring before growth begins. Remove the older canes to ground level. Overgrown plantings can be pruned back to several inches above ground level. The fragrant sumac, especially 'Gro-Low' is less aggressive than Staghorn sumac. Reserve that planting for contained or large areas where it can take control.

Companion Planting and Design
Use this fast grower en masse, to cover banks, and for erosion control. The low-growing cultivars can also be used as a ground cover or trailer over a wall. The 'Gro-Low' cultivar looks nice as a ground cover under crabapples, hawthorns, and other small ornamental trees.

My Personal Favorites
'Gro-Low' fragrant sumac forms mounds 2 feet tall and up to 6 feet wide. Its trailing growth habit makes it well suited as a ground cover, bank planting, or trailer over a wall. Staghorn sumac, *Rhus typhina*, is commonly seen on the freeway. It has large, ferny leaves that are the first to turn bright red in the fall. This large Minnesota native grows 15 feet or taller and is hardy in Zone 3b. Staghorn sumac is a fast-growing, aggressive plant that should only be used where it has lots of room to grow. The new 'Tiger Eyes' staghorn sumac has fern-like leaves that start out chartreuse and turn yellow for the summer.

Fragrant sumac is a tough plant that will provide lots of interest in the garden. In spring, the plant produces small yellow flowers before the leaves emerge. Don't be nervous when this plant remains bare after your other trees and shrubs leaf out. It is normal and worth the wait. Eventually the glossy green leaves emerge and make a nice back drop for the red berries that develop in summer and persist into winter. The Native Americans used the hairy red berries of sumac to make a pink sumacade (lemonade). They bruised the fruit and soaked it in hot water for fifteen minutes, cooled, strained, and enjoyed. Sumac ends the season with a spectacular display of orange to maroon fall color. And the fragrance? Well, crush a leaf and take a whiff. I think the name Rhus odoriferous is more fitting.

Other Common Name
Gro-Low Sumac

Bloom Period and Seasonal Color
Spring blooms in yellow; fall foliage in red, maroon, and orange.

Mature Height × Spread
$2^1/2$ to 5 ft. × 5 ft.

Honeysuckle

Lonicera species

Many of you may remember sipping the honeysuckle as a kid, or maybe the sweet fragrance filled your childhood landscape. The fragrant honeysuckles were once thought to be the answer to all our landscaping problems. This low-maintenance plant was promoted for its fragrant flowers, pest free nature, and tolerance of tough growing conditions. Does it sound too good to be true? It was. An insect pest and the invasive nature of the plant have reduced its value in the landscape. Avoid using Amur (Lonicera maackii), Tatarian (L. tatarica), Morrow's (L, morrowii), and Belle (L. × bella) in the landscape. These plants are invading our natural areas and crowding out our native plants. Use a cultivar of the non-invasive European fly honeysuckle or our native bush honeysuckle, Diervilla lonicera, to avoid these problems.

Other Common Name
Lonicera

Bloom Period and Seasonal Color
Spring blooms in white, pink, or yellow

Mature Height × Spread
3 to 12 ft. × 3 to 8 ft.

When, Where, and How to Plant
Honeysuckles are easily transplanted and are available as bare-root and container-grown plants. Plant bare-root plants in the spring before growth begins. Plant container-grown plants throughout the season. They prefer moist, well-drained soil but will grow in a variety of conditions. Avoid wet soils. Follow planting directions in the chapter introduction. Space plants 3 to 5 feet apart, depending on the species and cultivar selected.

Growing Tips
New plantings need an inch of water each week. Established plants are more drought tolerant. Minimal fertilizer is needed for new or established plantings.

Care
Prune established shrubs in early spring before growth begins, or prune right after flowering so you can enjoy the fragrant blooms. Remove the older canes to ground level to encourage new growth at the base of the plant. You can prune back any remaining stems by one-third. Honeysuckles will also tolerate severe pruning. Cut the entire plant back to several inches above ground level. The honeysuckle leaf-folding aphid is the biggest pest problem. This insect feeds on honeysuckle leaves from late April until frost, causing fine, twiggy growth (or brooms) to form on the ends of branches. Established plants will tolerate the damage. Remove and destroy the aphid-filled brooms. Or better yet, replace the plant.

Companion Planting and Design
Honeysuckles have long been sheared into formal hedges or allowed to grow naturally and used as a screen, backdrop, or bank covering. Always select non-invasive types.

My Personal Favorites
Clavey's dwarf honeysuckle, *Lonicera × xylosteoides* 'Clavey's Dwarf', is resistant to the leaf-folding aphid. This compact form grows 5 feet tall and 3 feet wide. It works well as a hedge and is hardy in Zone 4. 'Miniglobe' is hardy to Zone 3 and forms a dense globe 2 feet tall and wide. The dense foliage masks the flowers and fruit.

When, Where, and How to Plant

Plant balled-and-burlapped hydrangeas as soon as possible after they are purchased. Grow these shrubs in partial shade for best results. They will tolerate full sun as long as the soil is kept moist. Hydrangeas tolerate a wide range of growing conditions but prefer moist, well-drained soil. The plants do become ratty in drought conditions. Plant as recommended in the chapter introduction. Spacing depends on the type of hydrangea grown.

Growing Tips

Water thoroughly whenever the top 4 to 6 inches of soil feels crumbly and moist. Water established plants during dry periods. Mulch the soil to help conserve moisture and reduce weed problems. Wait a year to fertilize new plantings. Hydrangeas benefit from a light fertilization in the spring before growth begins. Use a low nitrogen, slow-release fertilizer to avoid overfertilization.

Care

Prune in spring before growth begins. Cut back the snowball-type hydrangeas to ground level every year. PeeGee hydrangea requires very little pruning. Cut back stems to maintain the desired size and shape. Improve flowering by pruning them back to their woody framework annually. Lack of flowers is the biggest problem on the blue and pink flowering hydrangeas. These plants (*Hydrangea macrophylla*) often die back to the ground over winter. Most flower on old growth, so you end up with all leaves and no flowers each year. 'Endless Summer' is a new introduction, hardy in Zone 4, that blooms on both old and new wood. Like all these types of hydrangeas, the flowers tend to be blue in acid soil and pink in alkaline soils.

Companion Planting and Design

The panicled hydrangeas make a nice focal point or combine nicely with ornamental grasses and perennials. Use the snowball types in the shade garden and foundation plantings. I have included 'Endless Summer' in my mixed border.

My Personal Favorites

Try one or more of these panicled hydgraneas. 'Tardiva' is later blooming. 'Angel's Blush'™ (white turning pink), 'Pink Diamond' (white, pink, and red flowers), and 'Limelight' (lime green blossoms) provide added color in the landscape.

Large, white hydrangea flowers remind many of us of our childhoods and perhaps visits to grandma's house. Hydrangeas are among the few shrubs that can put on a dramatic floral display even in the shade. The white flowers dry to beige and persist on the plants through winter. I like to leave mine on the plants for added winter interest. You have all season to plant container-grown hydrangeas. Cultivars of smooth hydrangeas, Hydrangea arborescens, are some of the more popular hydrangeas, covered with large, white snowball-type flowers in the summer. Cultivars of panicles hydrangea, Hydrangea paniculata (shown), are larger, hardier and often grown into a tree form. Its large, white, cone-shaped flowers develop a hint of pink color as they pass their peak. You can't make white hydrangeas pink or blue without the use of floral dyes and spray paint.

Other Common Name
Snowball Bush

Bloom Period and Seasonal Color
Summer blooms in white.

Mature Height × Spread
3 to 15 ft. × 10 to 15 ft.

Juniper

Juniperus species

Its wide variety of sizes, shapes, and foliage colors make juniper a valuable landscape plant. These tough ever-greens can be used as windbreaks, ground covers, screens, hedges, or rock garden plants. Use them alone as specimens or in groups for a mass display. There are hundreds of juniper species and cultivars available. They come in upright forms, spreading types, and low-growing ground huggers. Many junipers can spread to 20 feet wide. Save yourself a lot of work and frustration by selecting the juniper that fits the space available. Use the hardiest, most disease-resistant cultivars available. And don't forget to enjoy the fruit display. The blue, berry-like fruit add winter interest, feed the birds, and flavor gin. (Oil of juniper is used to flavor gin—explains that slightly "evergreen" smell.)

Other Common Name
Red Cedar

Bloom Period and Seasonal Color
Evergreen foliage.

Mature Height × Spread
20 ft. × 10 ft.

When, Where, and How to Plant
Plant balled-and-burlapped plants as soon as possible after they are purchased and container-grown junipers spring through September. Planting by October 1 gives the plants time to put down roots before winter. Grow junipers in well-drained soil. They tolerate a variety of soil conditions from sandy to clay. These tough plants grow in urban areas, dry soil, and windy locations. Be sure to wear long sleeves and gloves when planting this prickly evergreen (see chapter introduction).

Growing Tips
Water thoroughly whenever the top 4 to 6 inches start to dry. Established plantings can tolerate dry soil. Water junipers and other evergreens in the fall before the ground freezes. This, and mulching, will reduce winter damage. Wait a year to fertilize new plantings according to soil test recommendations. Once established, junipers need little, if any, fertilizer.

Care
Prune junipers in the spring before growth begins or in midsummer during their semi-dormant period. Wear long sleeves and gloves. When properly sited and spaced, junipers need little pruning. You can top overgrown junipers and reshape. Prune spreading and creeping junipers by selectively removing the longest branches. Cut these back to a side branch or main stem. Phomopsis blight is a fungal disease that causes tip dieback. Prune infected branches back to healthy side shoots with disinfected tools. Cedar rust is a common problem on red cedar, *Juniperus virginiana*. The disease spends half its life on the juniper and the other half damaging crabapples, hawthorns, and quince. Rust won't kill the plant but looks bad when the galls sprout their slimy orange tendrils in spring. Juniper may experience some browning after extremely cold winters. Prune out the damaged foliage.

Companion Planting and Design
Use low growing junipers as ground covers, trailers over wall, or en masse on a bank. Upright forms make nice backdrops, screens, and vertical accents in the mixed border.

My Personal Favorite
Select the most disease resistant cultivar that is the size and form that best fits your landscape design..

When, Where, and How to Plant

Plant balled-and-burlapped lilacs as soon as possible after they are purchased, and container-grown plants throughout the season. Grow lilacs in full sun and moist well-drained soil. Follow planting instructions at the beginning of this chapter. Spacing varies with species grown.

Growing Tips

Water thoroughly whenever the top 4 to 6 inches of soil is moist and crumbly. Mulch the soil to help conserve moisture and reduce weed problems. Wait a year to fertilize new plantings. Avoid high-nitrogen fertilizers that can prevent flowering. Established lilacs need little, if any, fertilizer.

Care

Remove old flower heads to encourage good flowering the following season. Lilacs bloom on the previous season's growth. Prune established lilacs after flowering so you won't interfere with next year's blooms. Remove 1/3 of the older canes to ground level. You can also prune remaining stems by 1/3. Regular pruning will reduce pest problems and control plant growth, while improving the overall appearance. Powdery mildew is the most common disease. Grow lilacs in full sun with good air circulation to reduce this problem. Proper pruning allows air and light in, reducing mildew problems. Bacterial blight and scale insects are easily controlled with proper pruning. These pests attack older, stressed stems. Regular pruning removes the susceptible stems and infected growth.

Companion Planting and Design

Lilacs can be used as hedges, screens, or as a backdrop for other plantings. Add a few specimen plantings to the mixed border as a spring accent. Grafted tree forms of 'Miss Kim' give the look of a tree on a smaller scale. Use them in a formal garden, as an open screen, or near a patio.

My Personal Favorites

'Blue Skies' will give you a lavender blue flower on bright green foliage and will tolerate light shade. *Syringa vulgaris* 'Dappled Dawn' has cream-mottled leathery leaves and mauve flowers. The wine-red flower buds of 'Tinkerbelle' open to a deep pink bloom that adds to its spring appeal. The deep pink, fragrant flowers of 'Miss Canada' appear in late spring or early summer.

Many lilacs end up in the landscape thanks to the fond memories they elicit. Other gardeners are lured by the sweet fragrance. For those who don't like the smell, less fragrant cultivars are available. That way everyone can enjoy a bouquet of freshly cut lilacs. There are hundreds of common lilacs, Syringa vulgaris, on the market. They grow up to 15 feet tall with white, blue, or purple flowers. Palabin lilac, Syringa meyeri 'Palabin', is a smaller plant, growing 4 to 5 feet tall and up to 7 feet wide. This easy-to-grow lilac is disease resistant. Miss Kim lilac, Syringa patula 'Miss Kim', grows up to 6 feet tall and 4 feet wide. It produces fragrant, icy-blue flowers and has purple fall color. It is disease resistant and hardy to Zone 3b.

Other Common Name
Syringa

Bloom Period and Seasonal Color
Spring blooms in white, blue, purple, pink, and magenta

Mature Height × Spread
4 to 15 ft. × 4 to 15 ft.

Mockorange
Philadelphus coronarius

The sweet, citrus fragrance of mockorange is the feature that won this plant a place in the landscape. The Greeks used them in garlands giving them the botanical name coronarius, *meaning crown. Select cultivars carefully. Many are subject to winter injury, eliminating the spring flower display. Other cultivars lack fragrance, which is the main reason gardeners grow this plant. The attractive blossoms are a wonderful addition to the spring landscape. Its appearance the rest of the year is less desirable, so consider limiting the number of plants used. Minnesota Snowflake mockorange,* Philadelphus × virginalis *'Minnesota', is flower hardy throughout the state. The 8-foot-tall shrub produces very fragrant, double-white flowers in midsummer. The dwarf variety grows 3 to 4 feet and puts on a good flower display even in poor soil.*

Other Common Name
Sweet Mockorange

Bloom Period and Seasonal Color
Spring blooms in white.

Mature Height × Spread
Up to 10 ft. × 10 ft.

When, Where, and How to Plant
Plant container-grown plants throughout the season. They prefer moist, well-drained soil. Dig a hole the same depth as, but wider than, the rootball. Carefully remove container-grown plants from the pot and loosen circling roots. Be sure to plant the shrub at the same depth it was growing in the container. Fill the hole with existing soil and water thoroughly. Space plants 3 to 6 feet apart depending on size of the variety you are growing.

Growing Tips
New plantings need an inch of water each week. Mulch with wood chips, shredded bark, or another organic material to help conserve moisture and reduce weed problems. Wait a year to fertilize new plantings. Follow soil test recommendations for the type and amount of fertilizer to use. Fertilize young shrubs in late fall after the plants are dormant, or early spring before growth begins. Avoid high-nitrogen fertilizers that can prevent flowering. Established shrubs need little, if any, fertilizer.

Care
Mockorange blooms on the previous season's growth. Prune established mockorange shrubs in the spring after flowering. Remove the older canes to ground level. You can prune back remaining stems by 1/3 to reduce overall height, or cut all of the stems on overgrown plants back near ground level.

Companion Planting and Design
Mockorange is an old-time favorite. It has traditionally been used as a hedge or for the spring color and fragrance it provides in shrub beds. Plant it in a location where it can be enjoyed if it blooms but not waste prime gardening space if it doesn't.

My Personal Favorites
Glacier mockorange, *Philadelphus × virginalis* 'Glacier', is hardy to Zone 4b. The fragrant, double blossoms appear in midsummer. The smaller, 5-foot-tall plant is a better size for most landscapes. Several variegated types will survive in Minnesota. They provide attractive foliage all season that will compensate for the years when the plant fails to bloom. *Philadelphus × lemoinei* 'Innocence' is an old French variety dating back to the early 1900s. Its leaves are splashed with creamy yellow.

Mugo Pine

Pinus mugo

When, Where, and How to Plant

Plant balled-and-burlapped plants as soon as possible. Plant container-grown plants spring through September. Planting mugo pines by October 1 will give them time to root before winter. Mugo pines will tolerate light shade. They prefer moist, well-drained soil but grow fine in well-drained to dry soil. See chapter introduction for more on planting. Spacing depends on the cultivar grown.

Growing Tips

Water thoroughly whenever the top 4 to 6 inches start to dry. Established mugo pines are drought tolerant. Water mugo and other pines in the fall before the ground freezes. Mulch to conserve moisture and reduce weed problems. Wait a year before fertilizing new plantings. Avoid excess fertilization that can stimulate more growth and bigger plants than desired. Established shrubs need little, if any, fertilizer.

Care

Prune mugo pines in the spring as the buds elongate into soft, new growth called candles. Remove $1/2$ to $2/3$ of each candle. Prune mugo pines yearly to control growth and ultimate size. Once the plant is overgrown, it is nearly impossible to greatly reduce its size. Pine needle scale is the major pest. It looks like flecks of white paint spilled on the needles. Treat with insecticidal soap or an insecticide when the shell-less immature scales are present about the middle of May (when the vanhoutte spirea are in full bloom). Repeat seven days later. European pine sawfly will also damage mugo pines by feeding on the needles. Smash the sawflies or prune off the infested branch and destroy the insects.

Companion Planting and Design

Use small cultivars of mugo pines in foundation plantings and rock gardens. These also make a nice addition to the perennial garden. Their texture and form provide a year-round framework that blends nicely with most perennials.

My Personal Favorites

'Aurea' is a true dwarf that turns gold in the winter. 'Sherwood Carpet' forms a uniform dense mound of dark green needles. *Pinus mugo pumilio* is a creeping form with shorter needles. This slow grower can eventually grow to 10 feet wide.

Mugo pine was once the only shrubby pine for the landscape. It has been a popular foundation plant for years. An increase in the number of cultivars has resulted in more uses for this durable plant. The straight mugo species is seldom grown in the landscape. There are quite a few cultivars and varieties that have been selected for their superior form or smaller size. Dwarf mugo pine, Pinus mugo mugo, is a lower-growing variety. Don't be fooled by its name—this dwarf is smaller than the species but can grow up to 8 feet tall. The mugo pine is native to the mountains of central and southern Europe, thus the other common name Swiss Mountain Pine. The name mugo refers to a mountainous region in western Austria and northern Italy where the mugo pine is native.

Other Common Name
Swiss Mountain Pine

Bloom Period and Seasonal Color
Evergreen foliage.

Mature Height × Spread
15 ft. × 8 to 15 ft.

Ninebark

Physocarpus opulifolius

Ninebark is a big bold plant that offers a dramatic silhouette against the winter sky. Or, as some gardeners feel, a coarse textured plant that is difficult to use. The new introduction 'Diablo' has elevated the status of this plant even among those who dislike ninebark. The straight species has pinkish-white flowers in spring. The fruit is an eye-catching angular dried capsule that starts out red eventually turning brown. The stout peeling stems are attractive though masked by the leaves in summer and tangled stems in winter. Regular pruning will help you get the most out of the winter show. This hardy native was introduced into the landscape trade in 1879.

Other Common Name
Eastern Ninebark

Bloom Period and Seasonal Color
Spring with white or pinkish flowers.

Mature Height × **Spread**
5 to 10 ft. tall and wide

When, Where, and How to Plant
Ninebark is usually sold as a container-grown plant. It responds well to transplanting and can be planted throughout the season. Grow this adaptable plant in full sun to partial shade location. This plant has the adaptability and toughness of the spirea. It tolerates acid to alkaline soils as well as drought. Follow planting directions in the chapter introduction. Space them 5 to 6 feet apart.

Growing Tips
Water established plants when the top 4 to 6 inches of soil begins to dry. Organic mulch will help conserve moisture and reduce weed problems. Wait a year to fertilize new plantings. Follow soil test recommendations. Established plants need little, if any, fertilizer.

Care
Minimal care is needed for these tough plants. Regular pruning will improve their appearance. Prune a few of the old (larger) stems to the ground every year. The total height can be reduced by one-third. Older and overgrown plants can be pruned back to ground level. I prefer the first method which results in more regulated regrowth. Plus it's easier on the gardener.

Companion Planting and Design
Gardeners looking for purple leafed plants should consider 'Diablo'. This hardy, basically pest-free plant will provide purple foliage without the problems of the purple leaf sand cherries and Newport plums. Dwarf ninebark form has more refined growth and can be trained into a hedge. The straight species is great in natural plantings and more informal gardens.

My Personal Favorites
The cultivar 'Diablo' (shown) is the reason I added this plant to my new edition. It is hugely popular. It maintains its purple color when grown in full sun location. Give this big plant, 8 to 10 feet tall and wide, plenty of room. The red fruit adds to the colorful summer display. Use this with ornamental grasses and silver and chartreuse flowers and foliage. I have seen this cultivar effectively used as a hedge or screen, or as an accent plant in the mixed border. The dwarf ninebark (*Physcarpus opulifolius nana*) has smaller less-lobed leaves and finer stem tips like bridal wreath spirea.

When, Where, and How to Plant

Potentillas are usually sold as container-grown plants at nurseries and garden centers. Plant them any time during the growing season. Grow potentillas in full sun and well drained soil for best results. See planting directions in the chapter introduction. Space plants 2¹/₂ to 3 feet apart.

Growing Tips

Water thoroughly whenever the top 4 to 6 inches of soil are crumbly and moist. Established potentillas can tolerate dry conditions. Mulch the soil to help conserve moisture and reduce weed problems. Wait a year to fertilize new plantings according to soil test recommendations or the general guidelines given in this chapter. Avoid high-nitrogen fertilizers that can prevent flowering and encourage floppy growth. Established shrubs need little, if any, fertilizer.

Care

Potentilla needs regular pruning to remain attactive. Prune overgrown and floppy potentillas in the spring before growth begins. Cut the plants back halfway to the ground. Remove about ¹/₃ to ¹/₂ of the larger stems to ground level, or prune all the stems back to just above ground level. This rejuvenation pruning can be done every second or third year as needed.

Companion Planting and Design

These shrubs are used in a shrub border, for mass plantings, mixed with perennials, or as a low hedge. They combine nicely with other sun loving, drought tolerant plants.

My Personal Favorites

The white flowers and smaller size of 'Frosty' make it a good addition to perennial and rock gardens. Or use it in front of shrub borders. A larger white cultivar is 'Abbotswood', with blue-green foliage and outstanding white flowers. It grows 3 feet tall. Others include 'McKay's White', developed at Wisconsin's McKay Nursery. It has more of a creamy-white flower with yellow-green leaves. 'Goldfinger' has large, bright yellow flowers that last into fall. This compact cultivar grows 3 to 4 feet tall and has dark green leaves. 'Pink Beauty' has bright pink flowers. Most of the red and pink varieties tend to fade to yellow in our hot summers unless grown in a cooler location.

Potentilla's bright yellow blossoms add color to the summer landscape. Its color, as well as its dense growth habit and pest free nature, make it a popular landscape plant. And just like with any tough plant, we gardeners push it beyond its limits. Proper cultivar and site selection and correct pruning will keep potentillas looking good in the landscape. Select the cultivar with the flower color, bloom time, and plant size that best suits the location. This is one of the few woody plants native throughout most of the Northern Hemisphere. You will find plants throughout the United States (including Minnesota), Great Britain, Europe, and China. The botanical name potentilla is from the Latin potens meaning powerful. It refers to its medicinal properties. The name fruticosa means shrubby.

Other Common Name
Bush Cinquefoil

Bloom Period and Seasonal Color
Summer blooms in yellow.

Mature Height × Spread
1 to 4 ft. × 4 ft.

Rhododendron

Rhododendron species

Rhododendrons like cool, moist, acidic soil and milder winters than we usually have. So why are so many Minnesota gardeners trying to grow them? The large, beautiful, and often fragrant flowers cannot be duplicated by another spring flowering plant. Their unique beauty has driven gardeners to expend time and money amending the soil and providing winter protection. This interest has encouraged plant breeders to develop more northern-hardy cultivars. There are over 900 species of rhododendrons and many more cultivars. So is it a rhododendron or an azalea? There is no clear distinction between them. In general, rhododendrons are evergreen, and azaleas are deciduous. Azalea flowers have 5 stamens (male flower parts) and rhododendron have 10 or more. Azaleas have funnel form flowers, while the rhododendron's are more bell shaped.

Other Common Name
Azalea

Bloom Period and Seasonal Color
Spring blooms in all colors.

Mature Height × Spread
5 ft. × 3 to 5 ft.

When, Where, and How to Plant
Plant balled-and-burlapped plants as soon as possible after purchasing. Plant container-grown plants in the spring or early summer to get them established before winter. Grow rhododendrons in moist, acidic soil. I have seen plants survive in the alkaline clay soil of Minnesota. Rhododendrons prefer full sun if the soil is kept moist. Avoid planting where the leaves will be subject to drying by winter wind and sun. An east facing location works well. Add several inches of organic matter to the top 12 inches of soil prior to planting to improve the drainage in heavy clay soil and the water-holding capacity of sandy soil. Alkaline soil may require adding granular sulfur or some other acidifying material prior to planting. See the chapter introduction for planting guidelines. Space them 3 feet apart.

Growing Tips
Established rhododendrons prefer moist soil. Water thoroughly whenever the top few inches of soil are moist but crumbly. Mulch the soil to conserve moisture, improve the soil, and reduce weed problems. Wait a year to fertilize new plantings.

Care
Rhododendrons require little pruning. Remove any winter damage and thin out overcrowded branches in the spring after flowering, or when they should have flowered. Winter injury is the biggest problem facing rhododendrons. Water them thoroughly in the fall before the ground freezes. Mulching insulates the roots. Young plants and those growing in exposed sites benefit from additional winter protection. Wrap them in burlap or surround with a hardware cloth cylinder filled with straw or evergreen boughs.

Companion Planting and Design
Rhododendrons are nice as a focal point in the spring garden or as an understory plant in woodland gardens.

My Personal Favorites
The University of Minnesota developed 'Northern Lights' azaleas and cultivar 'PJM' rhododendrons for hardiness. The 'Northern Lights' azaleas are hardy to Zone 3b. These compact plants grow up to 5 feet tall and have fragrant pink, orange, yellow, or white flowers. 'PJM' rhododendron is evergreen and hardy to Zone 4.

Spirea

Spiraea species

When, Where, and How to Plant

Plant balled-and-burlapped shrubs as soon as possible after they are purchased, and container-grown plants throughout the season. Spireas tolerate a wide range of soils, except for wet sites. Follow planting directions in the chapter introduction. Spacing varies with species grown.

Growing Tips

Established plants are drought tolerant. Water thoroughly whenever the top 4 to 6 inches feels slightly dry. Mulch to conserve moisture and reduce weed problems. Wait at least a year to fertilize new plantings. Follow soil test recommendations for the amount and type of fertilizer to use. Spireas are fast growers and need minimal fertilizer when young and very little, if any, once they are established.

Care

Spring-blooming spireas flower on the previous season's growth. Prune them just after flowering. Pruning at any other time will eliminate the flowers. Summer-blooming spireas flower on new growth. Prune in late winter before growth begins. Prune overgrown and floppy spireas back halfway to the ground. Remove about 1/3 to 1/2 of the older stems to ground level. Or prune all the stems back to ground level. This method is quick and easy, but the plants tend to be a bit more relaxed in their growth habit. Lightly shear summer-blooming spireas as the flowers fade to encourage a second and even third flush of flowers.

Companion Planting and Design

Bridal wreath spirea works well in heirloom landscapes and near older homes. Give it room to show off its natural form. All spireas can be used in mass plantings, as filler plants, and as bank cover. The smaller scale spireas work nicely in rock gardens and the mixed border.

My Personal Favorites

Select a cultivar that fits your garden design. Cultivars of the Japanese spirea are among the most popular of the summer-blooming spireas. They all produce pink, rose, or white flowers in the summer. For yellow foliage, try 'Limemound'®. The foliage starts out yellow with a russet tinge and matures to a lime green. The fall color is orange-red on red stems.

Spireas are tough, colorful plants that have been used extensively in the landscape. The summer-blooming spireas have become more prominent in recent years. These colorful shrubs require little maintenance and tolerate the stresses of urban landscapes. Let the plants stand for winter. The chestnut stems and dried seedheads can add to your winter landscape. Vanhoutte spirea, Spiraea × vanhouttei (shown), is the most popular spring bloomer. Many gardeners call this bridal wreath spirea. It is a large, arching shrub with long branches covered with white flowers in the spring. Snowmound spirea is a bit tidier in appearance and may be a good substitute for bridal wreath. It has similar white flowers in late May, dark blue-green leaves, dense habit, and is only 3 to 5 feet tall and wide.

Other Common Name
Bridal Wreath

Bloom Period and Seasonal Color
Spring or summer blooms in white, pink, and rose.

Mature Height × Spread
2 to 8 ft. × 2 to 8 ft.

Viburnum
Viburnum species

Viburnums are excellent landscape plants. Their white, sometimes pink-tinged, flowers provide spring interest. The leaves can be glossy and green, or slightly hairy, giving the plant a softer look. The red, blue, or black berries attract birds to your landscape. Some viburnums have spectacular red or purple fall color. These ornamental features combined with the diversity of sizes and shapes, make Viburnums good additions to any landscape. Our native American cranberrybush viburnum, Viburnum trilobum, is a large shrub that has white flowers in the spring, persistent red berries, red fall color, and is hardy statewide. The berries are edible, but I would need to add lots of sugar to add them to my diet. Avoid planting the look-a-like European cranberrybush, Viburnum opulus, and Wayfaring Viburnum, Viburnum lantana. These non-natives are starting to invade our natural areas.

Other Common Name
Cranberrybush Viburnum

Bloom Period and Seasonal Color
Spring blooms in white

Mature Height × Spread
2 to 15 ft. × 2 to 10 ft.

When, Where, and How to Plant
Plant balled-and-burlapped plants as soon as possible after purchasing, and container-grown plants throughout the season. Plant tender viburnums in spring or early summer to give them time to get established before winter. Viburnum species vary slightly in their light and soil requirements. Most tolerate full sun to partial shade. They prefer moist soil, but some species are drought tolerant. See the chapter introduction for planting information. Spacing varies with the species.

Growing Tips
Established viburnum species that require moist soil should be watered during dry periods. Water thoroughly whenever the top 4 to 6 inches is moist but crumbly. Mulch the soil to conserve moisture and reduce weed problems. Wait a year to fertilize new plantings. Established shrubs need little, if any, fertilizer.

Care
Slow-growing viburnums need little pruning. Remove unwanted branches back to an adjoining branch or main stem. For fast-growing suckering types, prune out old wood to ground level in the spring after flowering. You can prune the remaining stems by one-third. Viburnum borers are the most deadly pest, killing viburnum stems. Regular pruning and proper care will reduce the risk. Prune out and destroy infected stems as soon as they are discovered. Insecticides can be applied in early June.

Companion Planting and Design
Use viburnums as screens, hedges, backdrops, specimen plants, and wildlife plants. Most work well in formal, informal, or natural settings.

My Personal Favorites
Koreanspice viburnum, *Viburnum carlesii*, is used as a specimen plant. The pink buds open to white fragrant flowers, followed by blue-black fruit and spectacular red fall color. It's hardy in Zone 4. Arrowwood viburnum, *Viburnum dentatum*, has white spring flowers, blue fruit the birds love, and excellent fall color. It's a great choice for hedges, screens, and background plantings. It is hardy to Zone 4. 'Emerald Triumph' was developed by the University of Minnesota and selected for its hardiness and pest resistance (hardy through Zone 4).

Weigela
Weigela florida

When, Where, and How to Plant
Plant bare-root weigela in the spring before growth begins, and container-grown plants throughout the season. Planting in the spring or early summer gives the plants time to get established before winter. Grow weigela in full sun with well drained soil. Follow planting instructions in the chapter introduction. Space plants 3 to 4 feet apart.

Growing Tips
Water established plants thoroughly whenever the top 4 to 6 inches of soil is moist and crumbly. Mulch the soil to help conserve moisture and reduce weed problems. Wait a year before fertilizing new plantings. Follow soil test recommendations for the type and amount of fertilizer to use. Established shrubs need little, if any, fertilizer.

Care
Young weigelas need very little pruning. Remove any dead wood as it is discovered. Prune established shrubs in early summer after the first flush of flowers. Reduce the overall shrub size by cutting back long flowering stems to older upright growth. Remove several older stems to ground level each season. You can prune overgrown weigela back to ground level. Weigelas frequently suffer winter injury. Extensive damage will require major pruning. The plants will survive but you will lose the first and largest flush of flowers.

Companion Planting and Design
Weigela works best when used for massing, in the shrub border, or combined with other plants. The small size of 'Midnight Wine' fits well in my small yard and combines nicely with annuals, perennials, and my dwarf conifer garden.

My Personal Favorites
'Midnight Wine' has dark burgundy foliage and pink flowers. This weigela grows into a tidy mound 18 to 24 inches tall and 24 inches wide. The larger version, 'Wine and Roses', has similar foliage and flowers on a 4- to 5-foot plant. 'Pink Poppet' produces pale pink blooms on a 2-foot-tall plant that is hardy to Zone 3. 'Dark Horse' has bronze leaves with lime green venation that make an eyecatching backdrop for its magenta pink flowers. 'Bristol Snowflake' is a white-flowering cultivar. Compact 'Variegata' has green leaves with pale yellow-to-white edges.

Weigela is an old-time landscape plant that has remained a favorite for many years. The large arching growth habit looks to me like something I would find near an old farmhouse. Many gardeners include weigela to honor childhood memories while others are captivated by the many new cultivars with colorful foliage, intense flowers, and more compact growth habit. Whatever your motivation, this shrub provides flowers in spring and sporadically throughout the summer and into fall. My students and I have found a few stray weigela blossoms in November. You may see hummingbirds nectaring on the flowers and other birds feeding on the seeds. The leaves can be green, bronze, or variegated adding to the shrubs summer appeal. The dried seed capsules may look messy to some, but I think they add a bit of interest to the winter landscape.

Other Common Name
Old-Fashioned Weigela

Bloom Period and Seasonal Color
Spring through summer blooms in pink, red, white, and purplish-red

Mature Height × Spread
Up to 6 ft. × 9 to 12 ft.

Zones
Hardy to Zone 4

Witchhazel

Hamamelis virginiana

Witchhazel is found growing in shaded areas along the banks of streams in southeast Minnesota forests. In the landscape, it can tolerate a wider range of conditions. Its fragrant, yellow flowers are the last of the season. They open in mid-October or November as the leaves turn yellow and drop from the plant. Witchhazel fruits are dried capsules that form in November or December and persist for a year. The seeds ripen in twelve months and are literally shot out of the capsule. It is fun to listen to this unique seed-planting technique. Witchhazel also has an interesting and useful history. Divining rods made out of witchhazel are used to locate water. The witchhazel extract my grandma used to cure everything is still available in the pharmacy. It is made from distilled bark of young witchhazel stems and shoots.

Other Common Name
Common Witchhazel

Bloom Period and Seasonal Color
Fall blooms in yellow.

Mature Height × Spread
10 to 15 ft. × 10 to 15 ft.

When, Where, and How to Plant
Plant balled-and-burlapped shrubs as soon as possible after purchasing. You can plant container-grown plants throughout the season. I prefer to get them in the ground in spring or early summer to get them established before winter. Witchhazel grows well in sun or shade and performs best in moist soil though it will tolerate some extremes. Avoid growing witchhazel in very alkaline soil. See chapter introduction for planting tips. Space these large shrubs at least 5 to 6 feet apart.

Growing Tips
Water established plants thoroughly whenever the top 4 to 6 inches of soil is crumbly but moist. Mulch to help conserve moisture and reduce weed problems. Wait at least a year before fertilizing new plantings. Follow soil test recommendations for the type and amount of fertilizer to use. Avoid high-nitrogen fertilizers that may inhibit flowering. Witchhazel leaves may yellow in alkaline soil. Use acidifying fertilizers, such as ammonium sulfate, to minimize the problem. Established shrubs need little, if any, fertilizer.

Care
Keep pruning to a minimum with witchhazels. They are slow growing and respond slowly to pruning. Remove dead, damaged, or wayward branches in the spring. Prune them back to young healthy growth. Extensive feeding by rabbits will kill the plant. Fencing is the most effective way to protect these plants.

Companion Planting and Design
This large shrub is excellent for naturalizing large areas. It can also be included in shrub borders or near large buildings. I have seen it pruned up into a small tree and used in more formal settings. Place the plant where its fall color and fall flowers can be enjoyed.

My Personal Favorites
Vernal witchhazel, *Hamamelis vernalis* (shown), blooms in late winter instead of fall. The flowers are yellow to red, appear in late February or March, and hardy to Zone 4. Fothergilla is in the witchhazel family. It has lovely white fragrant bottlebrush flowers in spring and spectacular fall color. Plant the dwarf form in a protected location (in Zone 4) for best results.

When, Where, and How to Plant

Yews transplant best as balled-and-burlapped plants and should be planted as soon as possible after purchasing. Some nurseries and garden centers dig yews and place them in pots for easy handling. Others sell container-grown yews. Plant evergreens by October 1 to give them time to get established before winter. Avoid areas with drying winter winds to minimize the risk of winter burn. Good drainage is essential. Plants grown in poorly drained soils will eventually die. See the chapter introduction for planting tips. Spacing varies with type.

Growing Tips

Water thoroughly whenever the top 4 to 6 inches of soil is moist and crumbly. Be sure to water all evergreen plantings thoroughly in the fall before the ground freezes. Mulch the soil to help conserve moisture, insulate the roots, and reduce weed problems. Wait at least a year to fertilize new plantings. Established yews need little, if any, fertilizer.

Care

Yews are traditionally sheared into hedges, rectangles, and gumdrops but are quite attractive and healthier when grown in their natural form. They also require very little pruning if the right-sized plant is selected for the location. Prune yews in the spring before growth begins, or lightly in midsummer when they are semi-dormant. Maintain the yew's natural form by pruning branches back to a healthy bud, where the branch joins another branch, or back to the main trunk. Yews will also tolerate severe pruning, but be patient—it takes time for the plants to recover. Prune out any browning caused by winter damage or disease.

Companion Planting and Design

Yews are used as foundation plants, screens, and hedges. Combine yews with deciduous shrubs like chokeberry, serviceberry, and dogwoods for added beauty. The dark green foliage is a nice backdrop for perennial and annual flower gardens.

My Personal Favorites

There are hundreds of cultivars of yews on the market. Select one of the hardy Japanese *Taxus cuspidata* or Anglojap *Taxus × media* cultivars for your landscape. Look for the cultivar with the best size and shape for your landscape.

Evergreen yews can be found in most Midwest landscapes. Canadian yew, Taxus canadensis, is native to Minnesota. It is the hardiest of all the yews but is not well suited to most landscape situations. But the wide variety of shapes and sizes available, along with the yew's ability to grow in sun or shade, make the cultivated yew adaptable to many landscape situations. The soft, dark-green needles add texture to the landscape while the red fruit and bark provide additional interest. Pretty to look at but don't eat. The red fruit consists of a single seed covered by a fleshy red cup. It has a sweet but unpleasant taste that usually makes curious children spit it out. The red portion is not toxic but the seeds, bark, and foliage are.

Other Common Name
Taxus

Bloom Period and Seasonal Color
Evergreen foliage.

Mature Height × Spread
20 ft. × 10 ft.

Trees *for Minnesota*

Trees give structure to our landscape, providing form and year-round interest. They perform a variety of functions: offering privacy and shelter, serving as a habitat for wildlife, and providing a focal point for outdoor plantings. With proper selection, planting, and care, these plants can be an integral part of the Minnesota gardener's landscape for years to come.

Tree Selection

Planting the right tree in the right spot is a vital first step toward keeping it healthy throughout its life. Select the tree that is best suited to the soil, moisture, temperature, and other growing conditions of its location. Then choose a tree that will fit the available space, making sure the roots and crown will have enough room when they reach full size. Remember to check for overhead and underground utility lines.

With the choices narrowed down, the final consideration is selecting a tree appropriate for your landscape's design and function. Trees are available in upright, spreading, weeping, and irregular forms. Use the species and form best suited to your needs. Locate the planting site and call Gopher State One Call throughout Minnesota at 1-800-252-1166.

Purchasing the Tree

Now it's time to go shopping. Purchase your trees from a quality nursery or garden center. Trees are available bare root, balled and burlapped, or container grown. Bare-root plants are cheaper but should only be planted in the spring before growth begins. Balled-and-burlapped trees are dug in the spring and

A Row of Maples

Ash

fall. They are more expensive and are available for a longer period than bare-root trees. Container-grown trees are planted and grown in pots. They can be purchased and planted throughout the season.

Choose a tree with a straight trunk, good structure, and no signs of insect or disease problems. Smaller trees are easier to handle and recover more quickly from transplanting. A two-and-one-half-inch-diameter transplanted tree will soon surpass a 6-inch-diameter transplanted tree, plus you get the joy of watching it grow.

Transporting

Give your tree a safe ride home. Transporting the tree in a pickup truck or trailer is easier for you and better for the tree, or you can have it delivered. It is worth the extra effort or delivery cost to get your investment home safely.

Use a tarp to cover the top of the tree and prevent wind damage to leaves on the trip home. Cover the roots of bare-root trees to prevent drying. With a towel, wrap the trunk where it will rest on the vehicle. And always move the tree by the rootball, NOT the trunk, to prevent damage to the roots.

Plant your new trees as soon as possible. Keep them in a cool, shaded location until planting. Mulch bare-root and balled-and-burlapped trees with wood chips to keep their roots moist. Water these and container-grown trees daily or as needed.

Flowering Cherry

Planting

Locate the tree's root flare (the bell-shaped area where the roots angle away from the trunk). Plant the tree with the root flare at or slightly above the soil line. Dig a shallow planting hole the same depth as and three to five times wider than the root system. Roughen the sides of the planting hole to make it easier for the roots to enter the surrounding soil. Remove container-grown plants from the pot. Loosen or slice potbound and girdling roots. Place the tree in the planting hole. Be sure the tree is straight, moving it by the rootball, not the trunk, to minimize root damage. Remove the tags, twine, and metal baskets and cut away the burlap on balled-and-burlapped trees. Fill the hole with existing soil. Do not amend the backfill. The tree roots need to adjust to their new environment, and amended soils encourage roots to stay in the planting hole instead of moving out into the landscape. Water to settle the soil; mulch. Do not stake balled-and-burlapped or container-grown trees unless they have a large canopy and a small root system or are subject to high winds and vandalism. Stake bare-root plants. Install the stakes in undisturbed soil outside the planting hole. Use a soft strap rather than wire around the tree trunk. Remove the stakes one or two years after planting. (See the planting diagram on page 256).

Care for Newly Planted Trees

Do not prune newly planted trees. Research shows that the more leaves a tree has, the more energy it can produce, and the quicker it develops new roots and recovers from transplant shock. Do remove broken and damaged branches at planting time. Structural pruning will start in the next few years once the tree has adjusted to its new home.

Water the area near the trunk to beyond the planting hole. The key to success with watering is to water thoroughly but infrequently. Check the soil moisture before watering. It's time to break out the hose when the top six inches of soil is crumbly and moist. Apply enough water to wet the top twelve inches of soil. A thorough watering once every seven to ten days is usually enough for clay soils. Check quick drying, sandy soils twice a week.

Mulch the soil to conserve moisture, reduce competition from grass, and prevent weeds. Mulch also keeps the tree-damaging mowers and weed whip away from the tree trunk. Apply a three-inch layer of wood chips or shredded bark on the soil surface. Keep the mulch an inch or so away from the tree trunk.

Ongoing Care

Do not fertilize newly planted trees. Wait until the following spring to apply fertilizer. Use the amount recommended by soil test results or read and follow label directions on the fertilizer packet. Established trees do not need routine fertilization. They usually get plenty of nutrients from the fertilizers applied to surrounding lawns and gardens. Overfertilization can reduce flowering, increase risk of certain diseases and insects, damage tree roots, and actually reduce the plants health and vigor. Proper watering and mulching is the best care you can give your plants.

Everyone wants to know how much fertilizer to add without a soil test. The proper amount really depends on the health of the tree, growing location, and our climate. It is better to err on the side of underfertilizing; you can always add more at a later time. So if I must give a rate, here goes. Use a slow-release nitrogen fertilizer with little or no phosphorous and potassium. Apply two to three pounds of actual nitrogen fertilizer for every thousand square feet under the tree. This is equal to twenty to thirty pounds of a ten percent nitrogen fertilizer and ten to fifteen pounds of a twenty percent fertilizer. Get out the calculator to adjust the quantity for the percent nitrogen in the fertilizer you select and the size of the area you will be fertilizing.

Fertilizer can be applied over mulch. Water to move the fertilizer through the mulch and down to the tree roots. Place fertilizer in the soil for trees growing in the lawn areas. Remove small cores of soil six inches deep and two to three feet apart throughout the area around the tree. Start digging holes several feet away from the tree trunk. Divide needed fertilizer evenly between the holes. Water thoroughly, moistening the top twelve inches of soil.

Prune young trees to establish a strong framework, keeping the plant's growth habit in mind. Remove crossed, rubbing, and parallel branches. Select branches with wide crotch angles, the angle between the trunk and branch, to form the framework. Create a framework of branches that spiral upward around the trunk. Prune out competing central leaders. Pruning young trees results in smaller wounds that close faster. Do not apply pruning paint; it can trap in problems instead of keeping them out.

Despite your best efforts, pest problems may arise. Get a proper diagnosis and control recommendation from the local County University Extension Office or a certified arborist (tree care professional). Check out the International Society of Arboriculture (www.isa-arbor.com) for a list of certified arborists in your area.

Many problems that look bad to us are not really detrimental to healthy trees. If treatment is needed, select an effective method that is the safest for you, the tree, and the environment. Your efforts will be rewarded with years of enjoyment.

Alder

Alnus glutinosa

Alders are fast growing trees that can survive in difficult growing situations. They tolerate a wide range of conditions including wet soils. Alders are pyramidal in shape when young but tend to open up and become more rounded, like many of us, with age. Multistemmed plants are also available and are quite attractive. In spring, long, yellow-green catkin flowers appear. The fruit is a small, woody, egg-shaped strobile that resembles a small pinecone. In fact you often see these dipped in silver or gold and used for pendants or earrings. Fruits stay on the tree, providing winter interest. Alders are native to Europe, Western Asia, and northern Africa. They have escaped from our landscapes and established some pure stands along waterways, leading many to believe they are native.

Other Common Name
European Alder

Bloom Period and Seasonal Color
Early spring, with subtle yellow catkins.

Mature Height × Spread
40 ft. × 30 ft.

When, Where, and How to Plant
Alders adapt well to transplanting. Plant balled-and-burlapped trees as soon as possible after purchasing. Plant container-grown plants throughout the growing season. They prefer moist soil but tolerate both wet or dry and acidic or slightly alkaline soil conditions. Plant the tree with the root flare at, or slightly above, the soil line. Remove the container, twine, and the metal baskets. Cut away the burlap. Backfill, water to settle the soil, and mulch.

Growing Tips
Alder is a fairly low-maintenance tree. Water thoroughly whenever the top 4 to 6 inches of soil is crumbly and moist. Mulch to conserve moisture and improve tree health. Wait a year after planting to fertilize young trees. This fast growing tree is able to fix nitrogen from the atmosphere—it needs little if any supplemental fertilizer.

Care
This tree is very resistant to rot. In fact, the wood is so durable it has been used for bridges, sluice gates, and wooden shoes. Tent caterpillar, leafminer, and woolly aphids can be found feeding on this specimen. Prune out and destroy tent caterpillar nests to control this pest. Aders can tolerate damage caused by leafminers. Woolly aphids can create an unsightly mess. These aphids are covered with white fibers. As they feed, they secrete a clear, sticky substance called honeydew. A black, sooty mold can grow on the honeydew, creating sticky globs. Small populations are not a problem. Control large populations with several applications of insecticidal soap.

Companion Planting and Design
Alder can be short lived. Use it for quick impact and in areas subject to temporary flooding. The alder is a good substitute for the willow tree in wet locations. It isn't messy like the willow, nor does it create problems with invasive roots. The alder can be used alone as a specimen or planted in a group for mass effect. It looks nice growing in a backyard or next to a pond.

My Personal Favorites
'Pyramidalis' is an upright, columnar form growing 40 to 50 feet tall. 'Laciniata' is a large form growing 50 to 70 feet with lobed leaves.

Amur Corktree
Phellodendron amurense

When, Where, and How to Plant

Plant balled-and-burlapped trees as soon as possible after purchasing, and container-grown plants throughout the growing season. Use transplants less than 2 inches in diameter at breast height—the diameter of the tree at $4^{1}/_{2}$ feet aboveground (dbh)— for bare-root plantings. Grow corktrees in full sun. Their wide spreading root system adapts well to a variety of soils including acid, alkaline, and dry. Locate the tree's root flare. Dig a shallow planting hole the same depth and 3 to 5 times wider than the root system. Plant the tree with the root flare at, or slightly above, the soil line. Remove the container, twine, and the metal baskets. Cut away the burlap. Backfill, water to settle the soil, and mulch.

Growing Tips

Water thoroughly whenever the top 4 to 6 inches of soil begins to dry. Mulch to conserve moisture, suppress weeds, and reduce competition from grass. Wait a year to fertilize new plantings. Established trees need little, if any, fertilizer.

Care

Amur corktree is basically pest free. Prune young trees to establish a strong branch structure. Infrequent pruning is needed on mature trees. The fruit attracts birds but may cause a litter problem. Select a seedless variety to avoid the black fruit and the birds it attracts. Prune in winter for best results. Larger trees, bigger than $2^{1}/_{2}$ inches dbh may take a bit longer to establish.

Companion Planting and Design

A lone corktree against the winter sky is quite a site. Use this medium-sized tree for shade and ornamental value. Surround it with mulch or planting beds to mask falling fruit.

My Personal Favorites

'Macho' is a vigorous, fruitless, male cultivar. It has thick leathery leaves that are even more resistant to insects and drought than the species. 'His Majesty' was recently introduced by the University of Minnesota Landscape Arboretum. This fruitless hybrid has good yellow fall color, quickly grows into a mature vase-shaped habit, and is hardy throughout Minnesota. Sakhalin corktree (*Phellodedron sachalinense*), one of the parents of 'His Majesty', seems to be fast growing and hardier.

It's pretty to look at and tolerant of some pretty difficult northern conditions. The deeply furrowed corky bark led to this tree's common name, corktree, and its landscape appeal. The yellowish green flowers appear in late spring and are missed by most gardeners. The female trees bear fruit that ripens to black in fall. The berries persist into winter, adding interest and bird food to the winter landscape. Select a seedless cultivar if fruit does not sound appealing to you. The leaves put on a brief colorful display in fall as they turn from deep green to yellow or yellowy-bronze. The winter show is provided by the corky bark and picturesque form. The broad spreading canopy forms atop a shorter trunk. The few corky branches that reach out horizontally from the trunk are quite attractive against the winter sky.

Other Common Name
Corktree

Bloom Period and Seasonal Color
Late spring insignificant blooms, yellow fall color.

Mature Height and Spread
30 to 45 ft. × 30 to 45 ft.

Ash

Fraxinus species

Ash trees are commonly seen in nature and in land-scapes. *The yellow flowers create a subtle display in early spring. The green leaves that follow provide shade for home and land alike. In the fall, the leaves turn an attractive yellow or purple. White ash, Fraxinus americana, is native to Minnesota. This large tree has a wonderful reddish-purple fall color. Use it as a specimen in large landscapes. Sports enthusiasts and gardeners may know this tree for its strong wood used to make oars, paddles, bats, and handles for garden tools. Green ash, Fraxinus pennsylvanica, is native to other parts of the United States. It is much more tolerant of difficult sites but is twiggy and often irregularly shaped. Select a seedless form, like 'Patmore' with better growth habit. Green ash leaves turn yellow in the fall.*

Other Common Names
White Ash, Green Ash

Bloom Period and Seasonal Color
Early spring yellow flowers with yellow or red-purple fall color.

Mature Height × Spread
50 or more ft. × 25 or more ft.

When, Where, and How to Plant
Ash trees adapt well to transplanting. Plant balled-and-burlapped trees as soon as possible after they are purchased. Plant container-grown plants throughout the growing season. Ash trees tolerate a wide range of growing conditions. They prefer moist, well-drained soil. The green ash is tougher than the white ash. It will tolerate wet to dry soil. Follow planting directions in the chapter introduction.

Growing Tips
Keep ash trees healthy by mulching. Water trees thoroughly whenever the top 4 to 6 inches of soil are crumbly and moist. Wait a year to fertilize new plantings. Established trees need little, if any, fertilizer.

Care
Ash suffers from ash plant bug, borers, and Verticillium wilt. Its leaves may yellow and the plants decline if grown in an inappropriate spot. These trees produce lots of seeds, creating a weed problem in gardens and hedges. Select a male clone to avoid this problem. Ash flower gall is the other chief concern. It doesn't harm the plant, but it can be a nuisance in the landscape when the galls drop, creating a litter problem on walks and patios. Emerald Ash borer is a future concern. This insect attacks healthy trees, and the only cure is tree removal. Watch the news or contact your local County Cooperative Extension Service or Department of Natural Resources office for updates on the status of this potential pest.

Companion Planting and Design
Both trees make good medium- to fast-growing shade trees. Use them to shade a deck, picnic table, or the east and west side of the house.

My Personal Favorites
'Cimmaron' green ash is seedless, has rich red fall color, and grows to 60 feet tall and 30 feet wide. 'Leprechaun' green ash is dwarf in every way. It grows 18 feet tall and 16 feet wide with small leaves. I have seen these grafted on straight trunks to create a mini allee or small scale patio tree. 'Autumn Applause' and 'Autumn Purple' are seedless white ash cultivars with reliable fall color.

When, Where, and How to Plant

Transplant young trees in early spring. European beeches adapt better to transplanting and are more readily available. Beeches must have moist, well-drained soil. The European beech tends to be a little more tolerant of varied and urban conditions. Locate the tree's root flare. Dig a shallow planting hole the same depth as and 3 to 5 times wider than the root system. Plant the tree with the root flare at or slightly above the soil line. Remove the container, twine, and metal baskets. Cut away the burlap and fill the hole with existing soil. Water to settle the soil then mulch.

Growing Tips

Water thoroughly whenever the top 4 to 6 inches is crumbly and moist. Mulch the soil under these trees to conserve moisture, reduce weeds, and protect the shallow roots. Wait a year to fertilize new plantings.

Care

If planted in the proper location, beech trees are low maintenance and have no real problems, but remember this is a slow growing plant. Prune young trees to establish a framework.

Companion Planting and Design

Use American beeches as specimen plants or for naturalizing. The European beech also makes a nice specimen plant. It can be trimmed into a hedge, although it is difficult for many gardeners, including me, to severely prune such a lovely, sometimes hard-to-find, and expensive tree! Both the American and European beech trees will eventually grow into large shade trees. The beech tree is shallow rooted, making it nearly impossible to grow grass beneath its canopy. So give up the losing battle and mulch the area under the tree. Or, better yet, leave the beech branched to the ground. This is an attractive way to grow this large tree.

My Personal Favorites

The American beech, *Fagus grandifolia*, is native to Minnesota. It is hardy in Zones 4b and 5 and is becoming more readily available. European beeches are more available from nurseries. 'Atropunicea' ('Purpurea') is the most common of the purple-leaf forms. 'Roseomarginata' ('Purpurea Tricolor') has purple leaves with pinkish white and rose-colored leaf margins.

The beech tree is one of the majestic trees of the woods and landscape. These slow-growing trees carefully build a strong framework that lasts for many years. The smooth gray bark provides beauty and interest in all four seasons. Watch with great anticipation as the bronze leaves unfurl in the spring. Soon, they turn green for the summer and develop a rich brown hue in the fall. Some of the leaves persist on the tree through the winter to provide sound, color, and movement. The fruit on mature beeches is quickly devoured by a variety of birds. The words beech *and* book *are from the same root, which refers to the ancient practice of using beech wood for writing boards. Unfortunately, lovers and graffiti artists have also used the beech trunks for writing boards.*

Other Common Names
American Beech, European Beech

Bloom Period and Seasonal Color
Brown foliage in Fall

Mature Height × Spread
50 or more ft. × 35 or more ft.

Birch

Betula species

Paper birch is a very popular tree in Minnesota. When I moved north twenty-five years ago, I was amazed to see white birches in front of so many homes. I knew of the problems common to the birch, and I couldn't imagine why so many people grew them. I then went "up north" and realized that everyone wanted a piece of the north woods in their landscape. The paper birch, Betula papyrifera, is native to our north woods. It has been enjoyed and used by many cultures in the past. Native Americans used it to make canoes, baskets, utensils, and wigwam covers. It is a medium to fast grower with outstanding white exfoliating bark. River birch, Betula nigra, is also native and is resistant to bronze birch borer. The bark exfoliates, exposing multiple colors of gray, cinnamon, or reddish brown.

Other Common Names
Paper Birch, Canoe Birch

Bloom Period and Seasonal Color
Early spring not significant; yellow fall color.

Mature Height × Spread
40 to 50 ft. × 20 to 25 ft.

When, Where, and How to Plant
Transplant birch trees in the spring for best results. Plant container-grown birch early in the season so this slow-to-establish plant has time to root before winter. Grow birches in full sun to partial shade with moist, well-drained soil. This is especially critical in southern Minnesota where the summers can be too warm for this plant. Follow planting directions in the chapter introduction.

Growing Tips
Birches need cool, moist soil. Mulch or plant ground covers under the trees to create this environment. Water trees thoroughly whenever the top few inches are moist and crumbly. Wait a year to fertilize new plantings. Fertilizer is often included with insecticides used to treat leafminer and borer. Check labels before adding more nutrients. River birch prefers a slightly acidic soil. Use fertilizers like ammonium sulfate or Milorganite that don't increase the soil pH.

Care
Leafminers feed between the upper and lower leaf surface, causing the leaves to brown. Treat leafminer to reduce plant stress and borer problems. Bronze birch borer is the biggest killer of white birch. Plant species resistant to this pest or minimize plant stress to prevent problems. Consult a certified tree care professional for effective control. Birch trees will 'bleed' when pruned in the spring. It won't hurt the plant; it's just a messy job.

Companion Planting and Design
Birches prefer woodland-type settings. Plant them en masse to create a northern woodland in your backyard or include birches in planting beds. Plant the tree where you can enjoy the attractive bark year-round. Place it in front of an evergreen for an even better show. Keep the roots cool and moist by growing perennial ground covers or low-growing shrubs under your birches.

My Personal Favorite
Whitespire birch was promoted as a pest-resistant plant. Unfortunately many of these were started from seedlings that did not retain their parents' resistance. Look for 'Whitespire Senior' birch (*Betula platyphylla japonica* 'Whitespire Senior' that were started from cuttings or tissue culture and are suppose to be borer resistant.

When, Where, and How to Plant

Plant small balled-and-burlapped trees in the spring. Plant container-grown plants throughout the growing season. They prefer moist, fertile soil but will tolerate a variety of soils including wet and dry. They are a good choice for difficult conditions in large areas. See planting directions in the chapter introduction.

Growing Tips

Water established trees thoroughly whenever the top 4 to 6 inches are crumbly and moist. Wait a year to fertilize new plantings. Catalpas are medium to fast growers, so established trees need little if any fertilizer.

Care

Catalpas require some cleanup. They will lose small branches in wind and ice storms. A post-storm cleanup will take care of this problem. The falling flowers drive meticulous gardeners to distraction. Proper placement will allow you to enjoy the flowers without a mess. Catalpas are subject to Verticillium wilt. This fungal disease blocks the flow of water and nutrients between the roots and leaves, causing branch dieback. Contact a certified arborist for positive diagnosis. Do not plant catalpas in locations where other plants have died from this disease.

Companion Planting and Design

This is not a tree for my small city lot. Their size and coarse texture can be overwhelming in a small setting. Place catalpas in areas where the dropping twigs and falling flowers don't create a cleanup nightmare. Position them so the spring bloom and winter interest can be enjoyed. I remember a street planting of these I would pass each night returning from class. It elicited feelings of scary Halloween movies.

My Personal Favorites

Chinese catalpa, *Catalpa ovata*, has the same basic features of the hardy catalpa. It is smaller and has slightly finer-textured, longer, and thinner fruit. The yellowish-white flowers are less impressive than those of northern catalpa. Both are hardy in Zone 4.

You may also know this plant as cigartree or Indian-bean tree for its long bean-like fruit. The name Catalpa is the North American Indian name for this tree. Though brittle, the wood resists rot and was once used for railroad ties. The large size, coarse texture, and dropping flowers often limit its use in home landscapes. Those of us who like it enjoy the attractive, cone-shaped panicle of flowers that stands out against the large, heart-shaped leaves. The rough, furrowed bark and persistent bean-like fruit add texture and interest to the winter landscape. A close look at the flowers may have you thinking of orchids. Each flower is white with a purple blotch in the center. The ends of the bell-shaped flowers are frilled. The beauty of the individual catalpa flower is often missed on the large tree.

Other Common Names
Northern Catalpa, Cigartree

Bloom Period and Seasonal Color
Early summer blooms in white.

Mature Height × Spread
40 to 60 ft. × 20 to 40 ft.

Zones
Hardy to Zone 4.

Crabapple
Malus hybrids

Stop! Don't turn the page! If you have an old crabapple tree, you may be wondering what ever possessed me to recommend this plant. Many of you may have suffered through the mess of summer leaf drop and fallen fruit. Fortunately, there are many new disease-resistant crabapples with small, persistent fruit, eliminating the litter problem. Select crabapples for their year-round features. The colorful white, pink, or red flowers provide several weeks of beauty in the spring. The fruit, however, will give you months of enjoyment. Look for persistent fruit in many shades of yellow, orange, and red. The trees can be small and mounded, spreading, weeping, or upright. There are over 600 crabapples in cultivation, with new ones being introduced each season. I'm sure there is a crabapple out there for every gardener!

Other Common Name
Flowering Crabapple

Bloom Period and Seasonal Color
Spring blooms in white, pink, and red.

Mature Height × Spread
40 to 60 ft. × 20 to 40 ft.

When, Where, and How to Plant
Crabapples respond best to spring transplanting. Plant balled-and-burlapped trees as soon as possible after they are purchased. Plant container-grown plants throughout the growing season. Grow crabapples in moist, well-drained soil. See the chapter introduction for planting directions.

Growing Tips
Water established plants thoroughly whenever the top 4 to 6 inches of soil are moist and crumbly. Wait a year before fertilizing new plantings. Avoid excess fertilization, which can encourage disease problems and eliminate flowering and fruit.

Care
Prune only to establish and maintain the tree's structural framework. Excessive pruning will encourage water sprouts. Prune crabapple trees in late winter for quick wound closure that reduces the risk of disease. Select disease-resistant cultivars to avoid major problems. Fireblight is a bacterial disease that can eventually kill the tree. Prune out infected branches 12 inches beneath the canker, or sunken area, to control the disease. Disinfect tools with alcohol or with a bleach and water solution between cuts. Apple scab causes leaf spotting and dropping. Rake and destroy fallen leaves to reduce the source of infection. Several applications of a fungicide in early spring will help control this disease. Unfortunately, even some scab resistant cultivars are showing signs of disease. Talk to your County Cooperative Extension Agent for the most current recommendations. Crabapples are a favorite food for tent caterpillars. Physically remove the caterpillar-filled tent to control this pest.

Companion Planting and Design
Use them as specimen plants or in small groupings. The weeping cultivars complement water features, and the spreading types blend well in Japanese gardens. Include some of the smaller types in your perennial gardens. They can provide structure and year-round interest in large flower gardens.

My Personal Favorites
'Louisa' is a small scale, weeping form that fits into small yards, accents patios, and serves as a focal point for a mixed border. 'Firebird'® is a cultivar of sergeant crabapple with fragrant snow-white flowers and small red fruit that persists into late winter.

When, Where, and How to Plant

Douglasfir adapts well after transplanting when it is balled and burlapped. Plant the balled-and-burlapped tree as soon as possible after it is purchased. Container-grown trees can be planted throughout the growing season. Plant evergreens before October 1 for best results. Grow these evergreens in full sun with moist, well-drained soil. Douglasfir will not tolerate high winds or dry, rocky soil. Plant the tree with its root flare at or slightly above the soil line. Dig a shallow planting hole at the same depth as and 3 to 5 times wider than the root system. Place the tree in the planting hole. Be sure the tree is straight, but move it by the rootball, not the trunk, to minimize root damage. Remove the container, twine, and metal baskets. Cut away the burlap. Fill the hole with existing soil, water to settle the soil, then mulch.

Growing Tips

Douglasfir needs very little care if it is planted in the proper location. Water it during periods of drought. Water the whole area under the tree thoroughly, wetting the top 12 inches of the soil whenever the top 4 to 6 inches are moist and crumbly. Mulching will also help keep the roots cool and moist. Wait a year before fertilizing new plantings. Follow soil test recommendations and evaluate tree health before fertilizing established plantings.

Care

A variety of insects and diseases can attack. Proper watering and mulching will keep Douglasfirs healthy with fewer pest problems. Contact a certified arborist or your local County University Extension Service if pest problems arise.

Companion Planting and Design

Consider using this tree where a large vertical accent is needed. Don't use these trees as windbreaks. Take advantage of their form and stature by planting them as a specimen tree or en masse. Give Douglasfir plenty of room to grow and show off its beauty.

My Personal Favorites

Pseudotsuga menziesii glauca has reliably blue-green needles. It is more compact than the species and is hardy to Zone 4. 'Fastigiata' is a narrow, upright form.

Douglasfir's majestic appearance is striking. Nationally, it is one of the most popular Christmas trees, and you are more likely to see it in a Christmas tree lot than in Minnesota landscapes. Its green to bluish green needles have a camphor smell when crushed. It grows at a medium rate, adding 12 to 15 feet over a ten-year period. Like the Colorado blue spruce, this tree will outgrow most small city lots if not properly placed. You will then face the tough decision of cutting down the overgrown tree, limbing it up and ruining its appearance, or crawling under it to get to your front door. Douglasfir is native to the Rocky Mountains and the Pacific Coast. Plants from the Rocky Mountains tend to be shorter, tougher plants that do not live as long as those on the coast. They are, however, the best choice for our area.

Other Common Name
Douglas Fir

Bloom Period and Seasonal Color
Evergreen foliage.

Mature Height × Spread
70 ft. × 20 ft.

Elm

Ulmus species and hybrids

Do you remember the beautiful elm lined streets of the 1950s and early 1960s? Maybe you only saw the pictures. But the overuse of this tree followed by the advent of Dutch Elm Disease (DED) changed the urban forest and our memories forever. In the 1960s, the air was filled with the sound of dropping elms. The remaining American elms are still subject to an early death from this disease. Look for DED-resistant elms when adding them to your landscape. Several other elms are commonly used in the landscape. The Chinese or lacebark elm, Ulmus parvifolia (shown), is a tough tree that can tolerate a wide range of conditions. It is resistant to DED, as well as both elm leaf and Japanese beetle. The small leaves and beautiful bark make this an attractive and useful shade tree (borderline hardy in Zone 4).

Other Common Name
American Elm

Bloom Period and Seasonal Color
Deciduous foliage.

Mature Height × Spread
30 to 80 ft. × 40 ft.

When, Where, and How to Plant
Elms adapt well to transplanting. Plant balled-and-burlapped trees as soon as possible after purchasing. Plant container-grown plants throughout the growing season. Grow elms in full sun with moist soil, but many will tolerate wet soil and even temporary flooding. Follow planting directions in the chapter introduction. Water new plantings enough to keep the soil around the tree and beyond the planting hole moist.

Growing Tips
Water established trees thoroughly when the top 4 to 6 inches of soil are moist and crumbly. Mulch the soil around the tree to conserve moisture, reduce weeds, and eliminate grass competition. Wait a year to fertilize new plantings. Well-cared-for, established trees need minimal fertilization.

Care
Elms tend to be fast growers and weak wooded. Proper pruning throughout the tree's life will help reduce storm damage. American and red elms are susceptible to Dutch Elm Disease (DED). Avoid adding these disease-susceptible plants to your landscape. The red elm is often called slippery elm (*Ulmus rubra*) for its moist slimy inner bark. Pioneers used to chew the bark to quench their thirst. (You can still buy slippery elm throat lozenges.) Plant resistant species and hybrids to avoid DED. Use a preventative fungicide treatment to protect valuable trees. Lightly infected (5 percent or less) trees have been successfully treated. Contact a certified arborist for proper diagnosis and more details on treatment.

Companion Planting and Design
Large elms make good shade trees. Some species have been sheared into hedges. An elm relative, hackberry (*Celtis occidentalis*), has been used as an elm replacement. This large shade tree has a similar growth habit, is urban tolerant with textured bark, and DED resistance.

My Personal Favorites
The University of Wisconsin has developed and introduced several DED-resistant elms. 'New Horizon' and 'Regal' are two DED-resistant hybrids that are hardy to Zone 4. The 'American Liberty' elm is the result of crossing 6 different American elm clones.

European Mountain Ash

Sorbus aucuparia

When, Where, and How to Plant

Plant balled-and-burlapped trees as soon as possible after they are purchased. Plant container-grown trees throughout the growing season, though I prefer spring and early summer. Plant it in areas with cool, moist, but well-drained soil. It will not tolerate heat, drought, pollution, or compacted soil. Keep specimens away from heat-reflecting structures and pavement. Follow planting directions in the chapter introduction.

Growing Tips

Plant mountain ash in the right location to minimize maintenance. Mulch the roots with wood chips or another organic material to keep them cool and moist. Water mountain ash thoroughly whenever the top 4 to 6 inches are crumbly and moist. Wait a year after planting to fertilize. Avoid using fast-release and high-nitrogen fertilizers that can increase the risk of fireblight and interfere with flowering and fruiting.

Care

Mountain ash trees are susceptible to quite a few disease and insect problems. The shiny, smooth bark is susceptible to sunscald and frost cracking. The leaves often spot and drop from scab. Rake and destroy fallen leaves to reduce future risk. Fireblight can kill the tree one branch at a time or very quickly in one season. Remove wilted branches well below the canker, disinfecting your tools between cuts. Stressed trees can be finished off by borers. Proper watering and mulch will keep the trees healthy and borer-resistant.

Companion Planting and Design

Try planting them on the east, north, or cool side of your home in a spot where they can be enjoyed. They make a nice ornamental tree for small yards or for a mixed planting bed and wildlife garden.

My Personal Favorites

Korean mountain ash, *Sorbus alnifolia*, puts on a better flower and fruit display than the European mountain ash. This tree is more tolerant of our climate and is considered the best of the introduced mountain ash trees. American mountain ash, *Sorbus americana*, and Showy mountain ash, *Sorbus decora*, (hardy to Zone 2) are native in the Great Lakes region. Both have white flowers and orange-red to red fruit.

Mountain ash has long been a favorite tree for Minnesota gardens, providing seasonal interest. It has white flowers in the spring followed by showy orange-red fruit in the fall. The flower show is good, but not spectacular, and just a bit smelly. You may want to keep this tree away from open windows. The fall color is often a good reddish-purple, and the fruit display is excellent and attractive to birds. In fact, the botanical name Aucuparia comes from the Latin words avis meaning "bird" and capere meaning "to catch." This tree certainly catches the birds with its tasty fruit. Every December, the cedar waxwings join my students for their final exam. They fill the mountain ash tree and eat its fruit as the students identify the tree.

Other Common Name
Mountain Ash

Bloom Period and Seasonal Color
Spring blooms in white.

Mature Height × Spread
30 ft. × 20 ft.

Fir
Abies species

If you like the look of a blue spruce but are tired of fighting the pests, I have the perfect tree for you. The white fir, Abies concolor, *has blue-green needles and a pyramidal shape similar to the Colorado blue spruce. The broader, flat needles and growth habit of white fir give it a softer appearance, making it easier to blend with other plants. White fir is the best fir for home landscape situations. It prefers ideal growing conditions but is more tolerant of heat, drought, and urban conditions than other firs. Its name* concolor *means "same color," referring to the needles that are blue-green on both the upper and lower surfaces. The Fraser fir has become popular as a Christmas tree. Enjoy it for the holidays but don't count on it for the landscape.*

Other Common Name
White Fir, Balsam Fir

Bloom Period and Seasonal Color
Evergreen needles.

Mature Height × Spread
70 ft. × 30 ft.

When, Where, and How to Plant
For best results, plant balled-and-burlapped trees in the spring. Plant container-grown trees before October 1 so the plants will have time to root before the harsh winter. Grow firs in full sun or light shade. They prefer moist, well-drained soil in cool, humid locations. Firs do not tolerate hot, dry conditions. The white fir prefers ideal conditions but is the most tolerant of dry soil and city conditions. See the chapter introduction for planting directions.

Growing Tips
Proper site selection is critical for growing success. A well-placed fir will require little maintenance. Mulch the soil with wood chips or another organic material to keep the roots cool and moist. Water thoroughly whenever the top 4 to 6 inches of soil are crumbly and moist. Wait one year to fertilize new plantings. Properly watered and mulched firs need little, if any, fertilizer once established.

Care
Healthy fir trees suffer few pest problems and require very little pruning. Give this large tree plenty of room to grow so you won't be fighting to keep a large tree in a small space.

Companion Planting and Design
Use the white fir individually as a specimen plant or in small groupings. They make a nice backdrop to deciduous trees and shrubs. A flower bed with a group of white firs in the background is quite impressive.

My Personal Favorites
The introduction of new dwarf cultivars is allowing greater use of these picky trees. Most gardeners can find the perfect microclimate for a small scale tree but not always for their full size counterparts. 'Candicans' is a narrow, upright cultivar that grows 5 feet tall in ten years, eventually growing to 15 feet. Our native Balsam fir is a popular Christmas tree. The dwarf balsam fir, *Abies balsamea* 'Nana', can be carefully sited and enjoyed in a dwarf conifer or perennial garden. One of my favorites is the 'Silberlocke' Korean fir *Abies koreana* 'Silberlocke'. The curved needles show off the silver undersides of the needles. Protect it from the hot afternoon sun.

When, Where, and How to Plant

Ginkgo trees adapt easily to transplanting. Plant balled-and-burlapped trees as soon as possible after they are purchased. Plant container-grown plants throughout the growing season. Ginkgo is a tough tree that seems to thrive anywhere. It prefers full sun with slightly moist, well-drained soil. It is very tolerant of salt, pollution, and other urban conditions. It does surprisingly well in the hostile environment of sidewalk plantings in downtown areas. Follow planting directions in the chapter introduction.

Growing Tips

The ginkgo requires patience, adding about 10 to 15 feet of growth in ten to twelve years. You can speed things up by providing adequate, but not too much, water and fertilizer. Water the tree thoroughly whenever the top 4 to 6 inches of soil are moist and crumbly. Mulch to conserve moisture, suppress weeds, and eliminate competition from nearby grass. Wait a year to fertilize new plantings. Use moderate amounts of slow-release nitrogen fertilizer (see chapter introduction) to encourage faster growth on young trees. Established plants need little, if any, fertilization.

Care

Ginkgo trees have no real pest problems and tolerate a wide range of growing conditions. The slow growth and open habit eliminate the need for regular pruning.

Companion Planting and Design

Remember, this slow grower will eventually get big, so give it room. Ginkgo trees have an open growth habit. The light colored bark and interesting habit against the sky make it a nice addition to the winter landscape. Plant them where their fall color and winter interest can be appreciated.

My Personal Favorites

Select male clones or cultivars like one of these to avoid problems with messy fruit. *Ginkgo biloba* 'Fastigiata' and 'Princeton Sentry' are upright, male forms of ginkgo. 'Pendula' has strong, horizontal branching. Sold as a weeper, it actually spreads horizontally, creating an interesting look. I have seen its branches reach across a waterfall to create an attractive scene. 'Tuberiformis' is a dwarf male ginkgo with unique leaves. They emerge rounded like a tube curled upward.

Ginkgo trees are often called living fossils. They have been growing on the earth for over 150 million years. You may recognize the name from the ginkgo leaf extract sold to improve your memory. The ginkgo is also a beautiful landscape tree. The attractive, fan-shaped leaves add to the overall uniqueness of this plant. Its irregular shape and open appearance can make it difficult to blend in small landscapes. Mature specimens are breathtaking, especially in the fall. The leaves turn a clear yellow and, best of all, they all drop from the tree at the same time, making cleanup easier. Female ginkgo trees produce smelly, messy fruit. Called silver apricots, the seeds inside the smelly covering are edible. They have long been used in Oriental cooking and rituals. Plant male clones to avoid the problem. Otherwise, rake and compost the fruit.

Other Common Name
Maidenhair Tree

Bloom Period and Seasonal Color
Fall foliage in yellow.

Mature Height × Spread
50 or more ft. × 30 or more ft.

Zones
Hardy to Zone 4

Hawthorn
Crataegus species

Hawthorns are nice, small trees that provide year-round interest in both small and large settings. Their white flowers are effective for up to two weeks in May. But don't plant them next to your window unless you're sure you like the smell. The fruit is orange-red and usually quite showy in fall through winter and looks pretty when capped with snow. As the fruit softens over winter, the hungry birds will start eating them. It is quite entertaining to watch the birds feed on the fermented fruit. Whether flowering, fruiting, or bare, the horizontal habit is quite attractive. Select a native or introduced species that is best suited to your landscape. Grow them in planting or mulch beds to hide any fallen fruit and eliminate the risk of accidentally walking into a thorny branch.

Other Common Name
Thornapple

Bloom Period and Seasonal Color
May blooms in white.

Mature Height × Spread
20 to 30 ft. × 20 to 30 ft.

When, Where, and How to Plant
Plant small balled-and-burlapped trees in the spring. Plant container-grown plants throughout the growing season, though I prefer spring through early summer. Hawthorns prefer full sun and will tolerate a variety of soils as long as they are well drained (see the chapter introduction).

Growing Tips
Water established plants thoroughly whenever the top 4 to 6 inches of soil are starting to dry. Wait a year to fertilize new plantings. Avoid excess fertilization and fast-release, high-nitrogen fertilizers that can reduce flowering and fruiting and increase the risk of disease.

Care
Prune hawthorns in late winter when the pruning cuts will close quickly and minimize the risk of disease. Hawthorns are susceptible to several major diseases including fireblight, scab (see crabapples), and rust. Select the least susceptible species whenever possible. Rust is the most common disease. It causes leaves and fruit to develop orange spots and drop prematurely. Rust is usually harmless but looks bad. Rake and destroy infected leaves and fruit as they fall. Avoid planting red cedar (*Juniperus virginiana*), the alternate host for rust, in the same area. Falling fruit from the large fruited hawthorns can create a mess. Ground cover will allow it to compost out of sight. Avoid the area until the fruit rots and the German yellow jackets are done feeding.

Companion Planting and Design
Hawthorn's strong, horizontal branching helps anchor large buildings to the landscape. I have seen hawthorns used for screening, hedging, and as barrier plants. Avoid using these thorny plants next to entrances and walkways.

My Personal Favorites
Washington (*Crataegus phaenopyrum*) and 'Winter King' (*Crataegus viridis* 'Winter King') hawthorns are finer textured with smaller fruit. Both are quite effective in winter. Heavy snow loads may cause damage. I find Washington hawthorn to be a bit more attractive but the 'Winter King' has fewer thorns. Cockspur hawthorn, (*Crataegus crusgalli*), is native to Minnesota, has glossy green leaves, 1/2-inch red fruit, and long, sharp thorns. The variety *inermis* is thornless.

When, Where, and How to Plant

Plant balled-and-burlapped trees as soon as possible after purchasing. Plant container-grown trees by October 1 to allow root establishment before winter. Hemlocks are particular about their growing location. They are one of the few evergreens that prefer shade. Grow hemlocks in a sheltered location out of wind, drought, pollution, and water-logged soil. Winter winds and sun can be especially damaging. Follow the planting directions in the chapter introduction.

Growing Tips

Moisture and mulch are key to growing healthy, long-lived hemlocks. Water established trees thoroughly whenever the top 4 to 6 inches are crumbly and moist. Mulch the roots to keep the soil cool and moist. Wait a year to fertilize new plantings. Avoid fertilizing stressed trees. This can stimulate new growth instead of allowing the plant to focus its energy on repair. Established trees, especially those growing in shade, require little if any fertilizer.

Care

Stressed trees are susceptible to quite a few pests. Brown needles and branch dieback can occur when the plants are exposed to temperatures over 95 degrees Fahrenheit, drying winter winds, or drought. Prune out damaged branches, eliminate the stress, or move the plants to a more suitable location.

Companion Planting and Design

Hemlocks are attractive grown individually or in small groups. Dwarf cultivars are nice additions to small landscapes and perennial gardens. They provide structure and year-round interest. Use them as specimens, accents, screens, or transition plants on the woodland's edge. Their light, airy texture can soften surrounding plants and landscape structures.

My Personal Favorites

'Gentsch White' is a dwarf cultivar that only grows to 3 feet in ten years. The new growth has white tips. Prune this rounded plant for more compact growth habit. 'Cole's Prostrate' is a ground-hugging plant that grows 8 inches tall and up to 7 feet wide. It works well as a ground cover or rock garden plant in protected locations. There are several interesting weeping forms including 'Sargentii' and 'Pendula'.

Hemlock is a graceful beauty that is often overlooked for landscape use. Its shade tolerance extends the use of evergreens in the landscape. This native evergreen tree is pyramidal when young. With age, hemlock maintains its pyramidal shape, but the branches begin to weep, giving it a soft and graceful silhouette. The straight species is large and best suited for sizable landscapes. Many dwarf and uniquely shaped cultivars have recently been introduced, making hemlock an option for those with a small yard. This evergreen will tolerate pruning and can be used as a hedge. Before you reach for the shears, take a look at its beautiful shape. Maybe an informal hedge will work just as well. This not the infamous poison hemlock. That plant, Conium maculatum, *is herbaceous and looks more like Queen Anne's lace.*

Other Common Name
Canadian or Eastern Hemlock

Bloom Period and Seasonal Color
Evergreen foliage.

Mature Height × Spread
75 ft. or more × 25 ft. or more

Honey Locust

Gleditsia triacanthos var. inermis

Honey locust is a popular tree in the home landscape. This fast-growing tree provides fine texture and interesting form in both summer and winter. The small green leaves (actually leaflets) provide shade while allowing the sun to reach the grass below. The leaves turn a nice yellow in the fall. The flowers aren't showy, but they do provide a pleasant fragrance in early June. If you have a honey locust, take good care of it and keep it healthy. Mature specimens are quite impressive. The honey locust's fruit is a long brown pod. Some gardeners think they are ugly, but I think they can be ornamental in the winter. There is no debate about the mess they create when they fall. Many podless cultivars have been introduced to alleviate this problem.

Other Common Name
Thornless Honey Locust

Bloom Period and Seasonal Color
Fall foliage in yellow.

Mature Height × Spread
40 ft. × 30 ft.

When, Where, and How to Plant
Plant balled-and-burlapped trees as soon as possible after purchasing. Plant container-grown plants throughout the growing season. Grow honey locust in moist, well-drained soil. This tough plant tolerates a wide range of conditions including drought, salt, and high pH. Handle this tree with care and avoid damage when transporting and planting. Follow planting directions in the chapter introduction.

Growing Tips
Water established trees thoroughly whenever the top 4 to 6 inches of soil are crumbly and moist. Mulch the soil under the tree to conserve moisture, suppress weeds, eliminate grass competition, and prevent damage from mowers and weed whips.

Care
In spring, honey locusts are often attacked by plant bugs and leafhoppers. The insects won't kill the tree, but heavy populations can delay leaf development and cause twig dieback. The biggest problem is nectria canker. It causes sunken and discolored areas to develop on the branches and trunk, eventually killing them. Prevention is the best defense. Select healthy, disease-free trees and avoid injuries to the trunk and branches during transplanting and maintenance. Wounds serve as entryways for the disease. Prune in early summer when the weather is dry. Avoid pruning in fall or dormant seasons when the disease is present and wounds close slowly. Honey locusts also produce lots of sprouts off the main trunk. Remove these at the same time to maintain the tree's structure and appearance.

Companion Planting and Design
Honey locusts are frequently used in difficult growing spots. They are often used to shade patios, decks, and lawn areas. The filtered shade is cooling, but not detrimental to the grass.

My Personal Favorites
Almost all the honeylocust being sold are the variety *inermis*, thornless. Their long thin thorns were once used by Civil war soldiers as pins to fasten their coats. Today they create a painful nuisance when caring for the tree. Select podless cultivars if you want to avoid the mess. 'Skyline' develops a good upright habit. The new growth on 'Sunburst' (shown) emerges yellow before turning green.

Horsechestnut
Aesculus hippocastanum

When, Where, and How to Plant

Horsechestnuts respond best to spring transplanting, though container-grown plants can be planted throughout the growing season. Plant balled-and-burlapped trees as soon possible after purchasing. Horsechestnuts prefer moist, well-drained soil, although I have seen them growing in clay soil. See the chapter introduction for planting directions.

Growing Tips

Water established trees thoroughly whenever the top 4 to 6 inches of soil are crumbly and moist. Mulch the soil to conserve moisture, suppress weeds, and eliminate competition from grass. Wait a year to fertilize new plantings. Avoid excess fertilizing and fast-release, high nitrogen fertilizers that can interfere with flowering. Established trees need little, if any, fertilizer.

Care

Leaf blotch, anthracnose, and powdery mildew can all cause leaves to discolor and drop prematurely. Rake and destroy infected leaves as soon as they fall to reduce future infection. Healthy trees can tolerate these diseases. It's too late to treat the disease once symptoms appear.

Companion Planting and Design

Horsechestnuts are massive trees that need room to showcase their beauty. Place them where their late spring bloom can be enjoyed. Use them as a shade or large specimen tree in expansive lawn areas or on a woodland edge. Avoid planting these over sidewalks where falling fruit can create a messy hazard. Use mulch or ground covers under fruiting trees to minimize cleanup. Use fruitless varieties where you don't want to attract squirrels or children.

My Personal Favorites

Ohio buckeye, *Aesculus glabra*, is a shorter, 20 to 40 feet, cousin to the horsechestnut. The smaller size and fall color make it a better fit for most home landscapes. A close look at the horesechestnut-like nuts reveals the source of its common name. The University of Minnesota introduced the Autumn Splendor Ohio buckeye, *Aesculus glabra* 'Autumn Splendor'. It is a small- to medium-sized tree with very showy flowers in late spring. This tough cultivar is winter-hardy and tolerant of de-icing salts. The yellow buckeye is a large, beautiful tree with a cleaner appearance and pumpkin fall color.

Flowering horsechestnuts steal the show in late spring. Their large, cone-shaped blossoms make them a popular choice for gardeners. The horsechestnut's coarse texture, attractive platy bark, and large size make it a good fit in park-like settings. Horsechestnut trees produce light brown, spiny fruits that look like the spiked metal head of a mace. Inside are dark brown nuts with a light blotch. The falling fruit and seeds can create a mess. These are NOT the holiday chestnuts that are roasted on an open fire. Those edible chestnuts are from the American chestnut (Castanea dentata). The nuts and twigs of horsechestnut are poisonous. Select a fruitless cultivar to avoid the mess. 'Baumannii' has long-lasting double flowers without the messy fruit.

Other Common Names

European or Common Horsechestnut

Bloom Period and Seasonal Color

Late spring blooms in white with yellow and pink blotch at base.

Mature Height × Spread

50 or more ft. × 40 ft.

Zones

Hardy to Zone 4

Ironwood

Ostrya virginiana

Ironwood is an underutilized native tree. It is a slow grower, adding 10 to 15 feet of height in fifteen years. The slow growth rate and shade tolerance make it an appropriate tree for small settings and city lots. It is somewhat pyramidal when young, becoming more rounded with age. The fine, horizontal branches and finely shredded bark ensure year-round interest. Ironwood flowers in the early spring. It produces a subtle show providing a glimpse of other spring blooms yet to come. The long, narrow flowers (catkins) droop from the fine branches. These later develop into small, hop-like fruit, thus the other common name, hophornbeam. Ironwood may be a little difficult to find. Start by checking with nurseries and garden centers that specialize in native plants.

Other Common Name
Hophornbeam

Bloom Period and Seasonal Color
Spring flowers in greenish-yellow with good, yellow fall color.

Mature Height × Spread
30 ft. × 20 or more ft.

Zones
Hardy to Zone 3b

When, Where, and How to Plant
Plant balled-and-burlapped or container-grown trees in the early spring. Grow these trees in full sun or partial shade. They prefer moist, well-drained soil but can tolerate the dry, gravelly and sandy soils of central Minnesota. Dig a shallow planting hole the same depth as and 3 to 5 times wider than the root system. Plant ironwood trees with the root flare at or slightly above the soil line. Remove the container, twine, and metal baskets. Cut away the burlap. Backfill with existing soil then water and mulch. See the chapter introduction for more detailed directions.

Growing Tips
Though tolerant of dry soil, ironwoods do best when watered during extended drought periods. I observed quite a bit of damage on trees that were not watered during the drought of 1988. Water established trees thoroughly whenever the top few inches of soil begin to dry. Wait a year to fertilize new plantings. Though slow to get started, this tree will grow a bit faster once it's established. Properly watered and mulched established trees need little, if any, fertilizer.

Care
Ironwood has no serious pests. The wood is hard and durable, helping the plant resist wind and ice damage. It has been used for wedges, levers, and other tools.

Companion Planting and Design
These small trees are a good fit in small landscapes. Plant them in groupings for a bigger impact in larger settings. Ironwood's graceful growth habit helps soften vertical elements in the landscape. Take advantage of ironwood's shade tolerance. Use it in woodland gardens or as an understory plant for your larger shade trees. This native tree is at home in both natural and manicured landscapes.

My Personal Favorite
Hornbeam or blue beech (*Carpinus caroliniana*) is often called ironwood. It is another small, slow growing tree with a similar growth habit. Also called musclewood, *Carpinus* has smooth gray bark that looks like flexed muscles. It is another good native with yellow, orange, or red fall color. See the musclewood entry for more on this tree.

Japanese Tree Lilac

Syringa reticulata

When, Where, and How to Plant

Japanese tree lilacs recover quickly from transplanting. Plant balled-and-burlapped trees as soon as possible after purchase. Plant container-grown trees throughout the growing season. Grow Japanese tree lilacs in full sun and well-drained soil for best results. See the chapter introduction for specifics on planting.

Growing Tips

Japanese tree lilacs are the easiest lilacs to grow. Mulch the soil to eliminate weeds and to keep the roots cool and moist. Thoroughly water established trees anytime the top 4 to 6 inches of soil are moist and crumbly. Wait a year to fertilize new plantings. Avoid high nitrogen, fast-release fertilizer and excess fertilization.

Care

Once the framework is established, minimal pruning is needed. Remove dead wood and wayward growth. Tree lilacs tend to bloom heavily one year and lightly the next. Prevent this variation by removing spent flowers as the blossoms fade. The plant will then put its energy into producing next year's flower buds instead of setting seed. You may need a pole pruner to reach the flowers on top. Japanese tree lilacs are fairly trouble free in our state. They can occasionally suffer from borer, mildew, and scale like the common lilacs. Be sure to keep weed killers, including weed and feed products, away from this and other ornamental plants. Wilt has been a recent problem. Proper care is the best defense against this and other pests.

Companion Planting and Design

These small, flowering trees make nice specimen plants in both small and large settings. Plant them in small groups for greater impact. Use Japanese tree lilacs near large homes and buildings to soften and blend these structures into the landscape.

My Personal Favorites

'Ivory Silk' is a more compact plant with a rounded crown. 'Ivory Silk' starts flowering at an earlier age and produces more flowers than the species. Pekin lilac, *Syringa pekinensis,* is similar to Japanese tree lilac. This smaller plant has beautiful amber bark but a less impressive flower display.

Would you like large, white, fragrant, lilac blossoms in mid-June? You will have them once you plant a Japanese tree lilac in your landscape. The massive blossoms look just like common lilac, only bigger. They are fragrant, but not as sweet as lilac, perhaps more like privet (yes, privets have fragrant blossoms). The fragrance gets mixed reviews from gardeners. Japanese tree lilac offers more than just pretty flowers. The bark is smooth and shiny like a cherry tree, becoming gray and rough with age. The attractive bark adds year-round interest to the tree. The seedheads persist through the winter, adding texture to the winter silhouette. It's a small beauty that fits into most garden locations. Plants are available single or multistemmed. Avoid using this tree near native woodlands as there is some concern that it may become invasive.

Other Common Name

Tree lilac

Bloom Period and Seasonal Color

Mid-June blooms in white.

Mature Height × Spread

25 ft. × 15 ft.

Kentucky Coffee Tree

Gymnocladus dioicus

Kentucky coffee tree is a Minnesota native that makes an excellent landscape plant. It is a close relative to the Honeylocust with fewer pests. Both belong to the pea family, although it is hard to believe these big trees are related to the peas and beans in your garden. A close look at the fragrant flowers will reveal the family resemblance. Use the large Kentucky coffee tree to provide shade in the summer and an interesting silhouette in winter. Give it time and space to grow. This versatile plant tolerates a wide range of conditions while blending into formal and informal landscape designs. Early Kentucky settlers used the seeds as a coffee substitute. It is thought that the roasting helped eliminate the toxic properties. I hear the taste isn't that great—I think I'll stick to the real thing.

Other Common Name
Coffee tree

Bloom Period and Seasonal Color
Early June creamy flowers and yellow fall color.

Mature Height × Spread
75 ft. × 40 ft.

Zones
Hardy to Zone 3b

When, Where, and How to Plant

Spring transplanting is best, though container-grown plants can be planted throughout the season. Plant balled-and-burlapped trees as soon as possible after purchasing. Kentucky coffee trees prefer full sun and moist, well-drained soil but will tolerate wet and dry locations. Dig a shallow planting hole the same depth as and 3 to 5 times wider than the root system. Plant the tree with the root flare at or slightly above the soil line. Remove the container, twine, and metal baskets. Cut away the burlap. Fill the hole with existing soil. Water the tree and add mulch.

Growing Tips

Kentucky coffee tree is a low-maintenance plant. Water established plants thoroughly whenever the top few inches of soil begin to dry. Wait a year before fertilizing new plantings. Established trees that are properly watered and mulched require little, if any, fertilizer.

Care

There are no serious pests. The limited number in the landscape and fewer pest problems make this a superior choice to honeylocust. The fruit and leaves, however, can be messy. Fall leaves tend to drop over a long period of time. The small leaflets can easily be chopped with the mower. The long leaf stem (rachis) is what causes the mess. More meticulous gardeners may be annoyed by this extended fall cleanup (but it doesn't bother me).

Companion Planting and Design

This tough tree is a great choice for windy sites and urban areas. Use Kentucky coffee trees as specimen plants. Their large compound leaves can reach 36 inches in length and 24 inches in width. They are made up of many small, blue-green leaflets that are only $1^{1}/_{2}$ to 3 inches long. The feathery leaves help soften the coarse features of this plant. Once the leaves drop, the brown pods, scaly bark, and thick, stark branches stand out against the winter sky.

My Personal Favorites

Kentucky coffee tree may be hard to locate, so pick up the phone before you hop in the car. 'Espresso' is a fruitless (male) cultivar. It is smaller, with an elm-like growth habit.

When, Where, and How to Plant

Plant balled-and-burlapped trees in the spring when the plants are dormant. Plant container-grown plants throughout the growing season in moist, well-drained soil. Though our native larch tolerates wet, soggy soils in the wild, it performs best in landscapes with moist, well-drained soil. Avoid dry soil and polluted locations. Plant larch with the root flare at or slightly above the soil line. Remove containers, twine, and metal baskets; cut away burlap at time of planting. Backfill the hole with existing soil then water and mulch. See the chapter introduction for more planting details.

Growing Tips

Mulch to keep the roots cool and moist. Water established plants thoroughly whenever the top 4 to 6 inches of soil are crumbly and moist. Wait a year to fertilize young trees. Established trees need very little fertilizer.

Care

Properly placed larch trees need little maintenance. Insect and disease problems are few and infrequent. Healthy plants properly watered and mulched usually resist and tolerate any damage. I have had several distraught homeowners call panicked because their evergreen's needles turned yellow and dropped. I even know of a building manager who cut down several healthy trees because they lost all their needles in fall. I'm glad I didn't have to tell him this was an unnecessary waste.

Companion Planting and Design

Consider using one of these graceful plants near a pond or water feature. Larches are good plants for large landscapes and new dwarf cultivars are making them useful in small scale yards. The European and Japanese larches make attractive specimen plants. Plant individually or en masse. Groupings of larch make effective screens. Create a grove using a grouping of these plants.

My Personal Favorites

You may have trouble finding the American larch. Check with local nurseries specializing in native plants. The Japanese larch, *Larix kaempferi*, and European larch, *Larix decidua,* are the most ornamental, but both need lots of space to grow and show their beauty.

Driving through northern Minnesota, you are bound to pass a grove of our native larch trees. The American larch, Larix laricina, is also called tamarack and is a tall pyramidal plant. They are most noticeable in the fall when their needles turn a beautiful golden yellow. Look for them in wet, soggy locations. This adaptability is what makes tamarack wood so rot resistant. It was once used for water pipes. Parts of the tree were hollowed out and individual pieces were connected. In the landscape, you are more likely to see the European or Japanese larch. These beautiful trees are less tolerant of wet soil but are more adapted to transplanting than our American larch. Larches are deciduous conifers. The needles fall to the ground after their beautiful golden fall display. The tree silhouette is quite effective in the winter landscape. The dwarf variety Larix kaempferi 'Pendula' is shown in this photo.

Other Common Name

Tamarack

Bloom Period and Seasonal Color

Fall foliage in yellow.

Mature Height × Spread

75 ft. × 40 ft.

Linden

Tilia species

Lindens are a useful group of plants and provide several seasons of interest. Watch for the fragrant yellow flowers in late June or early July. You will probably smell them before you see them. The bees love them. In fact, the honey they make from these flowers is supposed to be some of the best. The fall color is usually a good yellow. All lindens have attractive forms, adding year-round interest. American linden, Tilia americana, is a large, irregularly shaped, upright native tree with large leaves. It's a good plant for large, informal yards and naturalized landscapes. Littleleaf linden, Tilia cordata, has small, glossy, heart-shaped leaves. Its smaller size and pyramidal shape make it suitable for landscapes. This tough tree is also very tolerant of pollution and city conditions.

Other Common Name
Basswood

Bloom Period and Seasonal Color
Late June to early July in yellow; yellow fall foliage.

Mature Height × Spread
Up to 75 ft. × 40 ft.

When, Where, and How to Plant
Lindens adapt well to transplanting. Plant balled-and-burlapped trees as soon as possible after purchasing. Plant container-grown plants throughout the growing season. Grow lindens in full sun with moist, well-drained soil. Most lindens tolerate heavy clay soil (see the chapter introduction).

Growing Tips
Lindens require minimal maintenance. Water established trees thoroughly whenever the top 4 to 6 inches of soil are moist and crumbly. Mulch to conserve moisture, suppress weeds, and eliminate competition from grass. Wait a year before fertilizing new plantings. Properly watered and mulched lindens usually need minimal fertilization.

Care
Little leaf lindens produce lots of side branches very close together. These will need to be thinned out to prevent future problems with rubbing branches. There are a few diseases and insects that attack lindens. It is not unusual to find a few holes chewed in their leaves. The damage is usually minimal and does not require treatment. This is not the case if Japanese beetles have invaded your landscape; however, healthy trees will survive. Some gardeners use contact or soil-applied systemic insecticides to reduce the population. Littleleaf linden is susceptible to nectria canker. Avoid damage when transporting, planting, and caring for this tree. See honeylocust for more details.

Companion Planting and Design
All of the lindens make good shade trees. The American linden is good for naturalized settings or woodland areas. The littleleaf linden is the most frequently used in the landscape. It is an excellent choice for street trees, planters, and planting beds. The strong, pyramidal shape and glossy, green leaves make this an attractive choice for most situations. Use littleleaf lindens to line a driveway or a wide walkway. Or you can trim them into a large hedge.

My Personal Favorites
Redmond linden, *Tilia americana* 'Redmond', is the American linden better suited for urban life.

Magnolia
Magnolia species

When, Where, and How to Plant

Magnolias do not respond well to transplanting. Plant balled-and-burlapped and container-grown plants in the early spring. Grow them in moist, well-drained soil. These trees will not tolerate wet or dry conditions. Avoid low spots and other areas subject to late spring frosts that can destroy the spring floral display. See the chapter introduction for planting directions.

Growing Tips

Mulch the soil with wood chips or another organic material to keep the roots cool and moist. Water established trees thoroughly whenever the top 4 to 6 inches of soil are moist but crumbly. Wait a year to fertilize new plantings. Avoid excess fertilization and fast-release, high nitrogen fertilizers.

Care

Pests are not a problem. Plants grown in poorly drained soil are subject to yellow leaves, poor growth, and even death. Magnolias are subject to snow and ice damage. Reduce the risk with proper training and pruning. Very little pruning is needed once the framework is established on young trees. Prune magnolias after flowering. Finish the job by early summer so you don't interfere with the next season's bloom.

Companion Planting and Design

Small magnolias can be used as an accent, a flowering specimen, or as a mass display in small or large yards. Include smaller trees near the house and patio or as part of a mixed border. Save the larger magnolias for bigger settings.

My Personal Favorites

The small star magnolia, *Magnolia stellata*, and long-time favorite saucer magnolia, *Magnolia × soulangiana*, are rated hardy to Zone 4. Both are earlier bloomers whose flowers are often damaged by early spring frosts. Merrill Magnolia, *Magnolia × loebneri* 'Merrill', has large white flowers, grows 25 to 30 feet tall, and has performed well in the Minnesota Landscape Arboretum. The cucumber magnolia, *Magnolia acuminata*, is the hardiest (Zone 3), growing into a large pyramidal tree. Not as ornamental in flower, the large leaves are reminiscent of the southern magnolia. 'Butterflies' magnolia is one of the best and hardiest (Zone 4) yellow-flowering magnolias.

When you hear the word magnolia you may think of the south and its trees with large fragrant flowers and huge, glossy, evergreen leaves. Or maybe the flowers conjure up visions of Chinese art. They were the first to grow these plants. They used the buds for flavoring rice and medicine. Many northern gardeners would also like to enjoy these beautiful plants. We can't enjoy the same species as our southern gardening friends, but we can enjoy magnolias. Select hardy types, plant them in the right location, and keep your fingers crossed that nature will cooperate. Sounds too risky? Once you have seen a blooming magnolia in a northern landscape, you will understand why gardeners grow this tree. The smooth, gray bark is beautiful year-round. When the blooms appear, they are spectacular.

Bloom Period and Seasonal Color
Early spring blooms in pink and white.

Mature Height × Spread
15 to 40 ft. × 30 ft.

Maple
Acer species

The familiar maple is one of the most widely used landscape plants. I'm sure you remember throwing maple seeds (we called them helicopters or whirleybirds) in the air as a child. Maples have the colorful yellow, orange, and red fall leaves used to decorate elementary schools' fall bulletin boards. Sugar maple sap is also used to make maple syrup. You need 40 gallons of sap for 1 gallon of syrup. These native trees grow best in moist, rich soil. They do not tolerate heat, drought, or salt. Use them as shade trees in lawn areas and other park-like settings. The true Red maple, Acer rubrum, gets it common name from its brilliant red fall color. This native tree will tolerate wet conditions but must have acidic (low pH) soils.

Bloom Period and Seasonal Color
Early spring flowers in red or yellow, with yellow-orange, and red fall color.

Mature Height × Spread
Up to 75 ft. × 40 ft.

When, Where, and How to Plant
Plant balled-and-burlapped trees as soon as possible after they are purchased. Plant container-grown plants throughout the growing season. Red and freeman maples respond best to spring planting. Grow maples in full sun with moist, well-drained soil. Some species are more tolerant of wet, dry, or other difficult conditions. See the chapter introduction for planting directions.

Growing Tips
Water established trees when the top 4 to 6 inches of soil are moist and crumbly. Mulch the area around maple trees. Avoid excess fertilization that can hinder fall color.

Care
Prune young trees to establish a central leader and sturdy framework. Maple trees will bleed when pruned in the spring. It won't hurt the plant, but makes most gardeners wince. Verticillium wilt can be deadly. Prune out infected branches, disinfecting tools between cuts. Do not replace trees killed by Verticillium wilt with other susceptible plants. Anthracnose, tar spot, petiole borer, cottony maple scale, aphids, and galls are a few of the problems maples are susceptible to. Healthy trees will tolerate all these pests. Rake and destroy spotted leaves as they fall to reduce future disease problems. Galls are just benign, colorful, and uniquely shaped bumps on leaves caused by insect feeding. They are harmless.

Companion Planting and Design
Maples are shallow-rooted trees that make it difficult to grow and maintain grass. Eliminate this frustration by mulching the roots or growing shade-tolerant ground covers under the tree. Do NOT cut or bury the roots. This can eventually kill the tree.

My Personal Favorites
Select the species and cultivars appropriate for your growing conditions and landscape design. Silver maple, *Acer saccharinum*, is a fast-growing, weak-wooded native plant that tolerates wet soil. Proper pruning can help extend the life of this tree. The Autumn Blaze freeman maple, *Acer × freemanii* 'Autumn Blaze', has stronger wood, red fall color, and tolerates alkaline soils. Amur maples (*Acer ginnala*) is a small scale tree with fragrant white flowers and orange-red fall color.

Musclewood

Carpinus caroliniana

When, Where, and How to Plant

Musclewood trees do not respond well to transplanting. Plant balled-and-burlapped and container-grown trees in the spring. Musclewood is native to the forests of Minnesota. It prefers partial shade and moist soil in the landscape but will tolerate heavy shade and temporary flooding. Locate the tree's root flare. That is the bell-shaped area where the roots angle away from the trunk. Plant the tree with the root flare at or slightly above the soil line in a hole as deep as and 3 to 5 times wider than the root system. See the chapter introduction for more planting details.

Growing Tips

Patience is the key to care. New trees take time to adjust to their new location. The slow-growing musclewood averages less than 1 foot of growth each year. Mulch the roots to keep the soil cool and moist. This also suppresses weeds and keeps away competitive grass that can further slow development. Water established trees thoroughly whenever the top 4 to 6 inches of soil are crumbly and moist. Wait a year to fertilize new plantings.

Care

Once established, musclewood requires little maintenance. Although trees are subject to damage from ice storms, properly trained trees will be less susceptible. Prune young trees to establish a structurally sound framework. Minimal pruning should be done after this.

Companion Planting and Design

Musclewood works equally well in a naturalized area or a more formal landscape. Its shade tolerance makes it a good choice for an understory tree in woodland settings or shady yards. The attractive bark, fine texture, and growth habit make them specimen-quality plants. Or you can use multistemmed forms of this wide plant to provide screening.

My Personal Favorite

Musclewood is available as single or multistemmed plants. It may be a challenge to find a local source. Call ahead to nurseries that specialize in native plants. The other tree known as ironwood, *Ostrya Virginia*, is about the same size and shape. It is more drought tolerant. See Ironwood for more details on this plant.

Musclewood is a beautiful element in nature that is often overlooked for use in the home landscape. It tolerates moist soil, even temporary flooding, and shade. That is quite unusual for specimen-quality shade trees. The fine texture and smooth, gray bark give this tree year-round appeal. The elm-like leaves turn yellow, orange, or red in the fall. The flowers are not very effective, but the papery fruit can persist and add winter interest. Musclewood goes by several common names. The slate gray, fluted bark looks like flexed muscles. That's how it got the name musclewood. The bark also resembles that of a beech, thus blue or water beech. And like the other ironwood, Ostrya virginiana, this tree has very hard and durable wood. It's worth the effort it may take to find one for your yard.

Other Common Name
American Hornbeam

Bloom Period and Seasonal Color
Fall foliage in yellow, orange, and red.

Mature Height × Spread
Up to 30 ft. × 30 ft.

Zones
Hardy to Zone 3b

Oak

Quercus species

Oaks are the majestic trees of nature, and they bring the same feeling of majesty to large landscapes. Oak trees are becoming more readily available thanks in part to an increased interest in native plants and greater transplanting success. These large trees are medium to slow growing but can still be enjoyed in our lifetime. Plus they are a great gift to leave to our children. Some oaks have good fall color. Many hold their leaves over the winter. That can add subtle interest and sound to the winter landscape. The nuts are ornamental and provide food for a variety of wildlife. Plus their coarse texture and dramatic silhouette provide year-round beauty. Members of the red or black oak group have leaves with pointed lobes, while members of the white oak group have rounded leaves.

Bloom Period and Seasonal Color
Fall foliage in yellow, brown, or red.

Mature Height × Spread
50 to 80 ft. × 50 to 80 ft.

When, Where, and How to Plant
Most oaks are difficult to transplant. Plant balled-and-burlapped trees in the spring soon after purchasing. In general, oaks prefer moist, well-drained soil. Some require acidic soil while others will tolerate alkaline soil. Select species adapted to your soil conditions.

Growing Tips
Most established oaks are drought tolerant. Water them thoroughly during extended dry periods. Mulch to conserve moisture, suppress weeds, and eliminate the frustration of trying to grow grass under oaks. Wait for one year after planting to fertilize.

Care
Prune oaks during the dormant season to minimize the risk of oak wilt infection. Oak wilt is a deadly disease that enters through wounds, such as pruning cuts. The upper leaves wilt then turn brown and drop from oak wilt-infected trees. Apply pruning paint to oaks pruned during the growing season. This is the only time you should use a pruning paint. Anthracnose and galls are common problems on oaks but are not harmful. (See Care under the maples entry.) Several oaks are very intolerant of alkaline (high pH) soil. They develop chlorosis, a yellowing of leaves. Avoid planting acidic-loving oaks in alkaline soils.

Companion Planting and Design
Plant these trees for future shade and specimen plants. Give them plenty of room; they will eventually need it.

My Personal Favorites
White oak, *Quercus alba*, is a native tree with beautiful, red fall color. It is hardy to Zone 4b but not tolerant of alkaline and compacted soils. The red oak, *Quercus rubra*, is a little faster growing than most oaks and a good choice for urban areas. The native swamp white oak, *Quercus bicolor*, tolerates moist, even wet, soil conditions. It is a good choice for urban areas, and the exfoliating bark is an added ornamental feature. This oak is hardy to Zone 4. Bur oak, *Quercus macrocarpa*, of our native oak-savannas will tolerate wet to dry soil. The coarse texture and furrowed bark provide year-round interest. Pin oak, *Quercus palustris*, is fast growing, finer textured, hardy to Zone 4b, and requires acidic soil.

Ornamental Plums and Cherries

Prunus species

When, Where, and How to Plant

Plant bare-root, balled-and-burlapped, and container-grown trees in the spring. Ornamental plums and cherries tend to be short lived in our area. Proper siting is important. They need moist, well-drained soil and have difficulty growing in heavy clay soil. Grow them in a protected site or on the east side of your home in full sun. That will reduce the risk of winter injury and flower damage from a late spring frost. Follow planting directions in the introduction.

Growing Tips

Water established trees thoroughly whenever the top 4 to 6 inches of soil are moist and crumbly. Mulch the roots to keep them cool and moist. Wait a year to fertilize new plantings. Avoid excess fertilization that can interfere with flowering.

Care

These ornamental plants have many insect and disease problems. Healthy plants are the best defense against these problems. Plant trees in protected areas with well-drained soil. Reduce problems by avoiding injuries caused by mowers, weed whips, or other items. Prune these trees during dry weather to avoid the spread of disease. These trees tend to be short lived and also sucker freely. You will discover little trees throughout your lawn. Cut them off below ground level to discourage resprouting. Treating the sprouts with total vegetation killers will kill the parent tree, too.

Companion Planting and Design

Use these ornamental trees as a temporary (ten to twenty years) specimen or accent plant. They also work well in patio and Japanese gardens.

My Personal Favorites

Schubert cherry *Prunus virginiana* 'Schubert' or its branch sport 'Canada Red' are the best of the purple-leafed prunus. The leaves emerge green and turn a deep purple for the season. These are hardy throughout the state. Purple-leafed sand cherry, *Prunus × cistena*, is more of a shrub than a tree. It is hardy throughout Minnesota. Renewal pruning will reduce pest problems and maintain the plant's leaf color and form. Amur chokecherry, *Prunus maackii*, is a reliable bloomer with shiny, amber-colored exfoliating bark. It's hardy throughout Minnesota.

Ornamental plums and cherries are grown for their impressive flowers or decorative foliage. These small trees can add early spring interest to both large and small landscapes. Many have decorative bark, fruit for the wildlife, and interesting form. After a mild winter and spring with no flower-killing frosts, we will have a beautiful spring floral display and a run on these plants at the garden center. Over time they fade away until the next glorious spring bloom. The native cherries and plums are often considered less ornamental but are more suited to our soils and climate. The black cherry (Prunus serotina) is native to our forests. It has distinct scaly bark that looks like someone glued burnt potato chips to the trunk. Its tight-grained, red wood has long been used for making cabinets and furniture.

Other Common Names

Flowering Almond, Cherry, Newport Plum, Purple Leaf, Sand Cherry

Bloom Period and Seasonal Color

Spring blooms in white or pink.

Mature Height × Spread

Up to 30 ft. × 30 ft.

Pine

Pinus species

Pines are an important evergreen in the landscape. They have long been used as windbreaks, screens, and wildlife habitats. Planted in the right location with sufficient space, pines provide years of beauty. White pine, Pinus strobus, is native to Minnesota. It was an important lumber tree here and throughout the United States. Carpenters like the wood because it is easy to work and finishes nicely. Landscapers like this beautiful tree because of its soft wispy texture. It starts out pyramidal and becomes picturesque with age. It is hardy statewide but will not tolerate salt, pollution, and alkaline soils. The red pine, Pinus resinosa, is the Minnesota state tree, and is a tough native used for windbreaks. Considered more of a workhorse than a beauty in the landscape, it has attractive red bark and green needles that turn yellow-green over the winter.

Bloom Period and Seasonal Color
Evergreen needles.

Mature Height × Spread
Up to 75 ft. × 40 ft.

When, Where, and How to Plant
Plant balled-and-burlapped trees in the spring or fall as soon as possible after they are purchased. Plant container-grown plants by October 1 to allow the plants to get established before winter. Pines prefer full sun and moist, well-drained soil. Most pines can tolerate dry conditions once established. Follow planting direction in the chapter introduction.

Growing Tips
Water established plants thoroughly whenever the top 4 to 6 inches of soil are crumbly and moist. Mulch to conserve moisture and suppress weeds since grass won't usually grow beneath these trees. Wait a year to fertilize new plantings. Properly managed trees need minimal fertilization.

Care
Pines need minimal pruning. Prune out dead and damaged branches and maintain a central leader. Pines can be pruned to limit growth. This is done in the spring as the new growth elongates. This tight, new growth is called a candle. Cut off $1/2$ or $2/3$ of the candles to shorten and thicken the new growth. There are several fungal diseases and insect problems that can be damaging. Contact your local University of Minnesota County Extension Office or a certified arborist for diagnosis and treatment recommendations.

Companion Planting and Design
Use these evergreens for windbreaks, screens, specimen plants, and winter color. Remember, these nice, small "Christmas" trees will grow into large, spreading trees sooner than you think. Use them as specimen plants or as a nice backdrop for deciduous plants. The dark green needles make the colorful bark of birches, dogwoods, and red maples stand out.

My Personal Favorites
The blue-green needles of Scotch pine, *Pinus sylvestris*, provide an attractive contrast to the orange bark. This tough tree tolerates a variety of soils, as long as they are well drained. The Swiss stone pine, *Pinus cembra*, is a good choice for small areas. It is a slow grower with a narrow upright growth habit. Limit the use of Austrian pine *Pinus nigra*. Once the workhorse of the landscape, it has recently been besieged by multiple pest problems.

Redbud
Cercis canadensis

When, Where, and How to Plant

Redbuds respond best to spring planting, which allows them to get established before winter. Grow redbuds in a protected location. They do best in full sun to part shade in moist, well-drained soil. Plant the tree with the root flare at or slightly above the soil line. Follow the planting directions in the chapter introduction.

Growing Tips

Growing a hardier strain of redbuds in a protected location will reduce maintenance needs. Water plants thoroughly whenever the top 4 to 6 inches of soil are crumbly and moist. Mulch the soil to keep the roots cool and moist. Wait a year to fertilize new plantings. Avoid excess amounts and fast-release, high nitrogen fertilizers. This can diminish flowering and winter hardiness.

Care

Prune young trees to establish a strong framework. Established trees need minimal pruning. Remove winter damaged and wayward branches. Prune in late winter or early spring when the wounds will close quickly and reduce the risk of disease. Winter injury is the biggest problem with these trees. Proper selection, siting, and care will help with this and reduce the risk of insect and disease. Verticillium wilt can be a problem. Remove infected branches, disinfecting your tools between cuts. Do not plant verticillium wilt-killed trees with susceptible plants.

Companion Planting and Design

Redbuds often grow wider than tall, so give them plenty of room to show off their attractive form. They are often used as specimen plants, along a woodland edge, or in a naturalized setting. Their strong, horizontal branching and flower display make them a good addition to a Japanese garden.

My Personal Favorites

Select a hardy strain for greatest success. Try the hardy "Minnesota strain," which was propagated from plants in the Minnesota Landscape Arboretum and introduced in 1992. These small trees have dark pink to purple flowers in early May. The "Columbus strain" was propagated from hardy redbuds in the city of Columbus, Wisconsin. You may want to stop by and enjoy their redbud festival.

The redbud is one of the most beautiful trees when it is in bud and bloom. The dark branches and trunk are covered with reddish-purple buds in early spring. The buds open into rosy pink flowers and put on quite a show. The flowers are edible as well as ornamental. Use them raw in salads or fried as an appetizer. Once the flowers are gone, the tree is covered with green heart-shaped leaves that turn a pretty yellow in the fall. After the leaves fall, a graceful silhouette is left to adorn the winter landscape. The redbud fruit is a dry, flat pod about 2 to 3 inches long and 1/2 inch wide. Redbuds can thrive in Minnesota, given the proper location and growing conditions. Redbuds are available as single or multistemmed plants.

Other Common Name
Eastern Redbud

Bloom Period and Seasonal Color
Early spring blooms in rosy pink; fall foliage in yellow.

Mature Height × Spread
Up to 30 ft. × 30 ft.

Zones
Hardy to Zone 4

Serviceberry
Amelanchier species

The Minnesota native serviceberry is among my favorite small trees. It provides four seasons of interest. The white flowers open in spring. Once done, they are followed by small berries. The fruit starts out pink and then turns purple-black. Don't worry about a mess; the birds will clean up the fruit before it hits the ground. I have robins lined up on my fence every June waiting for the fruit to ripen. And many gardeners tell me the cedar wax wings also love the fruit. Next comes the colorful fall display when the leaves turn a brilliant yellow, orange, or red. Serviceberries are edible. They have a nutty, blueberry flavor. The only trick is beating the birds to the fruit. One year, I was fortunate enough to gather enough berries for a pie. It was delicious.

Other Common Name
Juneberry

Bloom Period and Seasonal Color
Spring blooms in white; fall foliage in yellow, orange, and red.

Mature Height × Spread
Up to 40 ft. × 30 ft.

When, Where, and How to Plant
Plant balled-and-burlapped trees as soon as possible after purchase. Plant container-grown plants throughout the growing season. Serviceberries take time to establish after transplanting. Grow serviceberries in moist, well-drained soil. Dig a shallow planting hole the same depth as and 3 to 5 times wider than the root system. Plant the tree with the root flare at or slightly above the soil line. Remove the container, twine, and metal baskets, and cut away the burlap. Fill the hole with existing soil, water to settle the soil, and mulch.

Growing Tips
Serviceberries often take time to adjust to a new location. Be patient because the tree puts down roots before growing taller. Water established trees thoroughly whenever the top 4 to 6 inches of soil are crumbly and moist. Mulch the soil to conserve moisture, eliminate grass competition, and keep the roots cool. Wait a year to fertilize new plantings. Properly mulched and watered trees need minimal fertilizer.

Care
Serviceberries don't have serious insect or disease problems. Prune young trees to establish a strong framework. Mature trees will need minimal pruning. I prefer late winter or early spring pruning. The wounds close quickly, reducing the risk of pest problems.

Companion Planting and Design
Serviceberries are native to woodland edges, stream banks, fence rows, and hillsides. This adaptability helps them tolerate a wide range of landscape conditions. Use the shrub forms of serviceberry in groupings, as screens, or as an unsheared hedge. The small trees make good specimen plants near water features, in planting beds, or small landscapes. Larger trees can provide shade and ornamental value in larger settings.

My Personal Favorites
Downy serviceberry, *Amelanchier arborea*, is an upright, small tree. This slow grower can eventually reach heights of 30 feet. It is hardy to Zone 3b and is more tolerant of dry soil. Apple serviceberry, *Amelanchier × grandiflora*, is slow growing, tolerates partial shade, and is hardy to Zone 3. Allegany serviceberry, *Amelanchier laevis*, is hardy to Zone 4.

Spruce

Picea species

When, Where, and How to Plant

Plant balled-and-burlapped trees in the spring as soon as possible after purchasing. Plant container-grown trees by October 1 for greater chances of winter survival. Grow in moist, well-drained soil. Consult the chapter introduction for planting tips.

Growing Tips

Water established trees whenever the top 4 to 6 inches of soil are moist and crumbly. Mulch to conserve moisture and to suppress weeds (don't bother with grass under the trees). Wait a year to fertilize new plantings. Properly watered and mulched spruce need minimal fertilization.

Care

Spruce need very little pruning. Touch-up pruning can be done in the spring before growth begins. Make cuts on branch tips above a healthy bud. You do not have to prune off the lower branches of these trees. Limbing them up is for the gardener's benefit, not the plant's. Plants growing in optimum conditions are less susceptible to damage from disease. Mites can be a problem in hot dry weather. Spray infested plants once a week with a strong blast of water from the garden hose to keep these pests under control. Colorado blue spruce is susceptible to cytospora canker, rhizosphaera needle blight, and spruce galls. The first two diseases can greatly disfigure trees. Remove infested branches, disinfecting tools between cuts. Consider hiring a certified arborist if you decide to treat for needle blight. Galls don't harm the trees overall health.

Companion Planting and Design

These large trees provide a strong, pyramidal silhouette in the garden. Use them as screens, windbreaks, and specimens. Dwarf cultivars are suitable for smaller landscapes and for use in perennial and rock gardens.

My Personal Favorites

Serbian spruce, *Picea omorika,* has a narrow pyramidal shape and grows to 50 feet tall. Its pendulous branches make a graceful statement in the landscape. White spruce, *Picea glauca,* is native and hardy throughout Minnesota and needs moist soil. Black Hills Spruce is shorter, 20 feet, and slower growing. Dwarf Alberta spruce, *Picea glauca* 'Conica', needs protection from winter wind and sun to prevent browning.

Spruce trees start out and end up about the same shape: just bigger. These large trees provide a strong, pyramidal silhouette in the garden. Remember, these trees will get huge. Too many gardeners have planted a cute little spruce by their front entrance only to have it consume the whole yard. The most popular spruce for the home landscape is probably the Colorado blue spruce, Picea pungens f. glauca. It can reach a height of 60 feet and is hardy throughout Minnesota. It will tolerate dry soil and urban conditions. Its stiff, pyramidal shape and blue needles make it hard to blend with the rest of the landscape. Pices abies can also be found in many landscapes throughout Minnesota. This spruce needs moist soil. The dark green needles held on pendulous branches make this large tree a graceful specimen.

Bloom Period and Seasonal Color
Evergreen needles.

Mature Height × Spread
Up to 60 ft. × 30 ft.

Turfgrass *for* Minnesota

Grass is a unifying element and a functional part of any landscape design. Grassy areas provide walkways, play areas, and something to keep your feet from getting muddy when it rains. No matter how much effort and money you invest in grass seed or sod, your lawn will be only as good as the soil it is grown in. Taking the time to plan carefully before the first seed is sown or the sod is laid will help ensure a healthy, attractive lawn you can be proud of. After the soil is properly prepared, selecting the right grass for growing conditions in your area will also improve chances for a lush, green, outdoor carpet. Once the grass is established, mowing, watering, and fertilizing properly are the three keys to maintaining a healthy and attractive lawn.

The Grasses

Kentucky Bluegrass

Kentucky bluegrass (*Poa pratensis*) is a traditional favorite for Minnesota lawns. This cool-weather grass is well suited to our northern climate. It is green most of the year when the ground isn't frozen or covered with snow. Bluegrass may go dormant during hot, dry periods in July and August, but as soon as the weather cools and rains return, the grass turns green and begins to grow. Bluegrass lawns can be started from seed or sod. Grow it in full sun with moist, well-drained soil. It does not perform well in extremely

Kentucky Bluegrass

wet or dry locations. Bluegrass lawns will thin and eventually fail in heavily shaded areas. Use a blend of three to five cultivars to provide greater resistance to disease. 'Adelphi', 'Baron', 'Glade', 'Nasau', and 'Parade' are a few of the readily available disease-resistant bluegrasses.

Fescue

Fine fescues' (*Festuca* species) low-maintenance requirements and its shade and drought tolerance make it one of the top three grasses in Minnesota. It is much more tolerant of shade, drought, and acidic and infertile soils than bluegrass. You will find a large percentage of fine fescue in shade-tolerant lawn seed mixes. Although fescue will tolerate full sun, especially in northern Minnesota, it needs cool soil temperatures for best results. Overfertilization can lead to leaf spot and other fungal diseases. Fertilize pure stands of fescue growing in the shade only when the leaves are pale or the plants stop growing. One-half pound of actual nitrogen per thousand square feet applied in the fall is often enough for 100 percent fine fescue lawns growing in the shade.

Fine Fescue

The creeping red, *Fetuca rubra*, is the most commonly used fine fescue. It blends well with Kentucky bluegrass. Creeping red spreads slowly by rhizomes, so it is sluggish when recovering from injury. This fescue will tolerate drought and shade but not heat. Once established, it can be left unmowed for a meadow-like effect. Chewings fescue, *Festuca rubra commutata*, is a bunch-type fescue that has the same growth requirements as creeping red. Its bunching habit makes it more difficult to create an even stand. Hard fescue, *Festuca longifolia*, is often combined with sheep fescue, *Festuca ovina*, for low-maintenance lawns. Both are bunch-type grasses, and the lower-growing varieties require less frequent mowing.

Perennial Ryegrass

Turf-type perennial ryegrass (*Lolium perenne)* is an important part of lawn seed mixes in Minnesota. It germinates quickly and aids in the establishment of seeded lawns. The versatility of perennial rye, its improved quality, and the availability of hardier cultivars have made this a major component in most grass seed mixes. Straight ryegrass is often used to overseed high traffic or other thin areas of the lawn. Many new turf-type perennial ryegrasses are being introduced. Select the hardiest and most disease-resistant cultivars available. Annual ryegrass, *Lolium multiflorum,* is the quick-start grass of old mixtures. It is an annual that dies within the first year. Its coarse texture blends poorly with other grasses. Quick-fix miracle grasses contain a large percentage of this grass. They provide a quick-growing, short-lived lawn.

Perennial Ryegrass

Choices for Lawn Establishment

New lawns can be started from seed or sod. Seed mixes provide a wider variety of grasses and cultivars to choose from, allowing you to best match the grass with the growing conditions. Seed is cheaper than sod, but be patient—it takes about two months to establish a lawn from seed. Sod gives you an instant lawn at an additional cost. Most sod is best suited for sunny areas, though some growers are providing some that are more shade tolerant. Many gardeners sod the front yard and seed the back yard for fairly fast results at a lower overall cost.

Soil Preparation

Whether you seed or sod, start by taking a close look at the earth beneath your feet. Start with a soil test to determine how much and what type of fertilizer your lawn needs. Spread no more than the recommended lime, phosphorus, and potassium combination over the soil surface and till it into the top six inches of the soil. If soil test recommendations are not available, spread four to eight pounds of a starter fertilizer (no lime) over the soil surface. Lightly rake the fertilizer into the soil prior to seeding.

If your yard does not have at least four to six inches of good topsoil, you will also need to add blended topsoil or amend the existing soil by adding organic matter. Add two to three inches, equal to two to three cubic yards per thousand square feet, of peat moss, compost, aged manure, or another organic material to the top four to six inches of the existing soil. This can be incorporated at the same time as the fertilizer, lime, or sulfur recommended by the soil test. Do not add sand. Mixing sand into clay soil can result in poor growing conditions. Allow the soil to settle, and rake it smooth, leveling high areas and filling in low areas. With healthy soil in place, the next step is choosing the right grass for your yard.

A Well-Manicured Lawn and Garden

Seeding the Lawn

Use one or a mixture of the cool-weather grasses described above. Bluegrass works best in full sun while fescues really prefer the shade. Sun mixes contain mostly bluegrass and ryegrass with a smaller percent of fescue for shady areas. Shade mixes are the opposite, mostly fescues and ryegrass with a small percent of bluegrass to take over in sunny locations. Select a mix containing a variety of disease-resistant cultivars. Don't use zoysia, a warm-weather grass, it is better for southern states where the summers are long and hot. The best time to seed is August 15 through September 20. May is the second best time to seed. Apply half the seed over the entire lawn moving in *a north-south* direction. The remaining seed should be applied in an *east-west* direction to ensure good coverage.

Rake the seed into the soil surface and then roll the yard with an empty lawn roller, which will help guarantee good contact with the soil. Mulch the newly seeded lawn with straw, marsh hay, one of the season-extending fabrics, or other suitable mulch. Keep the surface of the soil moist until the grass seeds germinate, then water thoroughly but less frequently.

Seeding Rates

Pure bluegrass	1 to 1^1/$_2$ pounds per 1000 square feet
Pure fescue	3^1/$_2$ to 4^1/$_2$ pounds per 1000 square feet
Pure ryegrass	7 to 9 pounds per 1000 square feet
Sun mixes	3 to 4 pounds per 1000 square feet
Shade mixes	4 to 5 pounds per 1000 square feet

* Check package for specific guidelines for the mixture you purchase.

Sodding

Soil preparation is just as important for sodded lawns. Sod can be laid any time it is available and the ground is not frozen. Sod is purchased in rolls one-and-one-half by six feet (traditional size), though some garden centers now carry rolls two by four feet. Start by laying the first roll of sod next to a walk or driveway. Butt the ends of the sod pieces together, overlapping them slightly to compensate for shrinkage. Stagger the joints, just like you were laying bricks, for a nice finished look. Water frequently enough to

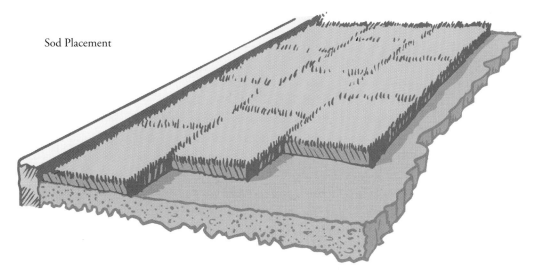

Sod Placement

keep the soil beneath the sod moist. Start watering thoroughly but less frequently once the sod roots into the soil and resists a light tug.

Caring for Your Lawn

Mowing

A healthy lawn is the best defense against weeds and disease. Proper mowing, watering, and fertilization will keep your grass green and healthy. Keep bluegrass lawns cut to a height of two-and-one-half to three-and-one-half inches. The taller grass will be more drought tolerant and better able to compete with weeds. No more than one-third of the total height should be cut at each mowing. Leave clippings on the lawn to decompose, adding moisture and nutrients to the soil. Be sure your mower blade is sharp. This will make your job easier, and the newly cut lawn will look better.

Watering

Ideally, lawns should receive one inch of water per week. Use a sprinkler, if needed, to supplement rainfall. Lawns in clay soils should be watered once a week. Yards in sandy soil should receive needed water in two applications per week. Avoid using quick-release, high nitrogen fertilizers (especially in summer) on non-irrigated lawns. This can damage the grass plants during the hot dry months of summer.

Fertilizing

Fertilizer is the third component of a healthy yard. Minnesota lawns generally need three to four pounds of actual nitrogen per thousand square feet a year. Use the annual holiday fertilization schedule: a light fertilization on Memorial Day (one-half pound actual nitrogen per thousand square feet), a heavier fertilization on Labor Day (one pound of actual nitrogen per thousand square feet), and the final application of fertilizer on Halloween (one pound of nitrogen per thousand square feet). Calculate the actual fertilizer needed using this formula:

One hundred divided by percent nitrogen in the fertilizer times the pounds of actual nitrogen needed equals the pounds of fertilizer needed.

For example, if we use a 6-2-0 fertilizer for our September application. Divide 100 by 6 (6% nitrogen in fertilizer) and multiply by 1 (we need 1 pound of actual nitrogen per 1000 square feet), so we need 16.7 pounds of 6-2-0 per 1000 square feet to provide the needed nutrients to the lawn.

Weed Control

When weeds appear, it's a sure sign that the grass isn't vigorous or healthy enough to keep them at bay. Do some detective work to determine why weeds have invaded your lawn. Is the area too shady? Is the soil compact, or is the grass not receiving needed water and nutrients? Correct the conditions for long-term weed control. You may decide instead to live with a few weeds rather than using chemicals or adjusting your yard-maintenance efforts in some other way. It's up to you to determine the quality desired and the time and effort you are willing to invest. If you do decide to use an herbicide, be sure to read and follow all label directions carefully. These really are plant killers. They can't tell the difference between a dandelion and a geranium, so use them carefully to minimize the risk to you, the landscape, and the environment. Timing is critical for successful treatment. Fall applications are most effective against perennial weeds like plantain and dandelions. Treat that bothersome creeping Charlie in spring when it is in full bloom or in fall, around late October, after a hard frost. All those chemicals you previously used unsuccessfully will work if applied at the right time. Crabgrass killers are applied in early spring before the seeds of this annual grass sprout. When the soil temperatures reach fifty degrees Fahrenheit (soon after the forsythia bloom), it is time to apply the crabgrass pre-emergent. Perennial grass weeds like quack and bent are more difficult. Anything that kills them will kill your good grass. Spot treat large infestations with a total vegetation killer such as Roundup® or Finale®. Then reseed to get new grass growing before the weeds take over.

Reduce your exposure by spot treating problem areas with broadleaf weedkillers. You do not need to treat the entire lawn and should not need to be treating it every year. Yearly applications indicate poor grass-growing conditions that need to be fixed. Gardeners looking for a safer option may want to try a new weed killer made of corn gluten meal. It interferes with the germination of many lawn weeds. It won't kill existing weeds, but it prevents weed seeds from germinating. This is an appealing alternative for many lawn owners whose children and pets play on the grass. Be patient, it takes several years to reduce the weed population by fifty percent.

Thatch Control

Thatch is a problem on highly managed lawns. Lots of fertilizer and water encourage thick, dense growth. As the old grass plants die, they have no way to reach the soil surface to decompose. The old grass stems, leaf coverings, and roots—*not grass clipping*—form the thatch layer. Control thatch when it becomes one-half inch or thicker. You can top-dress the lawn with one-fourth inch of soil to help compost the thatch in place. This is good for the lawn, but hard on your back! Core aeration is another method to control thatch. The core-aerating machine removes plugs from the soil. It opens the lawn, allowing the thatch to decompose. Dethatching machines and verti-cut mowers physically remove the thatch. Be

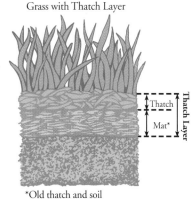

Grass with Thatch Layer

Thatch

Mat*

Thatch Layer

*Old thatch and soil

prepared: the lawn will look awful when you finish! But a couple of weeks later, you will be amazed at its recovery. Overseed thin lawns after dethatching or aeration to thicken up the lawn. You will have better seed germination once the thatch is removed. Core aeration and dethatching should be done in the spring or fall when the lawn is actively growing.

Pest Control

A healthy Minnesota lawn is relatively free of insects and disease. Use an Integrated Pest Management or Plant Health Care approach to preventing and managing insect and disease problems. Mow the grass high and often enough to remove no more than $1/3$ the total height of the leaf blades. Water thoroughly but only when the top 4 to 6 inches of soil are crumbly and moist. When your footprints are left in the grass - it is time to water. The follow a regular fertilization program based on soil test results. If these aren't available use the holiday schedule I provided.

Even with proper care your lawn may be attacked by disease or insects. Proper diagnosis is the first step in managing the problem. Check with your local University Extension service, the internet or The Perfect Minnesota Lawn for more details on possible problems.

These are a few of the symptoms and possible causes of problems that can be found in Minnesota lawns:

Scenario 1 – Grass affected in distinct circular patterns

Symptoms	Possible Cause
Ring of dark green grass with mushrooms	Fairy ring
Leaves chewed	Armyworm
Small bleached spots or circles	Dollar spot
Brown patch with tuft of green grass in center	Necrotic ring spot
Small brown patches	Dog urine
Brown grass with dead dandelion in center	Misuse of pesticide

Scenario 2 – Grass affected in irregular patterns

Symptoms	Possible Cause
Slow decline, yellowish area, shallow roots, wilt	Nematodes
Leaves have gray cast turn yellow-brown then slimy and mat together	Pythium
Grass comes out of winter matted white to brown and sometimes covered with pink or gray fuzz	Snowmold
Yellowish spots with fuzzy orange lesions shoes "turn" orange when walking across lawn	Rust
White powdery substance on leaves	Powdery Mildew
Spots on leaves, grass browns and melts away	Helminthosporium leaf spot
Yellowish or dead spots, grass easily pulls out no roots	Billbugs
Center dead, yellowish brown grass	Chinch bug
Grass blades cut and webbing near surface	Sod webworms
Grass fades in color or soil dries quickly	Septic tank, buried patio or change of oil texture
Weak, thin, leggy grass	Excess shade
Grass thin, wilts quickly, fertilizer doesn't help	Competition with trees
Brown grass along walks and drives in spring	De-icing salt
Runways of deadgrass in spring	Voles
Ridges in lawn in summer	Moles

Scenario 3 – Grass affected in streaked patterns:

Symptoms	Possible Cause
Grass bleached, yellow, brown or dead	Chemical (fertilizer, herbicide) burn

Scenario 4 – Grass affected but no particular pattern

Symptoms	Possible Cause
Roots cut off, dead areas in lawn, pulls up easily	Grubs
Stems chewed near soil surface, wilting and dead	Cutworms
Grass bleached or speckled, hopping insects	Leafhoppers
Small mounds of disturbed soil	Ants
Grass blades covered with gray chalky substance	Slime mold
Grass spongy	Thatch
Weeds	Compaction, shade, wet soils, poor management
Grass has grayish cast, tips of leaves split or frayed	Dull mower blade
Grass thin, weak and doesn't respond to proper care	Variety not suited to location
Grass yellowish green on older blades, eventually brown tips	Nitrogen deficiency
Yellowish foliage, especially new growth or between veins	Iron deficiency, high pH
Greyish green to brown grass, leaves rolled , soil dry	Drought
Yellow, thin blades and weak roots	Excessive water

Adjust the cultural practices if it is a water, fertilization or grass selection problem. Adjusting your care often corrects insect and disease problems. Overseed bare spots with disease resistant grass to improve the looks and disease resistance in your lawns. Proper care and disease resistant grass will take care of most diseases. If it continues you may decide to use a fungicide. Using the right product and applying it at the right time is critical to control. Be sure to read and follow all label directions carefully.

Insects can also invade Minnesota lawns. Most appear during hot dry weather. Proper care and change in the weather usually keep these pests under control. That is, except Japanese beetles. These are moving into our state feeding on many ornamental plants and the roots of our grass. Soil applied insecticides will help with their control. Milky spore is a fungus that will help minimize this pest. It takes several years to provide control but it is easier on the environment. DO not overuse insecticides. They kill the beneficial insects in the soil and can lead to other problems in the future.

Though the list of possibilities is long the problems are usually minimal. So get out and enjoy your carpet of green.

Armyworm Larva

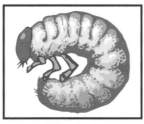
White Grub

Billbug

Vines *for Minnesota*

Are you running out of space in your garden? Do you need to mask a bad view? Try using some of the many annual and perennial vines that are available through catalogs, nurseries, and garden centers. Vines don't need much—just a little soil and a wall, fence, or other vertical support. Select vines that will tolerate the growing conditions, give the look you want, serve your needs, and climb on the type of support provided.

Vines attach themselves to structures in different ways. Some, like bittersweet and clematis, have twining stems and work well on chain-link fences, arbors, and trellises. Don't grow twining vines up tree trunks. They can encircle the trunk and kill the tree. Other vines have holdfasts. Boston ivy, climbing hydrangea, and other clinging vines have stick-tight tendrils, aerial rootlets, or adhesive pads for attaching to masonry or wood structures. Grow these vines on brick or stone walls and on wooden trellises, arbors, or pergolas. Do not grow these vines on wood-sided homes. They can damage the siding and must be removed every time your home needs painting or repair.

Supporting Your Vines

Use your imagination when selecting a support structure suitable for the vines you have chosen. I have seen twining vines climb up mailbox posts, lampposts, and downspouts. Some gardeners use attractive antique grates, door frames, or discarded play structures. Others attach a sheet of plastic or wire mesh to a wall or fence to give the twining vines something to attach to. It also makes maintenance much easier. You can carefully remove the support from the wall, lay it on the ground, and make needed repairs to the fence or wall. When the work is complete, reattach the support, vine and all, to the structure. Very handy

Clematis

Wisteria

gardeners use hinged trellises, which have lockable hinges at the soil surface. The hinges make it possible to carefully bend the vine-clad trellis out of the way when repairing the wall or fence. Do all of those choices sound like too much work? Don't worry, garden centers and catalogues are full of standard or unusual, attractive, preassembled trellises.

No matter what type of support you select, make sure it is well anchored. Vine-covered structures can act like a sail and take off in a strong wind. The structure also must be strong enough to support the weight of the vine. Bittersweet, trumpet vine, and wisteria can become quite massive and heavy. These plants will need a strong, well-anchored structure for support.

Once the support is in place, it's time to select the best vine for the landscape design and maintenance. Rampant growers like Boston ivy may not be as showy as a clematis, but they can quickly cover an ugly wall or hide a bad view. They will need regular pruning to keep them in line. Dropmore scarlet honeysuckle is a beautiful flowering plant that needs very little pruning, but it may need occasional aphid control.

For added interest, mix several vines together on one support structure. Two clematis planted on the same trellis or several different vine species planted in an arbor can increase bloom time and have a dramatic visual effect. Select vines that are equally aggressive, or the stronger plant will engulf the weaker one, giving you a single-plant display. Vines can also be used as ground covers. Allow them to crawl unrestrained through the garden to create attractive and unexpected plant combinations. Monitor and prune vines to make sure they don't overrun or choke out their neighbors.

Getting Started

Get your vines off to a good growing start. Minimize transplant shock with proper planting. Carefully slide the plant out of the pot, or better yet, cut the pot away at planting to minimize root disturbance. Simply remove the bottom of the container. Set it in a planting hole that is the same depth and at least two to three times wider than the rootball. Slice down the side of the pot and peel it away, leaving the rootball intact. Loosen any circling roots, fill the hole with soil, and water. Pruning and training techniques vary. See the care information under each vine for specific directions. Now go outside and take a look around your landscape. I bet you can find a little vertical space just begging for a vine.

Arctic Beauty Kiwi

Actinidia kolomikta 'Arctic Beauty'

This vine is a hardy and ornamental relative of the edible kiwi you may have purchased in the grocery store. Grow this vine for its ornamental foliage. The emerging heart-shaped leaves start out purple then turn green with a white and pink blotch. In fall, the leaves turn yellow before dropping to the ground. The attractive foliage makes a nice seasonal screen, vertical accent, or backdrop for other plants. I have seen this twining vine trained on tall posts, trellises, and arbors. A close look in late May and early June will reveal small fragrant flowers. If you have both male and female plants, you will be rewarded with sweet edible kiwis the size of grapes. Just the right size for popping in your mouth as you work in the garden.

Other Common Name
Arctic Beauty

Bloom Period and Seasonal Color
Mid-May through June in white flowers; colorful foliage in spring through summer, with yellow fall color.

Mature Length
15 to 20 ft.

Zones
Hardy to Zone 4

When, Where, and How to plant

Plant container-grown plants any time during the growing season. I prefer spring through early summer so the plants have time to get established before winter. Arctic Beauty kiwi will have the best foliage color in partially shaded locations. The foliage tends to bleach out in full sun and fade in heavy shade. Grow in a protected spot with moist, well-drained soils for best results. You will need at least 1 male for every 5 female plants for fruit (gender is on the label). Gently loosen potbound roots prior to planting. Place the plant in a hole that is as deep as the rootball and at least 2 to 3 times wider.

Growing tips

Water established plants thoroughly when the top 4 to 6 inches is moist but crumbly. Avoid excess nitrogen fertilizer that will inhibit flowering, fruiting, and good foliage color.

Care

Hardiness is its biggest problem. Increase survival rates by providing winter protection the first year or two after planting. Wrap new plantings with burlap or surround the plants with hardware cloth sunk in the ground and filled with evergreen boughs or straw. Prune new plantings back to a strong bud about 12 to 16 inches above the ground. Train 5 to 7 strong shoots onto the support. Next spring, prune stout side shoots by $^{1}/_{3}$ and weak branches back to 1 to 2 buds. Prune established plants back by $^{1}/_{3}$ or $^{1}/_{2}$ in early spring. Occasionally remove an old stem to ground level to promote new growth at the base.

Companion Planting and Design

Train arctic beauty kiwi on a trellis, arbor, or other structure. It creates a colorful screen to mask bad views or a nice backdrop to any garden. Use white and pink flowers nearby to maximize the impact of the multicolored foliage.

My Personal Favorite

Tara vine, *Actinidia arguta,* is less ornamental but produces more fruit. The green leaves will quickly cover the support. Select the self-fruitful cultivar 'Issai' to eliminate the need for male and female plants.

Bittersweet
Celastrus scandens

When, Where, and How to Plant

Plant bare-root plants in early spring before growth begins. Plant container-grown plants any time during the growing season. Bittersweet thrives in full sun and well-drained soil. It will tolerate partial shade but produces a poor fruit display in heavy shade. You will need at least 1 male for every 5 female plants to have fruit. Since you can only tell the sex of the plants by the flowers, check the label for that information. Many nurseries include both a male and female plant in the same pot. Plant bare-root bittersweet with the crown even with the soil surface where the roots join the stem. Bare-root plants need moist soil to establish new roots. Gently loosen potbound roots of container-grown bittersweet prior to planting. Place the plant in a hole as deep as the rootball and at least 2 to 3 times wider.

Growing Tips

Water established plants thoroughly whenever the top few inches of soil starts to dry. If bittersweet receives lots of moisture and fertilizer, it will grow bigger and faster with lots of leaves but no fruit.

Care

Train new growth to a support after planting. Bittersweet needs regular pruning. Prune in the late winter or early spring before growth begins. Prune dead, damaged, or out-of-place stems back to where they join another stem. Long side shoots can be pruned back to within 3 or 4 buds of the main stem. Just prune enough to control growth. Overpruning can lead to excessive growth and poor fruit production.

Companion Planting and Design

Train bittersweet on to a large pergola or arbor, allow it to crawl over a rock pile, or use it to cover a fence. Just remember it grows quickly and needs a strong support and regular pruning to keep it under control.

My Personal Favorite

Dutchman's pipe (*Aristolochia macrophylla*) is another old fashioned favorite worthy of a second look. This vine has long been used to screen a porch or climb a trellis. The large heart shaped leaves form a dense screen. A look under the leaves in late May or early June will reveal the source of the common name. Small pipe shaped flowers provide a hidden treasure for children and visitors to uncover.

Bittersweet is the perfect vine for tough places. It is a fast-growing plant that will quickly cover a fence or trellis and mask a bad view. This ornamental native can add year-round interest. Bittersweet's yellow fall color can be effective, and the decorative fruit can be used in dried arrangements. Birds enjoy feeding on the seeds throughout the winter. Although bittersweet is a vigorous plant, it is illegal to collect fruit from these native plants growing on public property. Ask permission of private property owners before collecting fruit from their plants. Beware of the Chinese bittersweet, Celastrus orbiculatus. *It is very similar to American bittersweet, though a little less vigorous. It can be sheared into hedges or grown on arbors, fences, and pergolas. Although Chinese bittersweet is versatile, it should be avoided since it has become an invasive weed in Minnesota.*

Other Common Name
American Bittersweet

Bloom Period and Seasonal Color
May to June blooms in yellow-white; fall foliage in yellow.

Mature Length
20 to 30 ft.

Boston Ivy

Parthenocissus tricuspidata

You are probably looking at Boston ivy when you see a vine-covered cottage or an old university building in Minnesota. Though not a true ivy, this tough, fast-growing plant gives you the same look. It is an excellent vine for covering large areas quickly. It attaches itself to structures and plants with holdfast tipped tendrils. Boston ivy is one of the first plants to brighten up the fall landscape with its brilliant red fall color. The blue, grape-like, decorative fruit is apparent after the leaves drop. Leave them for the birds since they can make people ill. A close relative is the Virginia creeper, Parthenocissus quinquefolia. *It has 5-part leaves, grape-like fruits, and good fall color and often survives in Zone 3. Both provide food and shelter for the birds.*

Other Common Name
Japanese Creeper

Bloom Period and Seasonal Color
Insignificant bloom; red fall color.

Mature Length
50 to 60 ft.

Zones
Hardy to Zone 4

When, Where, and How to Plant

Plant container-grown Boston ivy any time during the growing season. This tough plant will tolerate most difficult growing conditions. Grow it in full sun to full shade. Boston ivy prefers well drained soil but can take just about any type of soil. It can survive pollution, road salt, and wind. Dig a planting hole the same depth as the rootball and 2 to 3 times wider. Plant container-grown Boston ivy at the same level it was growing in the pot. Gently loosen potbound roots. Water thoroughly and mulch.

Growing Tips

Established plants are drought tolerant. Water thoroughly whenever the top few inches of soil start to dry. Minimal fertilizer is needed for this grower. Excess nitrogen can result in even more rampant growth and poor fall color.

Care

Pruning is the only regular maintenance established plants need. They can grow as much as 6 to 10 feet in a year. Prune vines away from windows, eaves, and gutters. Remove stems that are no longer attached to the structure. Older overgrown plants can be renovated. Prune them back to 3 feet. Boston ivy is difficult to remove from buildings and other structures. You can pull the vines off a wall, but the holdfast suction cups will remain attached. There is no easy way to remove them. Rubbing them off the structure with leather glove-clad hands seems to be effective. Or you can wait until they eventually dry up and fall off, but that will take quite a while.

Companion Planting and Design

This fast-growing plant can be trained on stone and brick buildings, walls, or other structures. It attaches with suction cup-like pads and needs no additional support.

My Personal Favorites

The Boston ivy cultivar 'Veitchii' is less aggressive and finer textured. The leaves are purple when young, green for the summer, and red in fall. This cultivar is a better choice than the species for most landscape situations. 'Star Showers'® Virginia creeper is less aggressive and has white speckled variegation on the leaves.

Clematis

Clematis × jackmanii

When, Where, and How to Plant

Plant container-grown clematis in the spring and early summer. Plant dormant clematis outdoors as soon as the soil is workable. Grow clematis in moist, well-drained, alkaline soil. Do not add lime unless directed by your soil test. Clematis plants often come with a stake. This can be cumbersome and may even damage the plant. Remove the stake and plant at the same level it was growing in the container or in the nursery. Pinch off the growing tips of newly planted clematis. Carefully attach the young stems to the trellis or support.

Growing Tips

Mulch the soil around the clematis after planting to keep the roots cool and moist. Avoid piling mulch over the stems. Keep the soil moist, but not wet, throughout the growing season.

Care

Clematis is fairly pest free. Moving struggling plants to a new location, even a few feet, often helps. Yellow clematis leaves are common in early spring. Once the soil warms, the plants will green up and start to flourish. Avoid injuring stems with rough handling and tools. These wounds often lead to stem cankers can cause stems to wilt and turn brown. Prune infected stems to ground level in late winter or early spring before growth begins. The early spring blooming clematis bloom on old wood and are pruned after flowering. These are generally not hardy in our area. Most gardeners prune heavily each year to maintain a small flowering plant. Prune summer and fall bloomers during the dormant season. I prefer late winter. Prune stems above a set of healthy buds 6 to 12 inches above the soil.

Companion Planting and Design

Use clematis to brighten up any vertical space. Train the twining vines on trellises, mailboxes, and lampposts. Plant several clematis varieties on the same trellis or add a rose for double the bloom.

My Personal Favorites

Clematis viticella 'Betty Corning' is my favorite. It produces blue, downward facing blooms through most of the summer. Sweet autumn clematis, *Clematis terniflora*, provides fragrant white fall flowers on an easy care, fast growing plant.

Most gardeners can't resist clematis once they have seen it in full bloom. This small plant provides lots of summer color, even in very small spaces. The old saying, "Clematis like their face in the sun and their feet in the shade" is true. Find a sunny location for this plant. Mulch the soil or plant a ground cover around the clematis to keep the roots cool. Small, dormant clematis plants are a common sight in the garden center in early spring. They are often sold with their roots packed in peat moss-filled plastic bags. These plants often break dormancy and begin to grow on the shelves of garden centers. Plant the growing clematis in containers and keep it indoors or in a cold frame outside. Move outdoors after all danger of frost is past.

Other Common Name

Jackman Clematis

Bloom Period and Seasonal Color

Summer blooms in white, purple, pink, or red.

Mature Length

5 to 18 ft.

Climbing Hydrangea
Hydrangea anomala subsp. *petiolaris*

The climbing hydrangea is one of the best flowering vines. It provides interest during the summer, fall, and winter. Beautiful, fragrant, white flowers appear in mid-June to early July. These flowers last for two weeks or more. The plant also does not grow flat against its support, which adds texture, depth, and interesting shadows to the landscape. The green leaves drop off in the fall, exposing the hydrangea's beautiful bark. The cinnamon-brown peeling bark adds interest all winter long. I am sorry my northern Minnesota gardening friends can't enjoy this plant. But then again, they get to live Up North year-round. I grew my climbing hydrangea as a container plant for several years. Each winter, I buried the pot in my back garden. I would lift the pot in the spring and enjoy it on my patio all summer long.

Bloom Period and Seasonal Color
June or early July blooms in white.

Mature Length
60 to 80 ft.

Zone
Hardy in zone 4.

When, Where, and How to Plant

Climbing hydrangea is usually container grown. It is slow to recover from transplanting, so it should be planted in the spring. Climbing hydrangea is an excellent vine for shady locations in southern Minnesota. It prefers moist, well-drained soil. Plants may suffer from scorch or brown leaf edges if grown in full sun or dry soil. Plant container-grown climbing hydrangeas at the same level they were growing in the container. Handle them with care. To minimize root disturbance when transplanting, first cut off the bottom of the container. Place the plant in a hole that is the same depth and at least 2 to 3 times as wide as the rootball. Slice and peel the side of the pot, leaving the rootball intact. Fill the hole with soil and water.

Growing Tips

Climbing hydrangeas start off slowly. The first few years they may barely grow. But by the third or fourth year, the roots are established and the plant seems to take off. Mulch and keep the soil moist, but not wet, throughout the growing season. Avoid high nitrogen fertilizers that can inhibit bloom.

Care

Remove wayward branches in the summer right after flowering. Prune the stems back to a healthy bud. Avoid severe pruning; it can decrease flowering for several years. Tie young shoots to a support. They will climb on their own once aerial roots form. Established plants need minimal pruning.

Companion Planting and Design

Train this plant on a brick or stone wall, a fence, or an arbor. Use a sturdy support. A container planting of this vine is a good way to include this beauty in your landscape when limited by a lack of planting space or cold temperatures. Winter protection, especially for the roots, is critical to its survival.

My Personal Favorite

I am not aware of any cultivars. It may be difficult to find, so check with nurseries and specialty garden centers in your area. You may find this plant sold under its old name of *Hydrangea petiolaris.*

Dropmore Scarlet Honeysuckle

Lonicera × *brownii* 'Dropmore Scarlet'

When, Where, and How to Plant

Container-grown vines can be planted any time during the growing season but do best if planted in spring. This plant thrives in moist, well-drained soil. Minimize root disturbance especially on late-season plantings by cutting away the pot at transplant time. Cut off the bottom of the container. Set it in a planting hole that is the same depth and at least 2 to 3 times wider than the rootball. Slice the side of the pot and peel it away, leaving the rootball intact. Loosen any potbound roots and fill the hole with soil and water.

Growing Tips

Mulch and keep the soil moist, but not wet, throughout the growing season. Avoid excess nitrogen that encourages leaf growth and discourages flowering.

Care

Prune damaged shoots at planting time. Tie young shoots to a support. They will soon attach to the structure on their own. 'Dropmore Scarlet' honeysuckle is a low-maintenance vine but may have problems with aphids. The plants will survive, but an infestation can ruin many of the blossoms. Heavy rains and lady beetles may take care of this pest. Contact or systemic insecticides can be used on severe infestations. Carefully follow all label directions. Powdery mildew can be a problem, especially on vines grown in the shade. Thinning them will help improve air circulation and reduce disease problems. Prune overgrown plants to fit the available space. Trim them to where the branches join, or above a healthy bud. Prune older stems back to ground level. Renovate older plantings by pruning stems back to 2 feet above the ground.

Companion Planting and Design

Use it on a fence, arbor, or other upright structure. Plant a fuchsia 'Thalia' nearby to echo the flower shape and color.

My Personal Favorite

Trumpet honeysuckle, *Lonicera sempervirens*, is one of the parents of dropmore scarlet. This fast-growing vine produces colorful flowers from spring through summer. It has very attractive foliage and variable flowers of red-orange to orange on the outside and yellow to orange-yellow on the inside.

Here's a vine that will work in every Minnesota garden. 'Dropmore Scarlet' honeysuckle is hardy throughout the state and puts on a great show in full sun and partial shade. Single plants can be trained on an arbor creating lots of color in a small yard. Larger plantings can be used to mask a chain-link fence or create a fence full of blossoms. Plant it in an area where you can enjoy the fragrant flowers and hummingbirds that come to visit. There are several native honeysuckle vines. The hairy honeysuckle, Lonicera hirsuta, found growing in woods, thickets, and bluffs is one of one of the parents to 'Dropmore Scarlet' honeysuckle.

Other Common Name
Honeysuckle Vine

Bloom Period and Seasonal Color
June through October blooms in red.

Mature Length
12 ft.

Fiveleaf Akebia
Akebia quinata

Add a tropical or woodland feel to your landscape with this deciduous vine. Akebia leaves remind me of those on a schefflera houseplant. This twining vine will quickly cover a fence, trellis, or anything standing still. It is adaptable to a wide range of growing conditions. I have mine growing on my wrought iron fence in pretty heavy shade. Each spring, I am rewarded with fragrant rosy flowers. They are small, mixed with the emerging foliage, and are a welcome sight in early spring. The leaves emerge with a purple tinge turning a blue green for the season. Here in the north, the leaves drop green in fall with the first hard freeze. It occasionally produces purple fruit that looks like a flattened sausage. Though it is supposedly edible, you will need to do a bit of hand pollination for good fruit production.

Other Common Name
Chocolate Vine

Bloom Period and Seasonal Color
Early spring with rosy flowers.

Mature length
20 to 40 ft.

When, Where, and How to Plant
Plant container-grown vines anytime during the growing season. I prefer to get them in the ground by early summer so they will be well rooted by winter. Grow these adaptable plants in sun or shade and just about any soil conditions. Once established, they will tolerate drought and moist soils. To minimize root disturbance, carefully slide the plant out of the pot before planting, or set the potted plant in a hole that is the same depth and at least 2 to 3 times wider than the rootball. Slice down the side of the pot and peel it away, and remove the bottom of the pot, leaving the rootball intact. Loosen any circling roots, fill the hole with soil, and water.

Growing Tips
Water established plants thoroughly and whenever the top few inches of the soil starts to dry. Excess fertilization that will only make this plant grow more and flower less.

Care
Regular pruning is needed to keep this plant contained. Wait until after flowering to enjoy the blooms and contain the growth. Prune new plantings back to a strong bud about 12 to 16 inches above the ground. Train 5 to 7 strong shoots onto a support. Next spring, prune stout side shoots by 1/3 and weak branches back to 1 or 2 buds. Prune established plants back by 1/3 or 1/2 in early spring. Occasionally remove an old stem to ground level to promote new growth at the base.

Companion Planting and Design
This shade tolerant plant makes a nice backdrop for shade gardens filled with hostas, ferns, and astilbes, or sun loving tropicals like canna and banana. I have seen it used as a ground cover with equally assertive partners, and winding its way through garden art.

My Personal Favorites
This is an underused plant in the northern landscapes, so it may be difficult to find in your local garden center. Check specialty nurseries and catalogues. 'Alba' has white flowers and white fruit while 'Rosea' has lighter lavender flowers than the species.

Hyacinth Bean
Lablab purpureus

When, Where, and How to Plant
Start seeds indoors four to six weeks before the last spring frost for early summer bloom. Plant in 3- to 4-inch clean containers filled with sterile potting mix. Keep the soil warm, 65 to 70 degrees Fahrenheit, and moist. Or wait until the danger of frost has passed and sow the seeds one inch deep directly outdoors. If using transplants, remove the stake (if one was included) prior to planting to avoid damaging the vine. Slide the plant out of the container and loosen any potbound roots before planting. Grow hyacinth beans in full sun and moist, well-drained garden soil.

Growing Tips
Keep the soil moist during sprouting and the seedling stage of growth. Water established plants thoroughly whenever the top few inches of soil are crumbly and moist. Fertilize according to soil test recommendations or as you would for your other annual flowers.

Care
This low-maintenance vine will provide lots of color summer through frost. Tie young plants to a trellis, fence, or other support. Once it makes contact, it will climb up the structure with minimal guidance. Only remove ripe fruit if production slows. Hyacinth beans are edible, but too many can make you sick. North Carolina State recommends thoroughly boiling the seeds and pods, changing the water several times before eating. I think I will stick to my Kentucky wonder pole beans and just enjoy the hyacinth bean's colorful show.

Companion Planting and Design
Show off the flowers and fruit by training your vine on a white picket fence or other light colored structure. The herb gardener at Boerner Botanical Gardens grew these on several teepee type structures marching down the center of a bed. The beans were surrounded by parsley, purple alyssum, santolina, and other green, silver, and purple flowers and herbs.

My Personal Favorite
I am unaware of any cultivars. You may find this plant listed under its former name *Dolichos lablab*. Check the internet and garden catalogues if you have trouble finding seeds or transplants at your local garden center.

No, it isn't a typo or a joke on you. The botanical name and the plant are both quite eye catching. This annual twining vine is the fancy relative of our bean plant. The dark green, heart shaped leaves with purple veins are held on reddish stems. The fragrant, rosy-purple flowers are followed by dark purple beans. The plant will be covered with both flowers and fruit from summer through frost. Grown here as an ornamental, this is an important food crop in Africa and India. New to many gardeners, this old-fashioned favorite has been grown in the United States for many years. Thomas Jefferson apparently had it growing in his home in Monticello in the early 1800s. Plus you may even be rewarded, I have, with a few plants that self-seed and make a surprise appearance in next year's garden.

Other Common Name
Lablab

Bloom Period and Seasonal Color
Summer through fall with rosy-purple flowers and purple fruit.

Mature length
6 to 12 ft.

Morning Glory

Ipomoea purpurea

Morning glory is an old-fashioned favorite that is still popular in modern landscapes. This fast grower provides summer-long beauty with very little care and in very little space. The heart-shaped, green leaves provide a nice backdrop to the funnel-shaped flowers. Use fast-growing annual vines like morning glories to provide temporary screening or shade until your permanent trees and shrubs grow big enough to do the job. Their annual nature allows you the flexibility to add a little variety and try something new each season. Heavenly blue with its white throated, sky blue flowers revived the morning glory's garden status. New introductions, such as 'Early Call' produce earlier blossoms, eliminating the frustration many gardeners felt waiting for the first set of flowers. 'Minibar' rose brightens things up even more. It has pink flowers and ivy shaped variegated foliage.

Other Common Name
Common Morning Glory

Bloom Period and Seasonal Color
Summer blooms in purple, blue, pink, red, and white.

Mature Length
8 to 10 ft.

When, Where and How to Plant

Start morning glory vines from seeds indoors, four to six weeks prior to the last spring frost. Nick the seed or soak it in warm water for twenty-four hours before planting. The seeds need moist, warm temperatures, 70 to 85 degrees Fahrenheit, to germinate in five to seven days. Plant seeds outdoors after all danger of frost is past. Plant hardened-off transplants outdoors after the last spring frost. Grow morning glories in full sun with well drained soil. Plant seeds 6 inches apart and 1 inch deep. Thin 3-inch tall plants to 12 inches apart. Space transplants 12 inches apart. Morning glory will reseed; remove unwanted seedlings.

Growing Tips

Each flower opens in the morning and lasts only one day. But it is replaced the next day with new blossoms. The plants will remain in bloom all season long. The less care morning glories receive, the better the bloom. Excess water and fertilizer will result in lots of leaves, but no flowers.

Care

Guide young plants onto a support structure. But once they reach the support, stand back! They will take off on their own! Careful, all parts of morning glory are toxic—don't eat it!

Companion Planting and Design

Grow morning glory vines in areas you will see early in the day since the flowers tend to close in the low light of afternoon and on cloudy days. Try growing them on small trellises in large containers. They make great vertical accents and mix well with other plants. One of the gardeners at Boerner Botanical gardens used morning glories to hold his tomatoes to their metal stakes. It was attractive and effective.

My Personal Favorites

Moonflower, *Ipomoea alba*, has white flowers that open at dusk. Start indoors for earlier bloom. Star glory, *Ipomoea quamoclit*, and cardinal climber *Ipomoea × multifida* have attractive foliage and red, funnel-shaped flowers. Spanish flag, *Ipomoea lobata* formerly *Mina lobata*, is shade tolerant with narrow tubular flowers that start scarlet and mature to yellow and orange.

Trumpet Vine
Campsis radicans

When, Where, and How to Plant
Plant bare-root trumpet vines in the early spring before growth begins. Plant container-grown plants any time during the growing season. Grow them in full sun with well-drained moist to dry soil. You will, however, find the vines are tolerant of most growing situations. Gently loosen pot-bound roots. Plant trumpet vines at the same depth they were growing previously. Water thoroughly and mulch to help keep roots cool and moist. Train new growth to the support. Once aerial rootlets form, it will attach itself.

Growing Tips
It may take several years for your plant to bloom. Excessive shade and nitrogen can prevent flowering. Trumpet vines are luxury feeders, consuming all available nutrients. This results in lots of leaves and stems, but no flowers. Avoid high nitrogen fertilizers around or near trumpet vines.

Care
Trumpet vines are slow to leaf out and may suffer winter injury. This is not a problem since they grow so fast. You may need to provide additional help to keep this fast growing plant attached to its support structure. Yearly pruning is necessary to keep this plant under control. The best time to prune is late winter through early spring. Prune young plants to fit the support structure. This will be the plant's basic framework and your basis for future pruning. Cut back the side shoots on established plants each year. Prune back to within 3 or 4 buds of the main framework. Remove overcrowded shoots as needed.

Companion Planting and Design
Trumpet vines need strong structures for support. They are great on fences in the landscape or on more unusual supports. One family let the trumpet vine wind around their children's old play structure. The vine had the support it needed, and the family got to keep their memories neatly tucked away under this plant. A nearby bakery has trained its trumpet vine into a small tree.

My Personal Favorite
Yellow trumpet vine, *Campsis radicans* 'Flava', is readily available through garden centers and catalogues. It produces yellow flowers on a plant similar otherwise to the trumpet vine.

Trumpet vine's beautiful flowers and its appeal to hummingbirds make it a good addition to any landscape. The vine produces clusters of large, orange, trumpet-shaped flowers often featured in artwork, on book covers, and with articles on hummingbirds and nectar plants. Trumpet vines are excellent choices for large, difficult locations. These rampant growers will overtake anything in their path. Its aggressive nature means you will need to get out the pruners every year. They also spread underground. They occasionally develop suckers from underground runners. The suckers can appear quite a distance from the parent plant. Use a sharp shovel to prune out the suckers at ground level. But once the suckers are removed and the pruning is finished, so is the yearly maintenance for the trumpet vine. Just sit back, relax, and enjoy the show.

Other Common Name
Trumpet Creeper

Bloom Period and Seasonal Color
July blooms in orange and yellow.

Mature Length
40 ft. or more

Zones
Hardy to Zone 4

Wintercreeper

Euonymus fortunei

Wintercreeper can be grown as a ground cover, as a small shrub, or vine trained to a wall or structure. The variable growth habit provides flexibility and interest in the landscape. They are often trained and sheared for formal gardens, but if allowed to wander a bit, they can provide a more informal feel. Wintercreeper will crawl along the ground until it finds something to attach to. Then up it goes on a tree trunk, trellis, or wall. Rough surfaces make it easier for the clinging rootlets to attach and climb. Use vining types of wintercreeper to soften a brick wall or a garden structure. If it is put in a protected spot, the green leaves will persist and provide year-round interest. Hardiness varies with species and cultivars.

Other Common Name
Wintercreeper Euonymus

Bloom Period and Seasonal Color
Evergreen foliage in protected locations.

Mature Length
40 ft. or more

Zones
Hardy to Zone 4

When, Where, and How to Plant
Plant container-grown plants any time during the growing season. Spring planting will result in established plants with the greatest chance for winter survival. Plant wintercreeper in moist, well-drained soil. They tolerate full sun in the summer but can be damaged by winter sun and wind. Plant container-grown wintercreeper at the same level it was growing in the pot, gently loosening potbound roots. Water thoroughly and mulch. Gently guide the plant to the support structure. Once clinging rootlets form, wintercreeper will support itself.

Growing Tips
Proper cultivar selection and plant placement reduce maintenance and keep wintercreeper healthy. Select cultivars and varieties that are hardy for your location. Plant in a protected site or east exposure where wintercreeper will be safe from winter wind and sun.

Care
Prune wintercreeper in early spring. Remove weak, damaged, dead, and winter-injured branches back to a healthy branch. Train wintercreeper vines to a wall or trellis. Loosely tie the main stem and side branches of young plants to the support. Prune any stems that are growing directly away from or into the support. Scale insects and crown galls are the worst pest problems. Treat the shell-less immature scale with insecticidal soap when the Japanese tree lilacs are just starting to bloom. Repeat the application twice at ten- to twelve-day intervals. Or use a soil-applied insecticidal soap in fall. Read and follow all label directions carefully. Crown gall causes golf ball-like nodules on the roots and stems. Prune stems beneath the gall and disinfect tools with denatured alcohol between cuts. Remove and destroy badly infected plants.

Companion Planting and Design
The glossy green leaves of wintercreeper look great against a brick or lannon stone wall. The glossy green foliage makes a nice backdrop for any flowering annuals or perennials.

My Personal Favorite
The purple wintercreeper, *Euonymus fortunei coloratus*, is prized for its purple winter color. It is usually nonfruiting, a good feature of this potentially invasive plant.

Wisteria
Wisteria species

When, Where, and How to Plant

Plant container-grown wisteria in the spring in full sun to light shade and in moist, well-drained soil. Plant container-grown wisteria at the same level it was growing in the container. Handle wisteria with care to reduce transplant shock. Cut off the bottom of the container. Place the plant in a hole that is the same depth and at least 2 to 3 times as wide as the rootball. Slice the side of the pot and peel it away, leaving the rootball intact. Loosen any circling roots then fill the hole with soil and water.

Growing Tips

Mulch and keep the soil moist, but not wet, throughout the growing season. The Japanese and Chinese wisteria flower buds are usually killed by our cold winters. Every few years, after a mild winter, you may see one of their breathtaking flower displays. Kentucky wisteria is plant- and flowerbud-hardy to Zone 4, with reports of plants surviving and even blooming in Zone 3. Avoid overfertilizing wisteria.

Care

Pruning is the only real maintenance needed. Prune established Japanese and Chinese wisteria in the early summer after they flower, or should have flowered. Prune Kentucky wisteria in late winter before growth begins. Wisteria may not bloom for the first seven years. You can develop a tree-form wisteria by training the main stem to a stake. The tree takes shape after several years of pruning back the main stem and side shoots. Prune yearly to maintain size and shape.

Companion Planting and Design

Espalier wisteria vines on a wall, grow them on a pergola, or train them into a small tree. Use sturdy supports. These fast growers can cause weak structures to collapse.

My Personal Favorites

Grow Kentucky wisteria for most reliable bloom. 'Blue Moon' is a fast blooming variety that is hardy and blooms up to three times a season. Japanese wisteria, *Wisteria floribunda*, is sold for its extremely long, 12- to 20-inch, fragrant, purple flowers. The Chinese wisteria, *Wisteria sinensis*, is less hardy and has shorter, less fragrant flowers than the Japanese wisteria.

Wisteria is one of the most beautiful blooming vines. Unfortunately, the pictures in books look much better than the plants growing in Minnesota landscapes. Japanese and Chinese wisteria vines are sold as hardy in Zones 4 or 5. The plants will survive but seldom flower in Minnesota. Kentucky wisteria, Wisteria macrostachya, is a better choice. It's not quite as dramatic, but it is more reliable and still an impressive sight in bloom. Kentucky wisteria produces beautiful 12-inch purple flowers in the summer after the leaves emerge. The American Medical Association (AMA) reports that all parts of this plant are toxic. Some older gardening books talk about how the Chinese harvested, steamed, and ate the mature blossoms of Chinese wisteria. I'm going with the AMA on this one.

Other Common Names
Kentucky, Japanese, or Chinese Wisteria

Bloom Period and Seasonal Color
Late spring or summer blooms in purple to violet.

Mature Length
30 ft.

Zones
Hardy to Zone 4

Gardening Resources

University of Minnesota Extension Service

The University of Minnesota Extension Service is a great resource for gardeners. They bring researched-based information to you through classes, workshops, newspaper articles, and the Master Gardeners. Their printed publications are the best resource for gardeners and landscape professionals. The information and recommendations are based on the soils and climates of Minnesota. Contact your local county office, listed below, for a list of publications and other resources available in your county.

Aitkin – Courthouse, 209 2nd St NW, Rm 100, Aitkin, MN 56431-1257, (218) 927-7321, aitkin@extension.umn.edu

Anoka – Anoka County Activities Center, 550 Bunker Lake Blvd NW, Andover, MN 55304-4199, (763) 755-1280, anoka@extension.umn.edu

Becker – Agriculture Service Center, 915 Lake Ave, PO Box 787, Detroit Lakes, MN 56501-0787, (218) 846-7328, becker@extension.umn.edu

Beltrami – PO Box 1220, Bemidji, MN 56619-1220, (218) 444-5722, beltrami@extension.umn.edu

Benton – Courthouse, 531 Dewey St, PO Box 650, Foley, MN 56329-0650, (320) 968-5077, benton@extension.umn.edu

Big Stone – Courthouse, 11 SE 2nd St, Ortonville, MN 56278-1544, (320) 839-2518, bigstone@extension.umn.edu

Blue Earth – Extension Service, Nichols Building, Ste 100, 410 E Jackson, PO Box 8608, Mankato, MN 56002-8608, (507) 389-8325, blueearth@extension.umn.edu

Brown – 300 2nd Ave SW, Sleepy Eye, MN 56085-1402, (507) 794-7993, brown@extension.umn.edu

Carlton – 310 Chestnut Street, PO Box 307, Carlton, MN 55718-0307, (218) 384-3511, carlton@extension.umn.edu

Carver – 609 W 1st St, Waconia, MN 55387-1204, (952) 442-4496, carver@extension.umn.edu

Cass – Courthouse, 245 Barclay Ave, PO Box 709, Pine River, MN 56474-0709, (218) 587-8280, cass@extension.umn.edu

Chippewa – Courthouse, 629 N 11th St, Montevideo, MN 56265-1685, (320) 269-6521, chippewa@extension.umn.edu

Chisago – 38315 Harder Ave, Ste A, North Branch, MN 55056-5385, (651) 237-3057, chisago@extension.umn.edu

Clay – 715 11 St N, Ste 107B, PO Box 280, Moorhead, MN 56561-0280, (218) 299-5020, clay@extension.umn.edu

Clearwater – Courthouse Dept 106, 213 Main Ave N, Bagley, MN 56621-8304, (218) 694-6151, clearwater@extension.umn.edu

Cook – Community Center Building, 317 W 5th, Grand Marais, MN 55604-1150, (218) 387-3015, cook@extension.umn.edu

Cottonwood – 235 9th St, Windom, MN 56101-1642, (507) 831-4022, cottonwood@extension.umn.edu

Crow Wing – Courthouse, 326 Laurel St, Brainerd, MN 56401-3578, (218) 824-1065, crowwing@extension.umn.edu

Dakota – County Extension and Conservation Center, 4100 220th St W, Ste 101, Farmington, MN 55024-9539, (651) 480-7700

Dodge – 42 E Main St, PO Box 159, Dodge Center, MN 55927-0159, (507) 374-6435, dodge@extension.umn.edu

Douglas – 720 Filmore, Ste B090, Alexandria, MN 56308-1763, (320) 762-3890, douglas@extension.umn.edu

Faribault – 412 N Nicollet St, PO Box 130, Blue Earth, MN 56013-0130, (507) 526-6240, faribault@extension.umn.edu

Fillmore – 902 Houston St NW, Ste 3, Preston, MN 55965-1080, (507) 765-3896, fillmore@extension.umn.edu

Freeborn – Courthouse, 411 S Broadway, PO Box 1147, Albert Lea, MN 56007-1147, (507) 377-5660, freeborn@extension.umn.edu

Goodhue – Government Center, Rm 105, 509 5th St W, Red Wing, MN 55066, (651) 385-3100, goodhue@extension.umn.edu

Grant – 411 1st St SE, PO Box 1099, Elbow Lake, MN 56531-1099, (218) 685-4820, grant@extension.umn.edu

Hennepin – 1525 Glenwood Ave, Minneapolis, MN 55405-1264, (612) 374-8400, hennepin@extension.umn.edu

Houston – 620 N Hwy 44/76, PO Box 228, Caledonia, MN 55921-0228, (507) 725-5807, houston@extension.umn.edu

Hubbard – 201 Fair Ave, Park Rapids, MN 56470-1483, (218) 732-3391, hubbard@extension.umn.edu

Isanti – 555 18th Ave SW, Cambridge, MN 55008-9386, (763) 689-1810, isanti@extension.umn.edu

Itasca – Courthouse, 123 NE 4th St, Grand Rapids, MN 55744-2659, (218) 327-7486, itasca@extension.umn.edu

Jackson – 607 S Hwy 86, PO Box 309, Lakefield, MN 56150-0309, (507) 662-5293, jackson@extension.umn.edu

Kanabec – 905 E Forest Ave, Ste 140, Mora, MN 55051-1617, (320) 679-6340, kanabec@extension.umn.edu

Kandiyohi – 400 Benson Ave SW, Ste 6, Willmar, MN 56201-3467, (320) 231-7890, kandiyohi@extension.umn.edu

Kittson – Courthouse, 410 S 5th St, PO Box 369, Hallock, MN 56728-0369, (218) 843-3674, kittson@extension.umn.edu

Koochiching – 715 4th St, International Falls, MN 56649-2486, (218) 285-0962, koochiching@extension.umn.edu

Lac qui Parle – Courthouse, 600 6th St, Madison, MN 56256-1295, (320) 598-3325, lacquiparle@extension.umn.edu

Lake – Courthouse, 601 3rd Ave, Two Harbors, MN 55616-1517, (218) 834-8377, lake@extension.umn.edu

Lake of the Woods – County Extension, Courthouse, PO Box 808, Baudette, MN 56623-0808, (218) 634-1511, lakeofthewoods@extension.umn.edu

Le Sueur – 88 S Park, LeCenter, MN 56057-1620, (507) 357-8230, lesueur@extension.umn.edu

Lincoln – 402 N Harold, PO Box 130, Ivanhoe, MN 56142-0130, (507) 694-1470, lincoln@extension.umn.edu

Lyon – Courthouse, 607 W Main, Marshall, MN 56258-3099, (507) 537-6702, lyon@extension.umn.edu

Mahnomen – Courthouse, 311 Main, PO Box 477, Mahnomen, MN 56557-0477, (218) 935-2226, mahnomen@extension.umn.edu

Marshall – Courthouse, 208 E Colvin Ave, Warren, MN 56762-1698, (218) 745-5232, marshall@extension.umn.edu

Martin – 104 Courthouse, 201 Lake Ave, Fairmont, MN 56031-1845, (507) 235-3341, martin@extension.umn.edu

McLeod – 840 Century Ave, Ste B, Hutchinson, MN 55350-3754, (320) 587-0770, mcleod@extension.umn.edu

Meeker – Family Services Center, 114 N Holcombe Ave, Ste 260, Litchfield, MN 55355-2274, (320) 693-5275, meeker@extension.umn.edu

Mille Lacs – 620 Central Ave N, Milaca, MN 56353-1788, (320) 983-8317, millelacs@extension.umn.edu

Morrison – Government Center, 213 1st Ave SE, Little Falls, MN 56345-3100, (320) 632-0161, morrison@extension.umn.edu

Mower – Courthouse, 201 NE 1st St, Austin, MN 55912-3475, (507) 437-9552, mower@extension.umn.edu

Murray – 2848 Broadway Ave, PO Box 57, Slayton, MN 56172-0057, (507) 836-6927, murray@extension.umn.edu

Nicollet – Government Center, 501 S Minnesota Ave, St. Peter, MN 56082-2533, (507) 931-6800, nicollet@extension.umn.edu

Nobles – 315 10th St, PO Box 757, Worthington, MN 56187-0757, (507) 372-8210, nobles@extension.umn.edu

Norman – Courthouse, 16 3rd Ave E, Ste 101B, Ada, MN 56510-1362, (218) 784-5550, norman@extension.umn.edu

Olmsted – 1421 SE 3rd Ave, Rochester, MN 55904-7947, (507) 285-8250, olmsted@extension.umn.edu

Otter Tail - East – 118 N Main, PO Box 250, New York Mills, MN 56567-0250, (218) 385-3000, eottertail@extension.umn.edu

Pennington – Courthouse, PO Box 616, Thief River Falls, MN 56701-0616, (218) 683-7030, pennington@extension.umn.edu

Pine – Pine Technical College, 900 4th St SE, Pine City, MN 55063-1738, (320) 629-4545, pine@extension.umn.edu

Pipestone – Municipal Building, 119 SW 2nd Ave, Ste 2, Pipestone, MN 56164-1684, (507) 825-6715, pipestone@extension.umn.edu

Polk – Municipal Building, PO Box 69, McIntosh, MN 56556-0069, (218) 563-2465, polk@extension.umn.edu

Pope – Courthouse, 130 Minnesota Ave E, Glenwood, MN 56334-1628, (320) 634-5735, pope@extension.umn.edu

Ramsey – 2020 White Bear Ave, Saint Paul, MN 55109-3785, (651) 704-2080, ramsey@extension.umn.edu

Red Lake – Courthouse, PO Box 279, Red Lake Falls, MN 56750-0279, (218) 253-2895, redlake@extension.umn.edu

Redwood – Courthouse, PO Box 130, Redwood Falls, MN 56283-0130, (507) 637-4025, redwood@extension.umn.edu

Renville – Renville County Office Building, 410 E DePue Ave, Rm 320, Olivia, MN 56277-1483, (320) 523-3713, renville@extension.umn.edu

Rice – Government Services Building, 320 NW 3rd St, Ste 7, Faribault, MN 55021-6143, (507) 332-6109, rice@extension.umn.edu

Rock – 319 E Lincoln, PO Box 898, Luverne, MN 56156-0898, (507) 283-1302, rock@extension.umn.edu

Roseau – 606 5th Ave SW, Rm 130, Roseau, MN 56751-1477, (218) 463-1052, roseau@extension.umn.edu

Saint Louis – Government Service Center, Ste 111, 320 W 2nd St, Duluth, MN 55802-1495, (218) 733-2870, duluth.stlouis@extension.umn.edu

Scott – 7151 190th St W, Ste 100, Jordan, MN 55352-2104, (952) 492-5410, scott@extension.umn.edu

Sherburne – Sherburne County Government Center, 13880 Hwy 10, Elk River, MN 55330-4601, (763) 241-2720, sherburne@extension.umn.edu

Sibley – County Service Center, 111 8th St, PO Box 207, Gaylord, MN 55334-0207, (507) 237-4100, sibley@extension.umn.edu

Stearns – Midtown Office Buildings, 3400 1st St N, Ste 103, Saint Cloud, MN 56303-4000, (320) 255-6169, stearns@extension.umn.edu

Steele – 635 Florence Ave, PO Box 890, Owatonna, MN 55060-0890, (507) 444-7685, steele@extension.umn.edu

Stevens – Courthouse, 400 Colorado Ave, PO Box 269, Morris, MN 56267-0269, (320) 589-7423, stevens@extension.umn.edu

Swift – Courthouse, 301 14th St N, PO Box 305, Benson, MN 56215-0305, (320) 843-3796, swift@extension.umn.edu

Todd – Courthouse Annex, 119 3rd St S, Long Prairie, MN 56347-1354, (320) 732-4435, todd@extension.umn.edu

Traverse – Courthouse, 702 2nd Ave N, PO Box 457, Wheaton, MN 56296-0457, (320) 563-4515, traverse@extension.umn.edu

Wabasha – 625 Jefferson Ave, Wabasha, MN 55981-1529, (651) 565-5168, wabasha@extension.umn.edu

Wadena – Courthouse, 415 S Jefferson St, Wadena, MN 56482-1594, (218) 631-7623, wadena@extension.umn.edu

Waseca – 300 N State St, Ste 1, Waseca MN 56093-2933, (507) 835-0600

Washington – 14949 62nd St N, PO Box 6, Stillwater, MN 55082-0006, (651) 430-6800, washington@extension.umn.edu

Watonwan – 108 8th St S, Ste 1, St. James, MN 56081-1790, (507) 375-1275 watonwan@extension.umn.edu

Wilkin – PO Box 199, Breckenridge, MN 56520-0199, (218) 643-5481, wilkin@extension.umn.edu

Winona – 202 W 3rd St, Winona, MN 55987-3115, (507) 457-6440, winona@extension.umn.edu

Wright – County Government Center, 10 2nd St NW, Buffalo, MN 55313-1186, (763) 682-7394, wright@extension.umn.edu

Yellow Medicine – 1004 10th Ave, PO Box 128, Clarkfield, MN 56223-0128, (320) 669-4471, yellowmedicine@extension.umn.edu

Other Minnesota Resources

Answers to Plant Questions and Soil testing

Plant Disease Diagnostics University of Minnesota Yard and Garden Line
(612) 624-4771
http://www.extension.umn.edu/projects/yardandgarden/diagnostics

Minnesota State Horticulure Society

1755 Prior Avenue North
Falcon Heights, MN 55113-5549
(651) 643-3601 or (800 676-6747
http://www.northerngardener.org

Hiring a Landscape Professional

Some landscape tasks require the help of a professional. It can be a challenge to find a qualified professional best suited for the job. Check the yellow pages, talk to friends and then interview several professionals. Ask each company the education, training and experience of their staff. Ask for referrals and check out their portfolio of past projects.

Several professional organizations are working to help with this dilemma. Members of several professional organizations participate in voluntary certification programs. Certification shows a level of expertise and dedication to the profession. The Minnesota Chapter of the International Society of Arboriculture in conjunction with the International Society of Arboriculture has a certification program for arborists. Check the yellow pages under tree care or their websites (www.isa-arbor.com and www.waa-isa.org for a list of certified arborists in your area.

The Minnesota Nursery and Landscape Association provides helpful information and lists of professionals on their website. Find out more about hiring a landscape professional at: htpp://www.mnlandscape.org/.

Department of Natural Resources Urban and Community Forestry Program

The Minnesota Department of Natural Resources has helped communities build and care for their urban trees. They can provide tree care information to you and your community. Contact your regional office for more information:

DNR Information Center
500 Lafayette Road
St. Paul, MN 55155-4040
Phone: (651) 296-6157 or (888) MINNDNR
TTY: (651) 296-5484 or (800) 657-3929

State Urban Forestry
Minnesota DNR
1200 Warner Road
Saint Paul, MN 55106
http://www.dnr.state.mn.us/forestry/urban/

Gopher State One Call
Gopher State One Call is a FREE utility-locating service. They will mark the location of any underground utilities in the planting area. Give them three working days to complete the task. This is important for your safety and pocketbook. Digging into a utility line can be expensive and even deadly.
(800) 252-1166 throughout Minnesota
http://www.gopherstateonecall.org

Ordering Soils and Mulch

Garden Size in Square Feet	Cubic Yards of Material Needed to Cover Garden Space Depth of Desired Material			
	2"	4"	6"	8"
100	$^1/_2$	1+	2	$2^1/_2$
200	1+	$2^1/_2$	$3^1/_2$	5
300	2	$3^1/_2$	$5^1/_2$	$7^1/_2$
400	$2^1/_2$	5	$7^1/_2$	10
500	3+	6	9	12
600	$3^1/_2$	$7^1/_2$	11	15
700	4+	$8^1/_2$	13	17
800	5	10	15	20
900	$5^1/_2$	11	17	22
1000	6	12	$18^1/_2$	25

Peat Moss Bale Size	Area That Can Be Amended With:	
	1 inch	2 inches
1 cubic foot	24 square feet	12 square feet
2.2 cubic feet	50 square feet	25 square feet
3.8 cubic feet	90 square feet	45 square feet

Or calculate what you need:

Multiply the area (length times width measured in feet) by the desired depth (in feet) of mulch or compost. Convert this volume from cubic feet to cubic yards by dividing by 27 (the number of cubic feet in a cubic yard). This is the amount of material you will need to order.

Spacing Chart

Use this chart to calculate the number of plants needed. Divide the square footage of the garden by the spacing factor. The answer is the number of plants you need.

Spacing (Inches)	Spacing Factor	Plants Needed			
		25	50	75	100
4	0.11	227	454	682	909
6	0.25	100	200	300	400
8	0.44	57	114	170	227
10	0.70	36	72	107	143
12	1.00	12	50	75	100
15	1.56	16	32	48	64
18	2.25	11	22	33	44
24	4.00	6	13	19	25
30	6.25	4	8	12	16
36	9.00	3	6	8	11
48	16.00	2	3	5	6
60	26.00	1	2	3	4

Fertilizer Needs

(Based on Nitrogen Recommendations)

Your soil test will tell you how much of what type of fertilizer you need to add to your garden. If this information is not available, you may have to adapt general fertilization recommendations for your garden. Use the chart or formulas here to calculate the amount of fertilizer needed to add the recommended amount of actual nitrogen (N) to the soil.

Fertilizer Analysis (N-P-K)*	Pounds of Fertilizer Needed to Apply:			
	1 lb. Actual N	1¼ lb. Actual N	1½ lb. Actual N	2 lb. Actual N
45-0-0 Urea	2.2	2.7	3.3	4.4
33-0-0 Ammonium nitrate	3.0	3.7	4.5	6.0
21-0-0 Ammonium sulfate	4.8	5.9	7.1	9.6
6-2-0 Milorganite	16.6	23.3	25	33.3
10-10-10	10	12.5	15.0	20
5-10-5	20	25	30	40

*Nitrogen-Phosphorus-Potassium

Or calculate the amount of fertilizer you need to add to your planting area. See the Fertilizing section in the "Vines and Groundcovers" chapter introduction.

Tree Planting Diagram

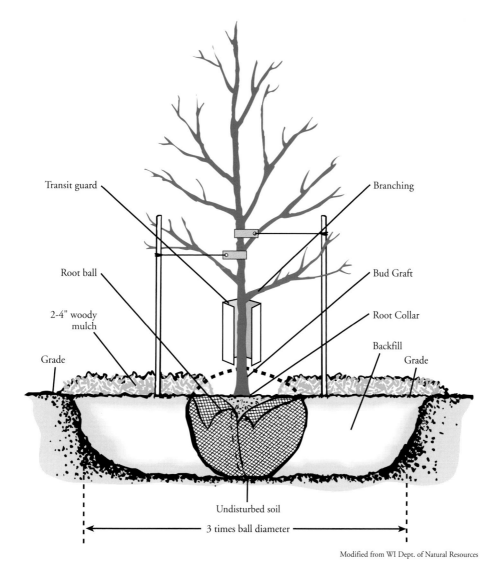

Transit guard

Branching

Root ball

Bud Graft

2-4" woody mulch

Root Collar

Grade

Backfill

Grade

Undisturbed soil

3 times ball diameter

Modified from WI Dept. of Natural Resources

- Remove transit guard, burlap, and wire baskets.
- Stake only if you must—bare root, large canopy with small rootball or similar situation.

Glossary

Acid soil: soil with a pH less than 7.0. Acid soil is sometimes called "sour soil" by gardeners. Most plants prefer a slightly acid soil between 6 and 7 where most essential nutrients are available.

Alkaline soil: soil with a pH greater than 7.0, usually formed from limestone bedrock. Alkaline soil is often referred to as *sweet soil.*

Annual: a plant that completes its entire life cycle in one season. It germinates, grows, flowers, sets seed, and dies within one year.

Balled and burlapped: describes a large tree whose roots have been wrapped tightly in protective burlap and twine after it is dug. It is wrapped in this manner to protect it for shipping, sales, and transplanting.

Bare root: trees, shrubs, and perennials that have been grown in soil, dug, and have had the soil removed prior to sales or shipping. Mail order plants are often shipped bare root with the roots packed in peat moss, sawdust, or similar material and wrapped in plastic.

Barrier plant: a plant that has thorns or impenetrable growth habit and is used to block foot traffic or other access to an area in the landscape.

Beneficial insects: insects or their larvae that prey on pest organisms and their eggs. They may be flying insects such as ladybugs, parasitic wasps, praying mantids, and soldier bugs; or soil dwellers such as predatory nematodes, spiders, and ants.

Berm: a low, artificial hill created in a landscape to elevate a portion of the landscape for functional and aesthetic reasons such as added interest, screening, and improved drainage.

Bract: a modified leaf resembling a flower petal, located just below the true flower. Often it is more colorful and visible than the actual flower, as in poinsettia.

Bud union: the place where the top of a plant was grafted to the rootstock; a term frequently used with roses.

Canopy: the total overhead area of a tree including the branches and leaves.

Cold hardiness: the ability of a perennial plant (including trees, shrubs, and vines) to survive the minimum winter temperature in a particular area.

Complete fertilizer: powdered, liquid, or granular fertilizer with a balanced proportion of the three key nutrients—nitrogen (N), phosphorus (P), and potassium (K).

Composite: an inflorescence (cluster of flowers) also referred to as a head container petal and disklike flowers. They are often daisylike with a flat (disk-like flowers) center and petal-like flowers surrounding the outside.

Compost: decomposed organic matter added to the soil to improve it's drainage and ability to retain moisture.

Corm: a modified bulblike stem. It is swollen, short, solid, and located underground. Crocus and Gladiolus are two such plants.

Crown: (*a*) the point where the stems and roots meet. Located at, or just below the soil surface. (*b*) the top part of the tree.

Cultivar: a CULTIvated VARiety. A unique form of a plant that has been identified as special or superior and has been selected for propagation and sale.

Deadhead: to remove faded flowers from plants to improve their appearance, prevent seed production, and stimulate further flowering.

Deciduous plants: trees and shrubs that lose their leaves in the fall.

Desiccation: drying out of foliage, usually due to drought or wind.

Division: splitting apart perennial plants to create several smaller rooted segments. The practice is useful for controlling the plant's size and for acquiring more plants.

Dormancy: the period, usually the winter, when perennial plants temporarily cease active growth and rest. **Dormant** is the verb form.

Established: the point at which a newly planted tree, shrub, or flower has recovered from transplant shock and begins to grow. Often indicated by the production of new leaves or stems.

Evergreen: perennial plants that do not lose their foliage annually with the onset of winter. Needled or broadleaf foliage will persist and continues to function on a plant through one or more winters, aging and dropping unnoticed in cycles of one, two, three, or more.

Foliar: of or about foliage—usually refers to the practice of spraying foliage with fertilizer or pesticide for absorption by the leaves.

Floret: a small individual flower, usually one of many forming an inflorescence considered the blossom.

Germinate: to sprout. Germination is a fertile seed's first stage of development.

Graft (union): the point on the stem of a woody plant where a stem or bud of a desirable plant is placed onto a hardier root system. Roses, apples, and some ornamental trees are commonly grafted.

Hardscape: the permanent, structural, nonplant part of a landscape; such as walls, sheds, pools, patios, arbors, and walkways.

Herbaceous: plants having fleshy or soft stems that die back with frost; the opposite of *woody*.

Hybrid: a plant produced by crossing two different varieties, species or genera. Usually indicated with a × in the name such as *Acer × fremanii.*

Inflorescence: a cluster of flowers occurring at the tip of a stem. This includes such arrangements as umbels ('Queen Anne's Lace'), composite or head (Daisy), spike (Salvia), raceme (Snapdragon) and panicle (Coral Bells).

Mulch: a layer of material used to cover bare soil to conserve moisture, discourage weeds, moderate soil temperature, and prevent erosion and soil compaction. It may be inorganic (gravel, fabric) or organic (wood chips, bark, pine needles, chopped leaves).

Naturalize: (*a*) to plant seeds, bulbs, or plants in a random, informal pattern as they would appear in their natural habitat; (*b*) to adapt to and spread throughout natural areas and appear as if native to that location (a tendency of some non-native plants).

Nectar: the sweet fluid produced by glands on flowers that attract pollinators such as hummingbirds and honeybees for whom it is a source of energy.

Organic material, organic matter: any material or debris that is derived from plants.

Peat moss: organic matter from peat sedges (United States) or sphagnum mosses (Canada), often used to improve soil drainage and water holding abilities.

Perennial: a flowering plant that lives over two or more seasons. Many die back with frost, but their roots survive the winter and generate new shoots in the spring.

pH: a measurement of the relative acidity (low pH) or alkalinity (high pH) of soil or water based on a scale of 1 to 14, with 7 being neutral. Individual plants require soil to be within a certain range so that nutrients can dissolve in moisture and be available to them.

Pinch: to remove tender stems and/or leaves by pressing them between thumb and forefinger. This pruning technique encourages branching, compactness, and flowering in plants.

Pollen: the yellow, powdery grains in the center of a flower. A plant's male sex cells, they are transferred to the female plant parts by means of wind, bees, or other animal pollinators to fertilize them and create seeds.

Raceme: an arrangement of single stalked flowers along an elongated, unbranched stem.

Rhizome: a swollen energy-storing stem structure, similar to a bulb, that lies horizontally in the soil. Roots emerge from its lower surface and stems emerge from a growing point at or near its tip, as in Bearded Iris.

Rootbound (or potbound): the condition of a plant that has been confined in a container too long, its roots are forced to wrap around themselves and even swell out of the container. Successful transplanting or repotting requires untangling and trimming away some of the matted roots.

Root flare: the transition at the base of a tree trunk where the bark tissue begins to differentiate and roots begin to form just before entering the soil. This area should not be covered with soil when planting a tree.

Self-seeding: the tendency of some plants to sow their seeds freely around the yard. It creates many seedlings the following season that may or may not be welcome.

Semievergreen: tending to be evergreen in a mild climate but deciduous in a harsher one.

Shearing: the pruning technique whereby plant stems and branches are cut uniformly with long-bladed pruning shears (hedge shears) or powered hedge trimmers. It is used when creating and maintaining hedges and topiary.

Slow-acting (slow-release) fertilizer: fertilizer that is water insoluble and releases its nutrients when acted on by soil temperature, moisture, and/or related microbial activity. Typically granular, it may be organic or synthetic.

Succulent growth: the sometimes undesirable production of fleshy, water-storing leaves or stems that results from overfertilization.

Sucker: a new growing shoot. Underground plant roots produce suckers to form new stems and spread by means of these suckering roots to form large plantings, or colonies. Some plants produce root suckers or branch suckers as a result of pruning or wounding.

Tuber: a thickened portion of underground stem used for energy storage and reproduction. Irish Potato is a tuber.

Tuberous root: a swollen root with one point of growth where stem joins the root. Sweet Potatoes and Dahlias grow from tuberous roots.

Variegated: having various colors or color patterns. The term usually refers to plant foliage that is streaked, edged, blotched, or mottled with a contrasting color, often green with yellow, cream, or white.

White grubs: fat, off-white, worm-like larvae of Japanese and other beetles. They live in the soil and feed on plant (especially grass) roots until summer when they emerge as beetles to feed on plant foliage.

Wings: (*a*) the corky tissue that forms edges along the twigs of some woody plants such as Winged Euonymus; (*b*) the flat, dried extension of tissue on some seeds, such as Maple, that catch the wind and help them disseminate.

Last Spring Freeze

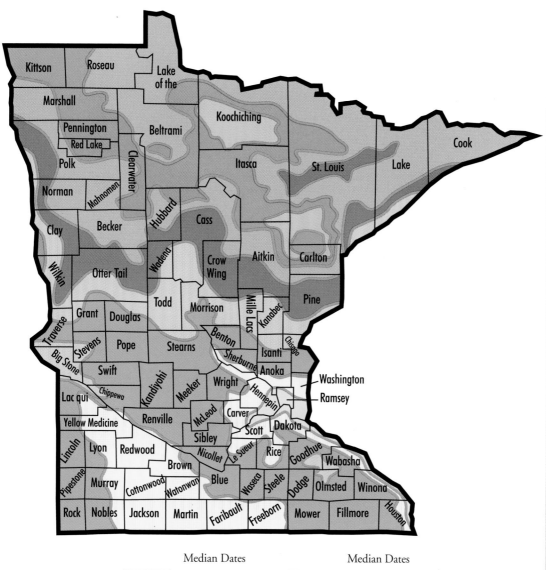

Median Dates

▨	Jun. 11 - 7
▨	Jun. 6 - 2
▨	Jun. 1 - May 28
▨	May 27 - 23
▨	May 22 - 18

Median Dates

▨	May 17 - 13
▨	May 12 - 8
▨	May 7 - 3
▨	May 2 - 6

First Fall Freeze

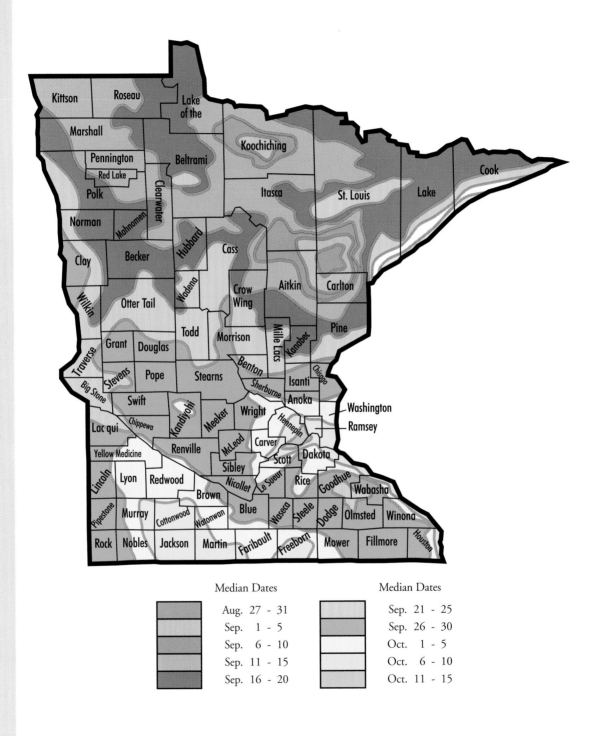

Median Dates

- Aug. 27 - 31
- Sep. 1 - 5
- Sep. 6 - 10
- Sep. 11 - 15
- Sep. 16 - 20

Median Dates

- Sep. 21 - 25
- Sep. 26 - 30
- Oct. 1 - 5
- Oct. 6 - 10
- Oct. 11 - 15

Bibliography

Brickell, Christopher and Judith D. Zuk, ed. *The American Horticultural Society: A-Z Encyclopedia of Garden Plants*. DK Publishing, Inc., New York, NY, 1997.

Brickell, Christopher, and David Joyce. *The American Horticultural Society: Pruning and Training*. DK Publishing, Inc., New York, NY, 1996.

Browne, Jim, William Radler, and Nelson Sterner, ed. *Rose Gardening*. Pantheon Books, New York, 1995.

Coombes, Allen J. *Dictionary of Plant Names*. Timber Press, Portland, OR, 1993.

Curtis, John T. *The Vegetation of Wisconsin*. The University of Wisconsin Press, 1978.

Dirr, Michael A. *Manual of Woody Landscape Plants*, 4th edition. Stipes Publishing Co., Urbana, IL, 1990.

DiSabato-Aust, Tracy. *The Well-Tended Perennial Garden*. Timber Press, Portland, Oregon, 1998.

Fell, Derek. *Annuals*. HP Books, Los Angeles, CA, 1983.

Martin, Laura. *The Folklore of Trees and Shrubs*. The Globe Pequot Press, Chester, Connecticut, 1992.

Reilly, Ann. *Park's Success with Seeds*. Geo. W. Park Seed Co., Inc., Greenwood, South Carolina, 1978.

Schneider, Donald. *Park's Success with Bulbs*. Geo. W. Park Seed Co., Inc., Greenwood, South Carolina, 1981.

Still, Steven M. *Manual of Herbaceous Plants*, 4th Edition. Stipes Publishing Company, Urbana, IL, 1994.

University of Minnesota Extension. Various publications.

Wyman, Donald. *Wyman's Gardening Encyclopedia*. McMillan Publishing Co., Inc., New York, 1977.

Photography Credits

Bill Adams: pages 42, 244

Liz Ball and Rick Ray: pages 8, 11, 17, 26, 24, 46, 47, 58, 64, 65, 90, 110, 112, 119, 123, 130, 131, 160, 168, 177, 182, 184, 185, 190, 192, 199, 206, 207, 210, 216, 218, 222, 223, 235, 239, 240, 247

Cathy Wilkinson Barash: page 212

Pam Beck: 100

Tim Boland and Laura Coit: page 201

Rob Cardillo: pages 82, 211

Mike Dirr: pages 162, 191, 194, 224, 236

Tom Eltzroth: pages 27, 28, 23, 29, 30, 32, 33, 34, 35, 36, 37, 38, 39, 40, 41, 43, 44, 45, 48, 55, 56, 51, 52, 60, 62, 66, 67, 69, 70, 72, 73, 74, 76, 77, 78, 79, 80, 81, 85, 87, 91, 92, 93, 96, 97, 101, 103, 114, 115, 118, 120, 121, 124, 125, 126, 127, 128, 129, 132, 133, 134, 137, 138, 140, 142, 144, 145, 146, 147, 148, 149, 150, 151, 154, 155, 156, 157, 158, 163, 165, 167, 170, 175, 178, 179, 181, 183, 187, 189, 196, 197, 203, 204, 205, 208, 209, 214, 215, 220, 221, 226, 227, 228, 238, 245, 246, backcover: 1st, 3rd, and 4th photos

Pamela Harper: pages 88, 102, 109, 116, 173, 174, 176, 198, 202, 217, 219, 242

Dency Kane: pages 104, 117, 166, 172, 243

Peter Loewer: page 107

Robert Lyons: pages 105, 237

Dave Mackenzie: pages 98, 108

Charles Mann: pages 54, 89, 164, 171, 200

Melinda Myers: page 53

Jerry Pavia: pages 31, 57, 59, 71, 75, 83, 86, 94, 95, 106, 111, 135, 139, 141, 143, 169, 213, 241, backcover: 2nd photo

Photo courtesy of the Conard-Pyle Company: page 159

Felder Rushing: pages 63, 84, 122, 136, 180

Ralph Snodsmith: pages 68, 186

Andre Viette: pages 11, 99, 113, 234

Mike Wendt: pages 195, 210, 223

Botanical Gardens and Arboreta

Botanical gardens and arboreta are the best places to find out which plants are hardy and suitable for your growing conditions. Pictures in books and catalogs often look very different from the actual plants that grow in Minnesota's challenging environment. I have a small yard, but I take home great ideas on plant combinations or unique plantings from botanical gardens. Visit often for landscaping ideas; plants change throughout the season. Below are many of the outstanding public gardens in Minnesota. For a more details on these and other Minnesota gardens visit http://horticulture.coafes.umn.edu/gardens/home.htm

August Schell Brewery
1860 Schell Road
New Ulm, MN 56073
(507) 354-5528

Carleton College's Cowling Arboretum
Carleton College
One North College Street
Northfield, MN 55057
(507) 646-4000

Como Conservatory
1225 Estabrook Drive
St. Paul, MN 55103
(651) 487-8201

Duluth Civic Center Gardens
411 West First Street
Duluth, MN 55801
(218) 723-3425

Eloise Butler Wildflower Gardens
Located in Theodore Wirth Park
4125 E. Lake Harriot Parkway
Minneapolis, MN 55422
(612) 370-4903

Enger Park
Sky Line Parkway
Duluth, MN 55802
(218) 723-3425

Historic Mayowood Mansion Gardens
1195 W. Circle Dr. SW
Rochester, MN 55902
(507) 282-9447

The Japanese Garden at Normandale
9700 France Avenue South
Bloomington, MN 55431
(952) 487-8145

Linnaeus Arboretum
Gustavus Adolphus College
St. Peter, MN 56082

Loring Park Garden of the Seasons
1382 Willow Street
Minneapolis, MN 55403

Minneapolis Sculpture Garden
726 Vineland Place
Minneapolis, MN
Phone: (612) 370-3996

Munsinger and Clemens Gardens
1339 Killian Blvd.
St. Cloud, MN 56301

Nokomis Naturescape Gardens
2401 E. Minnehaha Ave.
Minneapolis, MN 55417

Northland Arboretum
NW 7th St.
Brainerd, MN 56401
(218) 829-8770

Peace (Rock) and Rose Gardens
4125 E. Lake Harriet Parkway
Minneapolis, MN 55409

Pergola Garden
4801 Minnehaha Ave. South
Minneapolis, MN 55417

River Bend Nature Center Inc.
1000 Rustard Rd.
PO Box 186
Fairbault, MN 55021-0186
(507) 332-7151

The Rose Garden at Leif Erikson Park
13th Avenue East and London Road
Duluth, MN 55812
(218) 723-3425

Roseville Community Arboretum
Harrietville Alexander Nature Center
2520 N. Dale St.
Roseville, MN 55113-1701
(651) 415-2161

University of Minnesota Horticulture Display Gardens
1970 Folwell Avenue
St. Paul, MN 55108
(612) 624-5300

University of Minnesota Landscape Arboretum
3675 Arboretum Dr.
Chanhassen, MN 55317-0039
(952) 443-2460

All-America Selections Display Gardens

Lyndale Park Gardens
3900 Bryant Ave S
Minneapolis, MN 55409

Minnesota Landscape Arboretum
3675 Arboretum Drive
Chanhassen, MN 55317

North Central Research and Outreach Center
1861 Hwy. 169 East
Grand Rapids, MN 55744

University of Minnesota, St. Paul
1970 Folwell Avenue
St. Paul, MN 55108

West Central Research and Outreach Center
46353 State Hwy 329
Morris, MN 56267

Index

Meet Melinda Myers

Melinda Myers

Melinda Myers, best known for her gardener-friendly and practical approach to gardening, has more than 25 years of horticulture experience in both hands-on and instructional settings. She has a master's degree in horticulture, is a certified arborist, started the Master Gardener program in Milwaukee, and is a horticulture instructor at Milwaukee Area Technical College.

Outside the classroom, Melinda shares her expertise through a variety of media outlets. Her most recent books include Jackson and Perkins' *Beautiful Roses Made Easy: Midwestern Edition,* Jackson & Perkins' *Selecting, Growing and Combining Outstanding Perennials: Midwestern Edition* and the *Birds and Blooms Ultimate Garden Guide.* She hosts "Great Lakes Gardener," seen on PBS stations throughout the United States, the "Plant Doctor" show on WTMJ radio in Milwaukee, and appears regularly on WTMJ-TV, Milwaukee's NBC affiliate. She also writes the twice monthly "Gardeners' Questions" column for *The Milwaukee Journal Sentinel* and is a contributing editor and columnist for *Birds and Blooms* and *Backyard Living* magazines.

Melinda has written several other books, including *The Garden Book for Wisconsin, My Wisconsin Garden: A Gardener's Journal, Month-by-Month Gardening in Wisconsin, Minnesota Gardener's Guide, The Minnesota Horticultural Society's Month-by-Month Gardening in Minnesota,* and *The Perfect Lawn Midwest Series.*

Her 13 years of experience at the University of Wisconsin Extension allowed Melinda to work with backyard, community, and master gardeners throughout Wisconsin. In addition, she began the Master Gardener Program in Milwaukee County. As Milwaukee's Assistant City Forester, Melinda helped manage the city's street trees, boulevards, and green spaces. She worked with the Young Adult Conservation Corps supervising crews that maintain University of Wisconsin Extension urban test gardens and provide trail repair and other conservation work. She serves as a horticulture consultant to numerous community and beautification groups.

For her work and media presence, Melinda has received recognition and numerous awards, including the 2003 Garden Globe Award for radio talent and the 1998 Quill and Trowel award, both from the Garden Writers Association, and the 1998 Garden Communicator's Award from the American Nursery and Landscape Association.

white Pine any fast PS   F

Black Spruce Bog to Dry Shade M

Green ash heavy clay PS fast F

Yellow birch sandy   PS fast M

Red Osier Dogwood Shade

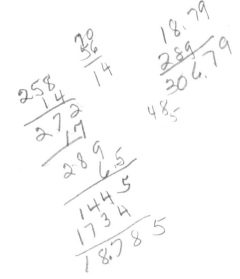